The American Shales

← ← ← ← ← → → → → →

From rich rock, unconventional ideas and
unwavering determination to a renewed world
energy future

Nissa Darbonne

Library of Congress Control Number:
2014907500

CreateSpace Independent Publishing Platform
North Charleston,
South Carolina

ISBN-13: 978-1497375628
ISBN-10:   1497375622

For Mom, Dad and explorers of all things

Text font is Garamond; title font is Times New Roman.
Energy-industry orthography is used,
such as its abridged form for fracturing.
Style is adapted, primarily from
The Associated Press Stylebook and Briefing on Media Law
and *The Chicago Manual of Style*.

CONTENTS

← ← ← ← ← → → → → →

INTRODUCTION

← ← ← ← ← → → → → →

Writing what was to be a three- or four-page feature in September 2011 of how Petrohawk Energy Corp. was launched with $60 million in 2004 and sold for $15.1 billion, the article became an eight-pager for all of the events—small, big and bigger—that led up to that.

"You should write a book!" Steve Herod, a Petrohawk executive vice president at the time, said, when asked to help fact-check it. The article was pared to four or five pages upon layout, of course, but the long version made it online.

A few weeks later, I ran into Jim Parkman, co-founder of energy investment-banking firms Petrie Parkman & Co. and, currently, Parkman Whaling LLC, as I often do on Texas Avenue alongside the Chase office tower downtown Houston. Jim had read the Petrohawk article. "You should write a book!" he said. "You should write a book about all of these guys!"

I admitted that, while working on the Petrohawk story, I had thought about it. The thought returned in January 2013 as I interviewed Dr. Bobby Lyle for the magazine's "Legends" feature. He had been important in the development of the Bakken; I had been familiar with this. In visiting with him, however, I better understood how and why. And I noted that the knowledge of what was learned there remains a valuable resource for continuing to figure out other troublesome formations.

Meanwhile, Bud Brigham was fact-checking a column I had written upon a platform of Ayn Rand's *Atlas Shrugged* on the renewed role of oil, rail and steel in the American economy. Bud was a co-executive producer of the 2012 movie *Atlas Shrugged II: The Strike* and gives lectures on Rand's work.

i

In a similarly small-big-bigger fashion, he and wife Anne had built Brigham Exploration Co. from a launch with $25,000 to a $4.7-billion sale. It occurred to me: Why does "fracing Brigham-style" continue to be industry short-hand for enormous frac jobs? Why was it that a small-cap E&P was the leader in pumping 30-plus frac stages? And how did that, in particular, play a role in putting it at the top of the list of companies Statoil ASA wanted to buy in 2011?

Having joined the magazine in 1998 from the oil and gas fields of South Louisiana, I had been there, writing and reading about the shales as they became economic in the Barnett, Bakken, Fayetteville, Marcellus, Haynesville and Eagle Ford.

But I had not paused during those 15 years to reflect upon the oeuvre of the past and, although extraordinary, what may yet still be prologue. Shale-play technology is being rolled out now into the Permian Basin and there are other basins—in the U.S. and abroad—that continue to host challenging, oil- and gas-rich rock as well.

I hope you find here, in the answer as to how the American shale plays have come to be, a lasting resource to turn to again and again in pursuit of *your* manifest destiny.

—Nissa Darbonne,
April 2014

"Explore! Do something!"
—*George Mitchell (1919-2013)*

BARNETT: 1996

← ← ← ← ← → → → → → →

"They were telling me--.
Well, they looked at it.
They could see no evidence of
...porosity...."
—George Mitchell

I t was 1946 and America had entered a new kind of manifest destiny. The great land push from sea to sea had long been achieved. Railroad service was from coast to coast and an unimpeded, interstate, highway system was under way. The world's tallest buildings had been completed a decade before in New York and one of these, the Empire State Building, would hold the title into the 1970s. Diego Rivera's commissioned mural, viewed as celebrating Marxism, in the lobby of Rockefeller Center had long been knocked down.

A nation—men, women and children—had pulled together to form and support a military of some 334,000 into one of more than 12 million to win wars against aggressors across two oceans in just 44 months. Hungry from more than 15 years of poverty—spawned by economic depression that was extended into rationing to fuel the war—goods and services were wanted.

These would require energy.

Oil had established itself in the prior several years as kingmaker—the key to a country's economic and political freedom. Neither Germany nor Japan had known what it should have been fighting for. The latter sought China, which was oil- and natural-gas-poor; its aggression against the U.S. was for being cut off from fuel for its march onshore Asia.[1] The former turned its eyes to the hydrocarbon bounty of Russia when it became clear that the Allied Forces' greater access to oil-fueled ships, tanks and aircraft would not be overcome.

George Phydias Mitchell was discharged from the U.S. Army in 1946. The 27-year-old had brought himself up from his Galveston, Texas, beginning as the son of a Greek immigrant by fishing to help support the family.[2] As an undergrad at Texas A&M University, he built bookshelves and made stationery, selling these to students of better means.

With his degree in petroleum engineering, emphasizing geology, he began offering consulting services, such as for wildcatter Roxie Wright at Roxoil Drilling Inc. He soon bought out one of the partners, going on with the group to discover new oil and gas plays along the U.S. Gulf Coast and extensions of existing plays.[3] Then, in 1952, "a Chicago-based bookie's tip, relayed through a friend, piques George Mitchell's interest in some North Texas acreage."[4]

Mitchell was well familiar with the gaming industry, having grown up in the 1920s and '30s era of prohibition in what was informally known as "The Free State of Galveston." There, the economy was supported in part by unprosecuted gambling and liquor sales, generating a tourism industry for the island community that had been

---

[1] Oil was not discovered in China until 1959. Relative to its demand, it remains oil- and gas-poor.
[2] Mitchell's father was Savvas Paraskevopoulos, who emigrated from Nestani, Greece, in 1901 at the age of 20. The Mitchell family says of the surname change, "He had no skills and spoke virtually no English. He found work, doing manual labor on a railroad gang. When he went to get his pay, the Irish paymaster felt his name was too difficult to pronounce so he told him that, from then on, his name would be the same as his, which was Mike Mitchell. George Mitchell was born approximately 18 years later."
[3] An extension is to prove commercially producible amounts of hydrocarbons outside the established boundaries of a known field.
[4] Mitchell Energy & Development Corp. annual report, 50th-anniversary edition, fiscal-year 1996.

nearly destroyed by the unnamed hurricane of 1900.[5]

A geologist, John A. Jackson, and a drilling-rig operator, Ellison Miles, were familiar with the North Texas prospect. They and Mitchell leased 3,000 acres in Wise County on the David J. Hughes ranch in Bridgeport about 50 miles northwest of Fort Worth. The partners and others were planning to target gas in the Bend conglomerate of formations overlying the Barnett shale in what would become known as Boonsville Field.

"The first well, the D.J. Hughes 1, is successful—as are the next 10 consecutive wells. Mitchell and Jackson perceive a huge stratigraphic trap underlying the entire area and Mitchell buys leases on 400,000 acres."[6] [7]

Fifty years later, in 1996, the company, now Mitchell Energy & Development Corp., had already made 1.5 trillion cubic feet of gas from the Wise County area.

And another tip was on its way to Mitchell's desk: "You should try the light-sand frac."

***

Ray Walker, a completions engineer for Union Pacific Resources Group Inc., passed this along to Nick Steinsberger, Mitchell's North Texas head of completion operations. In September 1981, Mitchell Energy had drilled a vertical well, C.W. Slay 1, in the deeper, Barnett-shale zone in southeastern Wise County. For all of its and others' gas production in the Fort Worth Basin, the source was this shale.[8]

---

[5] The storm remains the greatest U.S. natural disaster in terms of loss of life; more than 5,000 islanders are estimated to have died. The vibrant Galveston shipping industry immediately began to move north to what would become the Houston Ship Channel, one of the world's largest ports.

[6] Mitchell Energy & Development Corp. annual report, 50th-anniversary edition, fiscal-year 1996.

[7] Continental Oil Co., which is now ConocoPhillips, made the Boonsville Field discovery well, Bertha Flowers 1, in 1951 southwest of Bridgeport in Wise County.

[8] Oil- and gas-producing basins have one or more source rocks, which are considered the "kitchen."

This rock is so tight, though: Geologists who estimate where oil and gas are below the surface and the petroleum engineers who design a well for how it will be tapped just didn't even try to produce from it. A well might drain only yards of resources from around the hole, while a well in more porous layers of rock, such as limestone, at other depths, would more easily give up the oil and gas that had migrated into it for millions of years.

The Barnett shale lacked open, natural fractures. The rock had been naturally fractured but, over millions of years, the cracks had been healed by calcite; thus, they were no longer open. It would give up some gas, but the cost of drilling and completing the well would likely be more than the small amount of gas was worth.

So it just wouldn't be done.

However, Mitchell Energy wasn't operating in the North Texas area under the same cost/profit regime as most other oil and gas producers across the country. From some of its acreage, it had committed to provide a pre-determined amount of gas into a pipeline to Chicago. For this, it was rewarded under the contract with a higher-than-market price for the product, so its economics were different. And it was assured of always getting paid.

But, for this reward, it was unceasingly faced with a risk: It needed to always come up with the gas to put into the pipe. And this gas had to come from acreage that was part of the contract.

"We needed to produce more gas to Chicago and our reserves had begun to fall," Mitchell explained in a 2011 interview. "When you're trying to replace 100 million cubic feet of gas a day, that's quite a large amount of gas. We knew we were right on the big, tectonic belt that the gas supply in the whole Bend Arch came from. 'Where was the source of gas for all the Bend Arch fields?'

"That's what we were seeking. We needed to find another gas supply to supplement supply that was diminishing—and for one of our biggest contracts too. We were anxious to get something done."[9]

---

[9] George Mitchell was interviewed in April 2011. He passed away on July 26, 2013, in his hometown of Galveston. He was 94.

In 1980, Mitchell wasn't the only U.S. gas producer struggling to come up with as much new gas a day as it had produced that day. As U.S. oil-price regulations had been waged for decades, gas had undergone worse treatment. At first, beginning in the 1800s, it was regulated by municipalities that wanted to keep their local gas for streetlamps, heating and other uses. Then, it was regulated by states. When gas sales from one state to another came about in the 1920s, the federal government became involved.

In time, there were eras of market prices for some politically described types of gas and regulated prices for other types. For market prices, producers would rush to make that kind of gas, which would become oversupplied; the price would collapse. For the latter, producers weren't motivated to make much of it, usually because the prescribed price was too low for it to be profitable.

Mitchell said, "The government had control on gas, then it took control off gas and then it tried to compete with the independents. The program on energy from the federal government had been very poorly done. We had heard Washington saying, 'You can't sell this gas. You gotta cut the price. You gotta do this. You can't do that.' I never had any good angles out of that as to what should be done."[10]

Soon, natural gas was in short supply. In the winter of 1975-76, schools, other public facilities as well as private facilities, particularly in the northeastern U.S., were closed for lack of heating.

Vello Kuuskraa, chairman of research firm Advanced Resources International Inc., and Hugh Guthrie, an advisor to the U.S. Department of Energy, explain in a 2002 report, "(U.S. Geological Survey geoscientist) King Hubbert, who had gained considerable credibility (in the early 1970s) among energy-policy and Congressional staff by correctly forecasting the peak and subsequent decline in domestic oil production, applied his same forecasting methods to natural gas…

"He set forth a future of limited natural-gas resources and a pending crisis in…supplies. Hubbert viewed a low domestic natural-

---

[10] The cabinet-level U.S. Department of Energy did not exist until October 1977; until then, federal interest in energy matters consisted of myriad institutions and laws.

gas resource base of 1,050 trillion cubic feet of which nearly one-half had already been produced. He (correctly) predicted that the peak in gas production would occur shortly—in 1977—followed by a dramatic decline."

Further political pressure came upon President Carter's administration when, in Pennsylvania, a cooling system malfunctioned at the Three Mile Island nuclear-power plant, causing the core of one reactor to melt, resulting in a month-long national alert. Nuclear-power protests across the U.S. commenced; besides coal, the leading, alternative source of future power generation was natural gas.

But from where?

In 1978, Congress developed what was dubbed Section 29 tax credits to incent producers to try harder to make more gas. The relief was for making gas from tight rocks—coalbeds, shale, tight sandstones. The tax credit was for production through 2002 from wells spud before year-end 1992.

Kuuskraa and Guthrie write, "During a time when…gas prices were between $1.50 and $2.50 per Mcf (thousand cubic feet), the tax credit for (tight sandstone and shale gas) was about $0.50 per Mcf…and was on the order of $1 per Mcf for coalbed methane…Not surprisingly, industry's development and production of unconventional…gas responded strongly to these incentives…."[11]

In 1981, to replace the gas he needed to send to Chicago, Mitchell thought to challenge what the Barnett shale could do. Unlike some layers of rock in the Fort Worth Basin and in other basins, the shale is pervasive. It's where it is in Bridgeport, Texas, and in the same place 75 miles south in Cleburne. It doesn't appear, disappear and reappear. It isn't at 7,500 feet in this acre and at 10,000 feet in the next. It isn't 300 feet thick under City Hall and 30 feet thick under the high school.

It isn't under-pressured here—thus the gas would be perfectly

---

[11] The Reagan administration began deregulating oil, gas and other sectors, resulting in market-based pricing for all U.S. oil production beginning in April 1983. Free-market pricing for U.S. oil contributed to the 1980s price collapse. It also weighed in heavily on the decline of the Soviet Union. Legislation in 1989 removed all gas-price controls beginning Jan. 1, 1993.

happy to stay right where it is—and over-pressured there, just waiting to escape, waiting for something to unlock it, to give it relief.

Finding the Barnett—and again and again—was easy. Producing at least a little bit of gas from it was easy. Getting enough gas out of a single well to make that well worthwhile was a conundrum. Each molecule was jailed in trillions of tiny cells. In lieu of drilling a million tiny wells, what single key would unlock it all?

Generally, industry thought George Mitchell out of his mind. Some of his own team members were reluctant to get onboard. "While we were drilling through the Barnett, which is about 300 feet thick, we were having a slight gas show," Mitchell said. He had some of the company's North Texas-division geologists and engineers look at the rock samples.

"They were telling me--." He paused. "Well, they looked at it. They could see no evidence of gas in the cracks—the fissures—or any porosity for gas and, therefore, they couldn't see where it had any gas supply available.[12]

"They kept telling me, 'You're wasting your time.' That's what they kept telling me."

After that Slay well in 1981, Mitchell began building a team responsible for further investigation of the shale, while the balance of the North Texas division continued to make wells in conventional, less-tight formations—the shallower, Bend-conglomerate rocks.[13] During the next 17 years, the company completed more than 250 wells in the Barnett zone; none appeared to be worth much more than they cost.

Along the way, however, the Mitchell Energy team learned a great deal more, such as where to best land a well in the rock to prevent the subsequent fracture stimulation from penetrating the water-bearing Ellenburger formation that, in much of the basin, is immediately below. All that kind of well would make was water. If it made a

---

[12] Porosity is needed for a rock to contain oil or gas.

[13] C.W. Slay 1 was the discovery well of the Barnett-producing Newark East Field. A field is designated based on the zone from which it produces so another or several fields may overlap it, producing from other zones.

little gas, it wasn't worth it because water-disposal wells would have to be drilled to put the water back into Ellenburger—and it would just come right back to the surface. It would have to be plugged.[14]

Making the Barnett pay generously—and outside of a sweet spot just in Wise County—hadn't been figured out.

Into the 1990s, a few types of fracture-stimulation methods were commonly used across the U.S.—primarily one based on water with gelling additives known as the "cross-linked gel frac" or one using nitrogen foam and known as the "foam frac." The treatment was accompanied by tons of natural sand or more-expensive, higher-strength, manufactured, ceramic beads, some as small as table salt.

Altogether, it was expensive. An ordinary, unfraced, vertical well would cost about $250,000 to drill and complete. One with a "massive hydraulic frac," known in short as an MHF, would cost an extra half-million or so in the Barnett. Application of an MHF on a rock that is already brittle, such as in the Cotton Valley formation of East Texas, was highly economic even with drilling and completion costs there of up to $4 million.

In the stubborn Barnett, not so much.

"You should try the light-sand frac," Ray Walker and the UPR team told Nick Steinsberger in 1997. Walker had been involved with Mitchell Energy's attempts in the Barnett beginning with the Slay well. In 1982, he was a completions engineer for oilfield-service firm Halliburton Co. and knew many of the Mitchell team members from their engineering-school days at Texas A&M from which Walker graduated in 1979. Mitchell's Slay well had been drilled in 1981; Halliburton was brought in in 1982 to complete it—that is, to frac it. Walker was part of the Halliburton team.[15]

---

[14] Fracture stimulation—fracing, in short—is the use of pressured water to force rock to open. Mixed in are tiny, hard rocks—such as sand or ceramic beads—that stay behind to keep the cracks open—that is, to prop them, thus their moniker, "proppant."

[15] Completing a well is the process in which, after the hole is drilled, mechanical and other processes are involved in setting it up to flow hydrocarbons continuously. A Halliburton, Schlumberger Ltd. or Baker Hughes Inc. is usually involved in the well-completion process, while a rig operator, such as Helmerich & Payne Inc., is, usually, strictly there to drill the hole.

He continued to work with Mitchell on the Barnett wells on and off until 1991 when he left Halliburton to join Fort Worth-based Union Pacific Resources Group. Soon, he led the UPR team that was responsible for its East Texas portfolio, which was primarily targeting the sandstone members of the Cotton Valley formation southeast of Fort Worth.

UPR had been formed in 1987 from railroad operator Union Pacific Corp.'s natural-resources subsidiaries, which held its mineral interests. In the 1800s, the federal government had offered large land grants for railroad construction to incent coast-to-coast settlement, development, defense and trade. The grants included the mineral rights—ownership of whatever is below the land as well, from dirt to water, abelsonite to zinc. By the 1990s, Union Pacific owned rights under some 8 million acres as a result of the land grants and an additional 700,000 acres it gained over time.

In 1995, it spun out its land and exploration business as Union Pacific Resources Group in an IPO. No longer competing with other Union Pacific Corp. businesses for funding and leadership's attention, the newly independent oil and gas producer flourished. It was one of the country's most active explorers in the 1990s.

At the time, Walker and his UPR colleagues were giving a light-sand-frac idea a try in vertical wells in the tight, uber-gassy Cotton Valley sandstone. "We didn't invent the water frac because water fracs have been around for more than 60 years," Walker says, "but we kind of re-invented the water frac in the Cotton Valley."

The Cotton Valley was the first major, unconventional, gas reservoir to be developed on a large scale in the U.S. and it, like the Barnett shale, contained a lot of gas liquids—that is, it was "wet."[16] UPR had a large gas-processing plant in the midst of the Cotton Valley play in Carthage, Texas, where it was able to further profit from its gas production by stripping out the higher-value, wet molecules. As a profit-

---

[16] The simplest natural gas molecule is methane. The natural gas that is surfaced from a well, however, often contains more sophisticated gas molecules as well—such as ethane, propane and butane.

able play, its exploration team was able to try more expensive ideas.

"So it's an area where we learned how to frac really hard, tight rocks," Walker says. "We learned about ultra-low permeabilities and the ability to comingle (production from many) zones while trying to pump massive fracs to get a lot of drainage from a single, vertical wellbore. In the world of frac design—the fluids, proppants—virtually all of these advancements got started in the Cotton Valley at one time or another.[17]

"It was an application of state-of-the-art technology back then— the '80s and all through the '90s. If you wanted to see the latest, greatest thing, it was all operating in East Texas in the Cotton Valley."

At the time, fracing was all about putting more and more proppant into the cracks—at times as much as 2,500 tons in a single well. Sophisticated gelling fluids were developed to create more viscosity in the water for transporting the proppant into the high-temperature sandstone.

"But, when I left Halliburton and went to UPR, one of the things we were all thinking was that we didn't really need all that sand," Walker says. "We had kind of gone overboard and gas prices were getting weak. We needed to cut costs."

He and the UPR team launched an experiment. "We started cutting back on sand."

Instead of applying just less and less sand in each subsequent Cotton Valley well, "oftentimes we would go to the extreme on at least a well or two just to see what that looked like. We learned a lot pretty fast: As you got rid of the sand, you didn't need all those expensive gelling agents. We ended up with, essentially, just water— more water—and only a little bit of sand in 1995 or so.

"The well cost went from $4 million to about $1 million."

The Cotton Valley sandstone is so brittle that, when it is fraced, it shears apart and shifts, creating a void through which the gas can flow. Until the 1995 experiments, sand—and the gel to transport it— were deployed with the thinking that the rock needed a lot of prop-

---

[17] Permeability affects the ability of oil or gas to flow through a rock into the wellbore.

ping once cracked to keep it open; instead, the UPR team found that just a spot of sand would prop it. "A little bit of sand helps, but you may not need any sand in some cases," Walker says.

His and his colleagues' findings with this light-sand-frac or "LSF" technique led to their peer presentation, "Proppants? We Don't Need No Proppants," at the Society of Petroleum Engineers' annual technical conference in San Antonio in October 1997.[18] Did Cotton Valley sandstone, once fraced, need so much proppant to keep it cracked? They answered this for all of the petroleum-engineering community.

In their trials, they used half as much or even less sand than in the past—and, thus, even less gel to carry it into the cracks. In one, the well produced a higher initial rate of gas longer than wells that had undergone the MHF treatment. "The production rates of the (MHF) jobs are only better for the first two months," they reported. "The decline of the well with the (new, light-sand frac) is less steep. Its flow rate is about the same and higher, respectively, when compared with (two MHF) wells after 14 months."

In that timeframe, the LSF well made 312 million cubic feet of gas; the two MHF wells each made between 302- and 350 million. One of the old-styled wells had been given 1.1-million pounds of sand; the new well, 82,000 pounds.

"The treatment cost of the 1.1-million-pound job was $227,000. The (LSF) treatment cost was $40,000," they reported. "This is almost a sixfold cost reduction (but) with similar production results."

***

If using less proppant in a frac job was seemingly wrong-headed, a great place to give it a try should be similarly wrong-headed: making economic amounts of gas from the super-tight Barnett shale.

---

[18] Co-authors included engineers with Halliburton and with BJ Services Co., which is now owned by Baker Hughes Inc. The lead author, UPR's Mike Mayerhofer, soon went on to frac-mapping and -diagnostics firm Pinnacle Technologies Inc. Currently, he heads Halliburton's frac-technology center in Houston.

After the trials, UPR was testing the LSF in other formations across the country, such as the Olmos and Wilcox in South Texas. Walker and his colleagues enlisted other E&P companies to also give it a try. They made a follow-up presentation at the SPE annual convention a year later in 1998 in New Orleans: "Proppants, We Still Don't Need No Proppants."

Among producers trying it—all in the Cotton Valley—were Pennzoil Co., for which UPR had quit its hostile, $6.4-billion, cash bid a year earlier; Amoco Corp., which BP Plc was buying at the time for some $48 billion of stock; and privately held Valence Operating Co.

One more company participated: Mitchell Energy.

Nick Steinsberger had visited with Mike Mayerhofer, who had generated the LSF idea at UPR, as well as with Ray Walker and with frac-mapping and -diagnostics firm Pinnacle Technologies Inc.

"One of those formations that we wanted to get buying into the (LSF) idea was the Barnett," Walker says.

UPR didn't have oil and gas interests in the Fort Worth Basin in 1998; instead, peer-to-peer technology and intellectual transfer is commonplace in the oil and gas industry as successful—or unsuccessful—experimentation can serve to reduce the fail rate for all. The greater the LSF-sample population, the greater the odds of getting it right elsewhere or deciding to not even try it in some types of rock.[19]

And, indirectly, Walker's tip was also a return of a favor. Mitchell Energy had made a discovery in the limestone member of the Cotton Valley near Mexia, Texas, in 1969 in what became North Personville Field. But getting commercial amounts of gas out of the rock had been disappointing.[20]

In 1978, the company returned to the limestone with pumping nearly 1 million gallons of fluid and 1,400 tons of sand into a well in a research project with the newly created U.S. Department of Energy in

---

[19] As oil or gas made by one producer or another is not branded, the greatest competition among producers, instead, is for talented employees, the best leases, the best access to oilfield services and equipment, and the best net-asset-value appreciation.

[20] The roughly 2,200-foot-thick Cotton Valley group consists of Cretaceous-age sandstone on top and Jurassic-age shale and limestone intervals beneath.

what was dubbed the "massive hydraulic frac"—the MHF. Production more than doubled. The rock had some natural fracturing but not much; it had poor permeability but decent porosity. Pre-MHF, gas flow would decline to practically nothing within 24 months. The cracks were closing; they had needed more proppant.[21]

At the time, Walker was a year away from finishing his undergrad degree at Texas A&M just south of the MHF trial, which went on to catapult the tight Cotton Valley into a major producer—thus more work for Halliburton's frac services and a job for Walker.[22]

If Mitchell Energy could make the Barnett shale work, using the LSF recipe instead of the costly MHF, where else might a technological leap like this be applied in shales by UPR and others?

"So I spent a lot of time visiting with Nick Steinsberger about the (LSF) findings," Walker says. "I had actually tried to hire him away from Mitchell to work at UPR several years before."

A University of Texas petroleum-engineering graduate with Mitchell Energy since 1987, Steinsberger had worked with Walker on the Barnett completions while Walker was with Halliburton. Walker says of the LSF trial, "I was just encouraging him, showing him what we had seen in the Cotton Valley, building up enough evidence to say that they should try it in the Barnett.

"In the Barnett, it worked even better."

Steinsberger reported in the joint paper to petroleum-engineering peers in 1998, "Mitchell Energy…has a development program in Wise and Denton counties north of Fort Worth and has completed more than 250 Barnett shale wells, utilizing hydraulic-fracture treatments for the 300-foot interval. In a continuing effort to reduce completion costs, the (light-sand) fracs were implemented."

In 12 months of trials in several wells, the LSF was successful in all of them. "These designs consist of the same volume of fluid—

---

[21] As permeability allows oil and gas to flow through the rock, natural and induced fractures improve permeability.

[22] Hydraulic fracturing was begun in 1947 in Grant County, Kansas, by Halliburton for Stanolind Oil & Gas Co. on an experimental basis to unclog a gas well in the Hugoton Basin. Halliburton then applied it commercially in 1949 in Oklahoma and Texas.

water with a clay stabilizer and friction reducer—and 10% of the proppant volume as is normally pumped in the conventional jobs," Steinsberger reported.

The past frac recipe for the Barnett wells had been three pounds of sand per gallon of water; with the LSF, Mitchell Energy was finding good results from using less than half a pound of sand per gallon. "The decrease in chemicals and sand has led to savings of 60% of fracturing costs...."[23]

He concluded, "Mitchell Energy is cautiously optimistic with the results thus far and intends to pursue this cost-saving technique in the development of the (Barnett)...."

---

[23] Water-frac fluid consists some 99.5% of water; the balance consists of guar gum (gelling agent), a surfactant like dish detergent and a biocide like bleach.

BAKKEN: 1996

← ← ← ← ← → → → → →

"So I called it 'Sleeping Giant.'"
—*Dick Findley*

D ick Findley had an idea. Findley had been prospecting for oil and gas in some of the many formations of the Williston Basin of North Dakota and Montana beginning in 1975 for Tenneco Oil Co. in its Denver office.

In 1978, he landed in Billings, Montana, when answering an ad. Pat Patrick at Patrick Petroleum Co. was looking for a geologist with an interest in computer-based exploration. Findley was interested; he had done this in a summer internship with Union Oil Co. in Lafayette, Louisiana, in 1973. At the time, he had just received his bachelor's and was beginning work on his master's, both from Texas A&M.

"At Union Oil, we were using the Vax mainframe computer, the PDP 11," he says. "This was before the personal computer. My job was to look at the geology of a field and then build a database that was used for a pilot project for testing the feasibility of using computers for exploration."

The geologist Patrick sought would also be one with expertise in the Williston Basin's Mission Canyon—a member of the Madison group of intervals. Findley says, "Well, I was, luckily, on a team of geologists, engineers and geophysicists that had just discovered the Big Stick/Four Eyes fields, which were big Mission Canyon producers along the Billings (anticline) nose (in North Dakota).

15

"The only problem is they wanted somebody with 10 years of experience and I had three."

But Patrick hired him.

A few years later, before the oil- and gas-price bust that was under way was apparent to everyone in industry, Findley set out with his own firm, Prospector Oil Inc., as an independent geologist, generating ideas for other companies of where drilling a well might make enough oil and gas to produce a profit.

In 1996, now a career geologist in the Williston Basin, Findley was well familiar with the Bakken formation, which consists of three intervals: the uber-tight, upper-Bakken shale; the tight, middle-Bakken dolomite; and the uber-tight, lower-Bakken shale. Each layer is also extremely thin—about 30 or 40 feet thick—across the basin.[24]

And he had watched large, independent explorer Burlington Resources Inc. attempt to make a play of the upper-Bakken interval for a decade by now. In the mid-1980s, railroad operator Burlington Northern Inc. was emphasizing getting more value out of its businesses, including its E&P unit, Milestone Petroleum Inc., which held its mineral rights in a giant swath of land across the northern and southern Williston Basin.[25]

It bought El Paso Natural Gas Co. and Southland Royalty Co., rolling the E&P assets of these into Milestone and, with new management, primarily from Superior Oil Co., renamed it Meridian Oil Inc. In 1988, it IPOed the amalgamation of its E&P and other natural-resource operations as Burlington Resources.

The independent entity was in a unique position to explore: It had money and land. It sold or spun off its real-estate, gas-pipeline and forest-products businesses, raising $1.4 billion in five years, and reinvested the proceeds into oil and gas exploration. In the 225,000-

---

[24] As the continents were forming from the single landmass Pangea, the northernmost portion of the U.S. was at the equator during the Mississippian and Pennsylvanian ages, known as the carbon-rich Carboniferous Period. The uppermost Bakken member is at the bottom of Mississippian and at the top of the older, Devonian age.

[25] The railroad had been deeded this as part of an 1864 land grant of right of way by the Lincoln administration.

square mile Williston Basin under eastern Montana, southern Saskatchewan, western North Dakota and northwestern South Dakota, Burlington had 18 producing formations beneath its 3.7-million-net-acre leasehold at as shallow as 4,500 feet to more than 15,000 feet.

"Burlington had a strong management team with a lot of engineering and operations emphasis," says Taylor Reid. A petroleum engineer with a bachelor's from Stanford University, Reid worked for Burlington in the Williston and other basins from 1986 until its sale to ConocoPhillips Co. in 2006.[26] "After all those companies were put together (in the mid-1980s), they were looking at all the assets they had with a focus on operations, engineering and technology."

These were positions in the giant, gassy San Juan Basin that it gained from El Paso and Southland, the large mineral-rights position in the Williston Basin, a significant operation in the Anadarko Basin and its position in the gassy Pinedale anticline of western Wyoming.

In the San Juan, it was aiming to make a play of the bounty of the Fruitland coalbed. "There was a push, a real interest, at Burlington in the application of technology. That mostly started in the mid-1980s. They knew there was this incredible resource of gas in place in the Fruitland coal, he says.

"Through the application of new technology called 'cavitation,' the (Burlington) team started making incredible wells. They were gigantic; some were making more than 20 million cubic feet a day. Most other operators were fracing the formation without a lot of success. This new technique initiated a boom in the basin."

The coal-gas play was different from traditional oil and gas production in the U.S. in that it was a repeatable, resource play and it held trillions of cubic feet of gas that could be produced in a manufacturing type of process.

It wasn't wildcatting.

"It's what we call 'resource conversion,'" Reid says. "That's kind of what shale plays really are. There are massive resources in place.

---

[26] Upon the sale to ConocoPhillips, Reid went on to co-found Bakken-focused Oasis Petroleum Inc. with Tommy Nusz and other Burlington colleagues.

You know it's there. You can calculate the oil or gas in place, but the question is 'How do you economically get it out of the ground?'"

In 1988, in the oily, tight-limestone, Austin-chalk play in South Texas, operators were having some early success with new horizontal-drilling techniques, including by UPR.[27] Where else could Burlington apply horizontal drilling?[28]

"They were looking at all the places where they held property," Reid says. "The Bakken was kind of a natural. You had this shale—this source rock—in place that held this massive resource."

The company had a vast land-holding there and its staff was well familiar with the basin, having worked it for decades under one name or another. Its plan was to bore these horizontals—about 1,400 to 4,000 feet in length—in the upper-Bakken shale itself in western-central North Dakota where the shale is over-pressured and naturally fractured along the Billings Nose. The wells would produce naturally due to the pressure and natural fracturing.

"So they didn't stimulate the wells at that time. They didn't frac them."

On Sept. 25, 1987, Burlington, operating as Meridian Oil Inc., made the first horizontal wildcat in the upper shale in North Dakota with its MOI Elkhorn 33-11 on its land-grant leasehold in Elkhorn Ranch Field in Billings County for 258 barrels of oil in a first-24-hour "initial potential" (IP) test.[29] [30] It followed this with the BNRR 2-19 in June 1988 for 433 barrels in McKenzie County in Bicentennial Field.

---

[27] The first commercial horizontal wells were drilled by France-based Elf Aquitaine SA, which is now a part of Total SA, in southwestern France and offshore Italy beginning in 1980.

[28] Horizontal wells differ from what are known as "directional" wells in that the latter are slanted to reach a pocket of oil and gas, such as under a lake, but may produce from a vertical column of pay. A directional wellbore, however, could be turned laterally upon reaching the payzone to produce as a horizontal.

[29] The well went on to make 372,000 barrels of oil and 1.3 billion cubic feet of gas. It was still producing in 2013.

[30] A year earlier, Edwin and Berry Cox completed a horizontal re-entry of an old, vertical well in the Bakken formation with their Froholm 1-18 for 364 barrels of oil in nearby McKenzie County.

It attempted 11 more in the two counties with 10 coming on with between 19 and 435 barrels; only one of the 11 was deemed a dry hole.

Conoco Inc., as it was known prior to its merger with Phillips Petroleum Co., was curious. It tried one in May 1988, also putting it in Elkhorn Ranch Field, for 61 barrels. Privately held BWAB Inc. tried it in Golden Valley County, bringing one on in June 1989 with 95 barrels; another attempt, in McKenzie County, came on with 420 barrels.

Burlington's next 11 came on with between 44 and 547 barrels.

In 1989, more operators joined in the play, including American Hunter Exploration Ltd. and Slawson Exploration Co. Inc. Soon, five larger companies—Texaco Inc., Exxon Corp., Shell Oil Co., Oryx Energy Co. and UPR—tried it, each with one attempt. Then, Samson Resources Co. tried it, making a first attempt in October 1991. By then, everyone else had quit except for Burlington and Conoco.

After August 1993, only Burlington was still at it. In all, it made 103 attempts. It quit the horizontal Bakken program with the MOI Poker Jim 31-19H that came online on Feb. 4, 1995, with 60 barrels.[31]

In all, Burlington and others had attempted 175 horizontal, upper-Bakken-shale wells in North Dakota in just shy of seven years; all but 12 made oil. The success rate—more than 90% and involving so many wells—was remarkable for U.S. exploration at the time— particularly in North Dakota. Through 1994, some 12,700 wells had been spud in the state, beginning in 1922; among them, about 46% had been deemed dry holes.

But the horizontal, unfraced, upper-Bakken-shale play did not last. Thomas J. Heck, a geologist for the North Dakota Geological Survey, wrote in 1996 that it had peaked in 1990. Of the 274 wells drilled anywhere in the state in 1990, 77 were Bakken tests; in 1994, only eight.

"Success rates for Bakken tests, as judged solely by a well being completed as a producing oil well, remained high," Heck wrote in a

---

[31] Slawson made seven of the top eight upper-Bakken-shale wells, in terms of IP, with the best coming on with 1,914 barrels. Shell's one attempt was the second-best, coming on with 1,503 barrels.

state report. "The success rate during 1991 was 97% and the...rates during both 1992 and 1993 were 100%.

"(But) despite the appearance of success by this one measure, some of these wells will be economic failures because the volume of hydrocarbons recovered will not be sufficient to pay for...drilling and completion...Many Bakken wells declined faster than expected."

Operators were finding that the later-made wells' IPs were only about 150 barrels and their production was not as lasting as that of many of the early wells. Pumps were being brought in very soon after completion to help push the oil to the surface.

"These IPs and the change from (naturally) flowing to pumping wells indicate a significant change in reservoir performance has occurred," Heck wrote. "This apparent decrease in reservoir performance is also evidence that the ultimate recoveries of these wells will be low compared (with) earlier Bakken completions. Together, these changes were an indication that the horizontal Bakken play was dying because the play was no longer economically viable."

Reid says the play kicked off with a focus on some of the most naturally fractured and over-pressured areas; there, the oil wanted to get out. "Some were good wells—about 200,000-plus barrels (of ultimate recovery). And, because it was over-pressured, these were pretty lively wells. We tried to drill them near balance (with surface pressure, so the oil would remain in the formation until drilling was finished), but sometimes they were flowing while drilling.

"Then, once we got the hole drilled, we would run a liner, usually either pre-perforated or a slotted liner. We never cemented pipe in the open hole. We just ran a liner in it and then we would just open it up and flow it back. It was never (fracture-) stimulated."

Over time, however, explorers were drilling in areas where the reservoir had less pressure and less natural fracturing; there, the oil was more comfortable with staying right where it was. And oil prices had declined. At year-end 1993, Burlington was making only some 3,900 barrels a day from its nearly 100 horizontal Bakken wells—or about 39 barrels a day from each. It was getting an average of only $16.69 a barrel for its oil.

The unfraced, horizontal, upper-Bakken program was discontinued. "They weren't as prolific as the wells today that are fraced and in the middle-Bakken (member) rather than the shale," Reid says.

In the spring of 1995, in Burlington's year-end 1994 report, it didn't even mention Bakken. Heck concluded in his early 1996 summary of overall North Dakota drilling activity, "…Without a change in current circumstances, such as a new way to stimulate Bakken-formation reservoirs or the discovery of a new area with rock and/or reservoir properties similar to the (productive) fairway, completions in the Bakken formation will be made only for salvage…

"There will always be a few completions in the Bakken formation but, in those wells, the Bakken will be completed as bail-out zones."

***

That's what Dick Findley and partner Bob Robinson did in 1996 in Montana: They bailed out in the Bakken. At least, that's what it looked like on paper. And that was fortunate: They would need to quietly put together some more leasehold.

Burlington's and others' horizontal work in the shale interval in North Dakota had been fascinating, Findley says. "The Williston was one of the most unlikely places for a horizontal play to occur, primarily because, when we drilled vertical wells, it took us two weeks to even kick off and (turn the wellbore into a lateral). It was quite the deal what Burlington was doing. They were one of the pioneers of horizontal drilling and they were targeting the shale itself.

"It got a lot of people's attention."

Because the Bakken shale where Burlington was attempting these horizontals is naturally fractured, the wells produced with great power. "There were wells that would pay out while they were being drilled. They were flowing oil to the surface while they were drilling. So it wasn't even a closed system and, looking back on it, probably a little dangerous.

"But, certainly, that got the attention of a lot of people—myself included."

He was alarmed, actually: He wasn't in the play and, if it was successful, the leasehold to make wells in Bakken or any of the basin's many other formations for himself wouldn't be available. "It looked like I was finished. I wouldn't be able to get any acres for any other prospect ideas."

As the play evaporated, Findley continued to work. In 1996, he was looking for potential well locations for pay from the shallower Madison group of formations—Ratcliffe, Mission Canyon, Lodgepole, which kicked off North Dakota oil production in 1951—down to the deep Red River. With 10 stacked petroleum systems, the Williston is a "pick a payzone" basin.[32]

But pick carefully: Into the 1980s, the odds of success in the basin were about one in nine; the prospects were small in areal extent—they were traps with small, structural closures.[33]

"They had moderate reserves, multiple objectives and were fairly low-risk if you understood it. There was a reason to play it, but you had to understand it," Findley says. "They could encompass very small areas.

"So my world was that size.

"When we think of prospects, we think of structural closures or maybe a nose that would, hopefully, be three or four miles long—and that would be a big nose. So that was my world. And when you work for so many years and that's your trap—that's the size of your prospect—it's hard; you get these blinders on and it's hard to get these blinders off, so you can think beyond that and think big. I wasn't thinking big at the time.

"Based on its early history, the thinking was that the Williston would be one of the last places where a big play could be made."

Burlington's attempts to turn the areally pervasive upper-Bakken shale into a big play failed. "It really only worked in a couple of fairly small areas within the Billings County area. There were some attempts

---

[32] Until oil was discovered in North Dakota in 1951, production in the state was primarily gas from the shallow Pierre formation at fewer than 2,500 feet.

[33] A structural closure is one in which oil and gas are trapped in a pocket, primarily as a result of gravity, migration and tectonic events.

to extend it outside of that, but it just turned out to be an uneconomic play. 'The Bakken' really became a four-letter word in the early '90s.

"I never thought the Bakken would be a feasible, primary objective. That's based on what we knew at the time. And that was based on drilling in the shale (member) itself."

As an independent prospector beginning in 1983, Findley would generate ideas for wells, offer them to companies that would drill them and get a small interest as payment. In 1991, he decided to drill wells for himself, partnering with Bob Robinson, a landman based in Traverse City, Michigan, and whose Kelly Oil & Gas Inc. put acreage together to explore for bypassed pay.[34] Findley had met Robinson a couple of decades before while at Patrick Petroleum. Bob's brother, Charles "Red" Robinson, had been a vice president at Patrick.

In 1996, on the Montana side of the basin, Findley and Bob Robinson wanted to drill in Richland County down to Nisku, which is also known as Birdbear and is just below Bakken and the underlying Three Forks series of rock.[35] They spud Albin FLB 2-33 in what was known as Mustang Field. That March, they parked at the drillsite, as was customary for a well owner, looking at rock samples as the drillbit bored through one formation and, then, another.

With Nisku at about 11,000 feet, the pair had plenty to look at. "It was about two in the morning when we penetrated the upper-Bakken shale," Findley says. "We had a typical, 100-unit mud-log show. It's a source rock, so it's common to get shows out of the shale. I didn't think anything of it."

---

[34] Bypassed pay is oil and gas that were left behind because a formation higher or lower in the hole was more immediately appealing at the time or because producing from this zone and from a secondary formation might make a worse well, such as due to incompatible pressure variance from one zone to another. Less pressure in one zone could just enervate the other. Payzones can also be deemed dry simply because oil and gas prices are too low at the time.

[35] Within the 225,000-square-mile Williston Basin, the 15,000-square-mile Bakken petroleum system—incorporating the three pervasive layers of Bakken, the occasional Sanish, which sits below Bakken in one area, and four layers of Three Forks—is sealed by Lodgepole limestone at top and Nisku, aka Birdbear, at bottom, resulting in an overpressured system between the two normal-pressured seals.

Soon after, the drillbit was now in the middle Bakken—the do-lomite member. "About 40 minutes after we penetrated it, we got bot-toms up and had a 400-unit gas increase. And we encountered about a 10-foot drilling break, which indicated porosity. I didn't think there was any porosity to speak of in the middle member. That seemed pretty unusual."

Albeit pleasing, it disturbed him; he put it aside. Dawn was com-ing. "I was going to blame it on the early morning. I hoped that my mind was just fuzzy." The drillbit moved on. It finally landed in Nisku. The oil show was as expected.[36]

"That night, after we finished evaluating everything, we went back to the hotel in Sidney. It was maybe a dozen miles away. We were going to catch a little bit of sleep. I don't know how long I was asleep. My eyes popped open. I remember a kind of light-bulb thought going off.

"I was thinking, 'Wait a minute. Oil isn't in the shale' like most people thought, including myself. 'It looks like, in this area, the oil is in the middle member.'"

The middle-Bakken layer where Albin FLB 2-33 was drilled is a dolomite that is slightly shaley with grains of calcite and quartz. The well showed a little bit of oil out of Nisku, but it was uneconomic. "Bob and I said, 'Well, what do we do now?'"

Bail out.

Commonly, when the rock an E&P company is going after in a well doesn't work out, it hopes another formation along its path will have made a better offer. The well is completed in the better rock and the company hopes to at least make enough off that zone to cover its cost—thus, it's called a "bail-out zone." Findley and Robinson decid-ed to complete the well in the middle Bakken.

---

[36] At the Albin location, the lower-Bakken shale is not present. Findley explains, "The lower shale has the most limited areal extent and is located only in the deepest part of the basin." The middle member has a larger areal extent; the upper shale, even larger. "So wells drilled at the edge of the Bakken depositional system will encounter only the upper shale." Moving toward the basin's center, the upper and middle Bakken members are present. "The deepest parts of the basin will have all three zones."

"We were certainly hoping we could get part of our money back. That was typical at the time. Since 1951, when the first (well was drilled through the Bakken), that was the main thinking about it—that it was, at best, a bail-out zone. It was rarely a primary objective."[37]

He and Robinson called Halliburton to frac Albin FLB 2-33. The initial thought was to open the vertical hole to produce from both the upper- and middle-Bakken layers. Halliburton noted, however, that the shale member had a low fracture gradient: If fracing both the middle-Bakken dolomite and the upper-Bakken shale, it was estimated that the shale would break first and the frac fluid would go there—known as "losing your frac" and one of many, common types of disappointments when trying to make an oil or gas well.

"You wouldn't effectively fracture-stimulate the middle member, which is where we thought the productive oil primarily was. We decided to only perforate the middle-Bakken member."[38]

Worst-case expectations were that fracing the well just in the middle Bakken would still end up penetrating the shale; the middle Bakken is only about 30 feet thick there.[39] "As it turned out, the shale was actually an extremely good barrier to fluid migration upwards. That was awful good because, you know, the middle Bakken is where the oil turned out to be."

The well flowed back about 160 barrels of oil and officially IPed with 70 barrels on April 20, 1996. It was more than Findley and Robinson estimated they needed to at least get their money back.

---

[37] An exception to Bakken as a bail-out zone would be Antelope Field in North Dakota that produced 11 million barrels of oil and 20 billion cubic feet of gas primarily from the Sanish member of the system. Stanolind Oil & Gas Co. made the field discovery in December 1953 with its Woodrow Starr 1 in an eastern step-out from the Nesson anticline. The early, sweet-spot wells made 200,000 or more barrels. Findley says, "It was a bit of an anomaly. They were completing in natural fractures at the time." There, the anticline was steeply dipping. And the areal extent was, again, small—about 44 wells.

[38] To perforate is to open the wellbore in a zone to allow for production from that zone. At times, a well is perforated in more than one zone, allowing production from multiple layers of pay. The other, nonperforated zones—and their varying pressures and/or water content—are sealed off.

[39] The porosity is within only about 10 of the 30 feet.

***

Soon, that official IP rate of only 70 barrels would prove helpful. It looked like a mistake. It looked like an ordinary bail-out. In all of Montana in 1990 through 1995, three wells were completed in the Bakken, all in Richland County. One IPed just three barrels; another, 40; the third, 113. Albin FLB 2-33 didn't look like Findley and Robinson were onto something different—something big.

Normally, a well's highest production is in its first days and weeks online and it begins to decline. Findley and Robinson expected Albin FLB 2-33 would too.

"I remember—and this is probably one of the most profound things about the discovery—Bob called me a couple of months later and described the decline rate to me. He said, 'You know, this just isn't declining. Do you think we have someplace to develop this?'"

Could the same thing be done with many wells?

Findley went to the maps. Geologists first get an idea of what is below the surface by making visual observations of the surface, such as of natural outcrops and unnatural exposures.[40] Seismic studies are helpful as well. In this, a booming sound is made on the surface; instruments then measure how the layers of rock—or, at times, cavities—below reflect the sound wave back to the surface or refract it, suggesting the consistency of each layer.

When trying to decide where to place a well, oil and gas geologists also rely on logs of other wells—if any. Having access to these, which contain myriad data, as a preview of what lies beneath is known as "vertical control"—that is, to eliminate some blind risk by seeing what is nearby or, if considering re-entering an old well, seeing what was already encountered.

In the Richland County area of Montana, there were some to draw upon. The county is flanked on the south by the enormous Ce-

---

[40] The Grand Canyon is a natural outcrop where water has cut the rock for ages, showing its vertical composition in plain sight. Mount Rushmore is a natural outcrop but the carving that is the monument is an unnatural exposure.

dar Creek anticline, which first produced oil for Shell Oil Co. in 1951, and the state had been drilled beginning in the 1920s.

At times, geologists can also access physical samples of the rock a well encountered at core libraries. Oil and gas are usually found where they've been found before.[41]

Drawing upon all the available data and based on his own couple of decades of experience in the Williston Basin, Findley made a map of where else an Albin FLB 2-33 might work. He had initially told Robinson that the Albin just happened to tap a small, structural closure, thus the good porosity and slow decline.

An anomaly.

"But," he told Robinson that day on the phone, "I will look and see if we have any place to take it." Turning to past wells, he didn't feel that he had much to look at. "I started looking at the available 'control.' There wasn't a whole lot of control.[42]

"As I went north of our discovery well, the middle member had very low porosity. And it didn't have the higher resistivity we had in the Albin," he says. "I started thinking, 'Well, it looks like it's not going to go anywhere.'"[43]

Looking south, however, logs were showing the middle Bakken to have very persistent porosity—and between 8% and 12%—in a long trend.[44]

---

[41] This part of the process of deciding where to drill a well is called "close-ology." The term is also used when simply trying to lease in and around where a company with a good track record of exploration success is leasing.

[42] All the well logs for the area were available in state records; however, very few wells had been drilled that deep in the area of the Albin well.

[43] Resistivity is measured by electrical current in the wellbore and reported to the state as part of well files. It is an indicator of a rock's porosity—that is, its ability to contain a fluid, such as oil. Water is highly conductive of electricity; oil is a poor conductor. Differences in resistivity shown in well logs indicate what type of fluid is contained along the vertical column, if any. Meanwhile, permeability in a rock, which is needed for oil to be able to flow through it, is determined most reliably by analysis of a core sample. A frac job is to improve permeability.

[44] A core sample taken later from the formation showed extremely low permeability, averaging 0.05 millidarcy, which isn't much but better than that of granite, for example, and a max of 0.50 millidarcy.

"It took me a couple of days; there were maybe 20 to 25 wells I could look at. Every one of them had porosity and high resistivity for oil." Plugging each well into his map, it began to suggest a consistent northwest/southeast trend of producible pay; it began to look like a giant oil field.

He also noticed that the Albin had almost missed the trend. "As I mapped farther southeast, the middle member was gone. I found that we had drilled right close to the edge of what I later interpreted to be a 'shoreline trend.' It looked like a great stratigraphic trap. It looked like it was 40 miles long and 4.5 miles wide."[45]

As for the farthest northwestern extent of the trend, Findley "ran out of control;" there weren't any more well logs to look at. "I didn't really know how far to the northwest it went."

So Findley was right about the Albin being an anomaly—except it appeared it could be repeated and with far more than just a dozen wells. He called Robinson and suggested he sit down.

"I think we found a giant oil field."

Robinson was skeptical. "He said, 'I kind of doubt that.'"

But the pair proceeded with leasing acreage where there had been a dozen dry holes other companies had drilled in the area in the past while looking for other pay and not caring for what they saw in the middle Bakken.[46]

Before the revival in the past decade of oil and gas production onshore the U.S., land could be leased for as little as $10 an acre in areas where no other prospector is trying to do the same thing. Prospectors try to be quiet about it, though: A large E&P company could

---

[45] A shoreline trend is an ancient shore that has become buried in time along with all of the carbon-rich matter that had once existed alongside. A stratigraphic trap is one in which oil and gas are trapped within a rock between low-permeability rocks above and below it.

[46] A "dry hole" is rarely lacking in oil and gas entirely; instead, it usually just lacks sufficient amounts to produce profitably based on commodity prices and production technology at the time. What is deemed sufficient can also vary among producers: A small E&P company might find the small income worthwhile, such as to recover some of its cost of drilling the well; a larger E&P might not bother to further deal with the small well and just plug it. More often, "dry hole" is a financial designation rather than a geologic one.

run in and sweep up 100,000 acres on a whisper that a big play might be in the making; the $1-million spend is a penny to a company with $100 million in annual net profit.

Others drilling in Richland County in 1996 included the behemoth Burlington and about a dozen smaller companies, such as American Exploration Co., Armstrong Operating Inc. and Luff Exploration Co. For Findley and Robinson, with just their own resources, getting a starter amount of leasehold together was all they could manage. More wallets would be needed to lease more and to test the middle-Bakken idea.

"Bob and I didn't quite know what to do," Findley says. "It was going to take a couple million dollars to buy all the leases available on this trend and Bob didn't have that kind of money nor did I."

If the idea worked, they would want to have as much acreage as possible to make more of these wells for themselves and not just prove an idea from which everyone else would profit. Their secret couldn't last long, either. While E&P-company personnel, drilling crews, frac designers, pressure pumpers and others involved in making wells are to be mum about the rocks being targeted and plays that are being attempted, inevitably something slips out at the town diner or while waiting at the airport gate. Chatter happens.

If not securing the acreage to expand their idea and the money to make wells on it before the leases expire, Findley and Robinson could end up discovering a new oil field for someone else.

They had given the idea a name: Sleeping Giant. Findley admits, "You get pretty desperate when you start naming prospects after so many years. It really did look like a giant oil field that was just waiting to be developed.

"So I called it 'Sleeping Giant.'"

He and Robinson's initial plan for the play was to re-enter wells that had passed through the middle Bakken and test the idea that Sleeping Giant was, indeed, a continuous accumulation of oil. These wouldn't be inexpensive. They needed to spread the risk.

"I've drilled my share of dry holes, believe me. And there's that day you think you're going to find a really big structure—one that's going to be really productive—and it turns out to be a dry hole. Usually those are the ones you make when you put 100% of your dollars into them.

"Those are the ones that turn out to be a dry hole."

He told Robinson, "Well, there's only one guy I know who can deal in these kinds of numbers. His name is Cameron Smith out in New York."

BARNETT: 1996, PART TWO

← ← ← ← ← → → → → →

"This technique could reduce the
total cost to drill and complete a well
by as much as 20%."
—*Mitchell Energy & Development Corp.*

When Steinsberger took Walker and the UPR team's LSF idea to management, Mitchell Energy had just celebrated its 50th anniversary and undergone a major transformation. George Mitchell was approaching his 80s and the company's stock price had continued to experience the drag common of that of a conglomerate: Investors may understand one set of assets but not the other. The stock price didn't reflect the full value of Mitchell's diverse assets; the sum of the parts was greater than the whole.

While the company had been formed as an oil and gas producer in 1946, it came to also be a major real-estate developer—particularly of Mitchell's planned community, The Woodlands, north of Houston.[47] While real estate is an investor-philic, hard asset, most of Mitchell Energy's property-holding was in an economy—the Houston area—largely affected by the boom and bust of oil and gas prices. The portfolio wasn't a natural hedge against the E&P side of the business;

---

[47] The Woodlands is a result of Mitchell's and wife Cynthia Woods Mitchell's interest, beginning in the early 1960s, with a then-nascent idea now commonly known as "sustainability." The Mitchell family continues to support projects toward solving for a growing world population in the midst of diminishing resources.

if oil and gas prices declined, so did new-home sales in the region.

Understanding this, George Mitchell had begun to put the company into an intense, portfolio-reprofiling regime beginning in 1994 when he wrote to shareholders, "It's been a roller-coaster year."

Mitchell Energy had received an average of $2.86 per thousand cubic feet for its natural gas in 1993. About half was sold under the pipeline-to-Chicago contract for $3.52 per thousand; the balance went into the spot market at an average of $2.14, which is about what most every other gas producer got.

What the company was torn about, though, was an incongruity: Natural-gas prices had risen, but the price for natural-gas liquids (NGL) had fallen from $13.68 a barrel to $10.16. The boost the company received from higher gas prices was dragged down by what it wasn't receiving for the gas liquids it was stripping from it. And it had to strip the liquids before putting it into the pipe to Chicago.[48] In effect, in 1994, its gas-production and gas-processing businesses were upside down. Also, besides reducing revenue, the lower NGL price had reduced the paper value of Mitchell's gas reserves in the ground, lowering the company's overall worth.

Into 1994, the situation became even worse. George Mitchell and president Bill Stevens wrote to shareholders, "To say (the year) presented a number of difficulties would be a vast understatement."

The price for both dry gas and NGL had fallen yet more. For its contract and non-contract gas, Mitchell Energy had received an average of $2.71 per thousand cubic feet. The real-estate business was going well. "Even so...price changes mandated a close re-examination of all of our business segments and firm actions to adapt," they wrote.

The contract with the pipeline, Natural Gas Pipeline Company of America, was to expire at the end of 1997. Mitchell Energy would

---

[48] Processing removes the wet portion of the gas; fractionators then break the NGL into each type of molecule, such as ethane and propane. The liquids have to be stripped before the gas is shipped to the end-user. Gas that goes to a stovetop or industrial furnace is pure methane by law; impurities would result in a dangerously erratic flame. The entire process isn't inexpensive but it is normally profitable for the producer, processor and fractionator.

then lose its advantage of at least getting a better price than most other producers for half of its gas. Mitchell and Stevens set out to put the company to work on what it was doing best and letting go of the rest.

On the "doing best" side of the ledger was its half-million-acre Fort Worth Basin leasehold; it made 70 wells in it in 1994, most of them in the Barnett. Mitchell and Stevens concluded, "The events of the 1990s have convinced even the most optimistic that we shouldn't base future strategies and plans on a business climate much different from what we have been experiencing."

Buckle up: Rather than waiting for the gas contract to end, Mitchell ended it. On July 1, 1995, there was no more contract. Mitchell had been in an agreement in one form or another with the Chicago pipeline dating back to 1957—four-fifths of Mitchell Energy's existence. George Mitchell had been committed to sending natural gas to Chicago for half of his lifetime. He was now 76.

On June 30, the company was getting $4 per thousand cubic feet for the contract gas; on July 1, for all of its gas, it was getting market price: about $1.25.

This had been a big bet: The market price for gas in the prior six months averaged $1.57, down from an already-pitiful $2.07 in the first half of 1994. But the buy-out net the company a $205-million gain and operating control of thousands of miles of small-diameter pipe that was gathering gas from its 1,500 North Texas wells into bigger pipe and onto the processing plant.

Mitchell's thinking was that he was taking the profit from the contract up-front, rather than making it day by day for 30 more months. It also freed the company of ongoing, awkward, contract-related production limits in Newark East Field—the home of its difficult, yet still promising, Barnett-shale play.

Six months later, Mitchell celebrated the company's 50th anniversary. He wrote, "Fifty years ago, we started with a used drilling rig, some ideas and a whole lot of enthusiasm. Since then, Mitchell Energy & Development Corp. has drilled more than 8,500 wells, almost half of them in North Texas, to become one of the nation's largest independent producers and processors of natural gas.

"While we've had our ups and downs, we've always ended up each year in the black."

Without contract-related restriction on drilling in North Texas, production jumped to 238 million cubic feet a day from 180 million. The company made 40 extra wells that had been delayed while a production cap in the contract area had already been met. Of the more than 2 trillion cubic feet of gas Mitchell Energy produced in its first 50 years, more than 1.5 trillion were from North Texas alone.

Another surprise came in 1997: To further make transparent the value of the company's stock, he sold The Woodlands Corp.[49] The stock became an energy pure-play. Real-estate- and energy-securities analysts were no longer torn about whether to cover it or, if doing so, torn about how to value the part of the business in which they had less expertise. Oil and gas investors could better estimate what to expect from the company.[50]

In early 1998, gas prices improved. The company now had 1,125 employees, pared from nearly 3,000 in 1994. It held an interest in 16 gas-processing plants, reduced from more than 60. It had divested some small packages of oil and gas assets and made some bolt-on additions to its core holdings.

By now, it had drilled some 3,700 gas wells in North Texas; among them, 2,000 were producing and more than 250 were in the Barnett, where it was incessantly seeking the magic for how to make these. The company had tapped the uppermost section of the Barnett and the lowermost with vertical holes. In a study with the Gas Research Institute, it had attempted a horizontal well in 1991.[51]

It had fraced this way and that way. Every one of the wells had

---

[49] The Woodlands Corp. is now owned by The Howard Hughes Corp.

[50] The decision to exit real estate, rather than E&P, had been motivated in part by a $200-million Wise County court judgment in the spring of 1996, claiming Mitchell Energy had contaminated some water wells. Mitchell couldn't sell the E&P business for its full worth with an unresolved judgment attached. The judgment was dismissed entirely by a higher court in 1998. Other, similar claims ceased as attorneys for the plaintiffs were working on contingency.

[51] The institute was formed in 1976 to support research into creating new gas supply. It is now part of the privately funded, non-profit Gas Technology Institute.

made gas. None had been very impressive, based on their cost and what gas was worth in the 1980s and 1990s, which varied from a buck to $3.50 and generally was about $2. They were barely commercial even with the bonus of the higher-priced gas contract.[52]

But a breakthrough was under way.

In April 1998, the company disclosed in its annual report that it was trying something different in its Barnett-shale program that may prove meaningful. Until then, it didn't have much to report on its on-going experimentation in the Barnett.[53]

That Mitchell Energy chose in the spring of 1998 to reveal promising new Barnett attempts suggested that the early findings could favorably affect the company's worth. It reported, "Mitchell also is experimenting with new fracturing techniques in an effort to reduce costs and enhance profitability. One new technique uses mainly water, instead of polymer gel and large amounts of sand, to crack tight rock, so gas can flow into the well.

"This technique could reduce the total cost to drill and complete a well by as much as 20%."

The 61 words portended the most tremendous transformation of the company's net worth and that of every other U.S. oil and gas producer. But, having been 17 years on the Barnett bus by then, Wall Street just sighed.

---

[52] Natural-gas prices fluctuate seasonally, rising in the winter on greater demand for heating and declining each spring. In December 1996, it was about $3.60; three months later, about $1.90.

[53] Through 2000, Mitchell Energy was the only publicly held company that discussed the Barnett in any SEC filing—based on digital files available beginning in 1994—with one exception: Miller Exploration Co. was drilling the gassy, naturally fractured, Antrim shale in Michigan; it referenced Mitchell's Barnett work when filing to IPO in 1997.

BAKKEN: 1996, PART TWO

← ← ← ← ← → → → → →

"So I called Dick Cheney."
—Bobby Lyle

D
ick Findley and Cameron Smith had met in the 1980s when Findley was working at Patrick Petroleum and Smith had an E&P company, Taconic Petroleum Corp. A New York-based financier, Smith was born in the newly discovered oil fields of western Canada after his grandfather, William F. Buckley, had sent Smith's father and a couple of uncles there in the 1940s with a missive: "Get me some of that."[54]

A Texas-born attorney, Buckley founded Mexico-focused Pantepec Oil Co. in 1908 and ran it successfully throughout the early years of the Mexican revolution. After backing an unsuccessful counter-revolution in 1921, he moved the company to New York, taking up oil exploration in Venezuela, instead, as Mexico began to limit non-national ownership of its natural resources.[55]

Upon receiving an undergrad degree from Princeton and a master's in geology from Penn State, Smith worked in the family's oil companies and formed Taconic Petroleum in Oklahoma in 1978. Back in New York in 1991, he formed Cosco Capital Management LLC to connect geologists, engineers and MBAs with capital.

---

[54] One of Smith's uncles was William F. (Bill) Buckley Jr., founder of the *National Review*.

[55] Presciently, Buckley didn't return to Mexico when invited back by the president in the late 1920s; Mexico nationalized its natural resources in the 1930s.

After meeting in the 1980s, Findley and Smith remained in touch about one matter or another. More recently, Smith had contacted Findley to assist in evaluating an offer to lease some mineral rights in Montana that were owned by a royalty trust he managed on behalf of the Buckley family.

Upon developing the Sleeping Giant idea, Findley gave him a call. "Cameron, I think we found a giant oil field, but we don't know how to proceed from here, financially."

Smith said, "Well, it sounds to me like you need two things: You need an operator that can operate a lot of wells and you need money."[56] Findley replied, "Well, I think you're right about that."

Smith had been in touch with Bobby Lyle, the founder of Lyco Energy Corp. based in Dallas, over the years. Using 3-D seismic, Lyle had made a well in 1995 in Montana north of Richland County in the Red River formation that sits below Bakken. The well came on with 91 barrels of oil. A couple more attempts were dry holes.[57]

Lyle says, "Cameron and I had met some years before. We had never done a deal together. We had looked at a number of things."

Born in Kilgore, in the midst of the giant East Texas oil field that was the platform for the H.L. Hunt oil fortune, Lyle's father died while Lyle was just an infant. His mother moved the family to southern Arkansas to El Dorado, home of the 1920s Smackover oil boom where Hunt had gotten his start in the oil and gas business.

Eventually, the Lyles settled about 100 miles southwest in Shreveport, Louisiana. He enrolled in Louisiana Tech University, which had a well recognized engineering program and that, as a state university and fairly near Shreveport, he could afford to attend.

Receiving a bachelor's in mechanical engineering, he went to

---

[56] The operator is the E&P company that, usually, carries the most working interest in a well idea, thus most of the cost and exposure to the risk or reward. Also, it is usually an established company with active drilling operations, thus having ready access to rigs and other equipment and services.

[57] As computer-processing capacity advanced in the late 20th century, increasingly sophisticated 3-D interpretation of the subsurface was possible while 2-D seismic shows only height and depth.

work in Dallas while pursuing a master's in engineering administration at Southern Methodist University. Upon receiving the graduate degree in 1967, he was invited to join the business school's faculty. In the early 1970s, he became dean as Jack Grayson was called to Washington by President Nixon to chair the U.S. Price Commission.

After Grayson returned to SMU, he was called by Paul McCracken to help develop economic policy for President Ford; Grayson asked Lyle to join him at the White House. With that work done, Lyle set off in 1975 for the University of Massachusetts at Amherst for a doctorate in strategic planning and leadership.

As he was concluding his studies, he was considering three post-doctorate endeavors: a return to teaching and university administration, work for the government or starting his own business. The lattermost would test his doctoral findings. Could his theories on strategy and leadership be a successful recipe? He chose to find out.

But Vester Hughes, an attorney and director of privately held, Dallas-based Cornell Oil Co., was asking Lyle to lead Cornell as its chief executive officer. Lyle says, "My first reaction was 'That's not what I want to do. I want to start and run my own business.'" But Hughes reminded him of something: "He said, 'Well, Bobby, you're going to need some money to do that.' He was absolutely right."

During the following four years, Lyle worked on diversifying Cornell's assets, putting together a land deal that became the Dallas version of real-estate developer Gerald Hines' highly successful Galleria retail, hotel and office complex in Houston.

Also, he and other operators worked with the newly formed U.S. Department of Energy on developing a program in which oil that was produced from an old field could be sold at the market—versus government-controlled—price. "Old oil" could be sold for about $3.50 a barrel; "new oil" could get as much as $17 on the open market.

The Department of Energy approved a plan in which old oil could be sold at the market price if the price difference was invested in a qualified, enhanced-oil-recovery (EOR) program.[58] Cornell's and more than 450 other companies' projects qualified under the program. The first permit, #001, that was issued was for a Cornell field in southern California.

Lyle says of getting the field to make more oil, "we drilled a six-foot-diameter, vertical shaft into the producing formation, excavated a 25-foot-diameter room, built a platform and lowered mining equipment into the room, from which we drilled eight horizontal wells into the formation.

"After casing the wellbores and installing production equipment, we removed all of the drilling and completion equipment and began a huff-and-puff steam-flood, using four horizontal wells as injectors and four as producers."

Doing well at Cornell, Lyle had put together funds by September 1981 to launch his own E&P company, Lyco Energy. While intending to explore for new oil and gas reserves, he ended up buying a great deal of them instead, as oil prices trended down and owners of wells began putting them up for sale.

In the early 1990s, Lyle was seeking to raise more capital for Lyco and told a friend. "He immediately said, 'I know where we can place this.' I said, 'Okay. Where?' He said, 'Bill Buckley's nephew, Cameron Smith. He's in New York. Cameron will do this deal.'"

Smith's newly formed firm wasn't a fit just yet for what Lyco sought. "So that was a dead end. But as we talked through that, Cameron and I really resonated. I liked him very much and respected what he had to say. That meeting established a relationship that led to, some years later, Cameron bringing Dick Findley and Bob Robinson to my office."

After years of acquiring and exploiting existing properties, Lyle had been able to position Lyco to work on what he intended: finding new oil and gas fields. He was already looking in Montana.

Findley says of when he spoke to Smith about the giant oil field

---

[58] Water-flooding, injection of carbon dioxide and other EOR methods help to get more oil out of a formation.

he thought he and Robinson had found, "Cameron took my opinion on the middle-Bakken porosity trend on blind faith; he hadn't looked at my data." Actually, Robinson hadn't either at that point. Findley's reputation as an oil and gas finder was enough.

Only a few months since the Albin well had been completed, Lyle, Findley, Robinson and Smith gathered in Dallas. Findley says, "Bob and I didn't know Bobby Lyle and Bob didn't know Cameron Smith, but I knew Cameron and Cameron knew Bobby. Cameron said, 'Look, you can trust Bobby. He's going to look at your data, but he's not going to go out and go around you or anything.'"[59]

Findley had made a brochure. It described the resistivity in each formation in the Albin FLB 2-33 down to Nisku, the deepest it was drilled. It showed the well's production history and that it wasn't declining. Findley added details from logs of neighboring wells that had traveled through the middle Bakken. "It took quite a few hours," Findley says.

That was in the morning. Lyle liked the idea and wanted his team of engineers as well as a consulting geologist to look at it. They were quickly gathered and Findley made the presentation again.

Approaching 5 p.m., Lyle walked around the conference table, whispering in each Lyco team member's ear. "Bob and I were looking at each other. 'What is he doing? What is he whispering?'"

Lyle was asking each if he could work through the evening on evaluating the idea. At breakfast the next morning, Lyle told Findley and Robinson, "The good news is that the engineers reviewed your data and feel that you probably understated the potential. They think the potential may be even greater than what you said."

But the consulting geologist couldn't work into the evening; it had been his wedding anniversary. Lyle asked, "Would you mind giving me one more day, so the geologist can review it? If it holds up, we'll take your deal."

The next morning, Lyle told Findley and Robinson, "We'll take the deal." Robinson handled the terms of the arrangement.

---

[59] This meant that Lyle wouldn't just take Findley's idea and make the play for himself.

Findley says, "Essentially, they had agreed to re-enter 10 of the wells that had bypassed the middle Bakken to confirm that the oil was there. And we bought quite a few leases—at least 50,000 acres—along the trend. We were trying to be as selective as we could to stay in what we had defined as the porosity-trend fairway."

Lyco would have 75% working interest in the deal; Findley and Robinson, forming an entity named Sleeping Giant LLC, would own 25%. What acreage Findley and Robinson held was contributed to the partnership with Lyco. Lyle says, "It was a fair deal and we liked the people and the concept. We thought it was worth the risk and that, if it worked, there was potentially a lot of oil there."

Nine re-entries were attempted in 1997 and a tenth in early 1998. Three met with mechanical failure and were abandoned. Seven others came on with between 30 and 86 barrels—not very dissimilar to the Albin. While not commercially successful, they proved Findley's theory that the middle Bakken would produce from one end of the northwest/southeast trend to the other.

"We confirmed that we had a giant oil field," Findley says.

The science project was a geologic success; new well engineering would be needed to make it a financial success. Lyle and the Lyco team set out to solve the problem.

Lyle believed that the sweet spot—just 10 to 15 feet—of the roughly 30-foot-thick zone would have to be produced horizontally and—unlike the Burlington wells in North Dakota that were made in the upper-Bakken shale—the middle-Bakken wells in Montana would have to be fraced.

"But no one had ever attempted to fracture-stimulate (a horizontal in) the Bakken," he says.

A vertical, middle-Bakken well would cost about $450,000 to drill and complete and it might make between 20,000 and 70,000 barrels of oil in its lifetime. "If you're getting $17 a barrel against 50,000 barrels, you're not too anxious to do that.

"So we knew we had a reservoir here that seemed willing to give up commercial quantities of oil, but it wasn't going to work from a vertical well. If we could drill a horizontal for, let's say, 3,000 feet, instead of just 15 vertical feet of exposure to the middle Bakken, we would have 3,000.

"You run the economics on that and it begins to get interesting."

***

Lyco's engineers began looking for some example, some analog, of a fraced horizontal that was made in a similar environment.

"Finally, we found a Texaco field in California." Texaco had drilled some horizontal wells in a shallow formation and fracture-stimulated them. "It seemed to have worked, so we were further convinced that this was clearly a possibility.

"However, no one had ever attempted what we were proposing to do at a depth of 10,000 to 11,000 feet. And there was one other problem: We didn't have any money to really test this (horizontal-plus-frac) idea."

The horizontal well Lyle had in mind would cost at least $1.75 million. It was a lot of risk for a small, privately held company.

"So I called Dick Cheney."

Lyle and Cheney were on the Southern Methodist University board of trustees. Cheney was chairman of Halliburton, based in Dallas, at the time, after serving as U.S. secretary of defense for President George H.W. Bush until 1993 and before serving as vice president to George W. Bush beginning in 2001.

Halliburton had just announced that it was interested in taking a working interest in certain types of exploration projects, particularly ones in which Halliburton could test, prove and further develop technology for complex reservoirs.

Lyle says, "I told Dick what we wanted to do and asked if Halliburton was interested in participating."

Cheney shared Lyle's idea with a Halliburton well-completions team based in Denver that focused on serving operators in the Rockies area. Lyle, Findley and others on Lyco's middle-Bakken project met in a room in Denver filled with Halliburton engineers, geologists, geophysicists and frac gurus.

The presentation took the day to complete, followed by robust conversation. Lyle says, "At the end of the day, they said, 'We think this has potential.'" It was run up to Halliburton headquarters. Some weeks later, Lyle received the call.

"They said, 'We think this will work.'" Lyle wanted to try the concept with three horizontal tests. "They said, 'No. We won't do three. We'll only do one.'"

It was one well or no well; Lyle agreed to the one well.[60]

But oil prices were falling now. In early 1997, a barrel had pushed past $25 but, propelled by the 1997-98 "Asian contagion" of inflated estimates of Pacific Rim economic growth, a barrel was ticking down to what became as little as $11 in December 1999.[61]

And that was the Nymex price; what most producers actually net is less. The Halliburton group asked, "What do you want to do?" Lyle replied, "I'm not drilling a well up there with oil at $8.75 a barrel."

Halliburton agreed. Instead, it would take the idea apart and look at it all over again. "I said, 'I'm not going anywhere. If you need to do that, then, by all means, go do it.'"

Lyle let Sleeping Giant rest. Proving the enormous, new, U.S., oil field would have to wait.

---

[60] Halliburton's arrangement for an interest-share of the project remains confidential.

[61] Oppressing oil prices further was that OPEC members were increasing their unwanted production through 1998.

BARNETT: 1999

← ← ← ← ← → → → → →

"I'm thinking, 'Holy!'...
How much gas is in this rock that it could...
cause those things to balloon like that?"
—Kent Bowker

1 998 was the newest of many punishing years in the oil and gas industry. As the price of oil was still diving while entering the winter of 1998-99, natural gas was less than $2. Mitchell Energy's gas contract would have been nice now, but it would have expired a year earlier anyway.

Meanwhile, because oil prices were low, the price for NGL was as well. Ethane, a component of gas liquids, can be used in making petrochemicals just as with oil-based naphtha, so the price of one tends to track the price of the other.[62]

But the company was in good shape. By early 1999, George Mitchell had streamlined it to consist now of its best oil- and gas-producing properties and just six gas-processing plants.[63] Lawsuits

---

[62] Because of new NGL supply from the shale plays as well as from horizontals in other formations, such as Mississippian-age limestone in Oklahoma, the price of NGL decoupled from that of crude oil and collapsed in 2012. As of early 2014, the SEC and producers were developing guidelines on differentiating "liquids" production and reserves in reports to state what was oil and what was NGL.

[63] It also held an interest in a newly built MTBE plant, just as the federal government began to consider banning most use of MTBE within the U.S. A partner, Enterprise Products Partners LP, bought Mitchell Energy's interest and exports the production.

claiming the company had contaminated well water in Wise County were dismissed; insurers had reimbursed the company for most of its defense cost.

And he and Stevens revealed on April 16, 1999, that the Barnett science project had had a breakthrough; the new, light-sand-frac technique it had begun testing in mid-1997 was now being applied across the Barnett field, Newark East. Of its inventory of about 1,000 more development wells to drill on its leasehold, about 450 of these were targeting Barnett, "which now appears to hold considerably more (economically) recoverable gas reserves than once thought," the company reported.[64]

Besides switching the frac to the LSF, there had been reconsideration of estimates of how much gas might be in the Barnett.

Chevron Corp. had tried one vertical, wildcat, Barnett attempt, Mildred Atlas 1, in 1997 in southeastern Johnson County, far south of where Mitchell Energy had been coaxing the black rock. Kent Bowker was on the Chevron team at the time. With a bachelor's from Adrian College in Michigan and a master's from Oklahoma State University, both in geology, Bowker went to work in Appalachia in 1980 for Gulf Oil Corp., which was bought by Chevron in 1985.

"You know, it's a shame," he says. "I mean, it's kind of ironic that Chevron is spending billions of dollars to get into all of these shale plays now and they had information about the Barnett that no one else had back in 1997. At one time, Gulf and Chevron had the biggest acreage position in Appalachia and Chevron decided (in the late 1980s) that there was nothing left there.

"When I was at Chevron, we had a guy come through from the overseas business (unit). They were recruiting to get people to work overseas. He actually told us he felt sorry that we had to try and find oil and gas in the United States because it was obvious that there really wasn't anything left. He said we could work overseas, instead, and do exciting projects.

---

[64] Exploratory wells are wildcats in unproven acreage and may be dry holes; development wells are in proven acreage and are more likely to be successful.

"Now, the rest of the world is trying to emulate what we've done here in the United States."

Upon Chevron quitting its experimental, unconventional-resource attempts in 1997, Bowker left the company and its downtown-Houston office to work for Mitchell Energy near his home in The Woodlands as head of geology for the Barnett team. "My son was born in December of '97 and it looked like, for my career to go anywhere with Chevron, I was going to have to move overseas. I didn't want to do that with a newborn. And I had some information on the Barnett that no one else had. They (at Mitchell) were looking to hire another geologist, so the timing worked out perfectly for me.

"And I had always admired Mr. Mitchell—what he had done in building The Woodlands and for his persistence in the Barnett and other plays. I mean, he was still drilling Bend-conglomerate wells after a lot of people had walked away from it, saying it was finished.

"He was easy to admire; he was so far-sighted."

Mitchell Energy's Barnett team had become familiar with Bowker in 1995 when discussing with him Chevron's interest in the Barnett. Dan Steward, Mitchell's vice president of Midcontinent-region exploration, writes in his documentary of Mitchell's Barnett work, "He had more specific technical training in unconventional gas in general—and organic shale in particular—than anyone we had encountered."

Bowker had calculated gas in place in the Barnett from Chevron's 60-foot core that was taken from the Johnson County hole. The thinking had been that the Barnett contained 53 billion cubic feet of gas per square mile based on a 1991 core Mitchell Energy had pulled and a subsequent Gas Research Institute evaluation. Instead, Bowker estimated it could be four times that, if taking the gas in place in both the upper- and lower-Barnett-shale sections into consideration.

"I knew this thing could be huge," Bowker says the new math suggested. "The gas-in-place numbers were so much larger than what were reported by the GRI."

He had suspected this before the Chevron numbers arrived. "On a coring job, the core comes out of the ground in an aluminum barrel about 30 feet long and four inches in diameter. You lay that down and cut it into three-foot sections, so you can easily transport it. You put these rubber caps on the end of each section, so they don't fall out. At the Chevron well, we used hose clamps—like radiator-hose clamps—to keep the rubber caps on.

"As we were continuing to do our work, I looked over and these rubber caps were starting to balloon out. I'm thinking, 'Holy!' First, it's kind of dangerous because that's like a pipe bomb. Secondly, how much gas is in this rock that it could—and this is not thin rubber; this is thick rubber—cause those things to balloon like that?

"That piece of rock had already been exposed to decreasing pressure as we were bringing it up through the wellbore and it had been sitting out on the rig floor for at least an hour before those caps were put on. It had been de-gassing for many, many hours. There was that much gas in that rock—even after it had been exposed to atmospheric pressure for that long.

"Then, you have to wonder. 'Where does all of this gas come from? Where is all of this gas stored? How is it stored in there?'"

Meanwhile, Nick Steinsberger was switching the completion program to the LSF. "These two things were a happy coincidence," Bowker says.

"We learned that we were only getting 7% or 8% of the gas out; we had thought we were getting 30%. We could go back in and do re-fracs and tighter spacing and start perforating and fracing in the upper Barnett. Nick's work permitted that to happen because it basically cut our costs in half.

"Our re-fracs of old vertical wells—I mean, it would have cost more money to set up a printing press to print money than the amount of capital it took to re-frac those wells. It was like printing money but better."

Mitchell Energy was also spending about $10,000 per frac job on clay stabilizer. "I told them, 'We don't need the stabilizer because we don't have that much clay. If you put a piece of Barnett shale in a bucket of water and let it sit there over the weekend, nothing happens; the Barnett isn't affected at all by that water. A lot of shales will start falling apart within minutes, but the Barnett is like Pyrex."

Further experimentation was with the size of the sand and with an additional change in the gel recipe. Changing the recipe had been a sizable risk. "If it ruined the rock in that wellbore, you were never going to get the well back."

Based on new economics and new gas-in-place estimates, they began down-spacing the Barnett wells—drilling one per 50 acres versus one per 100 to reach more of the stuck gas. With the LSF, the Barnett wells were costing less, thus they were economic. And it appeared the new technique could make the Barnett productive east—toward Denton—and south—toward Fort Worth—of the core play in Wise County. It could result in several hundred more potential Barnett-well locations.

The company reported in the spring of 1999, "(The LSF), a better and cheaper method of fracturing the rock around each wellbore to enhance productivity, has made many Barnett locations once considered marginal now economic to drill. These (LSF) treatments use mostly water instead of polymer gel to crack open the rock and they rely on smaller quantities of sand to prop open the cracks…

"This new technique has reduced the cost of a standard…fracture treatment by 60%—or roughly $140,000 per well—and will enable the company to apply larger treatments at minimal additional cost to improve the productivity…."

George Mitchell had pared the company into a lean, energy pure-play, wrapped in profit with a Barnett-bonus bow on top. In the fall of 1999, he was now 80 and owned more than 60% of the shares. He put the company up for sale, hiring Goldman Sachs to negotiate with potential buyers.

Natural gas had improved to nearly $3 and crude oil to more than $20. A fifth rig was being brought in to drill more of its new Barnett potential. Employees were fewer than 900. It had interests in nearly 4,400 oil and gas wells and 1.1 million acres of land, about half of this over Barnett.

But no one showed up with a worthy offer.

On April 6, 2000, he announced the company would continue as it was, particularly in the Barnett. And he had more work to do. The company's two classes of shares would be consolidated into one; its fiscal year would become the same as the calendar year.

Twelve months later, with 70 new wells using the LSF, the potential was proving to be yet greater. He and Stevens wrote to shareholders, "Even after last year's breakthrough in the application of light-sand-fracture technology…studies indicate that only a small portion of the gas in place is being recovered."

Making the wells yet closer could add another 1,000 locations; these were in addition to the more than 500 potential and more than 300 proven locations it already had.

The company added 240 billion cubic feet to its proved-reserves column in 1999 using the LSF in the Barnett and now also in its Cotton Valley wells—the most reserves it had added in a single year in its 53 years. Its proved reserves now totaled 1.1 trillion cubic feet.[65]

In the Barnett, which consists of an upper section and a lower section, the old MHF technique had been too costly to make wells in the upper section. The company reported that the LSF now made economic production possible from that as well as the lower section, meaning both could be tapped from a single wellbore—further increasing production.

The new Barnett well costs made the program profitable at $2 gas and could make "an outstanding return at $3," it reported.

It planned 135 Barnett wells in 2000. It had six rigs at work. And 300 of its old wells that had been completed in the lower Barnett or other formations were being re-entered to add an opening in the upper-Barnett layer as well. Each was estimated now to ultimately produce between 1- and 1.25 billion cubic feet of gas.

And it was testing whether the rock would make just as much from wells as close as within 27 acres of each other, down from 100-

---

[65] The company, which had pioneered the MHF technique in the limestone member of the Cotton Valley in 1978, reported that it was paring costs by 30% there now by using the LSF instead. The savings were some $350,000 per well. Also, it had begun to make these wells closer than within 160 acres to drain more of the newly economic, stuck gas.

acre spacing just two years earlier.[66] If it worked, Mitchell would have more than 2,000 potential, Barnett-well locations.

Its production from the Barnett alone was now more than 266 million cubic feet a day compared with about 180 million in mid-1995 when it cut loose of the gas contract.

At the same time, industry leaders and federal law- and policy-makers were beginning to note that new U.S. gas supply was becoming even harder to come by—despite the tax-incented efforts of the 1980s and the application of new technology that resulted. And gas demand was growing, particularly from new gas-fired power plants, which had become favored over coal and nuclear.[67]

As days, weeks and months elapsed, a winning bidder would have to pay even more for Mitchell Energy now. The company's long-term debt had declined to $300 million from some $700 million in 1994. It had ordered two more rigs to work its Barnett acreage, bringing the total to eight. Its aim was to make 135 wells in the rock in 2000; by July, it had already completed 69 of these, up from 77 in all of 1999.

Gas had pushed past $4. And higher oil prices—about $21— meant a better price for its NGL.

The company was now making more than 300 million cubic feet a day with about 179 million of that from just the Barnett—roughly as much as from all of its wells across its portfolio in 1995.

Its stock price pushed past $45 in September—double that of earlier in the year. Suddenly, news of the play was reaching securities analysts and investors other than those who had only followed Mitchell Energy's stock.

---

[66] Spacing of wells on a per-acre basis is in reference to the areal extent the well is estimated to be draining. Developing a play too densely can affect other wells' performance. In the case of a super-low-permeability rock like the Barnett, however, denser development is necessary to capture as much of the gas as possible.

[67] When the Section 29 tax incentive to produce unconventional gas took effect in 1980, U.S. production from any kind of rock was about 53 billion cubic feet a day; in 2000, it was unchanged—about 53 billion—despite that the number of U.S. gas wells had more than doubled. In 2003, more than half of U.S. gas output was from wells fewer than three years old. Adding in gas from the new shale plays, U.S. production soared to 66 billion a day in 2012.

In November 2000, drilling-rig operator Patterson Energy Inc., which would later become Patterson UTI Energy Inc., was purchasing 21 rigs from Jones Drilling Corp. It reported that the rigs were working in the Permian Basin "and the Barnett shale area of north-central Texas." Four months later, international E&P operator Pogo Producing Co. mentioned in its annual report that it was active in the Barnett.

A week later, in its annual report, Mitchell Energy reported it produced 116 billion cubic feet of gas and 20.2 million barrels of oil, condensate and NGL in 2000. It now held 9,100 miles of gas-gathering pipe. Its share price hit $64. Fourth-quarter gas averaged $5.52 and briefly exceeded $10 on winter demand.

The company planned 276 more Barnett wells in 2001, expanding farther southeast and testing north; it had already expanded south and east. It reported, "...For years, the greatest technological obstacle to more rapid growth of Mitchell Energy has been the extremely dense shale of the Newark East (Field)...that only very reluctantly releases its natural gas.

"The use of (LSF) technology...has made it economical to expand development of the Barnett and promises to add even more opportunities in the future."

Old wells were being re-fraced; new production was coming on at eight times that of original production and they were declining less rapidly. Eight wells that were re-fraced and back online for at least six months were making an average of a half-million cubic feet a day each—more than twice what they had originally come on with.

And nearby wells were getting a production bump off the new frac jobs that were being done on other wells.

"To date, 61 offset wells have received incidental stimulation, with production rates nearly tripling to 721,999 cubic feet per day after offset-well stimulation and averaging 372,000 per day six months later," the company reported.

Overall, Mitchell Energy was making more gas from its new Barnett wells at less cost. It was doubling its productive targets by being able to add in the thinner, upper-Barnett section. Nearby wells were making incidental, additional production.

If dropping to 27-acre spacing, it had 4,000 potential, additional well locations. This was just for where the company had proven the Barnett to work in the core area where an underlying, Viola-limestone frac barrier was present; altogether, it had more than 550,000 net acres in North Texas.

***

What was going on at Mitchell Energy?

Larry Nichols wanted to know.

Nichols was well familiar with what a repeatable gas play could do for a company. One of these, the Fruitland coal in the San Juan Basin, had catapulted it from being a small, privately held E&P in the 1980s into a multi-billion-dollar enterprise.

In 1950, John Nichols had created the first publicly registered oil and gas drilling fund. It and those that would be formed in the decades to come involved private investments in a pool of money that would be spent on drilling wells, usually in a particular region of the country. The return on investment would be paid from production from wells in that program.[68]

By 1971, son Larry Nichols had a geology degree from Princeton and a law degree from the University of Michigan. He had served as a law clerk to U.S. Supreme Court Chief Justice Earl Warren and as an assistant in the Department of Justice to future Supreme Court Chief Justice William Rehnquist. He was soon called to his father's oil and gas business, forming Oklahoma City-based Devon Energy Corp. In 1989, he was its chairman and chief executive and the small company was in the biggest gas play in the country.

The Fruitland coal of the San Juan Basin in northwestern New Mexico had long been known by wildcatters looking to make gas from sandstones above and below. A Devon team, economically enabled in part by the Section 29 tax credits, had looked at how to profitably

---

[68] Fund promoters didn't always have a keen sense of the oil and gas business. Or they did and the fund was built to fail at the expense of investors. Funds like those John Nichols developed were among the trusted like those that Raymond Plank led, also beginning in the 1950s, that was the platform for what is Apache Corp. today.

produce the gas that was trapped in the coal. The tax credit for this kind of gas was about 83 cents per thousand cubic feet produced.

It began making wells of 20 million cubic feet a day—just from vertical holes. Nichols says, "The San Juan is an unusual basin. It's massive in geographic extent and there are several formations."

With success there, Devon went on to explore abroad in Canada, Azerbaijan, South America, southeastern Asia, Egypt and West Africa. By 2001, it was a Top 5 U.S. independent E&P as measured by reserves, production, market cap and enterprise value.[69]

Entering the Barnett-shale play would be a natural fit for the company. It already had experience with working unconventional rock, such as coal, and it was aiming to grow its North American gas weighting. All real-time and forecasted gas-demand data were clear by 2001 that the U.S. was long on future gas demand and short of new, additional supply.

By early 2001, oil and gas prices had found a trifecta of profitability: Natural gas was an incredible $7; oil, $27; NGL, $25. Mitchell Energy's long-term debt had been pared to only $218 million. Its bank line of credit of $250 million was unused.

Oilfield-service costs had grown as producers were getting back to work in the higher-commodity-price regime. But Mitchell Energy reported that "the increasing-cost trend is not expected to cause the company to curtail its drilling program in the near term since even below-average Barnett wells are economic at natural-gas prices as low as $2.50 per (thousand cubic feet)."

The figure was remarkable for the time. For example, some Gulf of Mexico gas producers were reporting that they couldn't make economic gas wells for less than $3.50 now. One of these quit exploring and set out to build an LNG-import plant instead.[70]

It was looking for five more rigs to take its Barnett rig count to

---

[69] An "independent" E&P company is one that only explores for and produces oil and gas; a "major" or "integrated" oil and gas company is one that is also involved in processing, refining and marketing its and others' oil, gas and byproducts.

[70] Dozens of power companies began applying for permits to build facilities to import gas as liquefied natural gas (LNG) via tanker.

20. Company-wide production was more than 400 million cubic feet a day. And this was gas onshore the U.S. The pipelines to take it to market were already in place. It didn't have to be produced offshore West Africa, for example, liquefied, put in a ship, landed on the Gulf or Atlantic coast and regasified before sold.

When George Mitchell put the company up for sale in the fall of 1999, Devon Energy had taken a look but not bid. By the spring of 2001, Mitchell Energy's proved reserves had grown to 2.5 trillion cubic feet of gas equivalent—more than double that of 18 months earlier.[71] He asked Goldman Sachs to check in on a few prospective buyers on if they were interested now.

Nichols took the call.

On June 14, he visited Mitchell in Houston and confirmed his interest. On Aug. 7, he proposed $30 and 0.585 Devon share per Mitchell share. George Mitchell asked for more. Two days later, he increased the cash portion to $31 a share. Mitchell asked him to increase it more. Nichols replied that it was as high as Devon would go.

The deal was done on Aug. 13. It valued Mitchell Energy at $62.12 a share for a total of about $3.5 billion. To further seal the deal, Devon bought 100 shares from Mitchell himself the evening before the deal was announced.

Three weeks later, the morning after the Labor Day holiday, Devon announced it would buy Calgary-based Anderson Exploration Ltd. for $3.5 billion in cash for a deal value, including debt assumption, of $4.6 billion. Besides Mitchell's 2.5 trillion cubic feet equivalent of proved reserves, Devon would gain Anderson's 3.2 trillion in the prolific Western Canadian Sedimentary Basin.

To make it clear that George Mitchell was still onboard, he was called upon to remark on it in the Devon announcement. He said, "Speaking as someone who looks forward to becoming Devon's larg-

---

[71] "Equivalent" is based on converting oil reserves and production into the Btu equivalent of natural gas, consolidating the two figures. When "barrels of oil equivalent" is used, it is the consolidation of the Btu value of the natural gas into the number of barrels of oil. Btu is a British thermal unit. It is a measure of the energy contained in oil or gas rather than of just its physical volume, which is measured in barrels and cubic feet.

est shareholder, I fully support the acquisition of Anderson. This transaction creates the preeminent North American independent."[72]

Completing both deals, Devon would have 12.3 trillion cubic feet of proved reserves, 87% in North America and the most held by any independent E&P. Its North American gas production would be 2.2 billion a day, making it the No. 1 independent North American gas producer. Oil and NGL production would be 180,000 barrels a day—again, No. 1.

A day later, Nichols presented at a Lehman Brothers-hosted energy-investment conference in New York. He recalls a securities analyst's introduction of him. "It was the worst introduction I've ever had. He said, 'And our next speaker is Larry Nichols. He just blew his brains out.'" Devon had announced $8.1 billion of deals—both betting on natural gas—in one month.

Laughing, Nichols told him, "You could have said 'I have doubts about it.' You didn't need to get personal."[73]

The Anderson deal had come about because of the Mitchell deal, he says. "It was one of those mixed blessings. We had been wanting to expand in Canada for a long time. I had talked to (chairman and chief executive) J.C. Anderson repeatedly and he had rejected our solicitation.

"When we announced Mitchell in August of 2001, while we were in New York and Boston explaining the deal to our (fund-manager) shareholders, he called and said, 'That's really great.'

"He understood the potential there. He looked at Mitchell's gas plus Devon's gas plus his and he said, 'We could really create a North American powerhouse. I've changed my mind. I'd like to sell Anderson to you.'"

---

[72] Upon closing, the Mitchell family held 13.9 million Devon shares or 8.9% of those outstanding. In the spring of 2013, the family held 22.7 million shares or 5.58% of those outstanding as a result of a 2-for-1 stock split in November 2004 and a 5-million-share sell-down.

[73] The analyst changed his rating of Devon shares some six months later to "Buy." Nichols says, "To his credit, he saw that what we were doing looked like it was going to work and changed his mind. We had begun to get converts."

Nichols was glad but had mixed thoughts. He recalls, "Half of my brain said, 'Great.' And half of my brain said, 'Why now?'"

Stock-market reaction to the Mitchell deal had already been mixed. "If you looked at what was there—proved, producing—you paid a full price. It didn't dilute shareholders much. If you had someone with an explorationist background (looking at it), who saw the potential, you were excited about it.

"So some shareholders thought it was a great deal and others thought, 'Eh. It sounds interesting, but I'll wait 'til you get farther down the road and then I'll buy your stock if you prove that you can grow it.'"[74]

In 1999, when Mitchell was for sale, potential buyers were still uncertain of whether the LSF technique could be repeated across the core area of the Barnett or successfully taken outside that core area. Nichols says, "Our people were convinced at the time that it didn't work. We didn't want to buy it. Devon and everyone else went in, looked at it and said, 'The hydraulic fracturing doesn't work—or it's *uncertain* that it works.'"

Tony Vaughn, Devon executive vice president, E&P, says, "It hadn't been replicated very many times yet." But Mitchell went on to repeat it across the core, expand it to additional Fort Worth Basin acreage and to use it in its Cotton Valley play south of there.

"Goldman Sachs ran a rare, failed auction (in 1999)," Nichols says. "And then, after a couple of years, you saw the production growing." He was surprised. "We asked, 'How's their production growing?' We went back there to Mitchell and looked at it and said, 'Yeah, the hydraulic fracturing is working—or it looks like it's working.'"

But that was only certain in the heart of the play. Nichols says he figured that the $3.5-billion offer would make a tiny return on the potential of using the light-sand fracs in vertical wells in the acreage.

"We would have gotten our money back."

---

[74] With softening gas prices and the 9/11 attack just a few days after the Lehman conference, Devon shares tumbled to about $18 (adjusted for a 2004 split). They turned north, then, to peak at $124 in June 2008 as the price of natural gas grew over the years to more than $12.

But it would need to make a return on investment and a 120,000-acre, vertical play wouldn't be enough.[75] "We paid a full purchase price for that area because we were betting and hoping we could make it work with horizontal drilling. Mitchell had tried a variety of horizontal wells but had never been able to do it successfully.

"The upside was the unknown: Could we take that horizontal? Could we combine the hydraulic fracturing that Mitchell was perfecting with horizontal drilling, which Mitchell had not yet figured out how to do there?"

Some 120,000 of Mitchell's more than 550,000 net acres in North Texas were in the Barnett core area. What if the vertical wells worked in at least 120,000 more acres? And what if it could produce yet more gas from horizontal wells?

This could be a world-class natural-gas field.

But it had to be expanded outside of the core and that would require horizontals. The core in Wise and Denton counties was where the Viola-limestone frac barrier sat above the water-bearing Ellenburger. "So, if you fraced a vertical well there, you didn't frac into the water. But if you drilled the well where the Viola was absent and fraced into it, some of those fractures would go into the water and you would get a water well.

"The solution—to make the Barnett work outside the core—we postulated was to drill a horizontal well to stay at the top of the formation. When you fraced it, you wouldn't go into the water. When we bought it, all we knew was that only the core acreage worked and only with vertical wells."

The Mitchell merger was completed in January 2002. In June, Devon completed its first horizontal in the Barnett. Nothing to it.

Nichols says, "Well, it wasn't quite 'nothing to it.'"

---

[75] Mitchell's sizable midstream-asset portfolio was solid but Devon assigned only face value to that. Nichols says, "Our philosophy on midstream has been that we always want to be able to get our gas or oil to a competitive place, where there's more than one outlet. If there's only one pipeline you're selling to, that pipeline can charge whatever they want. But owning midstream assets is not the end goal (for an E&P)."

BAKKEN: 2000

← ← ← ← ← → → → → →

"The driver got out and said,
Well, this is my second load of oil today."
—Dick Findley

Tom Lantz had joined Halliburton about two years before meeting Bobby Lyle, Dick Findley and Bob Robinson in Denver. A reservoir engineer with a bachelor's from the University of Southern California, Lantz had been working for Phillips Petroleum in Lafayette when Phillips decided to close that office. Employees were being relocated to Houston.

During U.S. oil- and gas-producer consolidation, beginning in the 1980s, with each round of price collapses, E&P companies would further expand offices in Houston, closing field offices. Further growth of Houston as U.S. energy headquarters was also driven by Shell Oil Co.'s development of how to produce oil and gas from beneath superdeep water in the Gulf of Mexico. Its and others' efforts required assembling large technical staff in one mind-trust location and where the most inter-E&P information-sharing was likely.

Lantz didn't want to relocate; his wife, Sharon, was the director at the time of the Educational Technology Review Center at the University of Southwestern Louisiana.[76] Having collaborated with Halliburton personnel who were based in Lafayette over the years on de-

---

[76] The school's name was changed to the University of Louisiana at Lafayette in 1999.

velopment projects for Phillips, he happened to have a meeting scheduled with them as the relocation news was announced.

"I half-jokingly commented, 'Do you guys have a job over here?'" Lantz says. "Well, the next day, I got a call."

As it happened, Halliburton was developing the new business unit that wanted to invest in E&P projects in which it could deploy new technology and further innovate to help make these and others possible. For Halliburton, Lantz worked with Chevron Corp. on an old gas field in the Gulf. A couple of years later, he was offered a post in Denver to head a Halliburton group that was involved in looking at Lyco's middle-Bakken project. Having lived in Denver in the past, he and his family accepted the transfer.

"Bobby (Lyle) had contacted Halliburton and posed a question of 'How would you try to complete these wells to effectively exploit this kind of reservoir?' That question was sent to the integrated-solutions group. We evaluated the project and made the decision to participate in it. We started putting our resources in to evaluate how to best go about developing this kind of a tight rock."

They agreed with Lyle that the play would have to be developed horizontally and fraced. The initial ideas at the time involved making select perforations along the wellbore and pushing a massive amount of water and sand into the formation.

"You would just pump into those perforations along the entire lateral length all at once and try to control the placement of the sand by the placement of the perforations."

The technique was used in vertical wells in which the targeted formation might be tens or even hundreds of feet thick. Several perforations would be made along, for example, 200 feet of vertical zone; the well would then produce from more than one opening along the column, capturing more of the resource.[77]

---

[77] This was "limited entry" fracing and pre-dated the modern, multiple-stage frac, in which perforations along the wellbore are fraced one at a time, usually starting with "the toe," which is at the farthest end of the lateral from the vertical "leg," and concluding with the one closest to the "the heel" where the vertical leg turns into a horizontal—that is, the "foot" or "shoe."

Meanwhile, oil prices had begun to improve, exceeding $26 in December 1999 and heading to $30. The price was the best since 1985.[78] Lyle says, "Finally, we started drilling the test well."

Burning Tree State 36-2H was placed about 17 miles northwest of the now four-year-old Albin FLB 2-33. The middle Bakken there was at about 10,000 feet below the surface. The decision was made that the lateral should be driven along the top half of the roughly 30-foot section, just below the upper-Bakken shale.

The drilling crew would need to keep the drillbit in that small window. "Today, with more than 8,000 horizontal Bakken wells in Montana and North Dakota, the task seems pretty simple. However, at the time, what we were doing had never been attempted.

"We were all a little nervous."

Lantz says, "The good news was that the upper shale has a very distinct gamma-ray signature, which is the main tool you're using to steer with." With this, it was apparent if the drillbit had deviated too close to or too far from the upper shale.

Findley recalls one of the engineers saying, "This permeability is so low there's no way this play is ever going to work. Let's walk away. It's just not worth doing." But "Bobby said, 'No. We've come this far. Let's go ahead and drill it horizontal.'"

The lateral reached about 1,700 feet; the plan had been to take it to about 3,000 feet. "The well started to torque up on us," Lyle says. "I was concerned we were going to lose it. I told the Halliburton group, 'We have enough exposure. Let's stop and test the idea. If we twist off now, we may never get back here again.'

"People might have gotten cold feet. 'If we lose the well, we're going to leave a lot of money in the hole. And we may not convince ourselves that we ought to try this again.' They said, 'We think that's a good idea.'

"So we stopped drilling."

It was time to complete the well. Perforations had been made in preparation for the frac job. From just open holes along the horizon-

---

[78] One exception was nearly $40 during the brief Iraq-Kuwait war.

tal wellbore, "we were surprised by the (natural) flowback we were getting," Lyle says. "It was better than we anticipated."

Findley and Robinson had decided to go out and watch the frac job. Findley, coming in from nearby Billings, and Robinson, from Michigan, arrived at the wellsite. "There was nobody out there. Nothing. We didn't know what was going on," Findley says.

They wandered around the site.

"There was this dust-covered gauge on the ground and it had 400 pounds on it. Bob looked over to the storage tank and saw this flap going up and down on the top. We put two and two together and said, 'My goodness. This well is flowing!'

"About that time, a tanker pulled up, onto the location. The driver got out and said, 'Well, this is my second load of oil today. I've already taken 400 barrels out of this thing.' Bob and I were pretty happy. It was flowing naturally, without a frac."

Still, it would be fraced; the flow, then, was even more impressive. Also, it turned out, again, that the upper-Bakken shale was a worthy barrier. Adding isotopes to the frac fluid, the completion engineers were able to log where the cracks went. Findley says, "Invariably, that frac would come right up to the shale and just stop; it just wouldn't go up into the shale."

They didn't lose their frac.

And, then, they waited. Would the well, like the horizontals in the upper-Bakken shale in North Dakota and the verticals in the middle-Bakken dolomite outside of Findley's porosity-trend fairway, just fizzle out? Lyle says, "We were cautiously optimistic.

"We didn't want to run out and get all excited about something that, overnight, was going to (begin producing) water."

Based on just the initial results, however, Halliburton was disappointed: It had signed on for one well. Lyle had wanted Halliburton in for at least three; Halliburton signed on for only one. Halliburton wanted to participate in testing further. Could it yet-further improve results from this generous rock?

After a couple months online, the rate just wasn't declining.

"From our standpoint, we were tickled: We had what appeared

to be a successful prototype and there were no real encumbrances in terms of a commitment (with Halliburton) on a go-forward basis.

"It gave us a little bit better negotiation position."

For Halliburton, should the play work out, the technology and expertise it could develop could translate across its business world-wide. More immediately, it would gain a position and advantage in the Williston Basin to serve other producers wanting to do a Lyco-type completion. Most frac jobs in the region had been just small ones on vertical wells. Burning Tree State 36-2H was the first fraced horizontal in the Williston Basin.[79]

Halliburton signed a new, 10-well deal in which it became the preferred service provider. "It opened that whole territory for them again," Lyle says.

"They had come back into the Williston Basin to do this project. See, when we first arrived, there were very few oilfield services in the area. They had closed their offices because nobody thought you could make any money up there anymore.

"I mean we (at Lyco) were foolish enough to think we could go into the basin with (newly available) 3-D seismic in the mid-1990s to find the elusive Red River bumps that had been overlooked when us-ing 2-D seismic. We shot the first 3-D seismic in the history of Divide County (in northwestern North Dakota).

"The problem was that we didn't have an analog. When we got the 3-D data, we didn't know what we were looking at. We were push-ing the frontier with new technology and, sometimes, being 'first' can be an expensive and painful learning experience."

But, from his nearly 20 years of experience since forming Lyco, Lyle knew there was still money to be made in old basins, having done it in the Texas Panhandle, Colorado, California and elsewhere. "We always stay with the reservoir until we figure it out."

Findley says of the middle Bakken, "Nobody would ever think

---

[79] Fraced horizontals had been made elsewhere, such as in 1994 in a tight sandstone in Germany by Mobil Corp. and in the tight, Clinton sandstone in Ohio by Belden & Blake Corp. The latter was part of a study co-funded by the U.S. Department of Energy.

you could produce oil out of such a low-permeability rock in (what became named) Elm Coulee Field."

He recalls that, after making the brochure about his Sleeping Giant idea and taking it to the Lyco group to review in the summer of 1996, "I was kind of embarrassed for naming it that. I thought it may have sounded a little hokey. Thinking back on it now, you know, it turned out to be correct."

On May 26, 2000, Burning Tree State 36-2H came on with an official IP of 196 barrels on a quarter-inch choke from three sets of perforations in the roughly 1,700-foot lateral at about 10,000 feet below the surface. The IP was about three times that of the vertical Albin FLB 2-33 and up to seven times the average of the vertical re-entries.

***

In 2000, only six wells were drilled in Richland County—Lyco's in the Bakken and five by others in Ratcliffe, Nisku, Red River or Stonewall. Lyco had managed to remain alone in the play into 2000, but other leaseholders were all around it, consisting of those exploring the other formations and those that simply owned acreage held by production (HBPed) from existing wells.

The neighbors were watching, though. What kind of decline curve would Lyco get from its middle-Bakken wells? Would the wells just sputter out? Or would they be economic?

Privately held, Dallas-based Headington Oil Co. had been curious. It made a vertical, Albin 31X-28, for 130 barrels in late 1997. The hole was bored to Red River; it was completed uphole in Bakken. The well's location was about a 15-minute stroll through a field north of Findley and Robinson's Albin of 18 months earlier.

In 2001, Lyco gave everyone more to talk about. It went 9-for-9 in its Bakken attempts, all fraced horizontals, bringing them online with between 190 and 368 barrels.

Armstrong Operating Inc. was curious now too. It attempted four wells in the county. Two were completed in the deeper Red River; one was a dry hole; a fourth, the vertical BR 29-1, was made in

Bakken for 150 barrels and averaged 124 barrels a day during its first 23 days online.[80]

Headington then went in with Dynneson 11X-5. The well flowed 181 barrels a day its first 12 days online; upon being fraced a couple months later, it came back on with 242 barrels.

In 2002, already 10-for-10, Lyco went another 10-for-10. Among them, it took its Peabody-Bahls 2-16H lateral about 8,500 feet for 576 barrels on Nov. 22, 2002—its biggest well yet and the longest-reach well yet in the state's history. Lyle says, "That gave us momentary bragging rights. It's always fun to be a part of something that is done for the first time."[81]

In 2002, however, the only other operator making a successful Bakken well in the county was Headington, which clearly was in the sweet spot too and now able to mimic Lyco's results: Its WCA Foundation 21X-1 came on with 445 barrels from dual laterals. One turned at 9,943 feet and went southeast for about 2,500 feet; a second went out about 4,000 feet.

By year-end 2002, Lyco had advanced to No. 5 oil producer in Montana, making 686,766 barrels that year or an average of some 1,880 barrels a day and advancing past several operators in the enormous Cedar Creek anticline fields that produce from deeper rock south of Richland County.

The state had named the play now: Elm Coulee Field. Its first appearance on the state's list of oil fields was at No. 5. In just 30 months and from fewer than 40 wells, it had already given up a cumulative 1,063,968 barrels—almost entirely for Lyco.

---

[80] Production declined and it was soon put on pump. Armstrong re-entered the well in 2004, making it a horizontal. It came back on with 223 barrels a day its first 20 days online. It was still producing in June 2013.

[81] It would be determined in further experimentation that, while more oil is made from the longer lateral in this zone in Richland County, it would economically make enough from a short lateral of about 4,400 feet.

BARNETT: 2002

← ← ← ← ← → → → → →

"I've always thought that, if you're a geologist,
you had to have amnesia...These notions you have
about basins tend to cloud your thinking...."
—*Larry Nichols*

O f Mitchell Energy's few horizontal attempts, one was the 1991 horizontal in a research partnership with the Gas Research Institute; two others were shortly before Devon bid for the company.[82]

Tony Vaughn, Devon executive vice president, E&P, says, "We could look at the few horizontals in comparison to the verticals and recognize a step-change improvement and we had experience with horizontal improvements in other plays in our careers.

"We had a guy run a conceptual model just to try to get a feel for that relative difference between the verticals and the horizontals. All of that started in the fall of '01. There was a team of us that would go to Mitchell's office every week for about half the week, working with those guys.

"We couldn't take over operatorship yet, but we were trying to get educated and set the transition so, as soon as we closed, we would be ready to go. We were talking about the relative difference and it took a while to get all these Mitchell guys onboard with this thought

---

[82] Mitchell Energy commenced drilling another horizontal in 2000 but, in this one, it was unable to turn the hole laterally.

process. They were comfortable with improving the process on the vertical wells that they had been making. They had been working on the vertical wells since 1981.

"They had spent from '81 to about '99 just trying to get repetitively commercial, vertical wells. They weren't ready to talk about horizontals, primarily because the pace of activity was high and the verticals were working.

"We were looking for a step-change improvement to commercialize a big portion of the acreage base and it was going take something different—we thought—than what they had done for 20 years."

Vaughn and Nichols had each experienced how technology can change the game. "It's a point you can make about this industry that has happened repeatedly over time—and will in the future," Nichols says. For example, in the San Juan Basin, explorers, including Nichols' father, had been making gas from the tight Mesaverde formation at about 5,000 feet since the 1950s. When making those holes, the wellbore was cased—that is, sealed off—while being drilled in the overlying Fruitland-coal interval, which was full of water. By the 1980s, industry thought the San Juan Basin was fully developed; except for the long-life gas wells already in Mesaverde, the basin was finished.

Nichols says, "The thinking was 'There's nothing more there. It's a tired, old, gas field that's sputtering out its last few bits of gas.'"

But, in the late 1980s, Amoco Corp. was experimenting with whether, if you let the coal produce out its water, the gas would follow. "It was a novel idea. We thought it might really work. So we bought an interest in a 33,000-acre unit. Here's big Amoco, sitting there with all this power they had at the time. A giant company. We go out there, see what's happening, pick it up, run with it and build ourselves up into an exciting little company."

Northeast Blanco Unit (NEBU) became Devon's most valuable property, catapulting it from an enterprise value of about $75 million into a Top 20-ranked independent U.S. gas producer. The acreage had proved to be in the sweetest spot of the Fruitland-coal play.

"Before that, I think we had ranked 260th of the public companies out there in our sector. We weren't even in the top half."

Co-developers Amoco and large, independent Burlington Resources urged Devon to divest its interest in NEBU, considering tiny Devon ill-equipped to fully develop the gas potential.

"The majors had developed a view that everything interesting in the U.S. had been fully developed. 'We'll keep what we have in the U.S. as a cash cow, but we're going to spend all our capital and all of our intellectual power worldwide. If, by chance, some little independent discovers something in North America, they'll have to come to us because only we—the majors—have the capital and the expertise to develop it.'

"Amoco and Burlington really didn't like us being there, but they didn't have the power to stop us."

Devon would not sell.[83]

"Along came new technology that defined a shallower formation that is more prolific than this historic basin was ever thought of being. You can say the same thing about the Fort Worth Basin—a tired, old area that was fully developed and poor George Mitchell was banging his head against the wall, trying to find something there.

"Everyone knew the Barnett was a marginal, uninteresting shale. We didn't think a lot about what George was doing there. We looked at it; it didn't work. That was that. He didn't seem to be making much progress in figuring that out.

"But one of the things you have to worry about in this industry is that we all have these notions, like about the San Juan Basin: 'It's old and tired; they did everything in the 1950s and there's nothing left there.' I've always thought that, if you're a geologist, you had to have amnesia, so that, wherever you were, you didn't have preconceived notions, such as in the Gulf of Mexico.

"The Permian Basin's the same thing: Pioneer (Natural Resources Co.) has been out there in this old, dull area. No one interested. Now they're a rock-star company because they have all these (unconventional-resource) acres there.

---

[83] In the company's new office tower in Oklahoma City, one of the restaurants is named Nebu; the other, Vast.

"These notions you have about basins tend to cloud your thinking, so that you want to go someplace *new* rather than just looking at new technology that might change where you *are*.

"New technology comes along."

And personnel with diverse experience. "The knowledge a company has is really the knowledge that its people have. They haven't necessarily been with your company all the time. So your company has an amalgamation of knowledge."

While at Kerr-McGee Corp., for example, prior to joining Devon in 1999, Vaughn had worked with a team that made horizontal wells in Breton Sound 21 in the shallow Gulf of Mexico. Vaughn says, "We had a very thin oil column on top of a lot of water, much like the Barnett (gas above the Ellenburger). Permeability was much higher and porosity was much higher, but we laid horizontal wells in that thin oil column to produce the oil and not the water.

"Some of the benefits of drilling horizontal—contacting more reservoir and minimizing pressure draw-down—are the same in tight rocks as they were in some of those conventional (Gulf) rocks. Looking at the Barnett, it was an idea that we put into our reservoir modeling. We thought we had a shot.

"And we weren't bashful about trying it. That's where we came to be with it. We were comfortable with failure."

Failure did not come.

In early 2003, Devon reported it had expanded the Barnett play beyond the core area Mitchell had long worked, which had been between the Mineral Wells fault system at the north and the Rhome Newark system at the south. It had six horizontals producing now; they had come on with between 2.5- and 4.5 million cubic feet of gas a day. They cost $1.3 million each, compared with Mitchell's verticals, which cost up to $600,000 for between 700,000 and 1 million a day.

Later that year, it had 34 of these horizontals online, making 51 million cubic feet a day combined—an average of 1.5 million a day each. In February 2004, it announced it had grown its Barnett production to some 575 million a day from more than 1,600 producing wells; among these, 53 were now horizontals. It added, "Horizontal wells

…will be the focus of future Barnett expansion."

By January 2005, Devon had 144 Barnett horizontals online. Alone, they were making 20% of Devon's Barnett production; 1,650 vertical wells were making 80%.[84]

There was the step change.

Meanwhile, gas was more than $5, up from about $2 upon consummation of the Mitchell merger. Devon shares were soon split 2-for-1 upon reaching about $80—up from about $50 when it closed the Mitchell deal.[85]

Vaughn says, "When the horizontal wells started working, we knew we were adding value beyond the acquisition evaluation—and pretty quickly."

By then, Devon was nearly done with a sell-down of some of its midstream assets for about $330 million. Among what it kept, roughly a third of its processing capacity was at Mitchell's Bridgeport, Texas, plant in the heart of the Barnett. There, it was handling 650 million cubic feet a day, stripping from it some 54,000 barrels of NGL a day.

The Barnett was now the largest gas field in Texas, making some 1.1 billion a day; explorers were trying the rock in 15 counties. Cumulative Barnett production had grown to more than 1 trillion cubic feet. Ninety rigs were at work in the play.

About a fifth of Devon's company-wide gas production was coming from its 1,950 Barnett wells alone and about a fifth of that was coming from just 144 new, horizontal wells.

For 2005, it planned 226 new wells with 156 of these horizontal and two-thirds of them outside the core. And it was taking well-spacing down to 20 acres.

---

[84] Devon's Barnett production declined briefly in 2004 to 556 million a day while converting the drilling program to horizontals, which require more drill days than verticals.

[85] Both figures are the price pre-split. Split-adjusted, Devon shares were about $25 when announcing the Mitchell deal.

BAKKEN: 2003

← ← ← ← ← → → → → →

*"Boy, when I saw that, I said,
'This game is on.' That did it."*
—Harold Hamm

The Bakken play in Montana was hot now. Other operators rushed in. After Burlington had quit trying the shale member of the formation in North Dakota in early 1995, the only mentions of the rock in SEC filings through 2002 were a few by Canadian oil companies, discussing formations on the Saskatchewan side of the Williston Basin.

Otherwise, mention was only by Burlington, while discussing its application of horizontal technology that it had learned from its Bakken attempts to the tight Red River B bench in its subsequent Cedar Hills Field discovery in southwestern North Dakota.

In July 2003, Whiting Petroleum Corp. called the new Bakken play out, revealing in its filing to IPO that it was in the middle of it in Richland County. The 23-year-old company was being spun out of Midwestern U.S. utility Alliant Energy Corp., which had bought it in 1992 for about $27 million. Whiting reported that its first two middle-Bakken wells, completed with dual laterals, appeared to be able to produce some 700,000 barrels of oil apiece.[86]

A month later, small-cap American Oil & Gas Inc. revealed the

---

[86] Whiting's 15-million-share offering was priced in November 2003 at $15.50 a share; in March 2014, the stock was $70, including a 2-for-1 split, for the equivalent worth of $140.

Richland County play in more detail. It was explaining, in an SEC fil-ing, its purchase of a 30% working interest in about 12,000 net acres in the county operated by privately held Slawson Exploration. A long-time Williston Basin explorer, Slawson had tried Burlington's Bakken-shale play in North Dakota in the early 1990s.

American Oil reported, about the new, middle-Bakken play in Montana, "this area has been very active since mid-2000, with up-wards of 50 horizontal wells having been drilled with no dry holes." [87]

No dry holes!

The two-year-old, horizontal, Montana play had already made 3.5 million barrels. The company explained why the Bakken had become interesting again—why one shouldn't cringe upon hearing of it again. "The North Dakota play succeeded or failed on the presence or lack of natural fractures in a poor-matrix reservoir. The Richland County play has a significant advantage in that it (is a) dolomitic, siltstone res-ervoir with modest porosity and permeability."

And the modern, horizontal, Bakken wells were being fraced.

Now, Lyco had lots of neighbors: 44 wells were attempted in Richland County in 2003; 38 of them were completed in Bakken. Eleven of these were by Lyco; its Cable-Leonard 29-14H came on on Dec. 16, 2003, with 1,086 barrels. Dallas-based, privately held Petro-Hunt LLC brought three online. Large-cap independent EOG Re-sources Inc. completed three, including Vairstep 1-22H for 624 bar-rels from two short laterals of approximately 3,200 feet each.

Nance Petroleum Corp. joined, making a couple for about 250 barrels each.[88] Headington went 20-for-20; one of them, the two-lateral BR-Hill 31X-29, came on with 975 barrels.

---

[87] Commonly, the smallest, publicly held, E&P companies will tell the most about wells or plays in explaining their upside and downside exposure, which is easily affected due to the company's size. This can have the effect of tipping others to—or warning others against—a new play. Internal events that may be "meaningful" by SEC definition to a small E&P is almost everything; to an ExxonMobil, rarely anything.

[88] Nance, a Rockies-focused subsidiary of SM Energy Co., had worked the Williston since 1991 from an office in Billings. In 2003, SM bought Flying J Oil and Gas Inc.'s Rockies-weighted E&P assets, including in Richland County, for $68.7 million and purchased Choctaw II Oil & Gas Ltd., adding the assets of both to its Nance portfolio.

Before year-end 2003, Continental Resources Inc. brought on the biggest well in the play yet: On Dec. 21, its Margaret 44-15H gave up a 1,280-barrel IP from two laterals.

Oil was about $33 a barrel now.

Lyle says, "Richland County was going from being one of the poorest-producing counties in Montana to the largest-producing county."

Elm Coulee became the state's No. 1 oil field, making 2.7 million barrels in 2003—exceeding that of the 52-year-old Cedar Creek anticline fields. Cumulative production was 3.7 million barrels; about 62% of this had been made by Lyco. Other operators were now taking a piece of the prize; Lyco's 2003 Elm Coulee production grew in total volume but declined in percent share of the field's total to about 42%. Lyle, Robinson and Findley had known they would need to lease all they could before attempting those first wells; others had quickly surrounded them.

In 2004, Burlington joined the play. All operators' attempts totaled 94. Eight of these came on with more than 1,000 barrels.

Continental Resources joined Whiting and others in mentioning the play. In its year-end 2003 report, it named it the "MB Project" and revealed it held 65,000 net acres in Richland County.[89] "Although this is a new venture for us," the company reported, "the activity in this area has been emerging during the past two years through the efforts of other operators. We delayed entry into this area and elected to monitor activity until the economics could be supported by results."

Its wells cost some $2.1 million each for a vertical depth of 9,500 feet and two laterals of about 5,000 feet each. "Wells typically take 45 days to drill and 30 days to complete," it added.

Ten rigs were now at work in the play, one of those for Continental, "and we believe more than 200 wells will ultimately be drilled within the potentially productive area…The potential size of the dis-

---

[89] The company was not public at the time but filed reports with the SEC as it had public debt.

covery could rival that of Cedar Hills."[90] Continental was moving a rig and crew from that play to Richland County. "We also have plans to add a third rig later in the year...," it reported. "Scheduled development of this prolific field is expected to take three years."

In 2004, Elm Coulee Field made 7.5 million barrels—about a half-million more than the second-, third-, fourth- and fifth-ranked Montana fields combined. Cumulative production was now 11.3 million. Of this, 4.7 million were Lyco's.

And oil was continuing to tick up: In January 2005, it was about $50 a barrel.

Lyco went 35-for-35 that year; Continental went 32-for-32; all operators combined were 143-for-143.[91] Slawson brought on Bearcat State 1-16H for a whopping 1,542 barrels.

In 2005, the field made 15.7 million barrels—roughly half of all the oil made in the state that year. Cumulative production was now 27.1 million barrels. Lyco advanced to No. 2 oil producer, making 4.1 million barrels that year, second only to Encore Acquisition Co. (6.4 million) and its enormous Cedar Creek anticline fields. Continental advanced to fifth (3.1 million).

Fellow oil and gas explorers had dismissed Lyco's early work, Lyle says. "They said, 'You're not going to make any money in Montana. You cannot make any money in the Bakken. That's absurd.' A few years later, they were buying acreage all around us."

Besides the 27 million barrels of oil the five-year-old field had made, it had also given up some 26 billion cubic feet of associated gas. It was making 30 million cubic feet a day.[92] Lyle had recognized early

---

[90] Cedar Hills Field in Bowman County in southwestern North Dakota was a horizontal, unfraced, deep, Red River B-bench play discovered by Burlington in 1994 on the eastern end of the Cedar Creek anticline.

[91] Two additional wells were drilled in the county—one by Nance; one by True Oil LLC—in a far-northeastern attempt to extend the play and were dry holes; each tested the stratigraphic column down to Red River C.

[92] Part of why the play worked is that the Sleeping Giant trend Findley discovered is a solution-gas-driven reservoir. In this, the gas is trapped within the oil molecules. As the oil enters the wellbore, the changing pressure causes the gas to come out of the oil and helps to push the oil to the surface.

in the Sleeping Giant program that gas-gathering infrastructure would be needed in addition to more oil-pipeline infrastructure. Gas flaring is allowed in the state from oil wells but not in perpetuity. Also, the gas the wells were making was full of NGL for stripping into ethane, propane and other high-value liquids.[93]

Lyle had gone to one of the gas-pipeline operators in the area and explained he would be needing gas take-away service. He was sent away. "They said, 'Well, we don't really think that's likely to happen. We think that's folly.'"

Lyle returned twice; the company refused to believe him.

Eventually, he went to Harold Hamm, who owned Continental Resources and oil-pipeliner Hiland Partners LLC. Hamm was the only pipeline operator who would listen to Lyle.

"We were," Hamm says. "We put in the oil-gathering pipe and we brought in the gas gathering. There was just one company gathering gas up there and they, basically, had no competition. The result had been that, whatever they offered you, you had to take it.

"That's not very attractive."

Continental was already an explorer in Montana and North Dakota and was familiar with what Lyco was achieving in Richland County. Lyle and Hamm agreed to dedicate their middle-Bakken gas to a new pipe; Burlington joined as well. Hiland's 85 miles of gas-gathering lines in eastern Montana were soon expanded to 200 miles. A processing plant to strip the liquids from the gas and the fractionators to separate them into individual components—ethane, propane and more—were also constructed.[94]

"Bobby—well, he just has very good common sense," Hamm says. "He had a good plan for what he thought he could do with Elm Coulee Field and he had Halliburton in there with him, willing to spend money on the technology and apply it. I have a great deal of respect for him.

---

[93] Some of the middle-Bakken wells were coming on with a bonus of as much as a half-million cubic feet of gas a day—about as much as the early, vertical, Barnett wells.

[94] Others producers could put gas into the pipe; the three initial commitments from Lyco, Continental and Burlington were for Hiland to financially justify building it.

"A lot of people just didn't give him a lot of credit. They should have."

***

By July 2005, Lyco and Sleeping Giant LLC had run their race—and won. Findley's idea in 1996 had made 8.8 million barrels for them. Every one of their horizontal attempts was a commercial success.

Best drilling and completion practices in the play had evolved by 2005 to determining that the tight Lodgepole formation on top of the upper-Bakken shale was a good place to turn the vertical leg into the lateral foot, and that polymer, rather than borate or gelled-oil, frac fluid was fine.

Also, simple sand versus resin-coated sand or ceramic was sufficient to keep the rock propped; an uncemented, perforated, lateral liner made more oil post-frac than a cemented liner and also allowed re-entry to re-frac any zones that weren't performing; and fracing the perforations in stages rather than all at once was better.[95]

Lyco had gone 83-for-83. Oil was heading to $60. It was time to sell. The company had proven Sleeping Giant from one end of Elm Coulee Field to the other. Its acreage—involving 80 square miles—was held by production from the 83 wells; the program would now become one of simply putting in additional wells. The likelihood of success was already demonstrated: 100%. Eighteen more wells were already spud or about to be spud.

As oil prices were on their way up, it could seem counter-intuitive to sell. Why not just continue to make money from the production? But the seller can fetch more for a property in a higher oil- or gas-price environment. And the buyer can bid more aggressively as it can hedge the proven, forward-production expectation three years out in the futures market.

---

[95] Lyle says, "The uncemented, perforated, lateral liner was Lyco's preferred completion design when the program started. However, Halliburton thought a cemented liner was a better design. It was only after 17 wells and many 'friendly,' technical discussions that the uncemented liner was tested. A meaningful production improvement followed."

The seller gets a bit of the higher, futures price as part of the bid and the buyer covers price-downside exposure by locking in the forward price. It was time to exit at the top and find another track to run.

Meanwhile, Canada-based, royalty trust Enerplus Resources Fund was fed up with the western Canadian market for oil and gas properties. Garry Tanner, Enerplus' chief operating officer at the time, says, "This was back in the golden era of Canadian royalty trusts. There were about 35 of us up there and everybody was, basically, trying to buy the same thing. We had given away our cost-of-capital advantage.

"People were, honestly, bidding PV5, maybe less, for the deals in Canada. So the last big deal we had done was when we bought Chevron out in 2004."[96]

"We continued to work the Canadian market for another year and just said, 'It's too frothy. We just can't find anything you can get at a reasonable price.'

"So we made a concerted effort to look in the U.S. market."

Formed in 1986, Enerplus was Canada's first royalty trust. To encourage new spending in oil and gas fields, the country had established a tax advantage for E&P companies that would take mature wells and acreage and re-invest in them, increasing production.[97] The law meant that trusts would pay most of their profits to investors, usually on a monthly basis. In exchange, the trusts did not pay Canadian corporate-income tax, which was as much as 31.5%, thus the profit available to distribute to investors was on a pre-tax basis.

This resulted in virtually all of the energy trusts focusing primarily on mature, low-risk oil and gas properties—and almost entirely in Canada. At the peak of deal-making, the trusts were producing some 15% of Canadian oil and gas yet they were driving about 85% of deals, Tanner notes.

They were insatiable. Leading into 2002, U.S. explorers had been buying Canadian E&Ps—the ones that were still exploring—as west-

---

[96] PV5 meant the offers were based on discounting the present value of the assets by 5%; traditionally, present value is discounted at least 10%.

[97] Mineral rights in Canada are owned by the government so new oil and gas production produces royalty income for it in addition to tax revenue from an improving economy.

ern Canada was relatively underexplored in contrast with the U.S. Also, the U.S./Canadian exchange rate favored the buying power of the U.S. dollar at the time.

That year, however, the currency differential began to diminish and the growing number of royalty trusts began offering heftier and heftier exit offers to owners of producing properties. Virtually every U.S. E&P company sold; their exploration assets went to the few, remaining Canadian explorers and their mature assets went to the trusts—either directly or when later turned out by the explorer.

Although the Western Canadian Sedimentary Basin is enormous, the supply of mature properties was rapidly declining.[98] Enerplus had to look beyond Canada.

Tanner was long familiar with U.S.-onshore E&P operations and operators. With a chemical-engineering degree from the University of Kansas and an MBA from the University of Texas at Austin, he began his oil and gas career in 1984 with Exxon Corp. In 1997, he joined energy private-equity-investment firm EnCap Investments LP in Houston and opened its Calgary office. As a major member of the investment group exited in 2002, Tanner and some fellow Calgary-office team members joined Enerplus.[99]

Enerplus considered buying in the Appalachian Basin for its long-life, conventional, gas fields. Privately held, West Virginia-based Triana Energy LLC was for sale. But competing bids for Triana were factoring for the possibility of the Marcellus shale there being commercial—as the Barnett play had proven itself to be—rather than just a straight-up valuation of the mature properties. While the Marcellus shale was interesting, it was still a rock for wildcatters—not for a divi-

---

[98] As hundreds of Canadian companies with any type of property that could be considered suitable had been converted into voracious trusts, the Canadian finance minister gave notice on Oct. 31, 2006, that the tax favoritism would end in 2011. This announcement was dubbed "the Halloween massacre." Several, including Enerplus, converted into traditional corporations; others merged with each other or liquidated.

[99] The exiting partner was El Paso Corp., which had entered a prolonged, portfolio-re-profiling phase as a result of energy-trading-shop failures in the wake of Enron Corp.'s disintegration in the fall of 2001.

dend-paying, acquire-and-exploit company like Enerplus.[100]

"And it was also just far afield from where we had operated before," Tanner says. Also, Enerplus was more eager to make an oily acquisition. "We thought oil might be better than gas. We had no crystal ball, just a bias to bringing in more oil."

It found Lyco's middle-Bakken play interesting. "We were already in the Williston Basin on the Canadian side. We'd be crossing the border, but we knew the rock and it was quite a bit closer to us, operationally.

"We landed on 'Let's chase the Bakken.'"

Seemingly, Enerplus would disadvantage itself amongst its royalty-trust peer group by buying outside of Canada. Profit earned in the U.S. would be taxed in the U.S. before it went to Calgary. But Enerplus had settled the issue by determining that the U.S. unit would be a subsidiary headquartered in Hungary, which had tax treaties with the U.S. and with Canada.

"And we had relatively high capex spending to do on a Bakken property, which gave further protection. At the end of the day, our tax leakage was a single-digit percentage. That tax hit coming across the border was a lot less than people expected."

On July 18, 2005, Enerplus bid $421 million for Lyco. Before the deal closed, Bob Robinson's estate sold its interest in Sleeping Giant LLC to Enerplus as well, for about $90 million.[101] [102]

The operating cost for Lyco's production was only $1.49 per barrel. Proved reserves were 22.5 million. The reserve life was 12 years. With 94 more wells to be drilled in the proven acreage, Enerplus estimated Lyco's current production rate of some 7,000 barrels of oil equivalent a day would grow to some 10,000, 92% oil, by year-end 2005 and continue at that pace into at least 2008.

---

[100] Chesapeake Energy Corp. bought Triana in September 2005 for $2.2 billion in cash and $75 million of debt assumption, putting itself in Appalachia on top of what became the Marcellus-shale play.

[101] Bob Robinson passed away on April 9, 2004. He was 68.

[102] Halliburton retained its working interest in the wells and undeveloped acreage. Findley had sold his working interest to another party but retained a royalty interest.

The wells cost—for a single lateral—about $3.5 million to drill and complete.[103] Each was estimated to ultimately make between 400,000 and 750,000 barrels equivalent.

More than 225 of these modern middle-Bakken wells had been made in Richland County by now in a roughly 325-square-mile area—all along the northwest/southeast, shoreline trend Findley had mapped. And with all of these holes already, reservoir pressure remained high. "It was overpressured at a 0.65 gradient or so," Tanner says.[104] Unlike the upper-Bakken play in North Dakota in the late 1980s and early 1990s, the newest wells just weren't sputtering out.

"For the first six months after we bought Lyco, there was an industry sentiment that 'Wow, you guys overpaid.'" While Lyco's acreage had been de-risked, Enerplus' oldest reference point on well decline in mid-2005 was that of the first fraced, horizontal Bobby Lyle had put in the rock in 2000. Others were younger, although performing just as well.

"About six months later, we were accused of stealing it. There was enough data where people said, 'These EURs are going to be significantly higher than we expected.'

"At least half a dozen different companies told me, then, that they were the No. 2 bidder."

***

Could the play be taken into North Dakota too?

Lyco held some 40,000 acres there as well. Lyle says, "We were convinced that the play moved across the state line into North Dakota and turned north toward Canada."

While he was re-entering vertical wells to produce from the middle Bakken in Montana in 1997, he had spud the vertical Plumer-

---

[103] Initial, Elm Coulee, fraced, horizontals cost between $1.75- and $2 million. That grew as they came to include dual laterals and additional frac stages. Also, increased drilling across North America as a result of rising oil and gas prices had created greater demand for oilfield services, pushing up vendor prices.

[104] Normal pressure is about 0.45.

Lundquist 25-2 in Divide County, North Dakota, northeast of Elm Coulee Field, completing it in Gunton (Stony Mountain) and Red River, both below Bakken. Some oil was made from both rocks.[105]

Lyle quit further attempts in North Dakota to focus on Lyco's new Montana potential. In February 2004, however, he went back, spudding Trigger-Kilbride 17-14—another vertical in Divide County. Drilling was stopped at 8,000 feet—about 2,000 feet short of its Bakken target. It was deemed a dry hole and plugged two days later.

He wanted one more attempt and with a fraced horizontal; in October 2004, he spud Titan A-Rase Ranch 4-2H in McKenzie County. Fraced by Halliburton with 600 tons of sand and 230,000 gallons of gelled water, it came on with 90 barrels and looked like it would sputter out.[106]

The middle Bakken in North Dakota was different. "The reservoir was different," Lyle says. "The rocks didn't look the same. The producing characteristics were not the same. It was not as prolific as we had found in Montana.

"Now, had we not sold the company, I think we would have stayed with it. That was the pattern with Lyco: We would have stayed with it until we figured it out. But, at the time, we had more than enough to say grace over in Richland County."

With a permit Lyco already held, Enerplus attempted a Bakken well in North Dakota in McKenzie County about 35 miles southwest of Lyco's earlier horizontal. Titan E-Gierke 20-1-H came on in January 2006 with 80 barrels.[107]

Some of Lyco's North Dakota acreage was near the Nesson anticline, along which the first North Dakota oil discovery had been made in 1951; some was near Findley's shoreline trend, but the trend of good permeability just quit at the North Dakota border.

---

[105] By 2013, the well, now owned by Newfield Exploration Co., had made about 78,000 barrels.

[106] The well ultimately produced only 21,000 barrels.

[107] The well was the Silverston Field discovery that later, when the North Dakota Bakken was figured out, went on to host 77 Bakken wells by mid-2013 that could recover at least 200,000 barrels each.

Tanner says, "We drilled a few wells and took a core. Our view at the time was that the science was telling us it wasn't going to be economic. We condemned it as were many others at the time. We said, 'This is too tight. We don't think this is going to produce.' We sold some of the acreage and some of it expired."

And wildcatting wasn't the energy trust's business model; instead, it worked proven, producing fields. "We had a small portion of our budget to do what we called 'Little E'—low-risk exploration—where you're trying to do extensional, small-step-out drilling but not wildcatting. North Dakota was going to require significant frac technology. Two or four stages weren't going to cut it.

"The North Dakota Bakken was still pretty much a pipe dream. In Montana, we had that dolomitic, middle Bakken, which was relatively unique and provided the enhanced porosity and permeability conduit that you needed for that to work.

"As you followed that shoreline trend east, it became a lot more sporadic. You saw some good wells and some bad wells right next to each other. In our minds, it stopped looking like a repeatable, resource play once you got outside of Elm Coulee Field proper."

The middle Bakken in North Dakota was more uniform in McKenzie County, but it was uber-tight. There wasn't technology possible yet to frac the rock enough.

"I remember we were wringing our hands about moving from two-stage fracs to four and I kind of laugh about that now," Tanner says. "That was going to be such a big move. Now, they're doing 38-stage fracs. The technology just wasn't there yet."

Capital markets were skeptical too. Even in 2006, when Crescent Point Energy Trust announced it would buy Mission Oil & Gas Inc. and its Bakken, migrated-oil position in Saskatchewan, the play was little understood by investors. Enerplus knew its value as a result of a 15% equity interest in Mission and because of its Bakken work in Montana via the Lyco acquisition.

In Viewfield in Saskatchewan, the Bakken play is more structural in nature. "On the Canadian side, there's a conventional component to it where you need a trapping mechanism versus being in the (repeatable, stratigraphic) resource play, 'the kitchen' of the Williston, in the center of the basin."

But it was still a good play with good returns. "We actually got into a bidding war on that one with Crescent Point; we tapped out before Crescent Point did." Crescent Point encountered investor disbelief like what Enerplus encountered when it bought Lyco. "People said, 'Wow, you paid too much.'

"They suffered a little bit of that market noise because the metrics looked high, but look at where Crescent Point is today: That was the company-making transaction."[108]

***

As the areal extent of Elm Coulee Field had been proven by 2005, getting into it would require buying in like Enerplus did or figuring out if it worked in another county. West Texas-focused producer Clayton Williams Energy Inc. reported in early 2006 that it tried the Bakken in Sheridan County north of Elm Coulee. Ruegsegger 24H 1 was taken short of the target and abandoned as a dry hole.[109]

And even with successful new wells in the core of the Sleeping Giant play, field production peaked in 2006 at 19 million barrels.[110] SM Energy Co., the owner of Nance Petroleum, reported in early 2007, "Our drilling (in Richland County), while successful overall, resulted in more marginally productive wells in the Bakken formation during 2006 as we near the end of that specific drilling program...

"This successful, grassroots program is nearing the end of primary development."

---

[108] A royalty trust like Enerplus, Crescent Point also converted into a traditional corporation.

[109] The company reported in early 2007, "We do not plan to spend any capital (on) drilling in Montana in 2007."

[110] Elm Coulee Field production declined to 18 million barrels in 2007 and 10 million in 2012. By year-end 2012, the field had made 125.6 million barrels and some 133.5 billion cubic feet of associated gas. Meanwhile, an extension, Elm Coulee Northeast, was figured out in Roosevelt County, giving up 3.7 million barrels in 2012. Elm Coulee and the northeastern extension were the No. 1 and No. 2 oil-producing fields in Montana in 2012.

The only place, then, that the middle-Bakken concept might be extended was into North Dakota. And going to give it a look was virtually any E&P that was in any kind of position to try—based on its existing acreage, existing knowledge, boots on the ground, ability to buy acreage and knowledge, and/or an internal mandate to grow an oil position.

Harold Hamm was among them.

Before joining Lyco in the Montana play in 2003, Hamm's Continental Resources was making about 952 barrels a day in the state, mostly from the deeper Red River formation in southeastern Montana along the Cedar Creek anticline. Its first horizontal, middle-Bakken well, Goss 34-26H, in Richland County came on in August 2003 for 459 barrels. It completed two more before year-end, including the 1,280-barrel-IP Margaret 44-15H.

In early 2004, its Williston Basin leasehold was 474,000 net acres, containing 76% of company-wide reserves. It had an interest in 332 gross, 296 net, wells and was operator of all of them.[111] It reported to public-debt-holders, "Using the (middle-Bakken) project (in Montana) as our model, we have expanded our search for Bakken oil reserves into North Dakota...Drilling evaluation of this leasehold has begun and will continue through year-end.

"The net reserve potential of these new leases could exceed those in the (Montana) project but remains unproven at this time."

It bought some additional leasehold in North Dakota for about $37.50 an acre; later in 2004, it leased another 10,000 net for about $100 an acre "in select areas in response to positive results."

While it was making its first Bakken wells in Montana, it had picked up a permit, using a pseudonym, to re-enter Southland Royalty Co.'s vertical Robert Heuer 1-17 that had been attempted in Divide County in January 1981 and deemed a dry hole. Southland had reached some 7,800 feet—passing through Ratcliffe, Midale and a series of limestones.

---

[111] Interest in 332 gross, 296 net, wells means it held a working interest averaging 89.1% in each.

It didn't come near the Bakken, which was some 2,500 feet farther below. The hole was plugged and the site restored to pasture.

In December 2003, a law office in Bismarck, North Dakota, submitted an application on behalf of a client—Canada-based Jolette Oil (USA) LLC—to re-enter the well. The request included the $100 fee and that the well file be confidential for up to six months after it was spud, which was customary and allowed by the state.[112]

Hamm had formed Jolette to not draw attention to the re-entry; it was formed in Canada to, hopefully, suggest to anyone who was curious that it was just a Canadian company that might be trying to extend the Bakken play of Saskatchewan into North Dakota. The well was just 19 miles from the border. It couldn't be readily known that Jolette was actually, highly successful, Williston Basin operator Continental Resources.

Jolette's plan was to drill 7,350 feet vertically and then deviate at the Madison formation—where Southland had quit—into a lateral of up to 5,000 feet. Cyclone Drilling Inc.'s Rig 16 turned—that is, "kicked off"—from the vertical at about 8,300 feet in Lodgepole instead. Lodgepole is where Burlington had kicked off its old upper-Bakken wells 15 years earlier and where Elm Coulee Field operators were kicking off.

From there, the lateral was taken some 5,000 feet at 90 degrees through the "Bakken sand," which is the lower portion of the thin, middle Bakken in Divide County.[113]

It was fraced with about 180,000 gallons of water and propped with 160 tons of sand. It came online March 5, 2004, averaging 87 barrels a day during its first 25 days online.[114] It was the first fraced horizontal in North Dakota.

---

[112] The permit-holder does still report well details to the state throughout that period.

[113] The sand, also known as "Banff sand," is described as a creamy, tan, sandstone that contains some dolomite, while the upper portion of the middle Bakken is mostly dolomite and about 10% sandstone.

[114] Continental revealed to the state in November 2004 that it was Jolette Oil. The well made about 107,000 barrels by mid-2013 and was still producing.

***

Hamm had founded Continental in 1967 in Enid, Oklahoma, northwest of Oklahoma City. In 1985, he purchased more than 500 wells producing from shallow formations in the Enid area from Petro-Lewis Corp., which had been squeezed by investors who had been expecting big returns that falling oil prices couldn't produce. Five years later, on the Petro-Lewis property, Continental discovered the nine-mile-wide Ames crater-astrobleme oil field when the company's senior geologist, Rex Olsen, suggested it drill to 10,000 feet—about 1,800 feet deeper than ever drilled in the area before.

Hamm pauses, reflecting on the result.

"That was tremendous," he says.

Jack Stark, now senior vice president, exploration, had just joined Continental in 1992 with a master's in geology from Colorado State University and years of experience with making holes in the Midcontinent region in which Continental operated. "It has a raised edge—the crater rim," Stark says of Ames Field. "It has a crater floor with a circumferential bottom that is a kind of moat. So it's this low area."

Upon the meteor's strike, the land and organic materials were compacted and, in time, became buried at about 9,000 feet.[115]

"Discovering that oil-producing astrobleme sitting underneath those producing properties really helped take Continental to another level," Stark says. "It immediately started to generate substantially more cash flow, which then allowed us to start thinking of going bigger than what we had been doing.

"I didn't see the opportunity to grow the company in Oklahoma. We could basically just kind of tread water because it was highly competitive and highly HBPed."

Upon Stark's arrival at Continental, it was otherwise attempting what were proving to be small, vertical, Charles C-bench wells at 6,000 feet in Valley County, Montana, northwest of Richland County.

---

[115] By 2013, operators had made 14.6 million barrels of oil equivalent—most of it by Continental—from the crater floor, a structural trap.

"When we looked at the Rockies, we focused on the Williston Basin because of its oil-prone nature. Harold had always liked oil over gas. He thought it just had more intrinsic value; it's worth more. And there's a lot of natural gas in the U.S. It's easier to find than oil."[116]

Hamm says, "Yeah, we came about that accidentally. Back in the early '80s, you know, natural gas went to nine bucks and everybody started drilling like it was a house fire and built up a small niche of unregulated gas. And the price fell back to $3. We started a project in Oklahoma in 1985 based on the economics of $2.50 gas. By the time we were done, two years later, it was a dollar and a quarter.

"The only way we made it out of that project was that we were lucky and ran across two oil zones: the Skinner and Red Fork. That paid the project off. We would have never paid it off with natural gas. So we got to thinking, 'Gosh, oil prices.'

"If you recall, they were still pretty decent until 1986. And, then, suddenly, they fell back to about $10 a barrel. They came back up to about $15. We got to thinking, 'Gosh, we'd better start looking for oil.' And that's what we did."

Following on the success Gulf Coast wildcatters were having with using 3-D seismic to find trapped oil and gas, Continental took 3-D to the Williston Basin. Stark says, "The basin had been explored since the 1920s. Our point was to find oil that was left behind, using this new technology. With 3-D, we were looking for very specific, structural features, particularly in the Red River (formation)."

In 1994, North Dakota explorers' newest fascination—as the old upper-Bakken play had peaked—was with a vertical, Kadrmas 75, that Conoco had completed for an IP of 520 barrels. The well had been made in the Lodgepole formation overlying Bakken in what was deemed a Waulsortian mound near Dickinson in Stark County.

Following it, Duncan Oil Inc.'s vertical Knopik 1-11 came on in December 1994 for 2,707 barrels. In 1995, producers were wildcatting

---

[116] Besides what producers make from gas wells, most oil wells also make associated gas.

for more mounds.[117] In the midst of the mound hunt, Continental turned its attention to what could be a deeper, substantive, stratigraphic trap instead: the B bench of the Red River.

In Bowman County in the southwestern corner of North Dakota, the Red River had given up oil since a Carter Oil Co. well was made in it for 195 barrels in 1958. Other operators tried five more in Red River through 1968 without success.

In March 1969, however, A.J. Hodges Industries Inc. made the Susag-Wick 1 for 165 barrels that went on to make some 500,000.[118] Another came on with 332 barrels.[119] Another 90 attempts met with widely varying results.

Then, in 1986, oil prices collapsed and drilling was quit.

Five years later, Koch Industries Inc., which had poked a last few holes in Red River in the 1980s, resumed attempts with a couple of verticals that were about as successful as past wells.

The formation piqued Continental's interest in 1993. The interval was deep—about 9,500 feet. It had produced oil—all from vertical wells. Continental thought the formation had an areal footprint that could make a sizable play.

Red River in the Williston Basin consists of four benches—A, B, C and D. The deepest two are more conventional with high porosity and high permeability that produce relatively easily from a vertical wellbore. The uppermost A and B are much tighter, having poor porosity and permeability.

"People would bail out in them if they were unsuccessful in C and D," Stark says. "They would come uphole and complete in the B zone and make a little bit of production. But, often, they just weren't stellar wells."

Stellar wells in B were on the way, however.

In 1994, as Burlington was quitting the Bakken play in the

---

[117] The Lodgepole-mound play made several enormous wells but, as a structural trap, explorers ran out of locations. Kadrmas 75 made more than 4 million barrels by mid-2013; Knopik 1-11, more than 1 million. Both wells were still producing.

[118] It was still producing in 2013.

[119] It went on to make more than 1 million barrels.

northwestern quarter of the state, only 111 wells were drilled anywhere for anything in North Dakota that year. But Thomas Heck, the geologist for the North Dakota Geological Survey, noted in early 1996 that "several that were drilled were important new discoveries."

Eight years earlier, Burlington had made an unfraced horizontal in Red River B along the Cedar Creek anticline in eastern Montana. The carbonate there was mostly dolomite with some limestone and the rock was pervasive, covering a large area. In 1994, it took the concept into the southwestern North Dakota corner of the anticline with the unfraced, horizontal Larkin 14-18H in Bowman County.

The well was made just northwest of the vertical Larkin 1-19 that Total Petroleum Inc. had drilled to 9,300 feet in 1985 to the bottom of Red River D. In it, the D bench was dolomite and limestone with little porosity.

In that hole, the thick, C bench of dolomite had some porosity but low permeability, despite that it was "usually the best zone of oil production in the Bowman County area," the on-site Total geologist noted in a log, while looking at rock samples as they surfaced from the wellbore.

The B bench was anhydrite and tight limestone with some dead oil and saltwater, lacking dolomite, which was needed for any porosity, he reported. The A contained limestone, dolomite and anhydrite. "The only significant shows of oil and gas in the 1-19 Larkin well were found in the Red River formation," he concluded.

But it wasn't enough. The well was plugged and abandoned.

In 1994, however, in Burlington's nearby horizontal wildcat, Larkin 14-18H, in what was known at the time as Austin Field, the lateral was put along the top of the roughly 10-foot-thick B bench. Unfraced, it came on with 250 barrels on Oct. 31, 1994.

The well was the discovery of the horizontal Cedar Hills Field.[120]

A new play was on.

Taylor Reid, the Burlington engineer who went on to co-found Bakken-focused Oasis Petroleum Inc. in 2007, says, "It was a classic

---

[120] It eventually produced about 285,000 barrels.

resource play. A huge resource was mapped with significant, known oil in place. The question had been 'How do you get oil out of this low-permeability rock?' That is where the (earlier) horizontal-drilling technique used in the Bakken shale came into play."

It wasn't a shale, "but the horizontal technique worked here as well." Again, the Burlington horizontals were unfraced; they flowed naturally.

North Dakota geologist Heck noted the discovery well in his January 1996 summary of drilling activity in the state. "Before the discovery of Cedar Hills Field, vertically drilled, Red River B-zone wells in Bowman County were not completed unless they were on or near the crests of structures because a combination of low oil and high water cuts made them uneconomic."

But Burlington placed the lateral along the top of B, tapping the oil, which had risen to the top, and not the water.

Heck reported, "The Larkin completion was proof that a horizontally drilled, Red River B-zone well could be productive because the greater borehole contact with the producing zone increased the oil cut and decreased the water cut.

"One of the theoretical benefits to drilling a horizontal well is that the coning of water into the productive wellbore is reduced and this has been shown to be true in this play," he concluded.

Early production suggested the wells would make between 200,000 and 500,000 barrels each.

Burlington followed the Larkin with two more horizontals, coming on with between 105 and 200 barrels. Continental joined with a horizontal, Peterson 1-26, for 497 barrels in May 1995.

Stark says, "It ended up that Burlington had the idea at about the same time we did." Through August 1994, Continental was, otherwise, drilling wildcat verticals on the other end of the state in Bottineau County, finally making one in Madison. It quit that. Continental also quit its vertical, Charles C-bench wells in northeastern Montana; they were proving to be small.

It went after Red River B in southwestern North Dakota instead. Burlington ended up owning about half of what would be delineated as the areal extent of the horizontal Cedar Hills Field; Continental, the other half. Other operators had room for making only eight attempts; two of these didn't work out.

Burlington made some 280 wells in the field; Continental, about 240. Of the more than 500 wells attempted, fewer than 10 were dry. Eventual production from the wells ranged from as little as some 15,000 barrels to more than 1 million with most making about 250,000 barrels.

By mid-2001, the first 199, horizontal B wells had made more than 25 million barrels.[121] Reid says, "Burlington had the biggest position, but the two companies kind of locked up that play. It produced more than 50,000 barrels a day—maybe a little bit more than that—at the peak."

The B success further transformed Continental, Stark says. "It was a technology evolution (over the years) that changed our focus from hunting conventionals to using 3-D to find structures to harvesting the Red River B with horizontal drilling."

The state's oil production grew from about 87,000 barrels a day in 1996 to nearly 100,000 a day in 1997 and Bowman became the state's top oil-producing county.[122] In 1995, auctions of leases for drilling on state land jumped to $12.7 million, totaling more than in the prior six years of lease sales combined and the most since 1981.

And the wells were incredibly inexpensive in comparison with their pay: Burlington reported in early 1998 that its first 70, unfraced B horizontals in 1997 cost only about $700,000 apiece.

It also noted that the new play was already finished. It reported, "The Cedar Hills Field should be fully delineated in 1998 and is planned for initial water-flood operations in 1999."[123]

As it turned out, Stark says, the field's peak production was reached in 1999 just as oil prices sank again. "It was kind of like Mur-

---

[121] Most were still producing in 2013.

[122] North Dakota oil production had peaked in 1984 at about 144,000 barrels a day.

[123] Delineation of the field was with the first, roughly 180 wells, which demonstrated the areal extent of the productive B bench. Water-flooding would be used to push more oil out of the wells.

phy's Law: We ended up getting the most production we'd ever had and oil prices fell below $13.

"But we survived that and continued on."

***

Still privately held at the time, Continental had begun preparing several years earlier for what might be its next growth play. As its production was more than ever, its expectations were greater than ever.

It had drilled a well in the 1980s in Sheridan County, northeastern Montana, proving Bakken could produce along a salt-dissolution feature there. But it wasn't a repeatable play. "It didn't work out," Stark says.

Now, in 1999, "we were basically just looking for an encore to the Red River discovery. The Red River was huge. I was concerned. Where's the encore? I mean—to find a field that covers a couple hundred square miles is not common. As big as it was, we did hit a limit.

"So where are we going to get something of this scale to continue to grow from? We were looking for a place where we could apply horizontal drilling to low-porosity, low-permeability rocks and with a wide areal extent that could be big fields."

It had considered other rocks: Duperow, Nisku, Lodgepole. "And we still look at these, but the Bakken was the one that had the earmarks of being a good horizontal candidate."

It had considered the middle Bakken in Richland County, Montana, for this and had mapped it. "There were some wells there that produced at low rates for long periods of time, which indicated there was a bigger tank out there, but there just wasn't much porosity or permeability."

Lyco had entered Richland County to do the 10, middle-Bakken, vertical re-entries at the time. Stark recalls suggesting to it and to long-time Richland County producer Headington Oil the idea of converting some existing verticals into air-injection wells to push more of the oil into new, horizontal wellbores.

"We weren't even thinking about fracing it at the time," Stark

91

says. "People in the day questioned if you could effectively frac a horizontal well."

Secondary recovery from Red River B in its North Dakota play would work with water injection. "We thought—because this middle-Bakken rock is so tight with such low permeability—that, although you couldn't shove water through it very easily, you could shove air through it. It would hit the rock and push oil out, into the horizontal wells. That was what our thought was.

"In other words, you could put some energy in there to push the oil out of the rock quicker." Neither Headington nor Lyco was interested, though. "So the idea just went away," Stark says.

Instead, Lyco developed its horizontal-plus-frac approach to Richland County. Stark says, "In the early days, the wells came on at nice rates, but the question was 'Would these wells sustain those rates?'"

Many hands had been burned by the Bakken in the past.

Hamm says, "Lyco just decided to frac it. Just frac it. Lyco turned it around in Montana. They were the leaders in applying the uncemented liner over there.

"These were short laterals—3,000-foot laterals—with a few frac stages. What turned it on over there was somebody just decided to frac it. And, then, Headington came in and, suddenly, you had large IPs—800 barrels or more.

"Boy, when I saw that, I said, 'This game is on.' That did it."

By early 2002, the first 10 of Lyco's wells had been online for more than a year. They held up.

Stark says, "We were very impressed with the rates. We immediately said, 'Well the big future and the big opportunity lies in North Dakota. The vast amount of Bakken is over there.'"

Hamm says, "In Montana, you had some pretty fair, natural porosity. In North Dakota, we didn't have that—for the most part. We knew it was going to be a different animal."

Therein lies the old, Southland Royalty dry hole: Robert Heuer 1-17 at the northernmost end of the Nesson anticline. Continental re-entered it, attempting a Lyco-style, horizontal-plus-frac in the middle

Bakken with a short lateral. "We knew it would produce," Stark says.

Continental had already begun leasing along the roughly 30-mile-wide and 100-mile-long anticline where oil had been made, primarily from the Madison formation just above Bakken, since Amerada Petroleum Corp. made the North Dakota oil-discovery well in 1951. The rock there was naturally fractured.

"It is, essentially, pressure-fractured by Mother Nature," Stark says. Thus, oil should flow more easily from it. "Actually there's better deliverability along the Nesson anticline than any place out there."

While the Robert Heuer re-entry came on with only 87 barrels in March 2004, it was commercial because, as a re-entry of an existing, vertical wellbore, it had been inexpensive. More important, though, is that it confirmed "for us that we were leasing on an idea that had merit," Stark says.

Hamm says, "We realized that this was going to work."

But it would need more science; it would be a climb.

Stark says, "We basically took the technology model that was successful in Montana and tried to apply it in North Dakota. It didn't work. Even though we knew the (middle) Bakken was there and that it was thermally mature and charged (with oil), we weren't able—right out of the chute—to make repeatable, commercial wells."

There would have to be a North Dakota variation on the Lyco-style frac. Stark says, "We were using open-hole completion technology. The rock mechanics in Elm Coulee Field were conducive to containing the fracture stimulation open-hole.

"In North Dakota, the rock mechanics were different. The fracs were not contained within the Bakken. They were going up into the overlying Lodgepole.

"You basically lost your frac into those zones. So we did have some early-times discouragements up there. It wasn't like we took that technology and walked right over into North Dakota, bought some leases, applied it and it worked.

"We had to work to break the code.

"What needed to be done was to not do an open-hole stimulation but to put a liner in the horizontal wellbore and then stage the

93

fracs. In other words, control the scale or the size of the fracs to contain them within the Bakken and not lose energy outside of it."

It had followed Robert Heuer 1-17 with a wildcat, Eleanore 1-5, far south in Stark County in November 2004 near the Little Knife anticline for 125 barrels. Called the "Normandy" area, Hamm says, "that was a pretty tough area for the Bakken. It still is today."

It resumed a year later with three in Billings County and one in Dunn at the Nesson's southern end for between 164 and 280 barrels.

How many wells before figuring it out?

"Several, at least," Stark says. "It wasn't just us; there were a bunch of people drilling wells out there."

Hamm says, "You know, it was somewhat discouraging to me. It was so big. The oil was there. A lot of times you want to look back and say, 'Gosh, why didn't I do this?' or 'Why didn't I do that?'

"There were times we were discouraged with this well or that well but, overall, we saw a continuous, gradual improvement with everything we were doing. We felt like we were onto something. We felt it was something huge. And it was going to happen.

"Early on, the fight was being waged with land. We started out with 300,000 acres by the time we drilled Robert Heuer. After we drilled that, we got a couple hundred thousand more acres.

"The reason I didn't do more early on is because I didn't have any money." There was a solution to that. In 2006, he decided to take the 39-year-old, private company public to fund its expansion. Oil prices had also continued to grow into the 2000s; Continental's production was mostly oil so, if the company was ever going public, this was a good commodity-price market in which to sell interest.

From being primarily an Oklahoma-area producer beginning in 1971, the Williston Basin now held 76% of its proved reserves, mostly producing from Red River B.

Hamm sold 20.7 million shares for $15 each in May 2007. The market didn't understand it, though. The stock closed at $14.10 in the first day of trading and hovered around $15 during the next three months before taking off.[124]

"We were very confident in the play," Stark says. "The market was still a little skeptical about the repeatability, but we had seen enough evidence to feel comfortable with that this was a play that had widespread repeatability and producibility."

---

[124] A share was $125 in March 2014.

BARNETT: 2006

← ← ← ← ← → → → → →

"It was foreign—the nature of an unconventional play—
to our thinking to think that
'Hey, this thing can go on and on and on.'"
—*Trevor Rees-Jones*

As Devon Energy announced its bid for Mitchell Energy in mid-2001, there had been only a third time Barnett was mentioned in an SEC filing other than by Mitchell since 1994. Micro-cap Empire Energy Corp. had purchased a Canadian company, gaining 3,000 lease acres in Parker County, just south of Wise County. It planned to explore whether it could produce "from the popular Barnett shale underlying the area." It had tried to lease more, but the other seller didn't have rights to produce from the Barnett zone.

Most of the companies exploring the Fort Worth Basin were targeting small pockets of leftover pay in the 50-year-old, Bend-conglomerate play overlying the Barnett. Any that were sampling the shale were privately held or, like Chevron, which made one in 1997 and quit the shale, weren't trying it in earnest.

Dan Steward, the former Mitchell vice president, writes in his documentary of the company's Barnett work, "Over the years, the Barnett play garnered only limited media coverage and hadn't sparked industry's interest. In May 1998, an article appeared in the *Oil & Gas Journal* that received some attention."

By then, Mitchell Energy and a few others were making some 80 million cubic feet a day from more than 300 Barnett wells in Wise and Denton counties. In the article, Vello Kuuskraa and a colleague at Advanced Resources International, along with two U.S. Geological Survey geoscientists, wrote, "However, very little publicly available information exists on resource potential and actual well performance."

In 1995, the USGS had recognized the Barnett as a gas play. In the 1998 report, it and Kuuskraa revealed their assessment of its technically recoverable gas: 10 trillion cubic feet. They noted as well that this much gas is the Btu equivalent of a 1.67-billion-barrel oil field. The article's headline: "Barnett shale rising star in Fort Worth Basin."

They concluded, "...Play boundaries are not yet delineated by drilling. The eventual productive area might be as small as 285 square miles or as large as 4,200 square miles."

By mid-1999, as gas improved to above $2 again, Mitchell was now joined by 11 other companies attempting Barnett wells. Further inspiration was gained from a symposium in September 2000 that was hosted by the Oil Information Library of Fort Worth. Its volunteer board was looking for a fund-raiser after years of declining exploration in the basin, according to Steward. It had hoped 125 people would attend; instead, more than 200 showed up at the Fort Worth Petroleum Club.

To not exceed fire code, "many had to be turned away," Steward writes. "...In addition to the local operators attending, there were representatives from some of the larger independents and the majors...The Barnett shale had now gained industry recognition as a significant resource play."

Among those chasing Barnett was Trevor Rees-Jones and his Dallas-based Chief Oil & Gas LLC. By mid-2004, when dozens of other companies, public and private, were on Devon's heels in the Barnett, trying to buy in, Rees-Jones was among those already there.

Rees-Jones had been chasing George Mitchell in the Fort Worth Basin for a decade already. He had been an oil and gas bankruptcy attorney in Dallas when oil was on its way up from about $15 to $40. He quit bankruptcy law in January 1984 to form his own oil and gas company. Oil had been trending at about $30 at the time. In the fall of 1985, it began to tumble, eventually finding bottom at less than $10 in the summer of 1986.

He chuckles about his timing. "Well, I didn't realize that. That's the great thing about youth: You don't realize some things that would have run you off. In the early '80s in Dallas, there was pretty much a boom going on in oil and gas and in real estate. The fact that oil was headed down—the fact that the boom had peaked and was on its way down—was kind of lost on me."

But half of his interest in starting an oil and gas company was to quit being a lawyer. "I was really miserable doing that. I couldn't imagine doing that the rest of my life. I hated being a lawyer. I wanted to be the businessman. I was in the meetings.

"I was supposed to be thinking about it as a lawyer. I was thinking about it as a businessman and wanting to be that guy who was drilling those wells. That struck me as a whole lot of fun, taking that risk. I was trying to find what I could do the rest of my life and that I would enjoy."

He began drilling some exploration prospects and buying others' prospects, raising money along the way. His six years in oil and gas law had been successful; success in drilling amazing oil and gas wells—and lots of them—would prove more elusive.

"I was dealing with drilling wells that were usually of a pretty high-risk nature (financially) and drilling a whole lot of dry holes."

Again, Rees-Jones had been contrarian—drilling wildcats when most of the oil and gas industry, beginning in 1986, was focused on buying producing properties as they were being shed in bankruptcy courts and by the largest oil companies that were heading overseas.

Then he bought a non-operated interest in a producing property for about $150,000. This was in July 1986; his timing had improved. That was the bottom of the oil-price collapse.

"Within about a year, oil popped back up to between $16 and $18 and the cash flow from that little purchase was what helped me stay in the game, putting drilling deals together."

It was some kind of journey, though. "About every two or three years, I'd find something that was good enough to repair the damage I'd done over the previous two years and carry me forward to go drill a whole bunch of other dry holes.

"And then, right before I got to the point of tumbling off the cliff and knocking myself out, I'd find something else that healed me up a little bit and kept me going.

"So the key was to stay in the game. I was always taking a risk, but I never took too much risk such that I was knocked out—which is, in hindsight, miraculous."

Rees-Jones had found the work he enjoyed. "Those were some tough years, but I loved it. I really loved putting deals together and taking a prospect from the idea or the very beginning through the mapping and the development, the raising of money from investors and then drilling the well."

That kind of fun was coming to an end, though, and another kind would begin: Shale! When starting out, "I was unmarried. The only thing throughout my first 10 years of putting prospects together and drilling wells that I can really claim to have become proficient at was setting myself on fire and barely putting the fire out, so I could live to fight another day, put another deal together and drill another well, at which time I set myself on fire again."

By the summer of 1994, "I'd been in the business 10 years now and didn't have a whole lot to show for it. And, most importantly, I was now married and had two kids."

Rees-Jones needed to figure out how to stay in oil and gas but reduce his financial risk. "It wouldn't be fair to my family to keep doing what I'd been doing."

George Mitchell had successfully worked the stacked pay of the Fort Worth Basin, particularly in Wise County, for more than 40 years by now. If Rees-Jones could get some acreage, which was difficult because so much of the basin was HBPed by old wells owned by other companies, he might be able to replicate Mitchell Energy's results or, at least, those of the basin's conventional-formation explorers, such as Republic Energy Inc. and Frank Pitts' Pitts Oil Co., both long-time, privately held, basin operators.[125] Although the field was just west of his Dallas office, Rees-Jones says, "I had never done anything there before."

He was looking for a statistical play, putting hit-or-miss-and-probably-miss-again wildcatting aside to build a base of gas reserves over a long period of time with lower risk. Searching for available leases, he put a small team together.

"I didn't have any money. Pretty much everybody was working for some type of little (royalty) override or an 'I'll pay you later' type of a Wimpy/Popeye hamburger kind of deal."[126]

With leasehold now, Rees-Jones went about drilling Bend-conglomerate wells just as Mitchell had done for decades. "Anybody would've probably told you that was the sorriest, most depleted oil and gas basin in the United States at the time."

He pared the office to about 500 square feet. On a contract basis, he had a geologist, landman, geological technician and a rep out in the field. The field rep was to help Rees-Jones drill the wells, since he was going to operate them now rather than just have an interest in them.

His newly part-time assistant needed a full-time job; Rees-Jones found one for her. "Then it was just me in the 500 square feet."

While making his Bend wells, Rees-Jones was well familiar with Mitchell's attempts in the Barnett. "In the 1980s, I think there were about 75 Barnett wells that were mostly, if not all, failures. So you'd look at the people drilling those and think, 'Man, these people have got to be crazy.'"

In the early 1990s, the gel-heavy frac method seemed to help but barely. "I wasn't there, challenging the Barnett, flailing against it like George Mitchell did all those years. He had to have been doing that for—if he could ever figure out a way to get that gas out—a monumental-profit standpoint. Everybody knew the rock held, locked within it, a tremendous amount of reserves in place."

---

[125] Frank Pitts was among industry members who urged deregulation of gas prices, resulting in the Natural Gas Act of 1978 and the eventual end to price controls.

[126] Wimpy often says, "I'd gladly pay you Tuesday for a hamburger today."

Dan Steward, the Mitchell vice president of geology, knew that figuring out how to repeatedly make commercial amounts of gas out of the Barnett shale would be important. But could it be done?

"Most of us geologists were well aware that there were hydrocarbons in the shales and they were the source rocks for the basins," he says.[127] "Most of the early work on shales pretty much proved that, while a lot of the hydrocarbons had leaked off (into neighboring rock), probably as much or more had stayed in the shale.

"When we would drill through the Barnett, we'd see a hellacious amount of gas, so there was no question hydrocarbons were there."

Contemporary thinking—as the result of myriad research by public and private entities—in the 1950s through the 1980s was that gas could only be prodded from shale that was naturally fractured. "You had to have open, natural fractures. You had to produce from the fractures (into which) gas had moved from the shale; you weren't actually getting much gas out of the shale itself.

"So when we went into the Barnett, we went in thinking that we were going to have to be able to find naturally fractured areas and drain those fractures. That's what we were expecting. Natural fracturing generally occurs around faults and structural anticlines or structural sinks, where you have rapid change in formation dips.

"So we started looking at the Barnett around faults and around structures. We found a lot of fracturing associated with those structures, but they were all healed with white calcite. In addition, we found some regional, basin fractures.

"Subsequent work has found that these are actually hydraulic fractures that occurred due to the maturation of the shale. We saw those too and they were healed with white calcite.[128]

"So we convinced management that what we need to do is back away from these structural features that have healed fractures. Then, by the time we found there were, essentially, no open fractures in the

---

[127] In the interview.

[128] Impure calcite can be other colors; because the calcite in the Barnett formation is white and the shale is black, it was easier to see in core samples.

Barnett, we had drilled and fraced quite a few wells. We fraced them because we felt like 'Okay, we're not seeing the fractures at the wellbore, so we need to induce fractures to reach out to find them.'

"By the time we found out that those open, natural fractures didn't exist, we had put larger and larger fracs on the wells and, over time, somehow or another, we were making a lot of gas, even though all the data said that we had no open fractures.

"It was fortunate because, if we had proven early on that all the natural fractures were healed and that there was no chance of finding open fractures, we probably would have shut down the play, because all the literature said that—without open, natural fractures—it wouldn't work."

Fracs on the earliest Barnett wells cracked the rock to about 125 feet from the hole; a larger job would crack it out about 250 feet. The frac jobs were with water and nitrogen or CO_2. The point of the latter, known as the "foam frac," was to help the frac fluid flow back to the surface and to also reduce the amount of exposure of freshwater to the shale.

"Well, the problem with these foam fracs is, once you get beyond 250 feet, they cannot effectively carry sand." Thus the switch to the MHF technique, which uses a large amount of gel to carry the sand farther into the fraced rock. "You have a breaker in that gel fluid that, after so many hours at the elevated temperature in the formation, causes the gel to break and goes back to water and then that water can flow back to the (surface)."

The earlier frac design that cracked the rock out about 125 feet would make a well of about 125,000 cubic feet of gas a day. Fracing out to about 1,500 feet would make a well of about 1 million a day. But it cost about $500,000.

"It looked like we were just trading dollars. This was 1986 or so. And we still didn't know what the wells were capable of doing over time. So management said, 'Let's drill a few each year and spread them out over the area to build our knowledge base.'

"We didn't know yet if they were even going to be commercial. I mean, for instance, let's say it comes on at 1 million a day and produces for three years and then something happens and you end up making only, say, 300 million cubic feet out of it. That wouldn't have been commercial."[129]

The LSF technique proposed by Nick Steinsberger was critical. "We had established that the Barnett was commercial for Mitchell Energy because we had a gas plant and we could make money on the (NGL) but not as a play that would garner industry interest.

"I'd say that, by '94, industry didn't give a damn. In the early 1980s, industry thought all it needed to understand about shales was that it was a source rock of hydrocarbons in a basin. It wasn't working on producing from the shale itself (outside of the naturally fractured Michigan and Appalachian shales).

"We were experimenting with things in the Barnett that we didn't really understand. I mean, when we tried the first (LSF), most people thought that was a stupid thing to do because, generally speaking, you don't put freshwater on shales.

"But they didn't understand that we already knew the Barnett was not sensitive to freshwater where we were working. Outside of the area we were working, the Barnett could be water-sensitive but not where we were working.

"So it was clear to us that 'Hey, let's try these water fracs.' We said, 'We're spending about $385,000 on the (higher-gel- and -sand-content) frac. Let's try three or four of these. We're going to spend $85,000 per well to frac it. We can save $300,000. Even if the reserves go down, we will probably improve the economics.

"And, even if the water fracs don't work, there's no reason why we can't go back and gel-frac them.' We decided that, if it was a failure, we were only out on the cost of the three or four wells. If it was a success, we were going to cut $300,000 off the frac cost of every Barnett well we would drill. And that looked real attractive.

"Management said, 'Yeah. Let's do it.'"

---

[129] At $2 natural gas, for example, a well that made 300 million cubic feet would gross only $600,000 in its lifetime. Also, oil and gas wells usually come online with their highest production rate and begin to decline; a 1-million-a-day-IP well may make 300 million cubic feet during its first three years.

103

***

In 1997, Rees-Jones wanted to give the Barnett a try and spud a well. "Unfortunately, it was a location that Mitchell would've easily passed on and perhaps that's why the lease was available because we ended up drilling into a fault and our completion failed," he says.

As would become known by others in shale plays in time—either by being told or having to learn the hard way with failed wells—a shale well is to be made exactly *not* where a traditional well that was chasing a structural trap would be made: a fault zone.

"So here I am again, taking too much risk and drilling just an absolutely horrible Barnett well, but, as sometimes happened, we had drilled through one of the best Bend-conglomerate zones that we ever found in the area."

The well was completed there, uphole, for 2 million cubic feet per day—Chief's highest-producing well it had ever made in the Bend. "So the investors were happy and we didn't see the Barnett as being anything better than what we were doing in the old, tired, Bend conglomerate."

And Chief didn't have what allowed Mitchell to keep drilling away at the Barnett. "They had a pretty high-priced gas contract. Ran up to about $4.25. They also had their plant that was stripping NGLs out of their richer gas. They were able to make more money."

In 1998, as oil and gas prices plummeted, "if you can believe it, my landman and I decided to shift our focus from the Bend to the Barnett." Some acreage was available at the intersection of northern Tarrant, southeastern Wise and southwestern Denton counties. This was south of where Chief knew Mitchell had denoted the fault zone— the Rhome Newark fault system that ran through the town of Rhome in southeastern Wise County.

Mitchell Energy had learned to not drill along that and focused its Barnett work north of the fault. Rees-Jones says, however, "We didn't see why the Barnett shouldn't work south of there as well as where Mitchell was drilling." He picked up some acreage in northern Tarrant County clear of the fault zone.

"One of the reasons we were able to get that leasehold in Tarrant County was because it was dry gas. Mitchell didn't want dry gas because it didn't do them any good; they couldn't take it to their (NGL) plant. They were a big gas-liquids producer. Dry gas was counter-productive to them."

Meanwhile, as Chief was ready in 2000 to begin a new Barnett attempt, Mitchell had well demonstrated by now success with the LSF. "Word got out that the 'water frac' was just as good, if not better, at freeing up the gas—and at a whole lot less cost."

Chief's first Barnett attempt had cost about $500,000 with some $250,000 of that for fracing the well, using the old, gel-heavy MHF technique. With the LSF, "we really kicked into gear. Gas prices were improving, the (LSF) had come into play and reduced the frac cost while overall service costs were still very low, having been beaten down over the previous 15 years."

With the idea of going south and using the lower-cost LSF, Chief hopped across the Rhome Newark fault with vertical wells and proved a second Barnett fairway. "I guess it's our claim to fame."

And it was with a smaller spend: Using the LSF technique lowered the completion portion of the cost to about $100,000. "You're talking about a huge reduction in cost. That was a pretty strong impetus to get more drilling kicked off."[130]

Soon, his work since 1984—and at something he enjoyed—would meet with great financial success too—and more than he imagined. Via its merger with Mitchell Energy, Devon had joined the play; dozens of other producers were as well.

In 2003, SEC filings began to pop with "Barnett" in them. A micro-cap paid $46 an acre for a non-exclusive option to purchase 3,231 acres in Montague County north of Wise to attempt Barnett wells.

---

[130] Kent Bowker, Mitchell Energy's Barnett geologist, says the reduction in operators' use of large amounts of gel in the Barnett, Cotton Valley and, soon, elsewhere "caused much consternation within Halliburton and the other frac companies we were using. They saw their profit margins drop because they weren't really charging for (frac-pumping) horsepower; they were charging for the chemicals. When we stopped using the chemicals and they stopped making money, they changed their pricing to more horsepower-driven."

Soon, it let the option expire to pursue acreage in northern Wise County with another micro-cap where the Barnett might be better.[131]

Another paid $100,000 for a 20% working interest in a Barnett prospect in Jack County, west of Wise. Another bought an interest in a well targeting Marble Falls overlying Barnett, mentioning to investors that Mitchell Energy had once drilled Marble Falls wells.

Tiny, Dallas-based, gas-pipeliner Crosstex Energy Inc. formed a joint venture to construct a gathering system in an area of the Barnett play for $3 million.[132] In February 2003, power company Progress Energy Inc. bought some 195 billion cubic feet of proved reserves from Fort Worth-based Republic Energy, which Dan Steward joined upon Devon's purchase of Mitchell and, then, Nick Steinsberger joined as well.

What Republic sold was its 23,000 acres in the traditional area of the Barnett play where the Viola-limestone frac barrier was present. It then leased west of there, where the Viola was eroded. Devon Energy was making horizontal Barnett wells now where Viola was absent by inducing fractures in the uppermost Barnett section, thus not penetrating the Ellenburger.

Midstream operator Enbridge Energy Partners LP bought into the Barnett story, paying $247 million for Cantera Resources Inc.'s more than 2,000 miles of gas-gathering pipe and processing capacity of 217 million cubic feet a day. Cantera had purchased the assets just three years earlier from Texas utility TXU Corp. for $105 million.

Enbridge reported in the announcement that "local markets for Fort Worth Basin production are nearing saturation and additional market outlets will be required."

Heritage Propane Partners LP, which was merging into Energy Transfer Partners LP, noted that capacity was being constrained in both North Texas and East Texas, which had been first to adopt the LSF technique. Barnett gas was going to East Texas, which was be-

---

[131] Part of Montague County ended up making oil from the Barnett.

[132] Upon merging with Devon's midstream assets in March 2014, Crosstex became EnLink Midstream LLC.

coming saturated with new Cotton Valley and Bossier-sandstone gas.

Pressure-pumper Key Energy Services Inc. ordered an additional 12,000 horsepower of pumping capacity to deploy in the Barnett. Rock-analysis firm Core Laboratories NV posted its most profitable quarter in its 68-year history; nearly 30 oil and gas producers signed up to participate in a study of Barnett and other shales.

By year-end 2004, producers were making more than 1 billion cubic feet of gas a day from the Barnett, which now hosted more than 3,000 wells. Applications for permits to drill totaled 75 in 1998; in 2004, more than 1,100.

And those who were successful were well rewarded.

Among them, Fort Worth-based, small-cap Quicksilver Resources Inc. had been exploring for coal gas in Alberta and producing from the naturally fractured Antrim shale in Michigan. In March 2004, it revealed it had put together more than 100,000 net acres over Barnett. Quickly, that grew to 207,000. It reported, "...Our initial production results, combined with (that of) surrounding, offset wells, are confirming the quality and large scale of this...shale play."

One of its horizontals cost $1.8 million, coming on with 1.5 million a day. Estimated ultimate recovery was 2.5 billion cubic feet, 20% NGL. "Modifications to fracturing techniques have resulted in improvements in each successive well...," it added. Four more came on with between 2.0- and 2.8 million a day. By mid-2005, it had 222,000 net acres in Hood, Johnson, Somervell, Bosque and Hill counties.

Larger-cap Denbury Resources Inc. noted in early 2002 that it owned Barnett acreage and had drilled a few wells. It drilled seven more verticals by March 2004, but its average 71% working interest was netting it less than 1 million a day. It planned to try horizontals. With five of these by early 2005, it was now netting 5.8 million a day from Barnett with wells coming on with an average rate of 2 million.

It reported, "We are still refining our fracturing technique, including an analysis of the best number of fracture treatments to adequately stimulate the entire length of our lateral sections, which can exceed 4,000 feet.

"Initial reserve estimates...appear to be three to four times greater than the vertical wells we initially drilled."

It was using 3-D seismic data "to better locate our wells, so that we encounter less faulting and underground sinkholes (karsting) which have been associated with fracture stimulations into zones outside of the Barnett shale that are typically water-bearing."

Its Barnett proved reserves grew to 62.3 billion cubic feet.

Soon, it determined there was minimal karsting—that is, collapsed structures in the underlying water-bearing Ellenburger—in its Parker County acreage. It was adding leasehold for about $500 an acre. It had a fifth rig on the way.

Permian Basin-focused Parallel Petroleum Corp. bought into the Barnett in April 2003. It then joined privately held, Dallas-based Dale Resources LLC in a first horizontal, Brentwood 1, to try the rock east of downtown Fort Worth. The well came on in July 2005 with an initial rate of 4 million cubic feet a day.

A few days earlier, adjacent to that lease, in a deal with privately held, Fort Worth-based Four Sevens Oil Co., its horizontal Parrot 1 came on with 5.1 million. Both were completed with staged fracs and cost about $2 million each. A couple more wells were brought on by its partners in the next couple of months, ranging from 2.2- and 5.2 million a day.

***

Rees-Jones joined in the new, horizontal Barnett play with a first lateral attempt in the summer of 2003. "And it was a disaster—not because it was horizontal," he says. "It was because we drilled along the south end of our second (fairway in Tarrant County) and we were running into another fault boundary. We had watched what Mitchell had done with the vertical wells and we were watching what Devon and others were doing now with the horizontals.

"In the first year or two of it, we had a real question of whether horizontal drilling delivered better economic results.

"In northern Tarrant County, a lot of our vertical wells were coming on at a million cubic feet a day and would ultimately make 1

Bcf (billion cubic feet). Going into 2005, it looked like the average horizontal would make 3 million a day and give you 3 Bcf of reserves. But it was at three times the cost of a vertical well.

"So we had a real question. If we were making vertical wells and bringing them on at a million a day for a Bcf, then 3 million a day and 3 Bcf at three times the cost is a push. But, getting into 2005, it was pretty clear that horizontal was the way to go."

As a small, privately held company, Chief had to let larger companies like Devon run through the trials and learn from them. "We had to pretty much follow these guys. We really couldn't stick our neck out, trying too many things new for fear of making too big of a costly mistake that would knock us out of the box.

"We tried to stay up. Boy, what an exciting time that was. Man!"

Rees-Jones had wanted more large companies to enter the play to further help figure out how to make it enormously profitable. Chesapeake Energy Corp., XTO Energy Inc. and Burlington soon arrived.

Large-cap Chesapeake had entered in June 2002 somewhat by chance via its $120-million roll-up of micro-cap, Oklahoma City-based Canaan Energy Corp.[133] Canaan had a Barnett arrangement with tiny, Dallas-based Hallwood Group Inc., which would get in and out of various businesses opportunistically, such as real estate, textiles and the ShoBiz Pizza restaurant franchise. In 2001, it had exited the oil and gas business, selling its assets in the San Juan, Permian and Gulf Coast basins to Pure Resources II Inc.

In 2002, it put together a new energy venture, Hallwood Energy Corp., to drill Barnett wells on some 28,329 net acres in Johnson and Hill counties—where the Viola-limestone frac barrier is absent, thus acreage was available for lease. It was a two-county, southern leap from where Mitchell Energy had made Barnett wells.

By the fall of 2004, it had 42 Barnett wells—31 vertical and 11 horizontal—making 25 million cubic feet a day, net. The horizontals were coming on with 5.5 million. It put this northern block of lease-

---

[133] Chesapeake had invested $14 million in Canaan in 2001; its buy-out in 2002 was via a direct appeal to fellow shareholders as Canaan management refused to negotiate.

hold in Johnson County up for sale.

The marketing brochure included a kicker: "Hallwood will share this unique completion expertise with the new operator."

How were fraced, horizontal Barnett wells being made in Johnson County without fracing into the underlying Ellenburger water?

Chesapeake was already a 45% partner in Hallwood's 27,000-acre "southern block," inheriting it from Canaan. Quickly, it went ahead and bought Hallwood's position in the northern block for $277 million in cash. Proved reserves were already 135 billion.

Aubrey McClendon, chairman and chief executive officer, noted, when announcing the deal, that Canaan's acreage over Barnett wasn't given any value when it bought the company in 2002. At the time, Johnson County was far from where Mitchell Energy had proven the play. "Today," he said, "it appears that Chesapeake's south-block Barnett shale position (it inherited) may be worth more than what we paid for the entire Canaan transaction."

Some six months later, it went ahead and bought out Hallwood in the south block too for $249 million. It estimated the $2.5-million wells would recover some 2- to 2.8 billion cubic feet each. Altogether, Chesapeake was making some 50 million cubic feet a day from Barnett now and looking to reach 80 million by year-end.

Gas was $8.

In 2004, large-cap XTO Energy entered the Barnett. The producer had been formed as Cross Timbers Oil Co. in Fort Worth at the bottom of the oil-price collapse in 1986. Jon Brumley, Bob Simpson and Steve Palko had been put out of their executive positions in Fort Worth at Southland Royalty Co. when Burlington Northern Railroad swept Southland up into its Burlington Resources unit.[134]

The trio and treasurer Louis Baldwin began acquiring producing,

---

[134] The deal had been a hostile takeover as were many others in the 1980s. For example, T. Boone Pickens bid on Cities Service Co., prompting Gulf Oil to bid more. Gulf won but then withdrew its bid. Pickens began buying shares of Gulf itself. Chevron stepped in and bought Gulf. Some members of Congress considered prohibiting oil-company mergers. It was withdrawn when Reagan said he would veto legislation that prevented mergers from being sorted out by the marketplace.

U.S. properties that were trickling down to small E&Ps from majors who were going to the deepwater Gulf of Mexico and abroad.[135]

The Barnett was under its Fort Worth headquarters and the company had long been a Cotton Valley producer in East Texas. It knew about tight-rock gas. But it wasn't the wildcatting type; as producers around it further proved the Barnett play, XTO bought into it, picking up 97.6 billion cubic feet of proved reserves for $120 million in February 2004 as an 11,000-acre, starter position in the play.

It reported, "Our technical teams have been assessing the long-term viability of the Barnett shale for the past two years—scrutinizing wellbore and reservoir dynamics along with economic feasibility. Given the conclusions, our development teams are enthusiastic...Our expertise in horizontal drilling and...fracturing techniques will find perfect application in developing the Barnett shale."

In the spring of 2005, it bought more, taking up Paul Rady and Glen Warren's privately held Antero Resources Corp. for $692 million. The deal made XTO the No. 2 Barnett producer, second to Devon, in what it called "the largest natural-gas field in Texas."[136]

Rady, whose career began as a geologist, and Warren, whose began as a landman, both at Amoco Corp., had formed Rockies-coalbed-methane-focused Pennaco Energy Inc. in 1998 with $28 million and sold it just three years later to Marathon Oil Co. for $500 million. They quickly formed Antero Resources Corp. in 2002, acquiring part of their Barnett entry via producing properties in the Vinson Ranch area from the Vinson family's Threshold Development Co. and from Sinclair Oil Corp.

In about three years, Antero had amassed 66,000 net acres in Tarrant, Parker and Johnson counties. Proved reserves totaled 440

---

[135] Brumley retired from XTO in 1996 to start another E&P, Encore Acquisition Co., operating along the oily Cedar Creek anticline in eastern Montana. It was sold in 2010 to Denbury Resources for $4.5 billion in cash, stock and debt assumption.

[136] XTO paid $342.5 million in cash, $218 million of debt assumption and 13.3 million shares, along with warrants to purchase 2 million shares at $27 each during the next five years.

billion cubic feet. Production was 65 million a day.[137]

Gas was heading to $15.

Burlington Resources had joined the Barnett play as well. In 2002, it spent $29 million on 40 verticals in Wise County for 6 million a day, net to its interest. It soon bought more acreage for $141 million, primarily just east in Denton County and it sold its upper-Bakken wells in the Williston Basin. By year-end 2003, it was making 34 million a day from Barnett. With up to nine rigs working for it there in 2003, it drilled 163 wells. And it launched an initial, two-well horizontal test.

Meanwhile, ConocoPhillips saw a future in a large, conventional- and unconventional-resource portfolio: On Dec. 12, 2005, it announced it was buying Burlington for $35.6 billion, primarily for its North American gas assets. It was the first major oil company to re-enter onshore-U.S. E&P after two decades of selling and the first to weigh in on the potential of U.S. shale.

In a conference call the morning of Dec. 13, Jim Mulva, chairman and chief executive, was asked at what gas price he based his valuation of Burlington. Gas was $14 and shot past $15 later that day as Gulf hurricanes Katrina and Rita had taken supply offline and strong, winter demand was under way.

Mulva replied, "…We don't see, necessarily, a continuation of gas prices that we've seen here recently…What we really look at is prices more in the $7 or $8 (range)…and, if they are north of that, it's all better…The numbers don't look particularly good at $5…but, on the other hand, we can live with it in terms of its presence in the portfolio. We don't think we're going to see $5…gas prices.

"Quite likely, we will see $7 or $8 and (we have) a pretty strong belief that we will see double-digit gas prices as we go out over the next year or two or three years…(But) this transaction is not done because gas prices are at $14…."

---

[137] Rady and Warren went on to build a Marcellus-shale portfolio. The company IPOed in 2013 at $44 a share, raising $1.6 billion.

***

By that time, much had changed—in gas price and in the Barnett: The Barnett was now giving up 1.7 billion cubic feet of gas a day. The horizontal code had been cracked. EOG Resources Inc. was bringing wells on with IPs of 10 million-plus.

In early 2003, EOG had mentioned to shareholders that it was looking at the Barnett; it had gone to Barnett school in 1999 when looking at Mitchell Energy's assets while Mitchell was for sale the first time. Formerly known as Enron Oil & Gas Co., the company was formed in 1985 and spun out of Enron Corp. in 1999—two years before the energy-trading firm's collapse.[138]

In May 2004, its earnings announcement carried this headline: "EOG...Announces Success in Texas Barnett Shale Natural Gas Play." The company revealed it had had horizontal-Barnett success in Johnson County—two counties south of Mitchell's original play. It held some 175,000 acres at nearly 100% working interest.[139]

The company estimated it had 400 to 800 potential well locations across its leasehold. "This play is expected to have a very significant impact on EOG's U.S., gas-production growth, reserve additions and re-investment rate of return," Mark Papa, chairman and chief executive, told shareholders. The stock jumped from about $49 to $54 in two trading days with some 12 million shares changing hands.[140]

It continued to add, soon holding 345,000 net acres—all in counties outside Mitchell's core area. Its Fricks 3H went into sales with 5.8 million a day. Papa reported, "The production rate and expected reserves of the Fricks completion indicate it may be one of the better wells that the industry has drilled in Johnson County, which is the focus of our current drilling activity."

---

[138] "All around the building there were cries of 'Free at last. Free at last,'" retired EOG chairman Forrest Hoglund says of EOG employee sentiment upon leaving Enron.

[139] Some of that Johnson County leasehold was owned by a limestone miner, micro-cap United States Lime & Minerals Inc., which received a royalty interest. The miner's stock was some $3 in 2003; in March 2014, about $56.

[140] Nine months later, the stock was split 2-for-1 as shares reached about $90.

By February 2005, it reported it had proven the Barnett's extension into Parker County too. It now had 400,000 net acres. Net production was 30 million a day. A couple of months later, it had success west of Wise County despite the absence of the Viola-limestone frac barrier. It also extended the play far southwest into Erath County. It had nine rigs drilling for it and it was looking at down-spacing its staged fracs to 500 feet apart along its laterals.

Soon, its Campbell Unit 1H in Johnson County came on with 7.7 million; Coppenger Unit 1H with 6.6 million; Kolar Unit 1H with 6.1 million; and Setback D Unit 1H with 7.5 million.

Then its Raam Unit 1H took the Barnett out of the park: The well came on with 10 million; more than a week later, it was still producing 8 million a day. "The flow is huge and the location is outside the traditional core area," *Oil and Gas Investor* reported in April 2006. "Thousands of acres held by EOG and others in the county are, theoretically, worth much more...So, just when prices for Barnett assets seemed high, there they grow again...."[141]

Papa said in a press release in early 2006, "The Raam 1H is one of the best natural-gas wells completed by any operator in the entire Barnett shale play—not just in Johnson County."[142]

Securities analyst Dave Pursell says a fund manager had asked him in the early 2000s about the Barnett in Johnson County where the Viola is absent. A petroleum engineer with a bachelor's and master's from Texas A&M, Pursell had worked in engineering and operations for Arco Alaska Inc. and had been a manager of petrophysics at S.A. Holditch & Associates Inc. before beginning his securities-research career.[143]

"That limestone barrier prevented or dampened the tendency for

---

[141] The report added, "The lease-expiration clock is ticking too fast for some acreage-owners who can't get their hands on enough rigs. Some 100 (rigs) were drilling there at year-end 2005 and most operators have announced plans to add more...."

[142] Across EOG's vast, multi-national portfolio, the 570-word, "operational highlights" portion of that press release included 282 words about the Barnett; the only other asset discussed was its holding in Trinidad.

[143] The firm, founded by Texas A&M petroleum-engineering professor Dr. Stephen Holditch, is now a division of Schlumberger Ltd.; as for Arco, it was bought by BP Plc.

the frac to grow down," Pursell says. "You wanted your frac to grow out and up. You didn't want it to grow down; you would end up hitting Ellenburger, which is a prolific water-producing interval. You'd get an ocean of water. As you move south in the play to Johnson County, you no longer have the Viola. It was either very thin there or nonexistent.

"There's very little distance between the bottom of the Barnett and this massive water-bearing zone. In a vertical well, your frac has to be pretty big to get enough contact with the reservoir to make that well economic. If you didn't have the Viola, you'd have to pump a very small frac to prevent it from growing down into the water."

The friend was being solicited to lease his mineral rights in Johnson County. "He called me and said an operator had drilled a well there and had a show in the Barnett, but there's no limestone barrier. He asked, 'How would you develop that?'"

Conceptually, Pursell replied, one would have to put in a horizontal well with four or five, small, frac stages. "Again, each frac has to be small, so it doesn't grow down into the water. I questioned at the time—and this was a long time ago—if anyone could do that economically." While the horizontal exposed the well to more of the shale, the additional cost could cancel the profit earned from the additional gas.

"And none of this technology was new. Horizontal wells had been drilled; hydraulic fracs had been done. But the ability to drill a horizontal well quickly—because there is a cost to how long the rig is out there—and put in multiple frac stages economically—because there is a cost to how long the pressure-pumping crew is out there— was a novel concept. EOG figured it out. There were others, but they were among the first."

The EOG news required that dozens of Barnett operators' worth would have to be re-examined. Among these was the worth of Houston-based Carrizo Oil & Gas Inc., which had been a micro-cap stock when Devon bought Mitchell Energy in 2001. Formed in 1993 to use 3-D seismic, particularly on the Gulf Coast, to find bright spots of pay in conventional rock, Carrizo bought 2,100 net Barnett acres in 2003.

Quickly, it went 14-for-14 in the play; its minority interest in the wells was netting it 1.4 million cubic feet a day. Gas was in the $6s.

By November 2004, its exposure had grown to 20,000 net acres in Wise, Parker, Denton and Tarrant counties. To fund drilling, it sold $18 million of senior notes due in just four years at 10%, secured by a second lien on its assets. It net just $16.2 million in proceeds after paying the broker. Within a year, it had 75,000 net acres and just $15 million of undrawn bank-line capacity to access. The horizontals were costing about $2 million each. Its first operated well, El Chico 2, came on with 3 million a day and it had 383 more locations to drill.

It reported, "Improvements in fracture techniques in recent years have dramatically changed the economics of producing reserves in the Barnett...The reserve profile from the typical, productive wells we drill in the Barnett...is notably longer-lived, compared (with) our wells drilled in our onshore Gulf Coast area."

Finally, its stock price improved; since selling the 10% senior notes, a share had gone from about $9 to $29. Other Barnett producers' stock prices were soaring as well. In four years by year-end 2005, EOG advanced 288%; Chesapeake, 397%; Carrizo, 443%; Quicksilver, 572%.

John Hancock Investment Trust noted in mid-2004 that its investment in Devon had served it well. "The vast acreage the company acquired in the Barnett...proved to be far more valuable than originally expected...," the portfolio manager reported. Scudder Portfolio Trust held EOG shares; it reported that, in 2004, it was "one of the best-performing stocks in the portfolio."

Other fund managers noted that oilfield-service firms' stock prices were gaining as well. Union Drilling Inc. and Bronco Drilling Co. each filed in 2005 to go public, citing growing onshore-U.S. rig demand for developing unconventional resources. By then, some 20 billion cubic feet of gas a day—about 40% of U.S. gas supply—was being produced from tight-sandstone, shale and coalbeds. In 1978, prior to federal Section 29 tax credits, U.S. gas production from these was only 4.4 billion a day.

***

By the spring of 2006, Trevor Rees-Jones held 169,000 net acres over Barnett in Wise, Denton, Tarrant, Parker, Hood and southern Johnson counties. Its proved reserves were 617 billion cubic feet; with putting about 800 more wells on the leasehold, the shale was estimated to give up 2 trillion cubic feet for the company.

"Tarrant County turned into one of the sweet spots of the Barnett, if not the sweetest," Rees-Jones says. "I don't know that Johnson, Wise and Denton counties—and they drilled out well—matches Tarrant County.

"As the Barnett progressed, we were always drawing these lines, projecting our fear of where it would stop. It was foreign—the nature of an unconventional play—to our thinking to think that 'Hey, this thing can go on and on and on.'

"We had a mindset based on conventional reservoirs and conventional exploration—always worried about where it was going to end. I felt a bit like Pavlov's dog going through the oil and gas business in the first 15 years, drilling all those dry holes and having things not work out so much. I was always waiting for the next shock.

"We were so attuned to the conventional, high-risk nature (of exploration at the time) that it was hard for us to grasp what was happening in the early years of the development of the Barnett."

Chief made its Jarvis-Chief 1 in 2002 three miles south of the dozen wells it had completed in northern Tarrant County. "Mitchell had developed this numerical calculation to indicate whether you had a good well. Well, our well calculated very well and we brought it on production at a million cubic feet a day. That advanced the field three miles south and we had a ton of acreage between and around that.

"That was pretty phenomenal to us.

"As we established production miles away, it was kind of bewildering that this thing could really be this big. When I realized this was really something different was when the larger companies—XTO, Chesapeake and the others—wanted to get involved. I remember when Bob Simpson (XTO chairman and chief executive) paid a visit to me and inquired as to whether we were for sale. At the time, we were not. That was early '05. Chesapeake made their first acquisition (after its inheritance from Canaan's portfolio) in late '04 in Johnson County.

"When these companies began to get involved, that was telling us something: We've really got something here.

"When Devon came in in 2001, I can't say that meant anything to me at the time. Mitchell Energy had been trying to sell itself for quite some time. For estate reasons or whatever, George Mitchell wanted to sell the company and along comes Devon to buy it.

"But I did not see that, at that time, as any big deal.

"The Barnett was looked upon as a--. Well, I don't think many people would have spoken of the Barnett very highly at the time. Even in 2002 and 2003, there wasn't much significance because no other big companies got involved."

In 2006, Rees-Jones thought it was now time to turn over what he had built to an operator with a bigger balance sheet that would leverage its greater access to public capital to drill the rest of the wells on his leasehold. And Devon was interested in buying Chief out.

On May 2, 2006, it bid $2.2 billion in cash for Rees-Jones' Barnett package, consisting of almost all of his holding.[144] By then, based on first-six-month production, Devon had drilled 22 of the Top 50 horizontal Barnett wells; Chief had drilled six. It was the No. 3 Barnett producer, making 120 million a day, gross, and had 31 more wells waiting for hook-up into a pipe that would add another 30 million.

With the Chief package, Devon would now hold 720,000 net Barnett acres. Larry Nichols said in a press release, "As with Mitchell Energy in 2002, the value of Chief to Devon is not fully reflected in current production or booked reserves. The true value lies in the trillions of cubic feet of natural gas underlying its acreage in the shale…that Devon has the knowledge, capital and resources to develop and produce."

---

[144] Rees-Jones sold his Barnett leasehold underlying the cargo- and private-air-service Alliance Airport area in far northern Tarrant County to Quicksilver Resources in 2008.

In four years since acquiring Mitchell, Devon now had 2,200 Barnett wells. It had drilled 1,300 of these itself, booking an additional 1.3 trillion cubic feet of reserves and, altogether, producing some 600 million a day.

It was placing wells now with 20-acre spacing. With 29 horizontal trials of this in the core Mitchell acreage, these denser-spaced wells would make an additional 1.8- to 2 billion cubic feet each, the company estimated. The position it gained from Mitchell alone could now, ultimately, make an additional 1 trillion-plus.

As for Rees-Jones' 400 miles of gas-gathering lines, he sold this for $460 million to Crosstex Energy, whose stock had grown to $84 since its IPO pricing of $19.50 in January 2004. Along Chief's gas-gathering system, some 330 producing wells were already hooked in.

Mile by mile, Crosstex had grown into one of the largest pipeline operators in the Barnett. Chief had been first in 2004 to commit gas into Crosstex's newbuild, 140-mile, 24-inch, North Texas pipeline that was shipping 250 million cubic feet a day by mid-2006 and being expanded to 375 million.

Rees-Jones' experience, before going after the lower-risk Bend conglomerate of rocks in Boonsville Field in 1994, was with chasing high-permeability, high-porosity, conventional, small, wildcatting, structural traps in several states.

Often, the extent of a play would come near his acreage and quit.

The Barnett didn't quit. It went on and on and on.

He thanks George Mitchell. "He spent decades banging away at that rock. It's really interesting to wonder, 'What if he had quit? What if he had raised a flag in surrender, called it a big failure and quit?' I guess, at some point, somebody would've tried it again and, possibly, made it work, but he's the guy who made it work.

"Devon did a lot in moving the needle on horizontal drilling but, of course, they had succeeded in the acreage position that Mitchell had made commercially exploitable to begin with."

FAYETTEVILLE: 2000

← ← ← ← ← → → → → →

"Did it get buried deep enough to be cooked?
Could this really be true?"
—Harold Korell

Where else might a shale play work? Harold Korell wasn't looking for one when J.B. Hunt called. The Southwestern Energy Co. chief executive had the exploration team looking at the coalbed-methane potential of the Arkoma Basin of eastern Oklahoma and western Arkansas.

Southwestern was formed as Arkansas Western Gas Co. in Fayetteville in 1929 by Dallas-based gas distributor Southern Union Co. Its purpose was to get Texas gas to northwestern Arkansas. The company began making gas for itself in 1943 with the discovery of White Oak Field in Franklin County, Arkansas, just east of Fort Smith in the valley between the Ozark and Ouachita mountain range.

As gas-utility regulation evolved, an E&P subsidiary was created in the 1950s as Arkansas Western Production Co.

In 1968, upon completing a degree in chemical and petroleum-refining engineering from the Colorado School of Mines, Korell began his oil and gas career with Mobil Corp., which sent him to work on the enormous, shallow, Kern River oil field in southern California's San Joaquin Valley.[145]

"At the time, oil companies were recruiting any kind of engineers

---

[145] Discovered in 1899, the field has produced more than 2 billion barrels of oil.

120

into the business because there was a shortage of these people in the industry. I had a lot of interviews. There were tons of jobs." He signed up with Mobil.

In a training program for a year, as was customary at the time, "I worked in every job in the field. I worked as a roughneck on a company rig up in the derrick. I worked as a pumper. And then you went into the office and worked in each engineering group—construction, drilling, production, reservoir—and in land, geophysics, geology.

"That's how you were trained in those years. It was a great learning experience for a guy right out of school with just a technical degree—getting that kind of exposure to all facets of the business."

Among his assignments was a summer at Mobil's downtown Los Angeles office, studying the climate in northern Alaska. Atlantic Richfield Co. (Arco) and Exxon had just discovered the Prudhoe Bay oil field. "This was right when North Slope exploration was beginning," Korell says.

"Companies like Mobil were trying to understand what the climate was really like up there. I was going back through 30 years of weather history and trying to sort it out."

He concluded that the weather 850 miles north of Anchorage in Deadhorse, Alaska, surprisingly wasn't as severe as in Greybull, Wyoming, where he grew up. The North Slope, on average, wasn't as cold. "It was unbelievable. Where I grew up, it was just so damned cold in Wyoming in those days. It's not now, but it sure was then."

Having worked in the field office amidst rigs and wells for several years by 1973, Mobil asked him and two colleagues to move to the Los Angeles office. "We were in Bakersfield and I was happy there. I was married now and couldn't afford to move to L.A. Gosh, we didn't have any money. We couldn't afford a home near downtown, so that would have meant at least an hour commute in heavy, heavy, stop-and-go traffic. And Los Angeles had really bad air pollution.

"None of us wanted to move. I told them 'no' at least once. Maybe twice. We were operations engineers, running the drilling and production in the field. From L.A., we'd have to drive an extra hour or more to get to the field. It didn't make sense to us young guys."

121

Finally, the boss drove out to Bakersfield and told them they were being transferred—whether they wanted to move or not. Korell got on the phone, calling Getty Oil Co. and Tenneco Oil Co., which also had offices in Bakersfield.

"Getty offered me a job in L.A., which didn't resolve anything. Tenneco offered me a job in Denver." Korell was ecstatic. Denver would be like going home; his alma mater was just west of there at the foot of the Rockies. And Tenneco was smaller than Mobil; Korell felt that he could make a difference. "In these big companies, you're just a--. Well, you're not even a cog in the wheel."

Tenneco immediately made him responsible for a profit area. "Now you're running a business. You're not just doing technical work and turning it in to somebody who turns it in to somebody else and it disappears.

"It was totally different. It was scary. I learned it just by doing it; that's the way Tenneco did it."

There, Korell also met Joe Foster, chairman and who would later lead his own E&P company, Newfield Exploration Co. "Tenneco was a good-size company at the time, but they really gave you a lot of responsibility. And Joe Foster was a great leader. I loved it any time he'd show up; I just loved to hear him talk."

After about eight years in Denver and five in Tenneco's southern California unit, Korell was transferred to Houston as vice president of production, responsible for meeting growth targets for the whole company. In committee meetings, he was sitting alongside the best exploration guys at Tenneco—and they were among the best in the industry.

"That is really where I learned a lot about exploration because I would just ask all the dumb questions I could think of. Throughout my career, I've tried to learn from people I've worked with—trying to take away the best of everyone I've been around."

While based in Denver, the Tenneco exploration group discovered Four Eyes Field in North Dakota in June 1978 on a Burlington mineral lease that became consolidated into Big Stick (Madison Unit) Field. The well, BN 1-29, came on with 880 barrels a day from

Duperow underlying Bakken in Billings County, North Dakota. Other wells were completed above Bakken in the Mission Canyon member of the Madison formation.

Tenneco had discovered a structural, stratigraphic and hydrodynamic trap. In short, it had all the trappings of a great field with a blanket of anhydrite as a seal on top; the oil was just beneath. "It was a big, big, big deal."

Here was a lesson Korell learned that was essential when inspired by the conversation with J.B. Hunt more than 20 years later. Lou Parish, general manager of Tenneco's Denver office, had been a landman. "Lou always believed, if you did your work and identified something of potential, then, if you were going to do it, you needed to have a big enough piece of it to make it worth something if it worked out."

Dick Findley, Bob Robinson and Bobby Lyle had known that too, in 1996, when deciding to try Findley's Sleeping Giant idea in Montana: In case it worked out, have as much acreage as possible already to be able to own the whole play; don't prove a play just for someone else to make all the wells in it.

"Lou had the courage to buy a big land position in that Big Stick/Four Eyes play," Korell says. And what was found to be productive—the Madison group—wasn't what they were looking for; it was a successful failure. They had been thinking the deeper Red River would produce.

"Prior to the discovery at Four Eyes, I wasn't really convinced that all this geophysics and geological stuff was valid. When that first well began producing big oil rates, I became a believer and that stuck with me throughout my career."

Generally, engineers have considered themselves the scientists; the geologists, artists. Their incessantly angst-filled relationship often results in productive skepticism and debate.

"After the initial discovery, we had drilled several wells and began to move locations up the structure. We eventually drilled a well that had high resistivity on the logs, indicating that it should be oil-productive, but it was producing water and very little oil—not a good thing. The geologists were questioning our well completion. 'It can't be,' they told me. 'You've got a bad cement job.' Blah, blah, blah."

The group eventually concluded that the cement job was fine. Instead, "we were updip, where the reservoir was filled with freshwater and not oil."

A structural and stratigraphic trap was hoped for; this was also a hydrodynamic trap. "Hydrodynamic was a new kind of a trap; our guys didn't explore this thinking of that kind of trap."

It changed things. "The Rocky Mountain division was Tenneco's smallest division at the time. In the corporate presentations, they would show a bar graph of the net income of each division. We were the puny, brown bar. We became the big, fat, green bar."

The company's Gulf of Mexico division was still bigger. "But we became the sweetheart and that felt really good. I think that imprinted on me that this exploration stuff can work and, if you do it right, you might find something big. And if you find something big, it changes everything.

"I've carried that around with me ever since."

***

Tenneco Oil was sold in pieces in the second half of the 1980s by parent Tenneco Inc., as oil and gas prices collapsed and it was looking to hang onto its tractor and auto-parts businesses. Korell went off to work in various oil- and gas-drilling endeavors. In 1997, he joined the Arkansas gas-distribution utility and its E&P company, which had become Southwestern Energy Co., as chief operating officer.

The utility's growth prospects were limited. Any upside for the stock would have to come out of the E&P group and the E&P group was foundering. Korell brought in new senior management and replaced more than 50% of technical staff. An Oklahoma City office was closed. Employees were re-aligned by the assets they managed.

In 2000, he was chief executive officer. About 56% of the company's 355 billion cubic feet equivalent of proved reserves were just west and south of Fayetteville headquarters in the conventional Arkoma Basin, where it was making gas from shallow formations, particularly the Pennsylvanian-age Atoka sandstones. The balance of its reserves and production was in the Midcontinent, in the Permian Basin and on the Gulf Coast.

To expand, Southwestern bought some 11,000 net acres in the old Overton Field in East Texas from Belgium-based Petrofina SA, which wasn't doing much with the property. It had discovered it in 1977 for gas from Cotton Valley at about 12,000 feet. About a dozen more wells were made and then it was left fallow. When Southwestern bought it in 2000 for $6.1 million, production was about 1.8 million cubic feet a day.[146]

Its shares were trading at about $2 at the time. The company began dropping in new wells in Overton Field, each of them proving about 2.2 billion cubic feet of gas. At the time, Korell was familiar with George Mitchell's work in the Barnett shale but, frankly, he wasn't giving it his attention.

"I didn't think it was worth paying attention to."

In South Louisiana, Southwestern was drilling deep wildcats, trying to tap structural traps using 3-D seismic as a guide. Statistically unusual, the company was successful in its first six attempts. "We thought we would be one for seven, but we were six for nine. We had unreasonable success. We had really good technical people doing this, but I swear that God was looking after us, helping us survive. I'm convinced of that."

The company had lost its appeal in June 2000 of a $109-million judgment against it involving how it paid royalty to Arkansas mineral-rights owners; its market cap had plummeted some 36% to about $190 million. "Some people thought we were gone. We put the utility on the market. We got some low-ball bids. We were busy trying to survive. We went through a near-death experience."

Bank of America had covered Southwestern on the lower-court judgment during the appeal process; essentially, all of tiny Southwest-

---

[146] Petrofina and Elf Aquitaine SA were rolled into France-based Total SA in 1999 and 2000. The consolidation was to keep up the presence of each at the international E&P table while other majors were merging, such as BP with Amoco and Exxon with Mobil.

ern—not just the utility—was collateral. When the appeal was lost, Southwestern's E&P portfolio had begun to show some life with the string of wildcat successes in South Louisiana and the new Overton Field wells. Bank of America continued to cover the company's debt.

Then, in August 2001, Devon bid $3.5 billion for Mitchell for its gas reserves and production. Korell says, "Suddenly, I knew the Barnett was worth paying attention to. We still couldn't play in that game. We didn't have any money. But it was interesting because it said, 'There's something new going on and it might work.'

"That was a seismic kind of event in the industry—when Devon bought Mitchell."

And that it was Devon buying Mitchell was particularly noteworthy, he adds. Larry Nichols and the Devon team had figured out how to get the Fruitland coal to pay in the San Juan Basin in the 1980s. Previously, the coalbed had been considered a nuisance when drilling the basin for deeper gas because of all of its water.

The shales were like this too. "In many cases, it was a problem because it was over-pressured. You'd have trouble (controlling the well while) drilling through it. The pressure in the Fruitland coal was a problem. At Tenneco, we'd get to it and it would kick on us and try to blow out on us.

"I remember asking our drilling guys in Denver, 'Well, why don't we try to produce it?' They thought it was hard enough just to try to drill *through* it."

Now Nichols thought Mitchell was onto something in the Barnett—and that the company was worth $3.5 billion. Korell took note.

"That couldn't help but get your attention."

At the time, Korell had a Southwestern team looking at the coalbeds of the Arkoma Basin for if they could profitably produce gas. While they were working on that, Korell got the call from J.B. Hunt. Hunt had founded his J.B. Hunt Transport Services Inc. in 1961 and grown it into one of the largest trucking companies in the U.S. With more than 16,000 employees, it was based in Lowell, Arkansas, some 18 miles north of Southwestern's office in Fayetteville.

Korell knew Hunt as part of the northwestern Arkansas business community, which includes Walmart's Waltons of Bentonville and Tyson Foods' Tysons of Springdale all along a 30-mile strip of Interstate 540 in the Ozark Mountains.

Hunt had retired from his company in 1995 and, while still its chairman through 2004, was working on new ideas. "He was off doing all kinds of investing," Korell says. "J.B. was the quintessential entrepreneur. If you would have met him, you would have loved him. He had an idea a minute. Big, white, cowboy hat. Cowboy boots. Big smile. Just a really fun guy. That was J.B."[147]

The gas-utility business was for sale; Hunt wanted to talk to Korell about buying it. "I said, 'Oh, really?' He said, 'Yeah, I want to buy it. Gas prices are high. You guys have got to be making loads of money in the utility business.'"

Helping Southwestern survive was its E&P business; gas had jumped to about $10 during the winter of 2000-01. But higher natural-gas prices don't affect a regulated gas-distribution utility; the price the utility pays for gas—up or down—is simply passed onto the consumer. The price mostly only affects the level of consumption.

Korell asked Hunt, "Well, do you know anything about utilities and how they make money? Because they're--. And he'd cut me off.

"'Well, no,' he said. 'But I know gas prices are high, so you must be making a big profit on that utility. And I know you need the money, so I ought to buy it.'"

Korell would try to explain it to Hunt. "I'm not a promoter kind of a guy to take advantage of somebody who doesn't know what they're doing." He explained that the utility isn't exposed to gas prices—neither the upside nor the downside.

"J.B said, 'Well, I don't understand what you mean about that, but gas prices are high, so you've got to be making a lot of money.' What I was telling him made no sense. It was this circular kind of conversation. He said, 'Well, I've got some other guys here with me. I'm going to put you on speakerphone.'

"I'm thinking, 'Oh my God!'"

---

[147] Hunt passed away on Dec. 7, 2006. He was 79.

Korell had an investment-banking firm marketing the utility and was struggling to keep the E&P company alive. "And here I am, talking to these guys. 'Well, who are they?' I asked. 'Well, it's Tim Graham and Gary Combs.' I said, 'I don't know who they are, but I guess I'll try to explain it to them. What kind of a return do you guys expect to earn on an investment?'"

Combs was a real-estate developer along that roughly 30-mile, Interstate 540 corridor of Waltons, Tysons and Hunts. Graham and Hunt were partners in Hunt's Hunt Ventures LLC, which had invested in some of Combs' projects.

Hunt told Korell they were looking for double-digit returns. Korell explained that a utility in those days might be allowed to earn an annual return of 8%. Hunt said, "Well, maybe we don't need to buy the utility. We know you're doing some drilling out at Overton Field in East Texas. We want to be your partner. We want to get in the energy business."

Korell said, "I don't know why you'd want to do that."[148]

But he agreed to talk about it over breakfast. "So we met in this little, country, family-owned, pink cafe on College Avenue (off Interstate 540) where truck drivers and people like me and J.B. go. They tell me they want to be in the oil and gas 'bidness.'

"I said, 'Well, J.B., you're going to be like every doctor and lawyer who gets in it while prices are high and you're going to wish you hadn't. And what do you know about it anyway?' He said, 'Well, Gary Combs here knows about drilling wells.'

"I looked at Gary. Gary was a good ol' boy from Fayetteville."[149] He had been successful in real-estate development, such as the J.B. Hunt Parkway Tower. His wife was Carla Tyson, grand-daughter of Tyson Foods founder John W. Tyson. "So he had access to some money," Korell surmised.

Combs had drilled a few, shallow, gas wells near Fayetteville in

---

[148] The gas-distribution utility, Arkansas Western Gas Co., with some 152,000 customer accounts in northern Arkansas, was sold in July 2008 to SourceGas LLC for about $230 million.

[149] Combs passed away in 2012. He was 59.

the mountains. "They were making a little bit of gas. It was biogenic gas. It's not anything that would last. It's going to be a little puff."

But the wells were interesting to Korell. They were producing gas and they shouldn't have. The Arkansas Oil & Gas Commission itself had refused to give Combs a permit for them as gas wells. "The commission said, 'There's none up there.'" They were permitted as water wells, instead.

"Later, the commission got 'hold of them and said, 'Hey, these are gas wells. You can't do this.' They hadn't drilled them on the proper spacing; they had drilled them all close together."

Hunt, Graham and Combs wanted to borrow Southwestern's shallow drilling rights in some of its legacy Arkoma Basin acreage. They wanted a farm-out to drill on the leasehold; if the wells were commercial, Southwestern could buy into it. It would have no risk if it didn't work out and could experience some reward if it did.

Southwestern was drilling for deeper—yet still relatively shallow—gas on the legacy acreage, targeting Atoka sandstone. Hunt told Korell, "Just give us the shallow rights in all that acreage. It's not any good to you."

Korell thought, "Well, we can't do that because what if something was there? We wouldn't own it all."

Hunt asked for a second breakfast, wanting to talk about it some more. "Seriously, J.B., I don't think you guys know what you're doing and I really don't think you know why you'd be doing this."

But Southwestern could use some money. Korell told John Thaeler, senior vice president, exploration, to talk to Hunt and Combs about a possible deal in Arkansas. "We needed money. If (Hunt, Graham and Combs) found something, we'd have a back-in. We'd have an interest, at least.[150]

"And, I told him, 'John, the other thing is that I do know they're producing some gas way up there—where there shouldn't be any—and I don't know what they're producing it out of."

---

[150] Hunt and Graham did form an E&P company, J.B. Hunt Gas & Oil Drilling LLC based in West Texas.

The conversations had prompted Korell to wonder: What else could the Arkoma Basin make that conventional wisdom would suggest it shouldn't?

He told Thaeler, "Maybe we should go back in and look at some of the wells we drilled 20 years ago."

Korell's predecessor, Charles Scharlau, had spoken of the Wedington sandstone in the few years Korell was at Southwestern prior to Scharlau's retirement. Scharlau had been chief executive beginning in 1968 and been with the company since 1951. The Mississippian-age Wedington is a thin layer of sandstone deeper than the Atoka and sits within the Fayetteville shale in western Arkansas, south of where Combs had made the shallow gas wells. Korell was thinking that, with higher gas prices, maybe Southwestern should take a new look at deeper rock in its old Arkoma Basin acreage.

Still, Southwestern's research into the potential for a new Arkansas gas play had nothing to do with what Mitchell was achieving in the Barnett. This was in early 2001. Larry Nichols hadn't made an offer for Mitchell yet; the Barnett wasn't interesting to Korell yet.

"Instead, the paradigm shift was higher gas prices," Korell says. "Could we do something that people had tried to do in the past but had failed because prices were too low?"

While Thaeler was talking to Hunt, one of Southwestern's Fayetteville-based geologists, Philip Shelby, went to work on looking at logs of old wells and mapping the ones that had been completed in Wedington sand. "That we had been in the basin for a long time is important here: We have all the data on all the wells that had ever been drilled in the Arkoma Basin because we'd been there since the beginning."

Southwestern had made that first gas well in 1943 in Franklin County south of Fayetteville in the valley between the Ozark and Ouachita mountains. Another early explorer was Arkansas entrepreneur Witt Stephens, whose portfolio became part of Little Rock-based Stephens Inc.

"We're the two who had been there forever and, in Arkansas, none of that stuff was digitized. The only people who had it were those of us who had it, right? Some other people could get it, but it was hard to get."

Shelby, who was mapping the Wedington wells for Thaeler, was a University of Arkansas graduate who had worked the Arkoma Basin his entire career. He sent his work to Thaeler, who sent it to Richard Lane, executive vice president, exploration and production. Southwestern had been studying the Arkoma Basin's coalbeds.

Thaeler says, "We were talking about that coalbed methane that didn't work. Richard goes, 'What else you got?' I said, 'Well, we've got this thing here.'"

Lane sent the Wedington findings to Korell: Wells Southwestern had drilled some 20 years earlier had made between four and six times more gas from Wedington than had been expected.

Korell says, "We had one of those significant incongruities, right? When anything looks strange, it might tell you there's an opportunity. That was the first light bulb. I still get goose bumps, thinking about it now."

By then, Devon had bid for Mitchell. Korell put Southwestern to work in earnest on what the potential of the Fayetteville shale might be. "This shale had to be contributing the gas in those Wedington wells," Korell says. "And, then, I'm thinking, 'This shale is Mississippian in age. It's the same age as the Barnett!'"[151] Southwestern sent rock samples out for analysis. Thaeler says, "We got a call. 'This shale looks really good. It looks as good as the Barnett. Where's it from?'"

The Barnett that Mitchell had been drilling was 300 to 400 feet thick. In the far-western Arkansas valley, the Fayetteville shale was 50 to 70 feet thick. That might not be thick enough to make a play. Korell says, "That might have stopped us there, but Richard (Lane) said, 'Well, what happens to the thickness of the shale as you move from this one little area here? What happens to it?'

"Someone said, 'It's probably about the same thickness.' Richard

---

[151] Formations made during the Mississippian age are among those favored by oil and gas explorers as the era is part of the Carboniferous Period in which Earth hosted a large concentration of carbon-rich matter.

said, 'Well, I don't care what the hell you *think*. Just map it! Don't just tell me what you think it is. Map it! Get all over that thing. Just map all of Arkansas and find out where it is.'"

Texaco Inc., formed as The Texas Co. in 1901 and bought by Chevron in 2001, had drilled some deep wells in the 1970s in the valley east of where Arkansas gas had been discovered in the 1940s. The attempts were unsuccessful, but Southwestern had the logs.

Further research found 50 wells that had penetrated Fayetteville. Pretty sparse. Lane says, "There were very few data points, but our geologists were good. They knew how to do big, basinal pictures."

Using these logs, a map was made across the state. "Lo and behold, the shale, instead of being 50 or 70 feet, just kept getting thicker and thicker to the east and got up to 400 or 500 feet thick out there." Acreage in that area was unleased and it wasn't held by existing production. The area had never produced commercial amounts of oil or gas; it was just full of dry holes, plugged and abandoned.

Korell wondered, "How big could this be? I remember sitting in a meeting and just calculating roughly that—if we could produce this amount per well and it's this big—this could be worth billions of dollars. It seemed too big to be true.

"A lot of times you get an idea; most of the time, they don't work. I said, 'We've got to get a clear understanding of this.'"

The company's ranking geologist, Thaeler, was put on the task as well as the company's geophysicists and reservoir engineers. "We put all the work papers, all the maps, everything in a room in Fayetteville. We made a war room up there."

The room, in a separate part of the office building, had been locked when Korell moved Southwestern's headquarters to Houston a year earlier to be near other E&P professionals and energy-securities analysts. About a third of its E&P staff remained in Fayetteville, working the Arkoma Basin.

"We sent our best minds up there," Korell says. "We said, 'Look, you've got to take this all the way back to the time of deposition and roll the geology forward. From there, we've got to understand the depth of burial. Did it get buried deep enough to be cooked? Could this really be true? What are the parameters for whether it is gas or water?' We spent nine or 10 months on this."

Thaeler says, "We went through the whole play." A geologist with an MBA, Thaeler had worked for 20 years for Occidental Petroleum Corp. across the U.S. and abroad before joining Southwestern.

Soon, every document, every file, everything the team could look at in the war room was reviewed and noted. The idea was holding up. It was time to start leasing. Korell says, "We couldn't afford to waste any money." It had to pick the best acreage. "We might have had $30- or $40 million of capital per year to re-invest. That was it. We were a tiny, tiny company."

Thaeler says, "I think my budget for the Arkoma Basin at the time was about $20 million." He asked for $7 million for leasing. "Harold said (to Richard Lane), 'You know, Richard, that last dry hole in South Louisiana cost us $7 million. What do you think?'"

Taking a $7-million risk on one Gulf Coast wildcat well would, if successful, pay tens of millions of dollars over its lifetime. The attention-deficient, public-equity market would only give credit for a fraction of its worth, however, as a third of the pay is made in just the well's first year. In contrast, taking a $7-million risk on a new play that might pay billions of dollars is a better gamble. And, after Southwestern had unusual success on the Gulf Coast with six consecutive wells, the following three had been failures.

Thaeler says of Korell's remark, "That put it in perspective. They all stood up and said, 'Let's go do it. In fact, we'll give you $11 million to get started.'"

In early 2003, with its stock price improved to $11.50, the company raised $103 million in an equity offering to fund its successful Overton Field program as gas prices were growing. The raise also freed some existing capital to deploy in leasing over Fayetteville shale.

***

The team was keeping the idea a secret, meanwhile—even internally. It was called, simply, Project Alpha. Korell says, "We didn't have any

133

money. If anyone in the industry would have found out, they would have blown us out of the saddle." The acreage would have been taken. "That worried us. The Barnett was starting to take off.

"How many times in your life have you had an idea someone else wasn't already working on? It's rare." The team wasn't worried that the Fayetteville would be a failure. "No, what we worried about was 'What if somebody else is looking at this?'"

The war room in Arkansas was 360 miles from the chatter centers of Fort Worth and Dallas, all abuzz about the Barnett play now, and 570 miles from the talkative Houston energy center. Meetings about continued progress on Fayetteville-shale analysis and leasing progress were held in the Arkansas office. When Korell, Lane, chief financial officer Greg Kerley and others from Southwestern's Houston headquarters would visit the Fayetteville office, it didn't seem unusual.

To further try to keep the idea a secret, Southwestern bought private abstract plants—that is, title libraries—in the targeted counties, giving it quick details on who owned the mineral rights and of any liens. "The county courthouses in Arkansas are small. They don't have much equipment," Thaeler says.

"Their records are old. So, to do this amount of brokerage work in the courthouses, it's almost impossible. You have to go to the abstract plants because they're a little more organized and they sometimes have better records and bigger facilities for doing your work."

Often, these plants are family-owned, handed down from generation to generation. Southwestern bought all the plants it could, making them unavailable to other E&P companies. "We left them open for people doing real estate and other, typical, title research. We didn't shut that down, but they had to get permission. So it made it more difficult for competitors."

Some counties had more than one plant, so other researchers could use those. "For other counties, it was just us."

Lane, who had worked with Korell at Tenneco years earlier, says, "It was an important competitive advantage." Landmen hired later by other oil and gas companies to get leases had to search the courthouse records in some counties. Thaeler says, "They had more of a gamble, guessing from different records whether or not people actually owned the leases; we had the real records."

In one county, the owner wouldn't sell the family business and it was the county's only title plant. Southwestern offered him an incredible price. "He just wouldn't do it," Thaeler says.

"But we heard that there had been a second plant that had closed 15 years earlier. We found the owner; she was in a nursing home. We asked her daughter, 'What happened to the plant?' She said, 'Oh, it's in a building. We just closed everything down. It's worthless.'

"We said, 'Not so fast.'"

Upon buying all the dusty records, Thaeler rented trucks with Oklahoma license plates to gather the records in the middle of the night and take them to the Fayetteville office. "I didn't want anyone to see trucks from Fayetteville. It turned out that that county was one of the core areas we ended up dominating."

As leasing was under way just one week, the lead Southwestern landmen for two of the four targeted counties called Jim Dewbre, a senior vice president, and said there was, suddenly, a bunch of brokers in those courthouses, looking at records for the same properties.

Thaeler says, "I thought, 'We're busted! And in just a week! Who do we shoot?'"

The landmen soon figured out the other brokers' client was just looking for land for placing cell-phone towers. Meanwhile, a Southwestern landman would run into a small oil and gas operator here and there, thinking about trying to make an old, traditional type of well in a conventional, long-explored rock.

"This stuff would startle us," Korell says. "We had this worry: What do we do if the cat gets out of the box? I had sleepless nights. What if somebody else is working on this? What if Chesapeake finds out what we're doing?"

Aubrey McClendon, Chesapeake chairman and chief executive, had co-founded the Oklahoma City-based company in 1989. In the 1990s, it had amassed enough fiscal bulk to enter the Austin-chalk play in southeastern Texas and aimed to expand it into Louisiana.

The company's shares soared 6,200% to $32 in November 1996 in about three years after four splits that were the equivalent of 10-for-6. The Louisiana chalk wells were fizzling out quickly, though, and the company's stock fell to about 75 cents. McClendon began rebuilding the company via the acquire-and-exploit model—buying existing oil and gas properties, reworking them and increasing production.

Korell knew McClendon could easily throw an army of landmen at Arkansas just as he had done in the chalk, buying up leasehold across as large a geographic footprint as possible. "Aubrey's view was that it doesn't matter what you pay for land," he says.

Quickly, while still leasing, Southwestern was ready to start testing the acreage. Keeping the leasing quiet was difficult enough. If dropping a rig in north-central Arkansas, it could just as well broadcast its plan over one of those cell-phone towers. The area along the Ozark foothills had barely been drilled in the roughly 80 years of the Arkansas oil and gas industry. And it hadn't been drilled in years.

An established operator like Southwestern rigging up in the area would be noteworthy. A small operator no one had heard of before would be dismissed as simply being optimistic. To resolve this, Southwestern formed Arkansas-based PV Exploration Co. that could only be traced back to Southwestern with the most earnest diligence.

"Yeah. PV. 'Present value.' That was Harold's idea. Harold 'PV' Korell," Thaeler says.[152] A drilling consultant was hired to run PV Exploration. "And there was a phone in the Southwestern office (in Houston) so, if anybody wanted to call PV Exploration, there was a real phone number."

The phone was placed near Lane's office; a sign was posted in the hallway: "Do not answer this phone!" It was left to roll into voice mail. Someone in the office would check the messages and return the calls—and only from that same phone.

Inevitably, however, McClendon began to stop in for lunch with

---

[152] Korell developed a formula as a motto for Southwestern that is "R squared over A equals V+." It means that the *right* people doing the *right* things with re-investing cash flow from the underlying *assets* will create *value-plus*. Korell had the logo placed on the company's headquarters in Houston.

Korell in Houston. "I was scared to death because we were like a tender baby still trying to learn to walk financially. Anybody could have taken us over and I was certainly suspect of Aubrey's intentions. I could tell he was just picking my brain. I would tell him some truths and some untruths.

"It was clear to me he was trying to figure out whether the Fayetteville was real—if it was going to work. I think I misled him enough for a while or made it ambiguous enough that he was afraid to enter, afraid he'd waste money.

"You know, he did the Austin chalk in a big way. He bought way too much acreage in Louisiana. He cautioned me about that. It was really positioning. He was trying to learn from me whether we were onto something and if he should make an offer for the company.

"I know that. Sort of a dance went on over a period of three or four months."

Finally, Chesapeake began leasing in the Arkansas valley. "He sent all of his landmen out there and started making big offers—prices we wouldn't pay. He picked up the things we wouldn't buy.

"By the time we drilled our very first well, our average lease cost was probably $50 an acre." Chesapeake paid $1,000 and more. "I'd said a number of times, 'It gets thicker to the east.' Well, Aubrey leased all the way to the Mississippi River."

Chesapeake became the biggest leaseholder in Arkansas, but Southwestern became the biggest producer. "They weren't in the best spot because we took it. They had to write a huge amount of it off. They were definitely not first at the party."

Lane was with Korell in New York for an investment symposium, explaining the company's profile and outlook. McClendon was there as well. Lane says, "Aubrey saw me, came over and said, 'What are you doing with those abstract plants?' I was like, 'I don't know what you're talking about.'

"He goes, 'Oh, yes, you do.' So he knew. And now I knew he knew. They had knocked on the door and we had said, 'We're closed.' They had said, 'It doesn't look like you're closed.'

"And we said, 'Well, we're closed to *you*.'"

Thaeler says, "Yeah, we got a lot of heat over that, but it's been repeated by others in other plays now. These title companies are private companies. They're for sale." Later, the Fort Smith Association of Landmen became involved. Lane says, "They said, 'We're not sure about this—what you've done. It might be unethical.' We said, 'No. It's a private enterprise.'"

By the time Southwestern drilled its first Fayetteville well in 2004, it had spent about $23 million on acreage; three years had elapsed since Korell suggested looking at old Wedington wells. Lane says, "And no one knew about it. We had been leasing for 18 months and no one found out. This was a part of the world no one cared about. It was in a part of the Arkoma Basin no one was working."

Thaeler says, "It turned out we never got busted. We didn't until we made the public announcement. And we had to make the announcement."

It was time to tell shareholders. Lane says, "A quarter would come up and we'd have long discussions with our SEC attorneys about this. We pushed them off for a couple quarters."

Finally, legal advised Korell that he had to mention the company was spending money on acreage. Korell did it in the year-end 2003 report filed with the SEC in February 2004. It simply said the company had spent $11 million on leasing some 345,000 acres of land in 2003. It didn't identify the location; it did mention that a small part of it was in Montana in a potential coalbed-methane project.

Securities analysts asked about it in a quarterly earnings call in the spring. One said, "We know about the acreage you have in Montana…but do you have any other acreage—either leased or under option—in other areas…?"

Korell mostly stated the vague language that was in the annual report, concluding "so that definitely fits in the category of, I think, answering your question."

In July, in the second-quarter earnings call, an analyst asked Korell if he would elaborate on what the company had simply called "new ventures," such as where the company was building acreage.

Korell answered, "No…I can't elaborate on that…at this time."

The analyst asked, "Can you give us any timeframe?"

Korell replied, "No."

But it was near. Lane says, "The attorneys were saying, 'This is hugely material. It's time!' We probably could have gone another quarter, but people were getting nervous."

On Aug. 17, 2004, three weeks after the quarterly earnings call and more than four years after Korell had received that unusual call from J.B. Hunt, the company issued a press release: "Southwestern Energy Announces Fayetteville Shale Play in Arkoma Basin."

It had leased some 455,000 net acres and already controlled about 120,000 net in western Arkansas that might be prospective and were HBPed by its conventional, shallow, sandstone-gas wells. It had acquired the new leases for an average of about $40 an acre. And the primary term on each averaged more than nine years, meaning it had that long to put a well in it or lose it.

Core samples showed the rock to be similar to the Barnett in terms of total organic content, thermal maturity and gas content. Southwestern's PV Exploration had already drilled four verticals. In Conway and Van Buren counties, the shale was 325 feet thick. But, with fracture stimulation, production was only between 150,000 and 500,000 cubic feet per day after flowing for up to 20 days.

Korell told shareholders, "Although there is a significant amount of data yet to be collected..., we are encouraged by what we have seen to this point." The company would keep drilling test wells to determine the geographic extent of the shale and the best way to frac the wells. "If our testing yields positive results, we expect that our activity in the play would increase significantly over the next several years."

***

The company's stock price jumped 13% that day. The Barnett was already making more than 1 billion cubic feet a day by then. What might this new Fayetteville play make?

But it was not yet proven. Fayetteville was indeed the very same rock as the Barnett, but Southwestern struggled with it.

Eventually, Korell got "the call." In all of Southwestern's secrecy, it had still not recruited someone from Devon, for example, or someone formerly with Mitchell Energy to help it find its way through making this shale pay—and as enormously as the Barnett.

"My thought was we needed to get as much of it as we could," Korell says. "If it worked, it was significant and, if we had trouble with making it work, we could always bring in a partner. We wouldn't have been able to hire someone from Devon anyway because we couldn't have interested a person to come with us without explaining what we were doing.

"So we learned everything we learned internally."

It wasn't going very well. Now it was 2007. The Barnett was making more than 2 billion cubic feet a day; the Fayetteville, less than a half-billion.

"My assistant came in one day and said, 'There's a George Mitchell who called and wanted to talk to you.' I said, '*The* George Mitchell?' She said, 'Well, I don't know. He said his name is George Mitchell.' I said, 'Will you call back and see if it's *the* George Mitchell from Mitchell Energy?' She came back in and said, 'Yes, it's George Mitchell. He wants to have lunch with you.'"

Mitchell was taking Korell to school. Korell was ready for class.

The test wells mentioned in Southwestern's August 2004 announcement, "at that point, were just poking around towards it," Thaeler says. The vertical Thomas 1-9, the official Fayetteville discovery, had come on in July 2004. From Arkansas, Thaeler called Lane and said, "Houston, we have gas."

After the well was drilled, he had waited for what seemed like a long time for the drilling fluid to flow out. "Once it did, you just can't wait to call it in. You've been working towards this for years now. You go out and find a place where you can use your cell phone. You didn't have very good cell-phone coverage back then."

The process was just begun, though. What types of facture stimulation fluid should be used? Can you drill horizontally in this rock? How far can you drill?

"We probably drilled more than 50 wells after the Thomas 1-9 before we were comfortable the play would be economic," Thaeler says. "And, in those 50 wells, you're not just finding sweet spots and non-sweet spots. You're finding out the techniques that will work best. That's the painful, learning-curve part. It just hurts because you try lots of things that fail.

"You get disappointed and you--. It's that 'It's always darkest before the dawn' thing. You go through an incredible amount of work and pain to get to where you're comfortable with that it's commercial and that you can replicate it."

Lane notes, "And then drilling them and completing them are whole different things. In hindsight, we drilled more vertical wells than we probably should have. We should have converted to (just horizontals) earlier."

In completions, the company tried different gels and it tried foam. But it had to learn, Lane says. "A challenge in these plays is that they're not as straightforward as 'Go do 10 this way and 10 that way and let's compare them and make a smart choice.' There are a lot of variables. You don't change too much at any one time or you won't be able to understand cause and effect.

"Was the well better because I changed A, B, C, D or E? It might be in a better part of the reservoir or it might be the completion technique. And we have 25 rigs running. We can't say 'Stop!' The world's running 24/7. It's running in real time. You apply what you've learned today to the next well, but you still have 25 wells that were completed in the past 100 days the other way.

"It's a challenge to discern what are the right changes and it's a constant thing that should happen the whole life of the play. There is still more to be learned about the Fayetteville, but it becomes more minutia."

By early 2007, Southwestern held some 900,000 net acres over Fayetteville. With the newer 300,000, its average lease term was now seven years; the cost, about $95 an acre; the royalty, 15%.[153]

---

[153] Southwestern was also testing the Mississippian-age Moorefield and Devonian-age Chattanooga shales underlying the Fayetteville in Arkansas.

It had spud 284 wells in the play now—196 of these in 2006 alone. Among the 172 completed by year-end 2006, 118 were horizontal.[154] Using gel fracs, it was finding improved results: The 90 wells completed this way came on with an average of 1.5 million cubic feet a day. But these newer wells were costing some $2.3 million each. Average vertical depth was only 3,500 feet; average lateral length, only 2,300 feet.

It was taking more than 18 days just to drill them. Gross production was some 100 million a day from 172 completed wells for an average of only about a half-million a day from each. The ex-Mitchell Energy team—scattered about now at Devon and elsewhere—knew the trade of making a successful shale play. But Southwestern didn't yet; it didn't have an ex-Barnett team member onboard.

In traditional wildcatting, explorers are looking for traps—areas where tectonic activity beneath the surface had pushed this layer of rock here and that layer there, forming a fault in which the oil and gas were stuck in a pocket, trapped.

The shales, however, "are the source rock," Korell notes. "They are where the oil and gas were created. They weren't created in the conventional, Mississippian sands, such as the Wedington. They migrated there from a source rock.

"That is the 'kitchen.' That's where the organic matter was deposited in a marine environment millions of years ago."

A "continuous accumulation" play like the gassy Barnett and oily Bakken comes without many dry holes, but they still have to be understood. Southwestern was advantaged by that it had spent very little on its 900,000 acres. And the Fayetteville shale was the same quality of rock as the Barnett.

Yet, that was still all it had going for it.

When George Mitchell asked to visit, Korell accepted.

"I met George and two of his guys at a club he belonged to in Houston." Mitchell had asked Dan Steward, who had been a Mitchell Energy vice president of geology until the sale to Devon, to write a

---

[154] Its first horizontal trial in Fayetteville was Vaughan 4-22H in February 2005.

book, documenting the work that led to the Barnett play. When Korell met Mitchell, the book had just been published.

"He wanted me to have a copy of it. And he said, 'Harold, you're really onto something big in the Fayetteville.'

"He thought we were onto something big! It was a really fun moment for me—for him to invite me to lunch and to, especially, give me a copy of that book. That was a very important book."

What Mitchell had done in the Barnett for 17 years wasn't just pushing a boulder up a hill for it to roll back to where it had been. It picked a different boulder each time and measured its success with it. One by one, those boulders—the mistakes—were demonstrating how to pick one that *would* make it over the hill. The book explains how the company had perfected the vertical, Barnett recipe—and it includes the recipe.[155]

As Korell began reading it, he ordered copies for all of the staff. It was a playbook for what to do in a shale like the Barnett—and what to absolutely *not* do.

"It's saying, 'Don't drill by the faults.' And, hell, that's what we were doing. So we started off without success with the vertical wells. We stayed with them a while. The important breakthrough was when we got away from the faults, when we tried to pick the quiet areas of the play."

To drill by the faults was how oil and gas wells had been made in the industry's nearly 150 years. To develop a play by avoiding the faults was counter to conventional wisdom.

But this wasn't a conventional reservoir.

"We had drilled near the faults where the rock would be broken up. The book straightened us out on that. Of course, it's clear now: You don't drill near the faults because you will lose the hydraulic pressure you are trying to apply to the rock to break it up. If we'd have known what they knew back then, we could have saved ourselves that

---

[155] George Mitchell had an interest in the Fayetteville's success; he was invested in another operator, privately held Alta Resources LLC, which was trying to make a play of it with publicly held Contango Oil & Gas Co.

step. We spent a lot of money early on because of that. But they were mostly vertical wells, so they weren't that expensive."

Updating its well-placement strategy, Southwestern also reconsidered how to drill the wells. It had encountered in the Fayetteville some geological exceptions to the Barnett.

"There was a sticky shale above it. We'd drill into it and try to make our turn into the lateral. We'd get stuck. We had to figure out how to engineer our way through that, how to run fewer casing strings to get the well cost down, how to drill horizontals and then how to extend the horizontals.

"The first horizontal wells we drilled, we had trouble initiating a fracture. We couldn't pump into them. We had to figure out how to orient the perforations, so that it initiated the fractures.

"All these things just piled on."

That part wasn't in the book—the part about how to complete a horizontal, shale well. The Mitchell team had tried just a few horizontals before the company's sale to Devon and they weren't economically better than the verticals.

"Devon had figured out the horizontal," Korell says. "We didn't know enough about what they were doing and they weren't publishing it. So we learned on our own. We got there independently. We didn't have their information; it was a competitive advantage for them."

From Korell's book order, Thaeler received one. Where to place the Fayetteville wells had been an internal debate for some time. "The advantage of natural fracturing is it has the capacity to store more gas," Thaeler says.

"You would think that, if you fraced it, you would have more pathways into your wellbore—so you should have better wells. What industry found out was that, even though you were closer to the natural-fracture systems and faults, the pressure regime changes when you frac it. It was hard to get your fractures propagated. You ended up with poor wells.

"So you stayed away from faulting; you didn't go near it."

BAKKEN: 2006

← ← ← ← ← → → → → →

"For those who don't have your calculators handy,
that's a $7.50-barrel, net, direct, finding cost."
—Mark Papa

Continental Resources and others made more than 60 fraced horizontals in North Dakota's middle-Bakken member by April 2006. They ranged from small to decent to four with IPs of more than 500 barrels—one each by Headington Oil, Petro-Hunt, Amerada Hess and EOG.[156]

The results were nothing like those of the first 60, fraced horizontals in the Montana play. Micro-cap, Denver-based Earthstone Energy Inc., which had been exploring the Williston Basin since the early 1980s, noted that the Richland County play was "depositionally distinct."

"…While great lessons have been learned in Montana in developing the resource there, challenges unique to North Dakota have stymied development…Several wells have been drilled in extremely promising areas in North Dakota that encountered mechanical, in addition to formation, difficulties."

Dick Findley, discoverer of the Montana play, says the natural frac barrier the upper-Bakken shale provided to the middle-Bakken porosity-trend wells in Richland County didn't work outside that area.

---

[156] Amerada Petroleum Corp. merged with oil-refiner and -marketer Hess Corp. in 1969, becoming Amerada Hess Corp., and is now known again as Hess Corp.

The same problem was encountered in Viewfield in southeastern Saskatchewan. It was a huge technology-transfer problem.

"In Viewfield, they would frac the Bakken in the middle member and it would travel up into Mission Canyon," Findley says. "They would produce just all kinds of freshwater with their oil."

When operators attempted to transfer the Bakken play into North Dakota, trying to find another Elm Coulee, "there were probably 90 wells drilled that were very uneconomic. It just didn't work that well."[157]

Bud Brigham was equally perplexed. The Bakken was hard; figuring it out would be harder.

Growing up in the booming oil and gas fields of West Texas, Brigham began his career in 1983 after getting a bachelor's in geophysics from the University of Texas at Austin. He went to work for oilfield-service firm Western Geophysical Co. as a seismic-data-processing geophysicist for about a year, converting billions of 3-D data points via computer into a format the client could read. He then worked for an independent E&P company, Dallas-based Rosewood Resources Inc., as an exploration geophysicist.

In 1990, now 29, he was ready to makes wells of his own.

"You can't be afraid of taking risks and you can learn as much or more from a failure than you can from a success," he says. He founded Brigham Exploration Co. in Dallas with his wife, Anne, who received her law degree from SMU and bachelor's in geology from the University of Texas.

"I believed that technology was going to be the biggest differentiator in our business," Brigham says. "And it was moving rapidly. I had already seen, just in the 1980s, computer technology advance quickly. My plan was to leverage technology to reduce exploration costs and enhance margins."

The technology that would make the difference at the time was

---

[157] Findley was named Explorer of the Year in 2006 by his peers within the American Association of Petroleum Geologists for his Elm Coulee Field discovery, the fourth-most productive oil field in Montana's history and still producing in 2013.

3-D, he believed. He set out, wildcatting at a time when other, new, E&P companies, such as XTO Energy, were being formed on the acquire/exploit model, buying producing properties that were being handed down by larger operators seeking new fields.

"Some people laughed. A number of people told me, 'You know, 3-D is not an exploration tool.' Like any entrepreneur, that just motivated me to work harder to make it successful. Though it was bold on the one hand, Anne and I had no children at the time and we had $25,000 to invest.

"We didn't have much to lose. Once you have a family, it's a lot harder to step out there and risk it all."

He began partnering with independent geologists to develop wildcat ideas and with landmen to assemble the acreage, primarily in the Permian and Anadarko basins and, later, along the Gulf Coast; together, they would sell majority interest to an oil and gas company that would drill the wells.

The wells might cost $200,000 to $300,000 to drill and complete; Brigham kept 6% to 12% interest to make his initial $25,000 last.

"Fortunately, we hit on our first 11 wells or I might not have made it."

By early 1997, Brigham Exploration had spotted more than 300 wildcats with a 63% success rate, proving some 120 billion cubic feet of gas and 24 million barrels of oil for it and its partners. Its share of this, which had grown to average 14%, had the potential to make an additional 22 billion cubic feet of gas equivalent. The company's 1996 production was 2.1 billion equivalent.

It had grown its reserves and production for five consecutive years, but it had also had a net loss each year. Its assets were about $28 million of oil and gas properties and about $1.45 million of cash on hand. It had some $24 million of debt. Private-equity investors General Atlantic Partners LLC and Rimco held 51% of the company's shares; Bud and Anne held 43%.

To further grow and to provide a liquidation vehicle for private investors, the Brighams needed to access the public-equity market. Oil had pushed past $26 in January 1997. The next month, they filed to

IPO the company. In May, selling roughly 3.3 million shares for $8 each, the raise was $24.7 million net of fees. The Brighams moved headquarters to Austin, which was quickly establishing itself as Texas' Silicon Valley.

"We had a great first year in '97, shooting 3-D and drilling wells at attractive finding costs." But, in early 1998, when the company was preparing to sell more shares to further fund drilling and pay down debt, oil had slipped to $17; in the second half of 1998, to about $14.

In January 1999, it dove to $11.

"Our stock got hammered," Brigham says. "All of a sudden, the banks were wanting us to pay down our debt and our stock price went down to as low as a dollar. A lot of people were questioning whether we would survive.

"It was a very difficult time. I worried a great deal."

And, he and Anne had more obligations than when they started the company in 1990. They had had one child since then. In November 1998, they had triplets. "So I was going home from a very difficult day at the office to three babies. It was a challenge, but it was motivational as well. We managed to work our way through and I think, ultimately, it made us a stronger company."

Brigham Exploration went on to build successful wildcat plays, including in the young, Oligocene-age Frio and the highly pressured Vicksburg trend in South Texas at some 13,500 feet, bringing on 10-million-cubic-foot-a-day wells. Now 15 years old, the company's cumulative 688 well attempts had met with a 73% success rate.

In 2005 alone, its success rate was 92%.

But hit-or-miss, conventional-trap chasing can easily turn from 9-and-1 to 1-and-9. In June 2005, Brigham had to tell shareholders that new attempts in making a 14,000-foot-deep producer in Frio "have been unsuccessful." The well was making 45,000 cubic feet a day—just a puff of gas.

"It appears that our (upper) Frio development program could disappoint us...."

He had already begun work on finding a new kind of play, though—one in which the company could apply technology and geology in a repeatable, unconventional, resource in a new frontier. The Barnett shale-gas play was transforming industry thinking about what was possible when inducing fractures and along a horizontal wellbore.

But he wanted oil.

He and the team had seen what Lyco Energy had achieved in the middle Bakken in Montana. Meanwhile, Brigham's gas wells on the Gulf Coast were in the midst of growing gas output from the Barnett and possibly more from the emerging Fayetteville play. If the Barnett continued to grow and the Fayetteville worked out, Brigham could foresee gas-on-gas competition in the future: There would be too much gas; prices would plummet.

"You know, operators were doing just an outstanding job in the gas-resource plays, delineating large, expansive, gas fields, and were going to provide a ready supply to the domestic market," Brigham says. "So we were very biased towards oil."

The Bakken was interesting. The acreage wasn't already leased up and the rock was pervasive "so we could put together, potentially, a very large position."

Also, the company had Lance Langford and Jeff Larson on its team. They had worked together at Burlington, which had led the Bakken-shale and Red River B plays in North Dakota as well as in tight rocks elsewhere. Langford was Brigham's executive vice president, operations; Larson, executive vice president, exploration.

Brigham picked Bakken.

In November 2005, shortly after Enerplus bought Lyco's Bakken play in Montana and prospective leasehold in North Dakota, Brigham announced the company had 46,000 gross and net acres in North Dakota, picking it up for about $100 an acre. Involving 126 sections in McKenzie and Williams counties about 30 miles east of the Montana play, the team estimated the acreage could take between 63 and 126 wells, costing between $3.5- and $4 million each with laterals of between 4,000 and 9,000 feet.

Brigham told shareholders, "Earlier this year, we undertook an internal initiative to evaluate numerous, emerging, non-conventional, domestic plays with the goal of building a diverse and attractive inventory of non-conventional projects to balance out our very successful but—by its nature—sometimes-less-predictable, conventional program." He concluded, "...The Bakken play could become a new focus trend for us."

The company's stock price had improved to $14 over the years, particularly in the prior few months. Brigham sold 7.5 million shares.[158] Now, how to make the Bakken in North Dakota work? Brigham and others were stumped.

PDC Energy Inc. brought on its Fedora 34-22H in Dunn County, averaging some 278 barrels a day during its first month online. The well cost $3.9 million, went to 10,780 feet and had a 7,465-foot lateral. "Additional production information for the Fedora well will be required to determine whether (it) will achieve results (like in Richland County)," PDC reported.[159]

Continental reported that a Bakken test in the southeastern corner of the Williston Basin showed that "the middle, dolomite member significantly thins...(It) was, essentially, not present." Overall for the North Dakota play, through February 2006, "results are limited but encouraging."

Micro-cap Earthstone Energy updated shareholders. While its State (Walleye) 16-1H attempt was put in the Bakken play in North Dakota, "the prospect is now headed in a different direction." The results "were not encouraging...

"Until such time as either offset Bakken production is demonstrated or a breakthrough in stimulation technology or application is made, (Earthstone) and its partners have little interest in pursuing Bakken development in this immediate area."

Having greater access to capital, as did Continental, Brigham Exploration remained optimistic. Its Field 18-19 1-H came on with 200 barrels just north of the Earthstone well. It reported, "As with any

---

[158] Brigham had also bought into the NGL-rich Granite Wash play in Oklahoma, 5,000 acres in the Barnett and a leasehold in a "stealth play" that was later revealed to be a horizontal attempt at the oily, 175-foot-thick Mowry shale in Wyoming. In operators' previous 18 verticals in Mowry, IPs had ranged from eight to 189 barrels.

[159] The well turned out to be marginal, making about 150,000 barrels by mid-2013.

unconventional play, it will take some time to learn how to optimize our drilling and completion techniques...." The company now had 80,000 net acres prospective for Bakken. And, it set out to raise more capital, offering senior notes.

Meanwhile, Continental brought in a partner, ConocoPhillips, which had just bought Burlington, in August 2006 to jointly drill Bakken wells on 97,000 of Continental's 256,000 net acres in North Dakota in Dunn, McKenzie, Mountrail and Williams counties. In the deal, either could buy 50% interest in the other's acreage for $500 a net acre.

Oil was $70 now and capital markets were frothy. The Dow was heading to 14,000. A lot of science could be funded. On Jan. 31, 2007, Brigham reported it had put together 55,000 net acres over Bakken in North Dakota. One day later, highly regarded explorer EOG Resources revealed it was in the play. Its Warberg 1-25H had come on in November 2006 with more than 1,553 barrels; its Bartelson 1-3H, a couple months earlier, with 1,800.

The code had been broken.

And Brigham had an inside track: It had an interest in some of EOG's leasehold. It was getting the well reports.

***

EOG had operated in North Dakota since 1987 but had had an increasingly small presence. At year-end 2000, it held only 4,203 net acres in the state. In 2003, it popped into Richland County, Montana, completing three wells in Lyco's middle-Bakken play there, including Vairstep 1-22H for a 624-barrel IP from two, short laterals.

In 2004, it made 13 more; in 2005, six more. In 2006, it made five more, but the IPs were smaller. The areal extent of Elm Coulee Field was proven now.

Meanwhile, it was adding to its North Dakota leasehold. In 2004, it took its position to 35,224 net acres. It added about 7,000 more in 2005. In early 2007, its 2006 annual report revealed it now had 144,212 net.

151

EOG had met Mike Johnson.

Findley, discoverer of the Montana play, says, "You need to give a lot of credit to Mr. Johnson." Until 2006, most operators' work on the Bakken in North Dakota had been on the Nesson anticline or west, nearer to Montana. Explorers needed to look east of the Nesson as well.

"Michael Johnson noticed that wireline logs of the middle Bakken in Mountrail County resembled those from the Elm Coulee Field in Montana," Stephan Nordeng, staff geologist for the North Dakota Geological Survey, wrote in a January 2010 report. "Even though the organic matter in the Bakken shales appeared incapable of oil generation, the recovery of free oil in drill-stem tests and some minor production led Johnson to pursue a Bakken play in Mountrail County."

Johnson had been an independent geologist since 1963 and, like Findley, generated oil-prospect ideas by looking at well records, physical rock samples and myriad other data. And, as was Findley's, Johnson's advantage in the Williston Basin was his extensive experience with the characteristics of each rock beneath the surface.

Born in 1926 in Missouri, his family moved to the bustling oil center of Tulsa, Oklahoma, where his father opened a pool hall and Johnson became a bit of a pool shark. Like George Mitchell, he was a son of Greek immigrants.[160]

In 1944, Johnson set off for college, receiving both bachelor's and master's degrees from Ohio State University in geology by March 1949. He wanted to work in the oil and gas industry, thinking he would land in Texas or Oklahoma.

"The Rockies never crossed my mind," he writes in his autobiography. And certainly not Montana; oil hadn't been discovered there yet. Yet, "I ended up spending my entire career in the Rockies."

He landed a job with Amerada Petroleum, which sent him to a new office in Billings, Montana, to work on what might be made from

---

[160] Johnson's father, Efstathios Giannakopoulos, changed his name to Sam Johnson.

the state.[161] Soon, though, Johnson was called up to the U.S. Army. Completing his service in 1953, he returned to Amerada but to its new office in Williston, North Dakota. While he had been gone, the company made the first commercial oil discovery in the state with its Clarence Iverson 1 that was completed in April 1951 for 165 barrels.

The roughly 11,000-foot well had been placed along the Nesson anticline in Williams County and completed in the Interlake formation. The formation sat below what was then an unnamed sequence dubbed "Kinderhook" at the bottom of the Mississippian age and top of the Devonian age.

A second Amerada well, Henry O. Bakken 1, was completed in April 1952 for 217 barrels. It had also traveled through the unnamed sequence. In 1953, it was given a name. In a report to the Billings (Montana) Geological Society, geologist J.W. Nordquist called it "Bakken," taking from the name of the well, which had been taken from the name of the landowner, Henry O. Bakken.[162]

Johnson worked for Amerada through 1958 and then with Apache Corp. into 1963. From there, he set out on his own, going on to discover fields across the Rockies. In the early 2000s, the horizontal Elm Coulee play in Montana captured his attention. Johnson had been well familiar with decades of mixed Bakken results.

"Horizontal drilling was emerging as the answer," he writes.

As Elm Coulee Field was clearly working, he began to look for another one. Generally, Johnson writes, his searches begin with considering the use of new drilling and completion techniques in an old, producing area or the application of old techniques in a new area.

"Best of all, however, would be using a *new* oil-finding technique in a *new* area. That was my goal."

---

[161] And much was to be made: Shell Oil discovered the first of many, enormous Cedar Creek anticline oil fields in the southeastern corner of the state a couple of years later.

[162] Sidney B. Anderson, a geologist for the North Dakota Geological Survey, named the formation Englewood in another document at the time but the Bakken name stuck. The well had been drilled to 13,709 feet, traveling through many rocks for which nomenclature was needed. The Kinderhook name was assigned to a limestone just above the upper-Bakken shale instead.

This would require land not already leased. Looking east of Elm Coulee toward the basin's center around Williston, North Dakota, this would exclude all the acreage along the Nesson anticline, which had been drilled since 1951; much of the acreage was HBPed by existing wells. Meanwhile, the middle Bakken wasn't appealing to him in far-western North Dakota based on what he could see of it in old well logs.

"Nothing fit my model."

He would have to look far east—east of Nesson. That's as far as he could take it, though; it would be the last place he could look. The Bakken becomes less and less thermally mature toward the outer boundaries of the basin. Toward the circumference, it is at about 8,500 feet rather than as much as 10,500 feet in the basin center.

"At this (shallower) depth, the Bakken shale becomes imma-ture...Earth's temperature...(has) decreased to a point that oil is not generated."

Eliminating acreage where wells had not been attempted in the past—thus there were no logs to review—Johnson was now looking at some 1,250 square miles in which only 25 wells had traveled through Bakken, "averaging about one well for every 32,000 acres."

None had been commercial. But, from some, he determined the middle Bakken in the area did contain oil. From others, he determined the interval was slightly over-pressured with a gradient of 0.52. "So I could chalk up another plus in my new area."

He concluded from his research that, "despite a few negative fea-tures, which I did not fully understand, this area was promising."

And the region—in eastern Mountrail County—wasn't leased already or HBPed. Virtually nothing had been produced way out there from any formation. By 2004, of the 468 wells that had been attempt-ed in the county since 1952, those that were commercial were made in the Madison group of formations overlying Bakken along the anticline on the far-western side of the county.[163]

---

[163] Going east of Mountrail, into Ward County, 453 wells have been attempted since 1922. Only 33 were commercial—all producing from Madison.

In 1990, during Burlington's Bakken play, privately held American Hunter Exploration Ltd. made one of these east of Nesson in Mountrail County for only 16 barrels; another, for 22 barrels.[164] In 1980, another operator had completed a vertical in Bakken in the county for 52 barrels; it was soon plugged there and completed uphole in Madison instead.

Using a well log, Johnson first targeted the northern portion of the county. Gulf Oil had attempted a wildcat, Nelson 1-24-2B, in 1982 near Stanley, taking it to 10,505 feet to Duperow below Bakken, Three Forks and Birdbear/Nisku. It was deemed a dry hole.

From what Johnson could see, he was concerned the Bakken was immature in the area. Is that why no one wanted to lease there?

"For a month or so, I was confounded. I would walk around downtown Denver's Seventeenth Street Mall, hands in my pocket and head down. One of the biggest questions was 'Why was all this acreage open?' The last oil and gas leases had expired three or four years previously."

Drilling in the county had ceased with a dry hole spud in December 2001. "What if there was some glaring geologic fact that I was missing?"

But Findley figured out the middle Bakken in Montana; Johnson was determined to figure it out in North Dakota. His capital partner, Denver-based stockbroker Henry Gordon, wanted to try it too. In 2004, they leased some 5,500 acres around the old Gulf Oil well for about $45,000—roughly $8 an acre. They sold it and their idea to Prima Exploration Inc. and Cordillera Energy Partners LLC, both privately held, for $75 an acre and a royalty interest.

Publicly held EOG had been making middle-Bakken wells in the Montana play and was looking to take the idea into North Dakota. It had some leasehold around what Johnson and Gordon had put to-

---

[164] One is in what became Whiting's Sanish Field north of New Town; the other, in what became Van Hook Field, south of New Town. When the Missouri River was dammed in 1956, creating Lake Sakakawea, two of the Fort Berthold native-American villages that were displaced were Van Hook and Sanish. The story goes that a name suggested for the new town was "Vanish." It was named New Town for the time being and still is.

gether and joined in the deal in one section—640 acres. There, it drilled the horizontal Nelson Farms 1-24H. Completed in October 2005, it came on with a modest 155 barrels from a 4,000-foot lateral as the Ross Field discovery.[165]

Meanwhile, Johnson had zeroed in on another old well, Lear Petroleum Exploration Inc.'s vertical Parshall SD 1 near New Town about 26 miles southeast of the Gulf well. It had been drilled past Bakken to 12,555 feet in 1980 and also deemed dry.

A geologist, John G. Larsen, had analyzed rock samples as the drillbit was boring the hole. He reported in the state's well file, "The top of the Bakken formation was reached at a drill depth of 9,130 feet. The formation (was) drilled (in fewer) than five minutes per foot in the shales (and)…nine minutes per foot in the sandier, siltier parts.

"No shows were reported throughout the formation nor was there any significant sandstone development. The shales in the Bakken were very dark grey to dark brown, soft, blocky, carbonaceous, some slightly calcareous and pyritic in part. Good amounts of gases were liberated from the shales as they were drilled…

"The shales were interbedded with thin sandstone stringers…predominantly clear to light grey (in color), sub-angular, very fine-grained, tight, calcareous, silty…."

The hole was plugged; the pasture was re-seeded with native grass. Johnson noted from the file that the well log indicated porosity in the middle Bakken. In mid-2004, just after beginning to lease what would become Ross Field, he and Gordon enlisted Tulsa-based geologist Bob Berry. Berry was also interested in the new Bakken attempts and financed the acquisition of some 38,000 acres around the Lear well, including some 1,900 state-owned acres for which Gordon bid $3 an acre and won. "We were the only bidder," Johnson writes.

He showed his idea to about a dozen operators, including EOG; none would buy. By November 2005, however, the Ross Field discovery well had been online for a month. EOG wanted another look at

---

[165] The Ross Field discovery, Nelson Farms 1-24H was the first commercial Bakken well in the county.

Johnson's other block. Berry sold 75% interest in it to EOG; Johnson and Gordon received a royalty interest.

In June 2006, about 1,200 feet northeast of the Lear dry hole—just across a state road—EOG made Parshall 1-36H for 463 barrels from the middle Bakken without yet fracing the roughly 1,650-foot lateral. The plan had been to take the horizontal at least 4,000 feet; it had to be quit: More than 12-pound mud was being used to stop the well from flowing oil while still being drilled.

It turned out that Johnson's concern about the thermal immaturity of the Bakken east of the Nesson anticline was justified: That characteristic resulted in a new type of trap. "Its unique feature is the trap—what caused the oil to accumulate—at the mature/immature boundary of the Bakken shales," Johnson writes.

On November 2006, having applied staged fracs in the Barnett for enormous gas wells, EOG came back to Parshall 1-36H and completed it with an uncemented liner, three swell packers, 109,000 gallons of gelled water and 148 tons of sand in four frac stages. The well was the discovery of Parshall Field.[166] And it was only EOG's second attempt in the new North Dakota play.

Johnson had shown his idea that became Parshall Field to about a dozen operators. After EOG bought it, others drilling North Dakota wanted to know what EOG would make of it. In September 2006, it followed the Parshall discovery with Parshall 2-36H for an IP of 883 barrels. In November, its Bartelson 1-3H came on with 1,800 barrels—not yet fraced. In January 2007, it brought on Warberg 1-25H for 1,553 barrels; in March, Patten 1-02H with 1,487.

Coming back in July to frac its nearly 10-month-old Parshall 2-32H, EOG used five swell packers, 1,100 tons of sand and 848,000 gallons of gelled water. Production had declined since September to 450 barrels a day; it came back on with 813.

What was EOG doing?

---

[166] The field had more than 300 producing wells by mid-2013. Johnson was named Explorer of the Year in 2009 by the American Association of Petroleum Geologists for his many discoveries—Parshall Field, in particular.

***

The key words in the EOG well reports were "swell packers." But it had become more and more difficult for other operators to know.

It was customary for the state to keep well details private for up to six months after spud. But EOG and others determined that the rule actually allowed the state to "tight hole" the file for up to six months after requested to do so and that the request could be made just prior to fracing it, instead. Other producers only knew that EOG was IPing some enormous Bakken wells and far east of the Nesson anticline; they didn't know how.

Bruce Hicks, assistant director of the oil and gas division of North Dakota's Department of Mineral Resources, explains, "EOG wanted to extend the confidentiality period out as long as they could. It would sometimes take two to five months after TDing the well before the well could be fraced and completed, which only allowed it to be on confidential status for a couple months after being placed on production.

"EOG starting requesting confidential status at the time the well was completed instead of requesting it with the AFD."[167]

Bud Brigham had information, however: Brigham Exploration owned an interest in some of EOG's and others' wells. EOG was using swell packers—a means of isolating each frac along the laterals.

In the early Montana play, a single frac was done in all perforations all at once along a short lateral of 4,000 feet. Next, this was done on a long lateral of up to 9,500 feet. Then, operators did it in multiple, short laterals from one wellbore.

In Parshall Field, EOG was using swell packers, which allowed it to frac perforations one at a time, usually starting with the one farthest—the one at the "toe" of the lateral "shoe" from the vertical "leg." The perforation would be plugged; the next area would be fraced, plugged and so on. Upon completion of all the fracs, the well would be opened to production. The technique is a "controlled" frac.

---

[167] TDing is to reach total well depth; AFD is the application for a permit to drill.

Until EOG's use of swell packers became clear, Brigham had remained stumped by the North Dakota play as were most others.[168] By March 2007, it had 144,212 net acres over Bakken. Its first three Bakken attempts, averaging lateral lengths of 8,000 feet, cost $17.5 million to drill and complete.

Its Field 18-19 1-H, spud in May 2006, was fraced now and making some 65 barrels a day. Mrachek 15-22 1H was making 30 barrels a day and wasn't fraced yet. Erickson 8-17 1-H that came on post-frac for 200 barrels quickly declined to about 45. Frac sand was blocking flow. Upon clean-out and put on a pump, it came back on with 227 barrels; that quickly declined to 82.

It was considering putting three laterals in its next well but waiting to see how that worked out for other operators.

Brigham says, "The first three wells we drilled were long laterals—two-section laterals. We did them with single, uncontrolled fracs because that was the current technology and that's what Bobby Lyle and Lyco had used, successfully, at Elm Coulee. But Elm Coulee had more porosity and more permeability. It really was a different kind of play—more of a truncation trap in an area that had more porosity and more perm.

"Unfortunately, ours in North Dakota didn't have enough perm for that method. The three pilot wells we drilled came on for about 200 barrels a day or less, which was a disappointing rate, given the cost of the wells. So the initial results were discouraging."

He worked out a deal with Fred Evans, the owner of scattered leasehold throughout the heart of the Mountrail County sweet spot, giving Brigham some "close-ology" to what EOG was doing. Meanwhile, micro-cap Northern Oil & Gas Inc. had acreage over Bakken, including in Mountrail County. In April 2007, after EOG had already brought on two Parshall Field wells of more than 1,000 barrels apiece, Brigham revealed it was participating in 5,120 gross, 3,000 net, Northern Oil acres in Mountrail County within four miles of EOG's wells.

---

[168] Whiting Petroleum, which had discovered Sanish Field next door to Parshall Field, was making EOG-size wells, using multiple, short laterals from a single wellbore.

In a report to shareholders, Brigham just came out with it: The deals put it alongside EOG. By then, EOG had spud 10 wells in Parshall Field. The first, which came on with 463 barrels, was making 304 a day after 10 months online. It and two other wells online between three and 10 months had already made 133,430 barrels.

The capital markets yawned, though. Brigham Exploration shares were $14 in November 2005 when announcing it was in the Bakken play; by early 2007, they had fallen to about $5 and continued to hover there—even after the close-ology news as EOG had not yet revealed its results.

On Aug. 2, 2007, however, EOG let it out. By then, it had 12 wells online—one in Ross Field and 11 in Parshall. Among the newest wells, peak 24-hour production ranged from 1,610 to 2,034 barrels; the official IPs were between 870 and 1,675.

In an earnings call the next morning, Mark Papa, chairman and chief executive, said EOG was completing the Bakken wells the way it had come to complete its Barnett wells. "…We've raised relative play economics to a standard that now exceeds those of the Barnett shale and that puts it—us—in the top class of high-return plays in North America."

Its wells in Mountrail County were costing some $5.25 million and each was expected to recover 700,000 barrels of oil, net to EOG. "For those who don't have your calculators handy, that's a $7.50-barrel, net, direct, finding cost," Papa said.

Oil was about $76 that day.

Securities analyst Tom Gardner asked about the completion technology EOG was using that was resulting in the higher-rate wells in the Barnett. Papa wouldn't disclose it and noted that none of EOG's neighbors to its monster wells in Johnson County, Texas, were getting the same results.

Gardner asked if the recipe was proprietary. Papa said it wasn't. "What we've done is just taken some of those concepts to North Dakota and some of them are, I'd say, known by everybody. I mean it's stage fracing. It's basically fracing multiple (sections) along the lateral in North Dakota—but…how we do that really is--." He stopped.

"...We had a play that was marginally economic—not anything that you could do back-flips over...We knew that there was a whole bunch of oil in place, but we had to do something to get the recoveries up...We (used) some of these Barnett techniques and suddenly we got the wells up where we're recovering now, roughly, 700,000 or so barrels, net, which is closer to about...850,000 barrels, gross...

"We've taken a project that now has turned into a 100% rate-of-return project."

Another securities analyst, John Herrlin, asked if EOG's middle-Bakken member in North Dakota is dolomitic and if it had the thermal maturity of the Montana play. Thus, was it the unique frac recipe that was resulting in the higher-rate wells?

Loren Leiker, EOG senior vice president, exploration, at the time, said, "John, that's the big question in the whole play...We feel like we understand what those sweet spots are, but we are going to keep that under our vest for today...

"I would say that there are...stratigraphic aspects of that that we feel like we understand. We are in the middle zone, John, and you got the shale above and a shale below that are fantastic oil-source rocks, maybe 20, 30 feet thick, each. And then you have the middle Bakken between those two, which is where all that oil is going and that is the zone that we are targeting.

"It has various lithologies and that's part of the trick—and that's why we are going to keep it close to our chest right now."

Gas had fallen to about $6 that day. Papa was aiming to shift EOG to more oil production, while still drilling its Barnett gas to HBP its acreage there. He said, "It's really hard to find oil in North America. That's the issue...With this horizontal drilling, we may have found a pretty sweet, oil project in North Dakota. The question is how big it is.

"We basically think, right now, it's 60 million barrels net (to EOG and at a) 100% rate of return...I will stack that up—on a net basis, again—to some of these deepwater discoveries that people are touting, which probably will turn out to be 5%- to 10%-after-tax rate of returns when (you) clear away the smoke and mirrors.

"Whether we can find more of these with horizontal drilling in the onshore U.S., we are looking…That's all I can say."

A month later, Brigham Exploration reported it now had 30,000 net acres east of the Nesson anticline with 22,000 of that in Mountrail County. The position gave it a 1.3% working interest in EOG's Risan 1-34H in Parshall Field that IPed 817 barrels. It also had a 0.5% working interest in a Hess Corp. well 35 miles north of that and 1.7% interest in a Petro-Hunt well some 15 miles farther north.[169]

Bud Brigham explained that, for a small share of the wells' cost, the company was getting a valuable look at the rock and how it changed across the area. He added that, "given the size of our company, we believe we've assembled what is potentially the most impactful acreage position of any public company in the play."

He was preparing to go all in. Of the company's drilling plans now, only four were Gulf Coast wildcats. It sold a position it had put together in the Granite Wash gas play in Oklahoma for $36 million, paying off all of its bank debt; its borrowing base was $101 million. To date, however, it only had—as the operator—three Bakken wells, all disappointing.

But the company continued to map it, including east of Nesson. He says, "To EOG's credit, they drilled the first successful wells on the east side of the Nesson in the Parshall area and they brought the swell packers up there from the Barnett. The swell packers provided the opportunity to isolate your stimulations along the lateral and, thus, more effectively break up the rock all along it.

"When we saw what they were doing over there—and we had already mapped east of the Nesson and knew the good areas that had the attributes we liked—we began buying leases. We assembled about 100,000 acres on the east side of the Nesson."

In late October 2007, EOG was increasing its Bakken-drilling program to eight rigs. Papa remained uncertain about future gas prices, however, and continued to plan to drill Barnett wells only to HBP

---

[169] The Petro-Hunt well, Torgerson 15B-2-2H, came on with 117 barrels in December 2007; the Hess well, En-Hegland 156-94-3229H-1, with 52 in April 2008.

the acreage. There, it was heading toward making 350 million cubic feet of gas a day by year-end and 450 million a day in 2008. It was pulling back on Rockies- and Canadian-gas drilling instead.

"We do not intend to increase our debt by drilling excess gas wells," he said in an earnings call.

In the Bakken, EOG now believed Parshall Field was at least 20 miles long and several miles wide and "probably going to be bigger." It held a majority of the acreage—more than 175,000 net.

"We try to be sly on that stuff…We're trying to camouflage our acreage position. We've got more than that," he added.[170]

A week later, Brigham reported it was about to spud its first, operated attempt in Mountrail County, the Bergstrom Family Trust 26-1H, and would use swell packers. Like EOG's wells, it would be made with a single lateral. In an earnings call, Bud Brigham broke it down this way: If each $5.2-million well made 800,000 barrels of oil, the finding cost is some $8.13 per barrel.

Oil was now $97. "At this point, the economics of this area look outstanding," he said.

Securities analyst Scott Hanold asked if there was any more acreage still available for grassroots leasing. Brigham said, "…Basically, in Mountrail County, if you're not already on the ground, it's pretty much done."

Analyst Jack Aydin asked if, in the EOG well in which Brigham had a 1.3% interest, EOG was sharing all the information. Lance Langford, head of operations, said, "I can't say that they are sharing everything because we don't know exactly what 'everything' is…Our operations people…are talking to their people who are actually doing the drilling and completions…We think they're freely sharing that information."

As for service companies, Langford added that, "although they won't tell you who is doing what, they will tell you what is being done

---

[170] EOG also reported that it had quit its attempts at making the Barnett work in West Texas. Papa described it as "a much-hyped play." The Barnett just didn't work there like in the Fort Worth Basin.

successfully in the area. So I think we have a really good feel (for what's being tried). We also have a partner...with a lot of interest with EOG in multiple wells and they're getting a lot of information.

"So I think there is a lot of sharing going on (among) everybody out there."

Brigham Exploration, which was founded upon pioneering the use of 3-D seismic to find relatively tiny, structural traps of oil and gas, was supplementing its Bakken research with only 2-D to select Bakken well locations. The Bakken was everywhere; the challenge was to put the best kind of hole in it to make an 800,000-barrel well rather than a 250,000-barrel well.

But, Bud Brigham told analysts and shareholders, "The great thing about this place is you're not going to drill a dry hole."

And Parshall Field and the area surrounding it east of the Nesson anticline were proving to be the sweetest spot of the play. By early November 2007, operators had completed 273 wells in the modern Bakken effort across western North Dakota. Only 16 of these came on with more than 1,000 barrels. Among them, 13 were EOG's—all in Parshall Field with single laterals and staged fracs.

Whiting made two—also east of Nesson and each with three, short laterals. Its Peery State 11-25H came on in May 2007 with 1,081 barrels five miles north of New Town in its Sanish Field. Altogether, the well involved 21,200 feet of pipe.[171] The other 1,000-barrel-plus well was made by ConocoPhillips in Dunn County along the anticline.

The east-of-Nesson code was clearly cracked. Brigham Exploration would soon take the code west of Nesson.

---

[171] Sanish Field took off. Whiting's next wells—with single, long laterals, instead—came on with up to 2,669 barrels. In June 2008, its Behr 11-34H came on with 3,207 barrels. The field hosted 425 wells by mid-2013, lined up north/south and the most wells in a Bakken-producing field in the state. By then, Behr 11-34H had made almost 1 million barrels and more than a half-billion cubic feet of gas. It was still producing.

MARCELLUS: 2003

← ← ← ← ← → → → → →

"I was scared, you know.
I'm the guy with the dry hole and
I'm asking him for more money."
—Bill Zagorski

A week after Devon Energy took in Chief Oil & Gas' Barnett assets in 2006, Range Resources Corp. added to its Barnett play as well. Trevor Rees-Jones would meet up with Range later, in Pennsylvania. He was going to the Marcellus; Range was already there.

"How did we know to go to the Marcellus?"

Rees-Jones laughs. "Well, we chose to go to the Marcellus without knowing what was going to come about from it. Of course, now—from a natural-gas standpoint—it's the granddaddy. The Barnett really pales in comparison."

"With all due respect to the Barnett, it pales in comparison to the Marcellus."

Range had been mostly missing until May 2006 from the Barnett story and the epic tale the shale was producing from under the company's Fort Worth headquarters.

Ray Walker had been missing as well.

The UPR engineer, who, with his colleagues, suggested the LSF to the Mitchell team in 1997, had left UPR when Anadarko Petroleum Corp. purchased it in July 2000. Meanwhile, Chris Wright and a partner, Bruce Baden, recapitalized small, privately held Stroud Energy Inc., which had an old, oil portfolio in Oklahoma.

Wright, who had founded frac-mapping and -diagnostics firm Pinnacle Technologies in 1992, had worked with the UPR team on the LSF trials in the Cotton Valley. Wright had quickly recruited UPR's Mike Mayerhofer, who had generated the LSF idea, to work for Pinnacle. In 2000, Wright recruited Walker to run Stroud Energy from Fort Worth.

Downtown Fort Worth property owners were repairing damage from a March 2000 tornado at the time. In September of that year, Walker was among presenters in the Barnett symposium that was a fund-raiser for the Oil Information Library, whose offices were among those damaged by the F3 cyclone. One tower, the Bank One building, had been swept away, except for its concrete-and-steel structure. It sat there, boarded up.[172] Fort Worth looked at the time like it was on its way out, just like the 50-year-old Boonsville gas field and 19th-century cattle drives that had brought cowboys to town along the storied Chisholm Trail.

Hiring other, former UPR colleagues, Walker put together for Stroud some Austin-chalk properties in southeast Texas and a couple of other small plays. UPR had made more than 1,000 unfraced horizontals in the naturally fractured chalk in the 1990s, producing more than 75,000 barrels of oil equivalent a day, 57% oil. It had named the play its "success story of the '90s" in a 1995 report—considerable recognition for one play within a company of UPR's size.

After a couple of years with Stroud, Walker joined another, small E&P that was also in the play. Wright and Braden then asked Pat Noyes to take over. Noyes had been with Mitchell Energy for more than 22 years, lastly as vice president, drilling and services, as it unleashed the LSF on the stubborn shale. Upon the sale to Devon, he had started, with fellow Mitchell vice president Chris Veeder, a small E&P to work the shale for themselves.

---

[172] As the Barnett renewed Fort Worth's economy, the tower was converted to host modern residences.

Joining Stroud in 2003, he and Veeder added Barnett assets from Dan A. Hughes Co. to the portfolio for some $35 million, bringing in some 23.5 billion cubic feet equivalent of proved reserves, all in Denton County.

By 2006, Stroud was looking to IPO, tapping the public-capital market to continue funding growth and to pay private investors. As it had come together in boot-strap fashion, including a private offering in 2005, selling shareholders were some 500 individuals and entities, ranging from holding as few as 900 shares to as many as 800,000 by GLG North American Opportunity Fund. Another 25,000 were held by T. Boone Pickens and 50,000 by his BP Capital Energy Funds.

Stroud's IPO was never completed, however. On May 10, 2006, Range put in a winning bid for it; the deal was closed on June 19. It paid some 6.5 million shares that were worth about $170 million at the time, $171 million in cash and $107 million of debt assumption. In return, it gained 171 billion cubic feet equivalent of proved reserves and interests in 126 wells in the Barnett, Cotton Valley and Austin chalk, producing 33 million a day, half of this from Barnett.[173]

With Stroud's 20,000 net Barnett acres, Range now had 35,300 net. It had 182 drilling locations identified. Yet, it was working on something else too—a new shale play. And the play—the Marcellus in Pennsylvania—just wasn't looking profitable yet.[174]

Would Ray Walker help it trouble-shoot this rock? "I really liked the people and the culture, so I took the job," he says. He happened to join the company the day Range closed its acquisition of Stroud.

Range had been formed in 1976 in the midst of severe Northeast U.S. natural-gas shortages as Lomak Petroleum Inc. with headquarters in Hartville, Ohio, in the midst of thousands of old, shallow, oil and gas wells. Lomak was drilling on leases farmed out to it by gas-distributor East Ohio Gas Co. that had been formed in 1898.[175]

It went public in 1980 on the nascent Nasdaq all-electronic stock

---

[173] Range sold the chalk properties for $82 million shortly after closing the Stroud deal.

[174] Range grew its Barnett business to 390 wells on only 52,000 net acres and sold it in 2011 for $900 million.

[175] East Ohio Gas is now part of Dominion Resources Inc.

market that was launched with the trading of Intel Corp. shares in 1971. The oil- and gas-bust of the 1980s resulted in Lomak's delisting. It was then bought by Fort Worth-based Snyder Oil Co. and Snyder senior vice president John Pinkerton took it over as president, relisting it on Nasdaq. It entered the new acquire-and-exploit era of independent E&Ps that were grabbing up the hand-me-downs of larger companies.

In 1998, Lomak merged with Domain Energy Corp., which had been formed just two years earlier in a management buyout of Tenneco Ventures Corp.[176]

Into the 2000s, Pinkerton saw the future was no longer in the acquire-and-exploit tack; the company, newly named Range Resources Corp., had to explore. Besides in the then-180-year-old Appalachian Basin, it held producing properties in the Gulf of Mexico and the Permian Basin in West Texas. Appalachia had made gas from shallow shale since the 1820s.[177]

In the Ohio office, Bill Zagorski knew the company's mission: Explore! He did explore and was thinking in early 2004 that he might be able to make good on a $6.5-million dry hole.

With a master's in geology from the University of Pittsburgh, Zagorski had been working the Appalachian Basin since 1980, when he joined Atlas Resources Inc. At the time, government-funded research—prompted by natural-gas shortages—into producing commercial amounts of gas from Appalachia's Devonian shale and from other, tight, U.S. formations was under way.

Zagorski had followed and studied the findings and, in 1983, while working for Mark Resources Corp., he had tried a new, revolutionary, "basin center" gas concept in Pennsylvania. The idea had been developed by geologist John Masters at Canadian Hunter Exploration Ltd. and demonstrated in 1976 with the discovery of Elmworth Field in western Canada.

---

[176] Tenneco Ventures consisted of Tenneco's remaining financial interests in E&P, which it had exited in the 1980s.

[177] It had made oil since 1859 with a well by Edwin L. Drake near Titusville, Pennsylvania, coming on with about 40 barrels a day. It was the first, commercial, U.S., oil well.

Masters' thinking was that gas could be produced from strati-graphic, low-permeability traps—an unconventional and controversial idea in the traditional world of searching for high-permeability, structurally trapped gas. Elmworth, a continuous accumulation, was estimated to hold 17 trillion cubic feet of gas and a billion barrels of NGL. He wrote in 1984 that it "opens many minds to…similar accumulations…

"Ten years ago, it would have seemed scientifically irresponsible to suggest that Canada had yet to see its largest gas field and that it would be found in a stratigraphic trap where gas lies downdip from water with no impermeable barrier between.

"Rational analysis of the future is always constrained by limited knowledge."

Zagorski was fascinated by the concept.

In northwestern Pennsylvania, he used the basin-center thinking for what became the trillion-cubic-foot Cooperstown Field. He went to the Uintah Basin in the Rockies and helped discover the Bluebell fields, holding trillions more cubic feet of gas.

In 2000 in Appalachia, wildcatting led by Canada-based Talisman Energy Inc. was producing some remarkable results in the deep, Ordovician-age, Trenton-Black River formation in northern New York.

"Everybody started focusing on the Appalachia Basin again because of these high-rate wells that a couple companies were getting in that deeper, Trenton-Black River play," says Zagorski, who had joined Range in the Ohio office as a result of Range's acquisition of Mark Resources in 1992.

He suggested Range also look at the basin's deeper rocks underlying Washington County, Pennsylvania, southwest of Pittsburgh. In 2003, on the way to taking the 8,000-foot well, Renz 1, to Silurian-age dolomite, it drilled through the Devonian-age Marcellus.

"When we drilled past the Marcellus, we got some really good shows and we noted them," he says. "But that wasn't the focus at that time." Instead, the company identified two other targets, both below Marcellus. One was the Devonian-age Ridgeley sandstone; the other was the yet-deeper, Silurian-age Lockport dolomite.

All indications from Renz 1—gas shows and pressure—were that Range had made a pretty decent, deep discovery. "But no matter what we seemed to do on that well, we failed to get commercial production. We tried sidetracking it; it was unsuccessful. We tried sidetracking it another time. Unsuccessful. We tried to treat other zones uphole—Salina and Oriskany. Unsuccessful.

"It just wasn't working."

The company had spent about $6.5 million on the well—a spend more like on a Gulf Coast wildcat. Appalachian wells tended to cost about $500,000. In 2003, the company-wide capital budget was only $105 million. The idea was put aside; Zagorski says he felt as though he became informally known as "the guy who made the dry hole."

He was perplexed.

"I mean, I had been a pretty successful exploration geologist in the basin. I was involved in a lot of big plays, but this particular well was frustrating for me as a geologist. We hit the target as we thought it should be hit. We hit more gas than we expected down there. But it was a failure in terms of capitalizing on an idea of the potential that I thought was there."

In early 2004, he traveled to Houston for the annual NAPE Expo, an oil and gas industry gathering in which geologists and landmen show their ideas for where to drill a well. E&P companies or investors might buy the idea or buy an interest in it. Zagorski visited there with Gary Kornegay with whom he had explored the Uintah Basin years earlier. Kornegay had an idea for the Floyd/Neal shale in Alabama's Black Warrior Basin at the southern end of Appalachia. The basin was already a known producer of conventional and coalbed-methane gas.

"At the time, I didn't know much about the Barnett shale and the Fayetteville shale hadn't shown up (in the news) yet," Zagorski says. Kornegay described the Floyd, about where gas had been demonstrated in the basin and why the shale was the source of that gas.

Zagorski was interested. "I said, 'That's great work, Gary. Why is this so exciting to you? What's the analog? What are you trying to imitate?'" Kornegay showed Zagorski how the Floyd had characteristics similar to the Barnett.

"In the last year or so, the economics of the Barnett play had really changed. They had lowered costs and were doing some successful horizontals there. It was a time when people in the industry were thinking, 'Wow. This Barnett shale—it's really something. But it's really leased up. Maybe we can find it somewhere else.'"

While Kornegay was showing Zagorski the Floyd and Barnett correlations, "that was a kind of 'Omg!' moment. I've got a light bulb going off: 'Holy cow! We just drilled through this stuff that looks just like this.' We had (gas) shows. It's everywhere up here (in Pennsylvania) and we never looked at it this way."

He had to tell the office. But his confidence was still shaken by his $6.5-million dry hole. "I'm thinking, 'What do I do now? I'm really excited about the potential of this Marcellus shale and what it could mean for us, but how many ideas are they going to listen to?'

"You know, you can't keep handing out money. I wasn't the only one spending it, but you know what I'm saying. So I was forced with making a decision. Do I bring this to my boss? How much work do I do on it?"

Range's capital budget had grown to $126 million in 2004. It had pared its $368 million of debt by $88 million on operational efficiencies and higher oil and gas prices. And it had reinstated dividends.

"At the end of the day, I just felt that it's the exploration geologist's job to find plays and find opportunities. It's someone else's job to say 'no' if they want to say 'no.' I was really charged up about it— and after so much failure."

Jeff Ventura had just joined Range in 2003 as chief operating officer at Fort Worth headquarters from six years with Matador Petroleum Corp., lastly as president and chief operating officer. He had begun his career in 1979 with Tenneco as a petroleum engineer with a bachelor's from Penn State. Upon his arrival at Range, Ventura had asked the team's geologists to find "the next Barnett."

Zagorski took the Marcellus idea to Ventura. "I was scared, you know. I'm the guy with the dry hole and I'm asking him for more money." Ventura was intrigued.

Zagorski says, "I would've expected someone to say, 'We'll do it, but we'll do it next year' or 'Well, we'll try your idea but, maybe, we'll put a small frac on it.' Instead, Jeff was pretty adamant about getting it tested and getting it tested soon.

"It was atypical. Spending a lot more money in this basin to get more production seems intuitive now and that's the way it should be. But that wasn't the way it worked several years ago. We were always concerned about drilling under AFE (authorization for expenditure)."

Zagorski believed the Marcellus test should be with an enormous, Barnett-style frac job to really get a comparison of the Pennsylvania and Fort Worth rocks. "And doing a massive stimulation on any reservoir was just a new concept."

Range's Appalachian operations were run out of the regional office in Ohio under Steve Gross. Ventura had arrived from Fort Worth headquarters for a regular meeting with Gross and others, going over production results and drilling ideas. Ventura had grown up in the Pittsburgh area not far from where Renz 1 had been drilled.

"Bill brought up the Marcellus idea," Ventura says. "It was very different from what Range had been doing—exploration in conventional plays that were higher risk and, theoretically, higher potential."

The company was wildcatting in high-temperature and high-pressure, deep formations, including the Norphlet in Mississippi, to 15,000 to 20,000 feet in the shallow Gulf of Mexico and to 10,000 feet for Trenton-Black River in Appalachia.

"The company's risk in those prospects was a 10% to 20% chance of success. When I joined Range in 2003, I knew we could never build a company that way," he says. "Historically, when you look for risky things, one, they tend to not work and, two, the industry's track record with looking for risky stuff was even lower than predicted."

Ventura's, president Pinkerton's and the board's vision for the company was to transform it, changing the structure to focus on lower-risk, resource plays like the Barnett. "I wanted to not only get into plays that are more repeatable and higher quality, in terms of production life, but plays that have better returns. It could have been a shale, a tight sandstone, coalbed methane.

"I saw Bill's work. I thought, 'This Marcellus could build a company.'" In the three years prior to 2004, prospectors were roughly 2,100-for-2,100 in Barnett attempts.[178] "The Barnett was growing into the largest gas field in the country at the time," Ventura notes.

"Bill Zagorski knew, when he had that 'Eureka!' moment, that it wasn't the Floyd shale over in Alabama that looked like the Barnett; it was the Marcellus that looked like the Barnett."

Both are black shales, which can be an indicator of containing a large amount of organic content. But the Marcellus was made about 40 million years earlier than the Barnett; this kitchen had been cooking for about 400 million years.

"I liked Bill's idea a lot because it had what I was looking for: His geologic thinking was very counter to the engineers and the operations people; it was counter to what the traditional thoughts in the basin had been."

When Zagorski asked for a Barnett-style, water-based frac on the Marcellus test, there was pushback by engineering and operations. Typically, the geologist determines where there might be oil or gas; the drilling and production engineers design the well and how it will be completed, including how it will be fraced—if it is fraced.

Renz 1 was scheduled for plugging and abandonment at the time and the land restored to its original condition. The operations team was tired of the well.

Ventura says, "The guys running the division said, 'Hey, we hear you, Bill, but we don't like it because we know the Marcellus is water-sensitive. We've drilled through it for decades. You put water on the Marcellus, it locks up. You put a big Barnett-style water frac on it, you're gonna lock it up.'

"And these were smart guys."

As shales, which are also known as mudstones, have varying amounts and types of clay content, the thinking was that getting it wet would cause any swelling clay to swell, further trapping the gas within the rock. Ventura says, "After listening to both sides, I decided to put

---

[178] By 2013, the Barnett hosted more than 16,000 producing wells.

a Barnett-style frac on it. Fortunately, it worked out."

He asked George Teer, an operations manager in the Fort Worth office, to convince one of the service companies there that was pumping a lot of Barnett fracs to have a crew in Appalachia "give us a Barnett job," using the Barnett recipe.

Renz 1 was re-entered in October 2004. It was perforated in the Marcellus interval uphole of the two deeper-target attempts and the Barnett-style, light-sand, water frac was put in it. The frac crew gathered for a photo. At the time, it was the largest frac job done east of the Mississippi River.

Zagorski says, "The test was pretty exciting." The peak, 24-hour rate from the Marcellus interval was 800,000 cubic feet of gas.

It had good indications by a second measure too: Could the Marcellus also produce a superior return on investment? Already, the U.S. Northeast paid a premium for natural gas as it is the nation's largest population center yet steeped in industrial demand for gas as well. Supply had been constrained by its location—far away from the Gulf Coast, Rockies and western Canada—that had contributed, along with counter-effective gas regulation, to winter-supply crises in the 1970s.

And there was another bonus: Marcellus gas was high-Btu, rich in strippable and marketable NGL.

Ventura says of the Renz 1 re-entry findings, "It was enough to keep us interested."

***

Until Oct. 18, 2004, Range's only mention of shales in its public filings had been in boiler-plate language about general aspects of the oil and gas business. In an operations update, it reported, after discussing its vast Appalachian Basin activity, "...The division is continuing to test a shale play in Pennsylvania."

It had 10 rigs working for it in the basin at the time, drilling shallow, upper-Devonian sandstones and testing the deeper Medina and Trenton-Black River formation. In the third quarter of 2004, the company had drilled 85 wells in the region.

And its position in the basin was growing. A few months earlier, Range had bought out partner Great Lakes Energy Partners LLC's 50% interest in a five-year-old joint venture for $200 million, assumption of $68 million of debt and retirement of roughly $22 million of hedges.[179]

In the deal, it added 664,000 net acres in Appalachia and became the third-largest operator in the basin. By year-end, it added more, buying interests at all depths from a private seller in 1,872 shallow, coal-gas wells in 417,000 acres in Virginia and West Virginia. The wells were netting 14.8 million cubic feet equivalent a day.

With this and the Great Lakes deal, Range's Appalachian leasehold had grown to 1.9 million gross, 1.7 million net, acres. Gas was about $7. Its stock had improved to about $20 from $1.80 in 2000.

In 2005, two more Marcellus verticals—Deiseroth 1 and Renz 2—came on just as well as Renz 1. Meanwhile, Renz 1 was shut in, waiting for pipe. A full year had elapsed by now. Ventura says, "We discovered the aging process at work."

Before being shut in, the well had a peak, 24-hour rate of about 800,000 cubic feet and then, naturally, declined. When re-opened a year later, after having connected it to a pipeline, it came back on with 800,000 a day again.

"And it was producing less water. Also, with the long shut-in, we established that we had a high-pressure gradient—we were over-pressured—in the Marcellus, which was critical. It was 0.69."

It didn't just sputter out: Several months after brought back online, it was making 200,000 cubic feet a day.

An advantage in advancing the play in these tests was that "we didn't 'over-science' the frac design," he says. The LSF that was being used in the Barnett was applied in all three vertical tests; slightly larger fracs were applied to the second and third wells.

"Typically, engineers design the frac jobs based upon available

---

[179] Great Lakes retained the right to participate, with up to 40% interest, in wells completed in Ohio in formations below Clinton and Medina, which sit below the Marcellus and above the Utica shale. When crossing the state line into Ohio, the Marcellus begins to disappear while the Utica remains present.

data. If that would have happened, the frac job would have been much smaller since the Marcellus in the Renz 1 had about a third of the thickness of the Barnett. Designing for the same fracture parameters and frac length, a job probably would have been about one third the volume of what we actually pumped.

"Had we gone that route, the reduced job might have resulted in a much lower flow rate and fewer reserves, which might have led us down a different path or may have even discouraged us."

That a company Range's size took on the cost of the large fracs was contrarian as well. "As a small operator, a more common practice would have been to pump a smaller frac job and attempt to keep the cost down, particularly since it was a new idea, so it had risk to it.

"Fortunately, we didn't do that nor did we over-science it."

And the company's ability to spend was growing: The 2004 capital budget had been only $126 million; the 2005 budget was $254 million. It went on to try three additional vertical tests in areas Zagorski thought should define the Marcellus' economic boundaries. But the wells ended up being completed in other zones.

One flowed 1.6 million cubic feet equivalent from a shallower formation. Drilling was stopped; the well was completed there. It didn't even get to Marcellus. The other two were taken past Marcellus to look at a tight, gassy sandstone while there. They tested 1.2- and 2.1 million a day; the wells were completed in that zone.

In 2006, its capex budget was now $429 million. Its share price had increased 750% since year-end 2001 on growing oil and gas prices and its Barnett results; the stock had been split 3-for-2. It planned five more vertical tests and a first horizontal try. The drilling and production team didn't think the horizontal would work.

And it didn't work.

Zagorski says, "It only made about 300,000 cubic feet of gas per day and it was real expensive. It wasn't as good as some of the vertical wells." The next one was worse. A third was better but still not much better than a vertical.

"And the whole reason for all of this investment and corporate interest was to develop a play that was par with the Barnett, in terms of horizontal potential and repeatable, long-term-growth potential."

Again, Zagorski was perplexed.

The first three Marcellus verticals, after five months online, were estimated to hold between 600 million and 1.1 billion cubic feet of gas—each. A fourth vertical came on with a peak rate of 1.2 million. The operations team based in Ohio wanted to just continue making verticals.

Verticals would continue to be made, but Ventura and Ray Walker, who was now onboard to help Range trouble-shoot the Marcellus, put an end to the completions in non-Marcellus zones. Ventura says, "The message from Ray and me was 'We don't care what you encounter. What will drive our company and this play is if we can make the Marcellus work.'"

To learn more about the Marcellus, Range needed more wells in the formation. And it opened an office in Pittsburgh with 100% focus on starting and running a Marcellus play. Ray Walker was sent to lead the new office, consisting at first of one employee: Ray Walker.

"It was the fall of 2006 and we had seen enough indications in the Marcellus that we would need a Marcellus-focused operation there," Walker says. "We tried for a month or so to find somebody local who was willing to and capable of starting that office. We just struck out. By now, it was around Thanksgiving."

Walker was having lunch with Ventura and Pinkerton. "We were talking about that. They looked at me and said, 'Would you do it?' So, in January of '07, I turned the lights on and it's been one of the best moves I've ever made."

By then, Range's capex budget had grown to $689 million. It was making some 300 million cubic feet of gas equivalent a day from across its portfolio. Proved reserves had grown to 1.76 trillion equivalent. Its stock was trading at about $30. It had sold its Gulf of Mexico and Austin-chalk properties and added to its positions in the Permian Basin and Barnett.

In Pittsburgh that spring of 2007, with the new office open just a few months, Ventura sat down with the Marcellus team. By then, Range had spent about $150 million on the vertical and horizontal tests. It appeared to be a somewhat successful vertical play but a yet-elusive horizontal play. He told the team it would have to make the Marcellus play work horizontally by year-end and cumulative spend was being capped at $200 million.

Zagorski says, "That meant we had about $50 million left to figure it out and it had to be done by the end of the year." The Renz 1 recompletion in the Marcellus was nearly three years old now. Ventura says, "And we didn't have the breakthrough yet that we wanted."

The company had been talking to investors about trying a shale play in Pennsylvania for three years. It had 420,000 net acres over Marcellus and 22 verticals and three horizontals online.

In the meeting, Zagorski drew a line in the shale. Each of the first three horizontal attempts had been completed at varying depths in the roughly 100-foot-thick Marcellus interval.

Ventura says, "The engineers were examining if they needed to pump more sand. Did we need more pressure-pumping rate? A longer lateral? Better perforation charges? There were dozens of variables."

But Zagorski walked up with a chart.

He noted that the deepest well, at about 40 feet above the bottom of the 100-foot Marcellus, made almost no gas, just 20,000 cubic feet a day; the middle well, about 20 feet higher, came on with about 350,000 cubic feet; the least-deep well, at about 30 feet from the top of the Marcellus, with about 600,000.

Ventura says, "I remember, when he put the graph up, everybody laughed and thought, 'Hey, that's hilarious, Bill.' Someone said, 'You know, if you had two points, you could get an even straighter line.'

"Bill had plotted the three points and drew a straight line. He concluded that we just needed to land the wells even higher and that would break the code.

"He was saying it had a great correlation—an R-squared of 0.98—and forget the lateral length for the time being and the sand and the stages. You just needed to land the well higher. Move it a little higher in the section and we'll get a breakthrough.

"After brainstorming on it, we decided to try it."

The fourth well was landed higher in the section. And, rather than just doing a Barnett-style frac job on this well, Range had imported a rig and frac crew from the Barnett itself.

Walker says, "One of the issues was that we were using equipment and services that were indigenous to Appalachia. Early on, I realized, 'This is just never gonna work.'

"I literally called in all kinds of favors, called everybody I ever had known, begged, borrowed—did everything I could to get some friends to move up there. We got some drilling rigs. We got some frac crews. We got some tool hands up there—the whole assembly of putting a well together.

"The Gulla 9 was the well where we finally got all of the parts right. Everything in life happens for a reason. That's one of those things that I learned in my career: Sometimes you've got to take the biggest leap of faith.

"We only had about $50 million more to make the Marcellus work. I'm really glad we got everybody's buy-in, took the major step and unlocked it on that Gulla 9."

The horizontal Gulla 9 came on with 3.2 million cubic feet a day—as much at the time as a good Barnett horizontal and very economic in the premium-price, northeastern-U.S., gas market.

Ventura says, "That well proved the concept that you could make the same level of commerciality in terms of production in the Marcellus that we could in the Barnett."

In December 2007, in an operations update, it identified its Appalachian-shale play as the Marcellus. It had completed four new horizontals by then: Gulla 9 had come on with 3.2 million a day; three others came on with 3.7-, 4.3- and 4.7 million.

Its stock price bolted from $43 to $51. It now had proved reserves of 2.2 trillion cubic feet equivalent. Its 2008 capital budget was $1.1 billion—nearly four times the company's 2000 market cap. It planned 60 net Marcellus wells in the new year.

Other operators were in the area, taking a look at the Marcellus by now too but not with Barnett-style fracs, equipment and crews, and not yet horizontally.

Zagorski says, "They were months behind in the science."

While half of the Marcellus' areal extent is as thick as the Barnett, the Marcellus has a larger geographic footprint—seven to 10 times that of the Barnett. "So," Ventura says, "it had the potential to become a bigger field."[180]

---

[180] The Marcellus produced some 3 trillion cubic feet of gas in 2013. As of March 2013, the U.S. Geological Survey estimated the Appalachian Basin, including Marcellus, contains 185 trillion cubic feet of recoverable gas; the Fort Worth Basin, including the Barnett, 26 trillion.

HAYNESVILLE: 2007

← ← ← ← ← → → → → →

> *"When it's time to make a decision, we make it...*
> *Floyd says, 'All the money's made before noon.'"*
> —Steve Herod

A s Range Resources revealed the new Marcellus play in late 2007, the Fayetteville was heading toward gross production of 2.6 billion cubic feet a day and the Barnett was heading to 5.7 billion a day. Petrohawk Energy Corp. had some experience with both of these. One experience was too soon; the other, just in time.

The company—a traditional, private-equity-backed, acquire-and-exploit E&P—had bought an operated position from Adexco Production Co. in the Barnett play in mid-2003 while the mechanics of it were still being worked out. At the time, it was working on proving the Barnett outside the sweet spot and where the Viola-limestone frac barrier was often absent.

"We didn't complete a single commercial well," says Dick Stoneburner, who had been Petrohawk's president and chief operating officer. "It was a very challenging period, from 2003 to '05, in completing these wells. The technology wasn't there yet."

Otherwise, Petrohawk only had an interest in a producing well offshore Louisiana and one that was shut in. It was making 1 million cubic feet a day. Its company-wide leasehold was 1,895 net acres. In

June 2003 and just formed, it was Floyd Wilson's third start-up and would become his biggest exit ever—a $15.1-billion sale to BHP Billiton Ltd. in 2011.

Wilson began his oil and gas career as a completions engineer in Houston in 1970 and packed up in 1976 for Wichita, Kansas, to make a business for himself in the Midcontinent's huge gas fields. There, he started several companies that, with $50,000 of his own and with some financial backing from Prudential Capital, culminated with forming Hugoton Energy Corp. in 1987 at the bottom of the 1980s oil-price bust.

He took Hugoton public in 1994 and sold it and its 246 billion cubic feet equivalent of proved reserves in Oklahoma, Kansas, Texas and North Dakota in 1998 for $326 million to Chesapeake.[181]

Days later, Wilson founded W/E Energy Co. LLC based in Dallas with $20 million of backing from EnCap Investments LP, himself and other founding managers. Rather than go through the process of an IPO, he bought a controlling interest in micro-cap, Houston-based Middle Bay Oil Co. With this, W/E emerged as 3Tec Energy Corp. in 1999 with immediate access to public capital.

"I built Hugoton bit by bit with bank financing and sweat equity," he said at the time. "This time, I arranged for the equity with EnCap first. Partners with cash are the best."

David Miller, EnCap managing director and co-founder, said, "Floyd had built a $350-million company, so we felt he had the skills to grow a half-billion-dollar company."

And he did. Wilson built 3Tec into 49 million barrels of oil equivalent of proved reserves, 87% gas, and sold it for $450 million in June 2003 to Plains Exploration & Production Co.

Days later, he formed Petrohawk Energy LLC with $54 million from EnCap and Liberty Mutual Insurance Co.'s Liberty Energy Holdings LLC. Another $6 million was put in by himself and fellow members of management, including Stoneburner, a geologist who had

---

[181] With the assets, Chesapeake's proved reserves came to exceed 1 trillion cubic feet equivalent.

worked with Wilson in the Hugoton days, and Steve Herod, who had joined Wilson and Stoneburner at 3Tec from Middle Bay.

Wilson rolled the $60 million into a controlling interest in micro-cap, Tulsa-based Beta Oil & Gas Inc., again accessing public-capital markets without an IPO. The tiny Beta's second-half 2003 drilling budget was a mere $4 million for 7.3 net wells; its production, about 7 million cubic feet equivalent a day.

When the deal closed in May 2004, the newly named Petrohawk Energy Corp. held some 33 billion cubic feet of gas equivalent in conventional fields in Oklahoma, Kansas and South Louisiana.

It was a platform for grander plans.

With the acquire-and-exploit model, Petrohawk bought into proven, oil- and gas-producing formations mostly within a five-state area: New Mexico, Oklahoma, Kansas, Louisiana and Texas. Stoneburner says, "And a little bit in the shallow Gulf if we could make a play out there. We'd sell anything else that we bought that wasn't in that geographical area—unless it was just great."

Wilson, now chairman and chief executive of his newest start-up, Halcon Resources Corp., says, "I use the 80/20 rule—always." That is, 20% of the assets make 80% of the money, thus Petrohawk's chameleon property set.

But, he adds, "the shales changed this old rule of thumb."

He had sold that small interest in the Barnett before closing the Beta deal. In mid-2004, the extension of Mitchell's core Barnett play was still one for explorers; it had not yet matured into a low-risk play suitable for an acquire/exploit E&P model.

Stoneburner says, "It was astute to sell it because you could see it wasn't a repeatable play at that time; the completion technology wasn't there yet." A year later, still, "nothing was repeatable. I mean, look at Southwestern's early efforts in the Fayetteville. Early on, it just wasn't working very well.

"So we flipped it, sold it to a company out of Denver pretty quickly. We were in and out of there quick; the technology wasn't there yet."

Three years later, by mid-2007, Petrohawk had amassed 1 trillion cubic feet equivalent of proved reserves. Oil and gas prices had climbed all the while. The company had entered the three- to five-year window for selling a build-and-flip start-up like 3Tec had been.

But, by way of one of its acquisitions, Petrohawk found itself in the Fayetteville shale—and the play was working by now. Sell or go shale? Wilson chose shale. The next day, Stoneburner was on a plane to Denver. There, he would discover a new play for Petrohawk.

With a bachelor's in geological sciences from the University of Texas at Austin, Stoneburner had gone to work in 1977 for Texas Oil & Gas Corp. in Wichita. He took leave for a couple years to complete his master's in geology at Wichita State University.

"I went back to Texas Oil for about a month in the summer of '79, but one of the senior geologists there had gone to work for Floyd. He recruited me to the company; at the time, it was called Kansas Oil Corp." Stoneburner worked with Wilson until 1985 when Wilson sold Kansas Oil.

"It was a very, very unfortunate time to be without a job in the oil business," Stoneburner says. "If there was one period of time when you didn't want to be out on the street looking for a job, it was then: The price of oil by January of 1986 was about $10 and it was a prolonged downturn—the toughest one in my career."

Stoneburner created some work for himself. Briefly, he and Wilson formed a small E&P. "It was kind of stupid on our part. We had some prospects I had generated. We got a couple of wells drilled and made some money, but there weren't enough of them.

"And we didn't have enough capital. We just had our own money and we had very little of it. Well, Floyd had some, but I didn't.

"It lasted about eight months."

Stoneburner started "just doing whatever I could to make a living—consulting work, well-site work, generating prospects. I ended up starting my own company, Stoneburner Exploration Inc., in 1990 and did that until '96. That whole time, I went without a paycheck—from '86 to '96. I got fees. Some of those years were really, really good, with overrides and whatnot, but there was nothing consistent about it."

Mrs. Stoneburner took a job hanging wallpaper. "She calls it our 'peanut butter and jelly days.' You had to really adjust. I was doing whatever I could to make ends meet. I was fortunate enough to have been able to make it through."

In 1996, Wilson called Stoneburner. His latest E&P, Hugoton Energy, had purchased some Austin-chalk properties in southeastern Texas. "And he didn't know anything about the chalk. Nobody in his company knew anything about the chalk and I had actually done quite a bit of chalk work."

Stoneburner had become familiar with the play while doing some consulting work in the late 1980s for Weber Energy Corp., which Ben Weber had founded in Dallas in 1983. Weber had been working on shallow oil in the area that would become the Giddings oil field.

At the time, Sun Oil Co. was targeting the naturally fractured chalk in Frio County with horizontal wellbores. In the play, a lateral would be drilled against the grain of the natural fractures, exposing the wellbore to more, natural pay. The wells produced from the natural fractures; thus, they weren't also fracture-stimulated.

"But it was very, very hush," Stoneburner recalls. "They were completing wells, but nobody knew anything more about it. They were re-entering old, vertical wells, milling a hole in the casing, drilling a 500-foot lateral and hoping to cut a couple of fractures."

Stoneburner suggested to Weber that he try some verticals in Pearsall Field. This met with success, despite that hitting a vertical fracture with a vertical wellbore requires making the hole in the most perfect place. Weber then tried some horizontals and hit more of the fractures. "If you drill the lateral long enough, you're bound to run into something," Stoneburner notes.

The deeper Buda formation in South Texas is similar: naturally fractured but hit or miss when making just verticals. One Buda well Stoneburner participated in was highly successful, contributing to the overrides that were keeping the lights on at home. "It was phenomenal; it was all fractured. You just had to find these fractures."

The yet-deeper Georgetown formation in Grimes and Washington counties was like this as well. "All of these Cretaceous carbonates—Georgetown, Buda, Austin chalk—were the same in terms of their reservoir make-up, which is zero (oil and gas) storage capacity; it has no primary porosity. But, when you found a fracture, you had infinite storage capacity—and I'm using that a little bit loosely—and almost infinite permeability (in those cracks).

"I mean, you have Darcy permeability in these fractures. You don't stimulate them; you just stand back and start flowing them."[182]

But, again, it's hit or miss. "A lot of people would run from the chalk. I would run from the chalk right now. It was one of those incredibly sexy but extremely, fiscally dangerous plays because you didn't really have the ability to predict these fractures. It was just a wing and a prayer to some degree that you would find the fractures."

The chalk produced very well in Giddings Field, in particular, which had faults that could be spotted with 3-D seismic. Otherwise, "the people who succeeded in the chalk were the exception. People who went at the chalk thinking they were going to hit a home run? Six or seven out of 10 walked away and said, 'What was I thinking?'

"The wells were expensive and their success was random. You just got heartbroken so many times when you thought you had a good place to drill and it turned out to suck.

"But we did learn a lot."

That was about horizontal-drilling technology—geo-steering, in particular. "Most people, early on, thought, 'The chalk's 400 feet thick and has all these fractures; it doesn't matter where you are in these 400 feet as long as you cross a fracture.' But that wasn't the case. The fractures were limited to specific members of the chalk and some of them are quite thin.

"You really had to be very careful about staying in zone."

As oil and gas wells are being drilled, samples—called cuttings—of the rock through which the drillbit is traveling are collected foot by foot and examined at the wellsite by a geologist to determine what kind of rock the bit is in.

---

[182] One Darcy is 1,000 millidarcies; in contrast, the Barnett shale, for example, has permeability of less than one millidarcy.

"You're out there catching samples and that's your best tool to see where you are. We didn't have gamma-ray technology at the time and we certainly didn't have a 3-D seismic grid to help us steer these wells. It was very low-tech stuff, but we learned a lot."[183]

Getting the call in 1996, Stoneburner rejoined Wilson to help with the chalk play and amassed 61,000 net acres over the rock by the time Wilson sold Hugoton Energy to Chesapeake. Stoneburner continued with Wilson into 3Tec Energy and then into Petrohawk.

***

By 2006, among Petrohawk's many acquisitions in just its first couple of years was an entry into the Elm Grove and Caspiana tight-gas fields that produced from the Cotton Valley and Hosston formations in northwestern Louisiana. From Shreveport-based Winwell Resources Inc. and Redley Co., Wilson had gained 106 billion cubic feet of proved reserves in the area for $294 million.

A few days after closing, he was talking to Jim Christmas, chairman and chief executive of KCS Energy Inc. It and Winwell had held the two largest positions in Elm Grove Field. Some six months later, Christmas sold KCS to Petrohawk to merge their positions in northwestern Louisiana for $1.9 billion in cash and stock. Petrohawk picked up an additional 463 billion of proved reserves.

"Floyd courted the heck out of Jim Christmas," Stoneburner says. "We did that deal because of that overlay of assets."

Elm Grove and KCS' position in nearby Caspiana Field represented some 40% of Petrohawk's reserves and 40% of production. Wilson saw them as an anchor property and massive cash cow for Petrohawk. The company went to work on new vertical wells in both the Cotton Valley and overlying Hosston zones and recompleting some old wells to bring Hosston gas up from those as well.

---

[183] Meanwhile, lessons in fracing shale weren't learned in the naturally fractured chalk; the wells weren't fraced with the purpose of inducing fractures, Stoneburner says. Instead, to prod more oil from partially depleted chalk wells, water would be pumped in at high rates in a method known as "dentritic fracturing" in which the water displaces additional oil.

Beneath these lay the Haynesville shale; it was the source rock.

Wilson says, "The Haynesville play had not developed yet. This was in 2006. No one knew of a Haynesville play yet."

Instead, Petrohawk aimed to deploy new technology in the two fields in which fewer than 400 wells had been drilled. Down-spacing to 40 acres meant room for more than 1,000 wells; if at 20-acre spacing, then 2,500.

He and Stoneburner had already had plenty of Cotton Valley experience, having built 3Tec on the Texas side of the rock. "All vertical but very repeatable," Stoneburner says. "Now, in 2006, all of a sudden you had the ability to down-space these Cotton Valley fields. And, while you encountered some interference (with production from neighboring wells), they were large enough that you could repeat yourself time after time and have consistent results.

"That was our experience—a tight-gas, repeatable play, which is what you wanted. Something like the Cotton Valley."

KCS also happened to have 15,000 net acres in Arkansas over the Fayetteville shale and had made a couple of vertical wells and a horizontal in it. It had come to own the lease because one mineral-rights owner, Joe Whisenhunt, had wanted a 40% royalty instead of the traditional 12.5%, forfeiting the cash-per-acre, upfront payment instead. Southwestern Energy had passed on the deal.

Whisenhunt called KCS, which wasn't looking to lease; it took the offer. In the arrangement, KCS would pay 100% of the cost; the mineral-rights owner would get 40% of the gross income.

"It's pretty hard to make anything work like that," Stoneburner says. "But it did work. That's how good the wells were: They could overcome a 40% royalty."

Petrohawk assumed drilling the lease. The wells were proving they could ultimately make 5 billion cubic feet apiece. The acreage, in Van Buren County, turned out to be in the sweet spot of the play.

Steve Herod, executive vice president, corporate development, added more to the holding, taking it to 43,500 net acres by June 2007.

The Fayetteville and Barnett were working economically now—and repeatably.[184]

Floyd Wilson had seen enough. He and the Petrohawk board decided to transform the acquire-and-exploit company's focus to resource plays. He announced it to shareholders on June 25, 2007.

Southwestern Energy's stock price had gained 480% since revealing its Fayetteville play in August 2004. Petrohawk's shares had only gained 98% in that time. This would have been a remarkable gain for an E&P—or any stock—in just 34 months. But the big returns were now in the shales—and they were history-making returns.

Herod says, "In a shale play, you might have 400 to 600 locations to drill—all the drilling you want for the next however-many years. In the conventional stuff, it's hard. You're drilling these amplitudes (as suggested by seismic study) in South Texas or wherever.

"You drill wells that are not all good. And it seems like you're always six months away from running out of inventory—more locations to drill. You're on such a treadmill for opportunities."

Stoneburner says, "You're just bouncing around the Gulf Coast, looking for amplitudes and they eventually run out. Actually, they have, basically, run out."

Herod, Wilson and Stoneburner had talked about getting into the shale plays for a while. Herod says, "It was just back and forth. It wasn't any movie type of moment where we all got together and had a revelation. It was more of a 'We're looking at this, looking at that. Let's think about it. Let's run some numbers.'"

The numbers checked out; the three concurred that it was time to make a decision: Shale or no shale?

Shale.

"That's something about Floyd," Herod says. "When it's time to make a decision, we make it. A big company would have taken four

---

[184] Petrohawk had also participated in some of Newfield Exploration's early Woodford-shale exploratory wells in Oklahoma where Beta Oil & Gas had some property. Stoneburner says, "The only reason we did that was because they brought us along for 35 cents on the dollar. We got some pretty cheap learning off that. What we learned was that it was still very early and challenging."

years to study whether they should get into shale plays. And, by the time they would make a decision, it was over.

"Floyd says, 'All the money's made before noon.'"

The Petrohawk team had a new missive: Build value from the Fayetteville exposure and find another shale play. Stoneburner calls the Winwell deal in northwestern Louisiana in early 2006 a seminal moment in Petrohawk's history.

"Nobody would think that, if they just saw the list of deals we made over the years. If we hadn't done that Winwell deal, we would not have done KCS. We probably would not have been in that shale pipeline by the time Haynesville rolled around. It was that one, little, $262-million acquisition that Floyd wasn't going to let get away.

"He knew we needed it."

Wilson had changed gears before. In 1993, he took Hugoton Energy beyond the low-risk Hugoton Basin into higher-risk exploration in the Williston and Permian basins and, with Stoneburner coming onboard, into the Austin chalk.

The day Wilson announced Petrohawk was going shale, the company joined a Core Laboratories shale-gas consortium. In these, participating companies view each other's rock data in plays of interest to each. Meetings were held twice a year. Stoneburner had signed Petrohawk up for it the day before registration was cut off.

The next morning, he was on a plane to Denver.

There, Randy Miller, a Core Lab vice president, presented an Encana Corp. well, J.W. Adcock Investments 1; it flowed up to 4 million cubic feet of gas a day. The vertical had been spud on Feb. 27, 2006, in Martin Field in Red River Parish and drilled to 12,878 feet. Encana had labeled the rock from which it produced as Jurassic-age "shale."

The well—one of three vertical tests Encana conducted in the shale in 2005 and 2006—had been drilled just southeast from Petrohawk's position in Elm Grove and Caspiana fields.[185]

Stoneburner and some fellow Petrohawk staff were sitting in the

---

[185] J.W. Adcock Investments 1 was not produced into sales; casing had collapsed uphole.

auditorium for the one-day-only meeting with about 180 other geologists and engineers, representing some 50 companies. Core Lab staff would present details of the rock of interest that was encountered in each of the wells that member companies had contributed. Without opining, they would simply state the findings of their analyses.

Separately, a core sample from the Encana well was there for consortium members to inspect. From the sample, it was clear it was shale. Mike Conway, president of Core Lab's Stim-Lab division and a renowned reservoir engineer, had analyzed the data.

Stoneburner recalls thinking, "This is an unbelievable reservoir. They got this (4 million cubic feet of gas a day) vertically. Imagine what it will do horizontally. It had an impressive—short-term but high-rate—flow test just vertically.

"I'm thinking, 'And that's just right down the street from our Elm Grove assets.' We had 50,000 acres in the neighborhood; we were right in the middle of it."

Back in the Houston office the next day, Stoneburner had staff start pulling logs of northwestern Louisiana wells that had penetrated Haynesville shale. KCS had once drilled in the area to 15,000 feet. With this, Stoneburner had a look at the entire stratigraphic column.

"We joined this consortium at the last hour. If we had joined one day later, we might not have become the Haynesville player that we became. We wouldn't have had that core data and as timely as we had it. We were a full year ahead of when the play blossomed. We had the ability to study it and become convinced of it instead of following a leader."

It also explained—if only to Petrohawk—why Chesapeake seemed to be stepping up its activity in the area. Like Petrohawk, Chesapeake already had acreage in the area by virtue of acquisitions.

In 2004, it had entered northwestern Louisiana with the purchase of 16,100 gross, contiguous acres in Sligo Field just west of Elm Grove for $425 million from privately held Greystone Petroleum LLC. The field, discovered in 1938, had produced some 1.6 trillion cubic feet of gas from along the stratigraphic column from Rodessa at about 4,100 feet to Cotton Valley at about 9,600 feet.

In 2007, suddenly, "Chesapeake was out there buying stuff that people couldn't understand," Herod says.

"'Why in the world are you paying that?' They bought a small deal in Caddo Parish from Rising Star (Energy LLC) that we looked at. It was a crummy, crummy asset. Chesapeake just blew it out of the water. They paid up for it."

Looking at the Encana core sample, Petrohawk now knew that Chesapeake knew about the Haynesville.

On Sept. 27, 2007, Chesapeake spud a horizontal, Bray 27-15-16H, in Bethany-Longstreet Field in Caddo Parish; it shut it in to tight-hole the details.[186] On Oct. 12, 2007, it spud a second horizontal, Feist 28-15-15H, and completed it Jan. 11, 2008.

Both had laterals of more than 4,000 feet. It was the first horizontal completed in Haynesville. It came on with 2.65 million cubic feet a day.[187] The pressure gradient in the Haynesville was 0.9; the temperature, up to 340 degrees Fahrenheit.

"None of the plays up to that point were in that realm of pressure, temperature and gas in place," Stoneburner says. "You're drilling through a relatively high-perm, shale reservoir with a 0.9 gradient at 11,000 feet and another 4,000 feet horizontally."[188]

Having mapped the shale based on old well logs, Petrohawk could determine the rock's nature in DeSoto, Bossier and Caddo parishes. "You know it's all going to work because you have enough subsurface control in these core areas," Stoneburner says.

Faults are rare in the Haynesville, unlike in the Barnett, thus suggesting there wouldn't be large areas of fail zones. "There weren't many geo-hazards. We had enough geophysical and subsurface support to feel confident that we weren't going to be surprised very much. And we weren't. It proved to be an accurate assumption."

---

[186] The well wasn't completed until June 14, 2008.

[187] The well's production peaked with 4.7 million a day in April 2008. Encana's first Haynesville horizontal, J.W. Adcock Investments 3-Alt, was spud earlier—on Oct. 9, 2007—but it was completed on Feb. 2, 2008—three weeks after the Chesapeake discovery well. It came on with 3.2 million.

[188] The Barnett and Fayetteville are at less than 7,000 feet.

If on 80-acre spacing, a well would make 8- or 10 billion cubic feet of gas. Based on this, Petrohawk could rationalize paying as much as $25,000 an acre for leasehold. "So $25,000 an acre times 80 acres, that's $2 million a well. Then, with your costs for drilling, completing and producing the wells, you're at $9 million. If an 8-Bcf well, you're still going to make a ton of money."[189]

And, in early 2008, gas was heading to $14.[190]

***

A land rush began. Running acquisitions and divestments—including leasing—fell to Herod, who was at Middle Bay when Wilson bought it and turned it into 3Tec. With a bachelor's in finance from Oklahoma State University, the Tulsa native had gone to work as a financial analyst at Superior Oil Co. in 1981. In the 1990s, he was president of small, privately held Shore Oil Co.

Middle Bay, which had been formed in 1992, had rolled up several small E&Ps, lastly of Shore Oil in 1997, taking in producing properties in Alabama, Mississippi, Louisiana and Texas. After the Shore deal, Herod stayed on with Middle Bay, leading property purchases and sales for it. In early 1999, though, oil was about $10 and gas was less than $2. Middle Bay was running out of money. Wilson saw it as the vehicle for taking his new 3Tec public.

When the merger was closed, Herod didn't know if he still had a job. "I wasn't counting on anything; I just kept working hard every day," he says.

That fall, 3Tec bought properties in Texas and Louisiana for $87 million in cash and 1.5 million shares. Oil had improved to about $26; gas, to about $3. 3Tec had a bank line of credit of $250 million.

---

[189] An 8-Bcf well at $5 natural gas would gross $40 million in its lifetime; with giving up even as much as 25% royalty to the mineral-rights owner, the operator would still gross $30 million.

[190] Natural gas had pushed past $15 in December 2005 and fallen back to the $7s as supply re-emerged from the Gulf of Mexico after hurricanes Katrina and Rita and as new gas supply was coming online from the Barnett and Fayetteville.

"I got involved with some of the work on that deal and I guess I did okay because, around Thanksgiving or so in 1999, Floyd came to me and said, 'We're going to do a public stock offering and we're going to name you CFO.'"

A few months later, Al Walker joined 3Tec as chief financial officer. Wilson needed Herod to run M&A for the company, which now had new access to more capital to fund deals. When Wilson sold 3Tec, Herod continued on with him to Petrohawk.[191]

In 2008, his job became one that he had never experienced before. In the past, he evaluated producing properties for purchase or sale for their upside potential from further drilling, recompletions and other prodding. The math involved existing production and proved reserves.

"To switch into the shale plays, you're buying acreage without any production. There's no reserve engineering; there are no proved reserves. The analysis of the production doesn't take very long because there isn't any.

"You may have a few type-curves for the area. You only *think* you know what wells will make; you only *think* you know what they're going to cost. It's much more subjective, what the economics are going to be."

First things first, though, bringing in acreage with existing production from Cotton Valley and other formations above Haynesville was an obvious way to add to Petrohawk's Haynesville potential. In January 2008, Herod won 83 billion cubic feet of proved reserves in a bolt-on Elm Grove Field deal from a private seller for $169 million, taking in another 3,000 net acres in the area. It now had interest in more than 150 square miles—that is, 150 sections—in the field.

The purchase didn't seem unusual to the market; Petrohawk was already in the field and it had just made a horizontal in the Cotton Valley there that came on with 16.5 million a day.

Wilson had sold the company's Gulf Coast division and, with it,

---

[191] Al Walker joined Anadarko Petroleum Corp. in 2005 and was chairman, president and chief executive in 2014.

204 billion of proved reserves for $825 million a couple of months earlier—after announcing its new focus on resource plays. Herod had picked up another 42,500 net Fayetteville acres, including 110 billion cubic feet of proved reserves, for $565.5 million from Alta Resources LLC, Contango Oil & Gas Co. and Aspect Energy LLC.

Petrohawk's position there was now 150,000 net acres. And there were rumors now of a Haynesville play. On Nov. 7, 2007, small-cap GMX Resources Inc. had mentioned in quarterly results that its Cotton Valley acreage in East Texas contained Bossier/Haynesville "gas shales." It didn't mention plans to drill it.

A week earlier, in an earnings call, Cabot Oil & Gas Corp. mentioned that it was looking at the entire stratigraphic column down to Haynesville at about 12,000 feet in its Trawick gas field in East Texas. That the Haynesville is a shale wasn't mentioned and no one asked about it. In an earnings call on Feb. 14, 2008, there was one question about Haynesville for which Cabot had no news.[192]

On Jan. 30, 2008, Exco Resources Inc. mentioned to securities analysts that it was evaluating deeper rock—Bossier, Haynesville and Smackover—in its Vernon Field position in northwestern Louisiana.

On Feb. 12, in a quarterly filing, micro-cap Cubic Energy Inc. reported it had drilled the vertical Hudson 10-1 in Caddo Parish to 11,650 feet, showing "an 1,100-foot interval of shale gas."

Later that morning, securities analyst Kim Pacanovsky was dialed into the Comstock Resources Inc. earnings call when the cell-signal failed. Upon redialing and her turn to ask a question, she said, "I don't know if you talked about the Bossier shale, but can you mention…what you found on your properties—maybe what the thicknesses are in your area versus north of you?[193]

---

[192] Questions were primarily about Cabot's upside exposure, via its existing Appalachian acreage, to the new Marcellus play, which Range had announced in late 2007 with its high-test-rate horizontals.

[193] Bossier and Haynesville were used interchangeably when the play first developed; the state deemed the Chesapeake discovery well as being completed in Haynesville, however. The overlying Bossier formation produces gas as well but its presence is less pervasive in the area.

"I know Chesapeake has done some drilling."

It hadn't been asked and it hadn't been discussed. Chairman, president and chief executive Jay Allison replied, "Good question." Mack Good, vice president of operations, confirmed that Chesapeake was drilling "Bossier shale" north of Comstock's acreage.

"We're also familiar with some other drilling activity to the south," he said. "There's been mixed results reported and so, as with any shale play, you better be careful…The shale plays require horizontal drilling to be successful. That's been shown in every shale play. The Bossier will be no exception…So we're in the process of doing the homework; we have an excellent lease position and we're evaluating the Bossier."

Allison confirmed Comstock did drill a Bossier test, deepening an existing well some 2,000 feet, but the results were not yet in. Other operators' Bossier wells about 10 miles south weren't good. "There was no reported production," Good said. "Wells were drilled through the Bossier and the logs were run and cores were taken and no gas rates reported…That's always a bad sign."

At the time, Petrohawk was already leasing for Haynesville in northwestern Louisiana; Steve Herod knew Chesapeake was as well. Its and Encana's new, horizontal-well results were not released yet in state records, but "there were a lot of rumors," Herod says.

"We'd heard—and some of this was 'Dairy Queen talk' in Shreveport—that Chesapeake had drilled a couple of pretty good wells and Encana had drilled a couple of pretty good wells. The cost was real high, though. That scared a lot of people off."

Petrohawk went ahead and pushed Chesapeake's button, looking to force its hand. On March 12, in an analyst-day presentation in New York, Stoneburner turned to slide 20. A Northrop Grumman B-2 Spirit jet, aka a "Stealth Bomber," appeared on the screen and there was a booming noise.

The slide stated, "New North Louisiana resource play. Organic-rich shale between Bossier and Smackover. Ranges in depth between 10,500-13,000 feet. Highly over-pressured in southern area of play. Elm Grove area only marginally over-pressured. Over 200 feet thick underlying Elm Grove. Encana J.W. Adcock core indicates favorable geochemical and petrophysical characteristics."

Herod says, "It got a big reaction. Floyd knew it would get (Aubrey) McClendon's ego that we had announced it ahead of him and that it would smoke him out.

"He'd have to say something about it. We really weren't sure how their wells were doing.

"Sure enough, two weeks later, Chesapeake came out and announced the discovery well, the Haynesville as their play and that it could be the biggest gas field in the country. So that sort of confirmed for us that they must be doing okay, which helped give us more conviction on our acreage-buying program."

In that announcement, on March 24, Chesapeake reported that it had been studying the Haynesville for two years and had drilled three horizontals and four verticals. "...Chesapeake believes the Haynesville shale play could potentially have a larger impact on the company than any other play in which it has participated to date."

By then, Chesapeake was already in the Barnett, Woodford, Fayetteville and Marcellus.[194]

And, now, McClendon looked to smoke Petrohawk out. He reported that Chesapeake already had four rigs at work on the Haynesville and planned to have 10 working on it by year-end. It held or had commitments for more than 200,000 net acres and its leasing effort's goal was to own up to 500,000. It was increasing its company-wide budget for leasing and drilling to $675 million.

Who could go stronger for longer?

Herod says, "That's when the great land rush got going. It was toward the end of March. Prices (per acre) started going up $1,000 or more a week."

Until then, there had been fewer than 50 references to Haynesville shale—and usually in reference to the underlying Smackover

---

[194] After Southwestern announced its Fayetteville discovery in 2004, Newfield Exploration revealed a third shale play, the Woodford in Oklahoma, within a smaller areal extent. Its first Woodford horizontal, Blevins 3H-9, came on on March 3, 2005, with 1.8 million cubic feet from a 1,500-foot lateral.

formation—in SEC filings in at least the prior 14 years. In the next 10 weeks, there were 140 mentions.

Any existing acreage-holder in the area had Haynesville. Anyone wanting more acreage would have to go up against Chesapeake and Petrohawk. Several, such as Encana and Royal Dutch Shell, whose existing acreage was held by production from shallower formations, didn't participate.

Stoneburner says, "Encana and Shell had plenty of capability of being aggressive and adding to their lease position. But they had big, legacy positions to begin with."

Who was in the leasing race came down to Chesapeake and Petrohawk. These six months would be the hardest Herod had ever worked. The pace was frenetic.

"From March through about August, it was really intense, really complicated," he says. "It was the most fun I ever had. We'd be working 15 deals of varying sizes at the same time. At one point, we had 300 lease brokers working for us, trying to pick up acreage.

"I worked, it seemed, almost around the clock. I had all of these maps laid out in my office. It was a sort of jigsaw puzzle. If you got Deal A, then you wanted Deal B because they fit together. But, if you didn't get A, you didn't want B and you had to try to keep them alive long enough to have both of them happen.

"It was complicated."

Petrohawk used eight brokerage firms, which provide title-search and on-the-ground negotiators. "Chesapeake had a reputation for hiring brokers who weren't exactly qualified. We would joke that some of their landmen had been working at Best Buy or Subway a week before. They'd put them out there and turn them into landmen."

Herod would visit Shreveport in the center of the play weekly to meet with the brokers and help close deals one-on-one. The buzz was palpable. "Everywhere I went, all the discussion was about the Haynesville. Every office I walked into, the receptionist would be talking to somebody about, 'Oh, yeah. My aunt's got 20 acres over here and she's talking to so and so.'

"You could feel it, the energy around it."

The city, with a population of about 200,000, was founded in 1836 at the intersection of the Red River and a cattle trail. Top employers were government, healthcare providers and casino operator Caesars Entertainment Corp.

"It was the lead story on the television and in the newspaper all the time. And there was this GoHaynesvilleShale.com website that became the conduit for lease owners' information. People would share. They'd say, 'Oh, wow. Chesapeake just offered me $15,000 an acre for my land, 16 North, 11 West.'

"So everybody knew what the market was. It was amazing."

Petrohawk won many; Chesapeake won many. "We were working hard with a guy with a furniture store, an older guy. He would come off as not sophisticated, but he was. He had a background in finance, I think. Sometime that summer, we had a deal worked out. I was going to Shreveport. He said he was ready to go with us.

"I called him again, while I was on my way. He said, 'Well, you can come on over, but I've got bad news for you. I committed to Chesapeake yesterday.' I said, 'How did that happen?'

"He said, 'Well, they sent their plane down here, picked me up, took me to Oklahoma City and sat me down with Aubrey. Anyway, I signed up with them.' There was plenty of that that went on."

Herod went to the store anyway. If the check wasn't already signed and deposited, the deal was not yet legally binding. The man had a modest office in the back, next to a warehouse.

"He had this acreage. He also owned three or four drilling rigs. Part of the deal he made with Chesapeake was that they were going to buy those rigs. I was trying to convince him that he made a mistake. He had pictures of the rigs."

Besides producing oil and gas, Chesapeake had integrated its business over the years to also own and operate rigs, frac equipment and other service operations, particularly as the shale plays took off. Like most E&Ps, Petrohawk didn't operate outside of producing oil and gas.

"I called Dick (Stoneburner). He said, 'Well, what do you think of the rigs?' I said, 'I'm looking at a picture. They look pretty *shiny*.

"'I don't know if they're any good, but the paint looks great.'"

Chesapeake paid $80- or $100 million, Herod recalls. "It was in late July, right ahead of when everything started going the other way. He got his money and there were tons of stories like this. Several billion dollars of lease-bonus money went into North Louisiana in five months."

Petrohawk alone paid $2 billion. "It was pretty amazing."

Stoneburner says, "We went toe to toe with Chesapeake from March to August, just a six-month period. But it was an incredible period to be involved in a play like that with Floyd and Aubrey going *mano y mano* to see who could end up with the best position.

"Every day, we were making multi-million-dollar decisions on taking leases for $10,000, $15,000, $20,000 and, then, $25,000 an acre. It was crazy, but it worked. I mean, it worked for us. I think it worked for them. It's hard to say.

"In the long run, it will. It certainly worked for us."

In early August 2008, Petrohawk reported its Elm Grove Plantation 63H in Bossier Parish came on with 16.8 million cubic feet of gas a day and averaged 13.7 million a day in its first 30 days online with casing pressure of some 5,100 psi on a 20/64-inch choke. Analysis of the rock indicated 1.26 million cubic feet of gas in place per acre-foot—the equivalent of 170 billion cubic feet per square mile.

A test in Caddo Parish, Hutchinson 9-5H, came on with 16.7 million cubic feet after nine frac stages. Soon after, its Elm Grove Plantation 64H came on with 15.7 million from a 4,100-foot, 12-frac-stage lateral. It was only its fourth Haynesville horizontal and the fourth of four to come on with more than 15 million.

By year-end, its 10 operated horizontals had IPs averaging 19.3 million cubic feet a day. By it and others, there would be thousands more of these. Floyd Wilson says of pre-emptively launching the Haynesville story in early 2008, "We weren't the first to drill a Haynesville well; we were the first to drill a headline, economic, horizontal, stage-fractured Haynesville well and release the information. We knew from our R&D and our mapping that the footprint of the Haynesville was extensive."

It had grown its land position in the play to 300,000 net acres—some 10 times the size of its pre-existing leasehold. Wilson was confident in the spend. "I think we spent $1 billion before we ever spud a well and $2 billion before we produced an Mcf of Haynesville gas. But we were comfortable with the research and, by this time, others were doing some drilling in the region. All of their results that we were able to find were consistent with our research."

Herod says, "We bet the company. We were 'all in.' People would say, 'Gosh, how could you take that much risk? How did you know?' The reason is that we didn't think it was that risky. Dick and his team had done their technical work. We all felt good about it.

"And this is what makes Floyd 'Floyd.' That's how you make real money. If all you're doing is buying in somewhere after it's already drilled up, where's the big upside? The vision is being able to go into a place ahead of everybody. That's where you really do well.

"Being in the Fayetteville helped us. We learned a lot in the Fayetteville. It convinced us that we could do it in the Haynesville.

"These completions and these fracs had been figured out in the Barnett and the Fayetteville. All of this was transferrable from play to play. They're all different in some way.

"But there was no reason why it wouldn't work."

***

Some mineral-rights owners held out too long, though.

"Some people--. Well, the greed got to them," Herod says. "When the leasing started, say in February, a lease in that part of the state was $300 an acre, which was a pretty good price (to get) in any other play that only had a few wells yet. Then, deals in April or May were at $5,000 an acre, which was an incredible number. Then, we saw it go to $20,000.

"Some people who had signed at $300 or $4,000 were thinking, 'God, we should have held out.'"

Gas was $12. Oil was heading to $150. Capital markets were wide open to oil and gas producers; stock prices were soaring. "It was this convergence of rising commodity prices, open capital markets and an incredibly fierce competition between Chesapeake and us."

Some offers included royalty of as much as 25%.

"It was a perfect storm where acreage can go from $300 to as much as $30,000 in six or seven months—and without a single well producing from the Haynesville already on or around that lease. That has never been seen before in the industry and probably will never be seen again. I mean, it was like an Oklahoma land rush."[195]

In July, however, natural-gas prices began to decline; oil prices did too. The days of $25,000 an acre were over. Petrohawk topped off at about there; it paid a bit more for some most-choice land.

"There were people in July and August who were turning down $25,000 because they wanted $30,000," Herod says. "The bottom started to fall out in August. Oil and gas prices were coming down. And then, after Lehman (Brothers' bankruptcy-protection filing) and all of what happened in September, it basically went to zero.

"It just stopped. There were people who thought they were going to get $30,000 and ended up with zero. They should have taken it. I would tell people that. They would say, 'Well, we're gonna pass.' Or whatever. I would say, 'You have a really good offer here.'

"These were individuals. These weren't Fortune 500 companies. These were families."

Herod would tell them, "You know, this is $40 million, $16 million, $20 million. You should be in my office tomorrow morning with a pen in your hand, asking, 'Where do I sign?' I would hear, 'Oh, we're gonna wait. We know it's a lot you're offering, but we're gonna keep going.'

"It's like any boom; it has an end."

---

[195] To populate central Oklahoma, the U.S. deeded land to settlers who, totaling an estimated 50,000 men and women, rushed in via foot, horse or wagon at an appointed time on April 22, 1889, to claim a 160-acre section. Oklahoma City was founded that day.

BAKKEN: 2008

← ← ← ← ← → → → → →

"It extended the play another 50 miles or so
into western North Dakota."
—Bud Brigham

In the Bakken, for Brigham Exploration and many others, it all came crashing down in September 2008 as well. The play was still nascent and money dried up. Entering 2008 in the Williston Basin, the east-of-Nesson code was clearly cracked. But Brigham Exploration didn't have a 1,000-barrel-plus well of its own yet.

In May 2008, it did: In Mountrail County, Brigham put 12 frac stages on its Carkuff 22-1H; it came on with 1,042 barrels and 1.15 million cubic feet of gas.

Bud Brigham reported to shareholders, "By increasing the number of stimulated intervals, we've seen substantially higher, early-production performance from our horizontal Bakken wells."

Halliburton, which had co-founded the new Bakken play with Lyco Energy's first, fraced horizontal in Montana in 2000, mentioned Bakken now—a first time in its SEC filings. It had set its 900th "Swellpacker" system. It reported, "The use of this packer system has allowed operators to compartmentalize their wellbores for fracture completions, resulting in improved production. 'Delta Stim' sleeves are also used with the 'Swellpacker' systems, greatly reducing the time required to complete a well."

Meanwhile, Brigham and others were still trying to make big Bakken wells west of the Nesson anticline. Investors weren't giving leasehold there much value; wells were just ordinary. At investment symposia from New York to Houston, the company was incessantly questioned about the acreage: Can "west of the Nesson" work? The middle Bakken there was even tighter than east of the Nesson where the rock had some natural fracturing.

"We were optimistic that we would figure it out," Brigham says. "It became apparent to us that the swell packers and the multi-stage, frac stimulations were likely to be a game changer."

In early 2008, west of Nesson, Brigham quietly re-entered its Mrachek 15-22 1H in McKenzie County; the well had come on in 2006 with an IP of only 80 barrels from a roughly 5,000-foot lateral. Taking from its 12-stage, Carkuff, east-of-Nesson lesson, the company put in seven frac stages, using swell packers; the well came back on on May 15, 2008, with 565 barrels.

"It was the first multi-stage well west of Nesson," he says. "We pulled everybody together within hours of it flowing back and said, 'We've got to shut that well in.' We were negotiating to buy another 40,000 acres out there."

The well was shut in. The completion report was sent to the state two months later. "We kept that well as tight as we could." It picked up the additional 40,000 acres for $100 an acre.

Now, Brigham had 93,000 net acres east of Nesson and 100,000 net west. In the western acreage, it planned to try two 10,000-foot-lateral wells near the Mrachek well—each with 20 frac stages. It picked up a second rig and expected to have five at work for it by year-end 2009.

Meanwhile, Continental was looking at making yet another Williston Basin oil play—the Three Forks layer underneath the lower-Bakken shale.[196] The four dolomitic benches of Three Forks are each

---

[196] Continental's test soon indicated that a lateral in the first Three Forks bench wasn't simply draining oil that would have been made from the middle Bakken above it. It was a whole new play.

separated at top and bottom by a shaley layer of rock. Each bench also has some porosity but low permeability.

Among all operators drilling for North Dakota Bakken now, 48 rigs were at work. All the while, Whiting Petroleum, Continental and other producers were giving data to the U.S. Geological Survey, which was gathering new information on Bakken from them as well as from the Montana and North Dakota geological surveys and other experts.

Its last assessment of the potential of the Bakken was in 1995 at the conclusion of Burlington's upper-shale play. Since then, by 2008, the fraced, middle-Bakken member had made 80.2 million barrels from the eight-year-old Elm Coulee Field in Montana. And the fraced, middle Bakken in North Dakota was making 1,000-barrel-plus wells east of Nesson.

Producers weren't supposed to be able to get this much oil out of the low-perm, low-porosity rock. But that was with old technology. In April 2008, the USGS issued a press release: "3 to 4.3 Billion Barrels of Technically Recoverable Oil Assessed in North Dakota and Montana's Bakken Formation—25 Times More Than 1995 Estimate."

The 1995 estimate had been just 151 million barrels.

It reported, "The Bakken-formation estimate is larger than all other current USGS oil assessments of the lower-48 states and is the largest 'continuous' oil accumulation ever assessed by the USGS. A 'continuous' oil accumulation means that the oil resource is dispersed throughout a geologic formation (stratigraphically) rather than existing as discrete, localized (structural) occurrences."

Two weeks later, the 16th annual Williston Basin Petroleum Conference in Minot, North Dakota, drew some 1,400 attendees. North Dakota's Department of Mineral Resources had also newly assessed the Bakken's potential. Lynn Helms, director, reported that, in the North Dakota portion of the Bakken, 2.1 billion barrels of oil could be produced using new technology. And, he added, this was only 1.4% of all the oil the state's geological survey believed the North Dakota Bakken contained.

Ed Murphy, state geologist, wrote in the department's newsletter of the two assessments, "The results of the (state) and USGS assessments come surprisingly close, given that they were done independent of each other, using somewhat different data and very different assessment techniques. I recalculated the USGS Bakken estimate based upon the segments of their assessment units that are within North Dakota and arrived at 2.6 billion barrels of oil.

"You could argue that 2.6- and 2.1 billion barrels are almost 20% apart, but we were relieved that the results were the same order of magnitude, given the number of educated assumptions that these assessments require.

"In addition, we were well aware that a 1995 USGS assessment of the Bakken (across the entire Williston Basin) concluded that it contained only 151 million barrels of producible oil. Of course, that assessment was completed at a time when horizontal drilling and fracturing techniques were not as advanced as they were in 2008."

He also noted the headlines the Williston Basin generated as a result of the USGS findings—"(more) than we have seen since the discovery of oil in the Clarence Iverson 1 in 1951, a distant second being the original horizontal play in the upper-Bakken shale during the early 1990s.

"Just the announcement on April 8, 2008, that the USGS Bakken assessment would be released later that week generated a number of front-page newspaper articles across the country. That led one (firm), specializing in investment opportunities in the energy sector, to lead with an editorial (at its website, titled) 'Less than 48 Hours Left to Get a Piece of the Bakken.'

"The rising price of crude oil, coupled with some exceptionally good Bakken wells in Mountrail County, already had a number of energy companies and investors looking at the Bakken. It appears that the results of these assessments spurred some of these people to act."

Stephan Nordeng, staff geologist for the North Dakota Geological Survey, noted separately that the state's last estimate of recoverable Bakken oil within its borders was 14 million barrels. He wrote, "Three years later, changing technology places the reserves at 2.089 billion barrels (in North Dakota)…

"Even though the Bakken itself has not changed, our ability to extract oil from it has so…our ideas concerning the future possibilities of this resource must as well."

Citing the USGS report, pipeline operator Enbridge Energy Partners LP reported that a further expansion to haul 161,000 barrels a day out of Bakken wells was proceeding. Until just a few months earlier, the pipe could only carry 30,000 barrels a day. All oil production from North Dakota was about 80,000 barrels a day in 2003; in 2008, it was already 172,000.

Soon, micro-cap Earthstone Energy noted that getting Bakken oil to market wasn't the only problem: Instead, there increasingly wasn't enough Midwest U.S. refining capacity at the end of the pipe to take all of this new oil. EOG Resources was arranging to haul its oil out by rail to the Gulf Coast.

XTO Energy jumped into the play, buying privately held, Dallas-based Headington Oil for $1.85 billion in cash and stock, gaining 352,000 net acres over Bakken in Montana and North Dakota. A few weeks later, it bought privately held, Dallas-based Hunt Petroleum Corp. for about $4.2 billion in stock and cash, gaining production and reserves throughout the U.S., including 15,000 net over Bakken in North Dakota. In other deals, it picked up another 100,000 net over Bakken for some $1,150 an acre.[197]

Hess Corp.—the successor to North Dakota oil discoverer Amerada Petroleum—now had some 500,000 net acres over Bakken in North Dakota and seven rigs running. Marathon Petroleum Corp. had seven rigs drilling for it.

With independent assessments of the Bakken's new potential, capital rushed into shares of Bakken players, increasing their ability to fund more drilling. In their first 12 months of trading by mid-May 2008, Continental's stock price had gained 265%.

Brigham's gained 184%.

Oil was $115 and heading to $150.

---

[197] XTO hedged the oil production from the Headington, Hunt and other deals at some $128 a barrel and the gas production at about $11 per million Btu through year-end 2010.

***

In 2008, by the morning of Sept. 15, operators had spud more than 650 wells in North Dakota in the modern Bakken play. Oil had now fallen from nearly $150 in July to about $95. Natural gas had declined from nearly $14 to about $7.40. Both were still profitable for most U.S. oil and gas producers. Also, many had hedged future production for up to three years at the July high.

Two mornings earlier, however, those headquartered in Houston and those with Gulf Coast or Gulf of Mexico assets had already entered a period of unthinkable circumstances. Hurricane Ike had made landfall near Galveston, traveling north along Interstate 45 into Houston and The Woodlands.

Darkness fell upon the roughly 80-mile corridor as power failed for more than 90% of Houston, primarily as a result of downed trees that had not been culled naturally by a significant windstorm in the area since the 1980s. Many areas would be dark for at least a week; some, a month.

Just two weeks earlier, Gulf and Gulf Coast producers had already been hit with production outages as a result of Hurricane Gustav that landed south of Houma, Louisiana, traveling along some 120 miles of oilfield-highway U.S. 90 into Lafayette.

The morning of Sept. 15, though, while working to find power for phones and laptops in Houston, oil and gas producers awoke to more news: At 12:45 a.m. CDT, Lehman Brothers had filed for Chapter 11 bankruptcy protection.

Public-equity investors had already begun to pull out of the market a year earlier after the Dow hit 14,000. When closing Sept. 12, 2008, the broad indicator had already tumbled to 11,421.

The Lehman news and other, subsequent failures, such as of AIG and Merrill Lynch, sent markets into a nosedive. A U.S. dollar in a money-market account was teetering on being worth 99 cents. The Dow was collapsing toward 6,547 by March 9, 2009.[198]

---

[198] Twelve years of gains were erased; the Dow had last been that low in April 1997.

The NYSE Arca Oil & Gas Index fell from 1,265 in just five weeks to 770.[199] Oil tumbled to $40 by mid-December.

Brigham Exploration was hit by all four storms—two hurricanes, the capital-markets crisis and collapsing oil and gas prices. Company-wide production was 36% less in the third quarter of 2008 than in the prior-year quarter as the September hurricanes suspended its Gulf Coast output. That further diminished revenue.

And capital markets were closed to virtually any company in any industry. Bud Brigham announced that the company's plan was to fund continued drilling from cash on hand, borrowing from the bank, getting working-interest partners to pay their bills, selling some projects and properties—"or alternative financing sources."

The company's stock price, which had soared past $18 in June 2008, was now foundering at about $3.50.

Brigham Exploration was in the middle of a world-class, predictably repeatable, oil play in which it and other operators had yet to fully define the productive limit. There were still trials to be done to determine what could be achieved with yet more frac stages, the areal extent of the east-of-Nesson play and of the west-of-Nesson play, and the potential of the underlying Three Forks.

Acreage could expire if it didn't keep drilling. Also, the company needed to pay its share of bills for wells that operators with more cash on hand—EOG, Slawson Exploration, Hess—were continuing to drill and in which it had a working interest.

He had to see the Bakken play through; it was too valuable. His first, big, east-of-Nesson well—the 12-frac-stage, 10,000-foot-lateral Carkuff 22-1H in Mountrail County in May—had made 25,000 barrels in its first three months. This was while having been choked back to 200 barrels a day for about six weeks during pipeline maintenance.

The company's first Three Forks test east of Nesson had made 13,000 barrels in just its first month online. The well, Adix 25-1H, had been fraced in 12 stages along 5,600 feet of lateral.

---

[199] The oil and gas index had already begun to decline from its all-time high in May 2008 of 1,630 as investors suspected oil and gas prices had outrun fundamentals.

He explained to shareholders that, even at $55 oil, the wells would make a roughly 40% return. And there was at least one bonus in this storm: Oilfield-service costs were declining as fiscally challenged operators and those whose acreage was already HBPed were dropping rigs in the Bakken and throughout North America.

He planned to focus on making yet-stronger wells and at a lower cost. That might see it through.

But oilfield costs had to come down and Brigham Exploration needed to contribute to that. In December 2008, he let both of the company's Bakken-rig contracts expire. The drilling program would consist for the time being of paying its share for wells other operators had already spud and were continuing to drill. Larger producers with more cash weren't letting up; from Sept. 15, 2008, through year-end 2009, they spud 635 more wells for Bakken—about as many as in the first 4.5 years of the new play.

And Brigham still wanted to make a giant well west of Nesson. Its Mrachek re-entry in May 2008 with seven frac stages had shown that more frac stages made more oil there—where wells had been underperforming in comparison with those drilled east of Nesson.

What could yet more frac stages west of Nesson—like the 12 he had put on the Carkuff and Adix wells east of Nesson—do? There still hadn't been a 1,000-barrel-plus well made west of Nesson, while it and other operators—primarily EOG and Whiting—had made 66 of these east of Nesson by now.

In January 2009, he went ahead and completed Olson 10-15H, which the company had spud as the first two-section, 9,500-foot lateral on Sept. 9, 2008. He put 20 frac stages on it—the most frac stages yet anywhere in North Dakota.

It came on with 1,160 barrels.[200] And it was west of Nesson—roughly 50 miles west of the giant wells of Parshall and Sanish fields.

"We had talked to the other operators," Brigham says. "They wanted to do it, wanted to try it, but they were worried: They didn't

---

[200] The Olson was near Brigham's first Bakken well, Erickson 8-17 1-H, which came on in 2006 without staged fracs for a disappointing IP of 156 barrels.

think they could get that many swell-packer stages into a two-mile-long lateral. And oil prices were down."

The company proceeded, however, doing the science and taking the risk that could buoy the worth of all the west-of-Nesson acreage-holders. "It extended the play another 50 miles or so into western North Dakota."

He needed more money.

Into 2008, the company had spent a cumulative $185 million on prospecting in its nascent Bakken acreage in the Williston Basin. "At the time, we were bullish on oil prices and, though we recognized there was some risk with the broader economy, we certainly did not anticipate what occurred.

"It was surprising to us how rapidly the economy turned south—and oil prices along with it."

He was sure oil would recover to at least $100. In early 2009, however, Wall Street wasn't sure of anything. Most investors were scared of everything; many had lost half or more of their portfolios.[201]

Oil quickly found bottom at $33 in mid-February; in mid-May, it was already $60—the price at which Brigham could make a more than 40% return on Bakken wells. And the calculation had been based on higher, pre-September-2008, oilfield-service costs. Meanwhile, with success both east and west of the Nesson, the company was proving itself to be a leading well-maker in what was proving to be one of the world's most interesting oil plays.

He bit the bullet: In May, the company sold 36 million shares to fund a renewed drilling program. In June 2008, that would have net some $650 million. Now it net some $100 million; the stock was $2.75.[202] But, encouragingly, the offering was oversubscribed. "Prior

---

[201] The losses, erasing gains earned dating back to 1997, using the Dow as a measure, did result in a bittersweet bonus to the U.S. oil and gas industry. In the mid-1980s until the advent of the shale plays, few students pursued geology and petroleum-engineering degrees as jobs had declined with oil and gas prices and industry consolidation. A roughly 20-year age gap had developed. After September 2008, many 40-year-plus veterans with newly discounted retirement funds continued to work, thus mentoring a new generation of oil and gas explorers.

[202] That was improved from as little as $1.04 in March 2009.

to that, the equity markets were not open at all—not to any industry," Brigham notes. "Everything was frozen or locked up.

"But there were a lot of visionary fund managers who, upon hearing our story, got excited. They saw it as an opportunity to step in, particularly given that we had a trump card with our acreage position in the play. So the offering added a lot of quality, longer-term, value- and growth-oriented investors into our stock."[203]

He used $35 million of the fund-raise to pare the company's bank debt below what the bank had set as the company's new, lower, credit line, based on the reduced value of oil and gas. "It was very painful at the time, suffering that kind of equity dilution, particularly given that we believed we had the premier acreage in the most promising oil play in the U.S.

"But the world had changed. We recognized that we couldn't be as dependent on bank debt. We wanted to have a strong balance sheet." He considered bringing in a joint-venture partner across the leasehold. "But we determined that the best source—well, the least-dilutive source—of capital for us was the equity market. We would have suffered more significant dilution, bringing in a JV partner."

Issuing stock privately was another option. "But capital was not moving. It was a really amazing time. The public-equity markets were a little bit in front; they moved prior to the private-equity players. In our case, some of the private-equity players that could have come in and benefited from our assets missed out big time."

The company rehired rigs and resumed drilling. Oilfield-service costs had fallen as much as 40% in the region. The company completed two more long-lateral wells in its Alger Field east of Nesson in which it had made the discovery well in January 2008 just north of Whiting's Sanish Field.

Strobeck 27-34 1H came on with 1,788 barrels from the underlying Three Forks with 20 frac stages. The completion cost alone was $3.9 million, down 33% from the 2008 estimate. Anderson 28 1H

---

[203] Among the offering's buyers were Bud Brigham and several additional members of management. "We believed strongly," he says, "in what we were doing."

came on with 1,756 barrels from 24 frac stages. It cost $6.25 million to drill and complete, down some 34% from the 2008 estimate.

And it returned to its Figaro 29-32 1H west of Nesson that—like the Olson well—had been spud in September 2008 and had been awaiting completion. In August, it put 20 frac stages on the 10,000-foot-lateral for 1,310 barrels and 1.5 million cubic feet of gas, proving a second time that big, Bakken wells could be made west of Nesson.

It also brought in a capital partner, U.S. Energy Corp., to pay 65% of the cost of six additional west-of-Nesson tests on acreage that was going to expire and Brigham believed to be prime real estate. After payout to U.S. Energy, Brigham would buy back 35% of the working interest to bring its total in each well to 70%.

It had 16 wells in its own name in Bakken now—four of them IPing more than 1,000 barrels.

The broader market was paying attention again. Securities analyst Subash Chandra reported that the Bakken play "will be one of the largest oil discoveries in North America."

In October 2009, oil pushed to $70. Brigham went back to the market, selling 16 million shares at $10.50 each to fund further drilling and to retire the company's $110 million of bank debt. While $10.50 was still off the $18.25 all-time high of June 2008, it was at least as good as in May 2008.

The company was going to 28 frac stages. The first well, Brad Olson 9-16 1H, in the U.S. Energy Corp. arrangement came on with 1,810 barrels from 28 frac stages. A couple of weeks later, the 28-stage BCD Farms 16-21 1H came on with 1,553 barrels.

Brigham explained in an earnings call in November that each additional frac stage—by reducing the spacing between them along the 10,000-foot lateral from 750 feet to 400 feet—appeared to be adding 35,000 barrels of reserves per stage. At a cost of $120,000 per extra stage at the time, the additional spend was the equivalent of some 60 cents per additional barrel.

He added, "We are going to monitor the results of our 28-frac-stage wells, but don't be surprised to see us increase the number of stages further."

The company went on to make 12 more wells west of Nesson around the Olson and Figaro—coming on with between 1,181 and 3,236 barrels from up to 30 frac stages. East of Nesson, three more came on with between 2,678 and 4,335 barrels. Then, its 27-frac-stage Sorenson 29-32 1-H came on in April 2010 with 4,335 barrels and 4.8 million cubic feet of gas for a record 5,133 barrels equivalent.[204]

Through year-end 2009, all it had invested in its Bakken program beginning in 2005 on land, wells and seismic was only $222 million. It held 283,000 net acres in the Williston Basin.

---

[204] Brigham later brought on a second Sorenson well with an IP of 4,661 barrels and 4 million cubic feet.

EAGLE FORD: 2008

← ← ← ← ← → → → → →

*"I mean, I have never seen—before or since—
a thick, continuous, high-quality,
shale reservoir than what we saw on that log."*
—Dick Stoneburner

When Floyd Wilson had asked for a new shale play in 2007, Dick Stoneburner returned from Denver two days later with the Haynesville idea. Wilson asked for yet another one. Stoneburner found another one.

On Oct. 21, 2008, just as the company was bringing online only its fourth Haynesville horizontal, it issued a press release: "Petrohawk Announces New Shale-Gas-Field Discovery; Eagle Ford Shale Well Placed on Production at 9.1 MMcfe/d."[205]

"Floyd is a big picture, strategy guy," Steve Herod says. "He thinks ahead in terms of what's going on in the business. And I'm pretty good at execution, making sure it's done right and timely. Our group also shares a work ethic that is a sense of urgency in everything we do. You know, every day matters. It's easy to say, 'Oh, well, we'll get that offer out or this thing out next Monday instead of today.'

"On a one-off basis, that probably doesn't matter. But, if everything you do is delayed because there's not enough of a sense of urgency, that compounds and it ends up costing you a year or two. It's all about getting it done quicker."

---

[205] Million cubic feet of gas equivalent a day.

Misses can result in a mess of market timing—the right time to raise capital through stock and debt offerings, the right time to buy properties, the right time to sell properties. Leading up to the U.S. financial-markets crisis of September 2008, Petrohawk had made a series of stock offerings, raising capital to fund its Haynesville play, and won an increased bank line of credit.[206]

"The August offering was right when gas prices were starting to come off from $13. We took a lot of criticism. 'Why are you guys raising more equity? What are you thinking?' As it turned out, a month later, Lehman went down and the whole market froze up for a while.

"We were glad we did what we did."[207]

In the midst of the heated Haynesville lease program during the first half of 2008, the company had quietly won 100,000 net acres in La Salle and McMullen counties in South Texas and was closing on another 50,000. In La Salle, its Eagle Ford discovery well, STS 241-1H, came on in October with the 9.1 million cubic feet of gas equivalent from a 3,200-foot lateral and 10 frac stages at about 11,300 feet. Of the initial production, 7.6 million cubic feet was gas; the balance, 251 barrels of high-value condensate.

A second well, Dora Martin 1H, was being completed about 15 miles west; the Eagle Ford appeared to be yet more superior there.[208]

Its Eagle Ford horizontals would cost about $7 million each, it estimated. And the wells' production was NGL-rich in a U.S. market increasingly awash with dry gas.

But the market price for NGL was tumbling in step with oil. Investor sentiment had turned cold to news of more oil, gas and NGL supply, while prices for these were down more than 50%. The attitude

---

[206] In January 2008, it had sold 20.7 million shares for $15 each; in May, 25 million for $26.39 each; in August, 25 million at $26.53 each. It also sold $500 million of senior notes. Five days before the beginning of the capital-markets meltdown, it had confirmed the new bank line: $1.1 billion with zero drawn.

[207] In four weeks post-Lehman, Petrohawk Energy drew $450 million from the bank line and put the cash in short-term securities. It cut capex from $1.5 billion to $1 billion. And it filed a shareholder-rights plan.

[208] Dora Martin 1H came on with 9.7 million; another on the lease came on with 8.3 million.

on Wall Street when Petrohawk announced the Eagle Ford discovery in October 2008 in the midst of the financial-markets crisis: "Just what we need: More shale gas."

***

For months leading to the Petrohawk announcement, Rod Lewis had been certain something odd was happening in South Texas. A rig had appeared in La Salle County that summer, drilling for Corpus Christi, Texas-based explorer First Rock Inc.

That wasn't what was unusual in the long-drilled area—not like when Southwestern Energy set up a rig in north-central Arkansas under the PV Exploration pseudonym to drill its Fayetteville tests. It was by no means concealed, either, on the South Texas landscape of oak and mesquite trees, scrub brush, deer stands and wild hogs.

Instead, Lewis noted how much drillpipe was at the site and that drilling had been under way for more than seven weeks now. Then, the frac crew and equipment showed up. The spread was enormous.

Drilling in La Salle County began in 1925 and commercial production commenced in 1940. The region's stacked pay above Eagle Ford includes the Wilcox, Escondido, Olmos and Austin chalk; below Eagle Ford, the Buda, Georgetown and Edwards. Vertical wells had been attempted in the Eagle Ford itself since the 1960s with marginal and unreliable success, particularly in areas where the rock contains more clay.

Besides drilling and studying his and others' well logs, Lewis had explored the region by air as well—stalking wells.[209] His fascination with the air had been inherited from his father, an Air Force pilot. In 1976, with a bachelor's degree in criminal justice from Texas A&I University, he wanted to become an FBI agent but was rejected for being near-sighted.[210]

---

[209] Lewis owns and operates 24 vintage aircraft, known as the Lewis Air Legends collection, and serves on the board of the National Air and Space Museum.

[210] Texas A&I became Texas A&M University-Kingsville in 1993.

He went to work, then, as a gauger, going from South Texas wellhead to wellhead, checking their vitals, for a small, Canadian oil company. In 1982, he bought a first well of his own, Williams & Williamson 1A, for $13,000.

As frac technology improved in the early 1990s, Lewis and others set out with it, making wells in the Escondido and Olmos some 4,000 feet above Eagle Ford. In one of these, he drilled deeper, making Dawson 1 in 1992 in Edwards limestone below Eagle Ford in an area dubbed "the Edwards split."

The production was unusual, though. The Edwards traditionally gave up high-sulfur-content gas in the area. Dawson 1 was making sweet gas—about 500,000 cubic feet a day.

"We were dumbfounded because the gas wasn't sour," Lewis says. "We were expecting sour gas."

Nevertheless, he moved on, putting horizontals—inspired by the horizontal success in the Austin chalk about 250 miles northeast—in the Edwards in Webb County that borders Mexico. The drillbit would hit the shaley Eagle Ford for about 150 feet, the underlying Buda limestone for about 200 feet and then be turned laterally into the limestone.

He took it another step, making dual horizontals—one lateral in one direction; another in the other. He then started stacking horizontals in the thick section: one in the upper part; the other in the lower.

"We drilled as many as five laterals from one well. The record was ours at the time."

In 1999, Lewis spied EOG Resources drilling a well, Cactus Jack 1, just northwest of his Dawson 1 in Tom Walsh Field. "I was watching it closely with my helicopter. This well was drilled to some formation that they couldn't even name. It was producing gas and large amounts of condensate, so it was tucked up under the Edwards reef.

"Later on, we figured out it was something between the Austin chalk (just above Eagle Ford) and Buda (just below Eagle Ford). It was probably a little bit of chalk and a little bit of Eagle Ford that was perforated because they perforated a large interval."

He was inspired. Besides that his Dawson 1 made sweet gas and not sour, he remembered the well because he had crashed at the site. "I was flying a little Super Cub in and out of the rig (locations) at the time. I basically lived on the drilling rigs in the early '90s."

He surmised that his vertical Dawson 1 was making its sweet gas from the Eagle Ford. "That was the beginning of my work with the Eagle Ford, which was well before anyone else and it was by mistake. We didn't know enough about what we were doing to understand we were even in the Eagle Ford."

In 2000, Lewis perforated a vertical in the Eagle Ford, putting a large frac into the opening. "It made about 1.2 million cubic feet a day and a little bit of condensate too, but it depleted very rapidly."

From it, though, Lewis determined that the formation would produce. In 2003, he went back to it, armed with grand plans and determination. This time, he plugged three Edwards laterals in his Pallet Fox 1H and went back in with the goal of making a horizontal uphole in Eagle Ford.

"I was told by everybody at the time, 'There's no way you can drill this zone because it'll kick your butt. It's blow-out city. You can't control the well. You're not going to have enough mud weight. You just can't drill it.'

"I said, 'I think I can drill it. I don't know if I can *complete* it, but I can *drill* it.'"

Lewis camped out at the wellsite "through the whole ordeal." He and Henry Boyte, who was Lewis' rig supervisor at the time, used 17-pound mud.[211] "It was kicking our butt the whole way." The lateral got to about 1,700 feet; rock samples indicated it had stayed in the shaley Eagle Ford zone. "I said, 'You know, this is enough to test it.'"

Lewis hadn't done much planning for the completion. "I was mostly concerned with 'Can we even drill this well?' Everybody had told me that there's no way in hell I could even get the well drilled. So I was really concentrating on the drilling portion."

A consultant who had worked on Austin-chalk completions for UPR suggested Lewis use a 2.875-inch slotted liner in the roughly 4.5-

---

[211] The greater the reservoir pressure, the heavier the mud that is needed.

inch slimhole. "We were getting ready for a huge amount of gas because it was flaring the whole time we were drilling.

"I told the guys, 'I'm a pretty good risk-taker. Let's just displace this 17-pound mud with diesel. We'll do it with coiled tubing to make sure we keep the well under control.'"

The completions team put 1.25-inch coiled tubing inside the 2.875-inch slotted liner within the 4.5-inch, roughly 13,000-foot wellbore. "This expert who worked for UPR at the time told me, 'This is the only way you can complete this well.'"

The tubing became stuck. "We tried to pull out of the hole and we couldn't. Now we had a well that didn't have any hydrostatic head on it and had very high pressure. We were stuck. It turned into a big fiasco—not any blow-out situation but a fiasco of a fishing job.[212]

"I decided, 'To hell with this. We'll just try to produce the well with the coiled tubing in the hole.' Well, the well produced maybe one day and then it just plugged off."

Lewis had spent $3.2 million on it—enough to drill and complete at least six, shallower Olmos or Escondido wells. "That was a huge amount of money for our company at the time. We were really sticking our heads out, experimenting. And this was in 2003—five years before the 'real' frac technology came around.

"So I called it quits."

He continued drilling Edwards wells. The sour gas had to be treated to get it into end-user-worthy shape and that contributed to higher costs. But the Edwards was fascinating.

"I enjoyed the challenge of drilling these horizontal wells balanced (with surface pressure); we were flowing them as we were drilling. Sometimes we'd flare 5- or 10 million a day for a short time. Then, we'd get the well under control and we'd keep drilling. It was like we were drilling in a controlled blow-out all the time."

Still, the Eagle Ford continued to taunt him. "For two years, I thought about this." Now, it was 2005. "I decided, 'Well, hell. Let's just plan better this time on our completion side. I want to set pipe

---

[212] Fishing is to remove equipment from the hole.

and I want to cement it.'" He attempted three wells, still on the reef where he had been drilling for Edwards.

"I thought you had to be on the Edwards reef to hit Eagle Ford. We didn't know anything about it. We didn't have 3-D seismic either. I thought everything north of the reef wasn't going to produce.

"That was our idea because the only place the Edwards actually produced was on the reef. You had to be on the reef or you weren't going to get the Edwards where it had natural fracturing, permeability and porosity. We thought that was what it took to have a good Eagle Ford well. And we were pretty much the expert on horizontal technology in this part of South Texas at the time.

"We were stretching our budget. We were a boot-strap company. We were really sticking our necks out."

He found a log on a vertical Edwards attempt, Rettig 34, from the 1980s that had been plugged as non-commercial while gas prices were low. Lewis sent a rig to make a horizontal nearby with plans for three frac stages.

"We fraced one zone and tried to flow it back. We fraced another zone. Tried to flow it back. We screened out on the third zone. It was pretty much a complete failure. We produced a little gas but, again, the well didn't have any longevity to it."[213]

Lewis asked a completions team with Schlumberger to drop by his Lewis Energy Group LP headquarters in San Antonio. By then, horizontal-completion technology in shales had improved exponentially with innovations in the Barnett play.

"They came in and said, 'Hey, we have the answer to your problem here with the Eagle Ford. You're not fracing it the right way.'"

Schlumberger offered to do a frac like what it was doing in Barnett wells. It would cost $3.5 million, which is mostly what a Barnett-type frac had come to cost if including the cost of sending a crew to South Texas to do it.

"I'll never forget this. I told them at the conference table, 'Guys, I just spent my last cent getting the damn well drilled. There's no way

---

[213] "Screened out" means the proppant clogged the perforation.

in hell I can spend $3.5 million to frac this well.' That was the end of that. I didn't want to spend $3 million drilling a well and $3.5 million fracing a well.

"We couldn't afford that. We just didn't have that kind of money. If we would have, it would have broken the Eagle Ford loose right then and there, back in 2005."

Already, Lewis had spent $25 million on the Eagle Ford. "We had tremendous drilling problems. One well, we had a near blow-out. We had to spend a lot of money just getting it under control."

In a management meeting, "I was told, 'Well, Rod, we can either keep going—trying to prove this Eagle Ford and break the company—or we can get back on our regular, bread-and-butter stuff and keep building the company.'

"I was convinced that we needed to be working on the Eagle Ford, but they shut me down. I mean, I owned the company; I could have over-ridden them. But you have a lot of very smart people saying, 'We just can't keep doing this.' So I gave it up in '05. That was it.

"I said, 'We're going to figure this out some day. We're going to come back to it and we're going to hold this acreage that we've got in the Eagle Ford until we figure this out.'"

In the summer of 2008, flying back and forth to his South Texas wells from San Antonio about 130 miles north, the rig drilling STS 241-1H for First Rock appeared on the La Salle County horizon near Fowlerton—population, 62.

"I thought they were drilling an Edwards well," Lewis says.

He assessed, day by day, how much pipe was still at the site compared with how much was initially there. It had been enough pipe to get to Edwards, which was about 200 feet below Eagle Ford, and, then, make a lateral. Once the drilling was done, the rig left.

Then, a Barnett-size frac crew showed up. Whoa!

"I started flying by every couple of days and this frac took a long time. There were a lot of tanks out there, a lot of sand and a lot of water. I was monitoring it." When the frac was done and First Rock, operating for Petrohawk, initiated flowback, Lewis hovered alongside the site.

"It got to the point where, when I was flying over, they would just shut the well down," he says. "They knew I was watching what they were doing."

Getting buzzed via air by Rod Lewis is commonplace in South Texas. Dick Stoneburner knew he was watching; he knew Lewis was even dropping in and visiting the site.

"Indeed," Stoneburner says. "He would set down, check flowing pressures and take back off!"

***

When Floyd Wilson had asked for another shale play—besides Haynesville—in 2007, Stoneburner contacted an old friend, Gregg Robertson. "In the Fayetteville, we knew we didn't have the dominant position," Stoneburner says. "We were in third place; it wasn't going to carry the day. And, in the Haynesville, we hadn't drilled our first well yet, although we were very confident in its commerciality.

"Floyd told me, 'Work with the guys and let's find another one.'"

Robertson had explored South Texas on foot and from First Rock's oceanfront headquarters in Corpus Christi for 30 years, learning the rocks first from his father, wildcatter Rock Robertson, who had mapped the Austin chalk from Mexico to Mississippi in the 1970s. Stoneburner had met Robertson while collaborating on chalk and other wells in South Texas during the peanut-butter-and-jelly days of the 1980s and '90s.

For Petrohawk, Robertson would look for a shale play in South Texas—a region Stoneburner knew Robertson knew from Darcy to nanodarcy. Robertson soon brought an idea by. "We fleshed it out. We didn't pass on it; we just put it in a corner to think about later," Robertson says.

He had also watched a well Burlington Resources drilled in 2006 in Live Oak County north of Corpus. "It was just out in the middle of nowhere." In talking to landowners, he learned that, based on that well, Burlington was leasing. In late 2007, the state released the file; ConocoPhillips, the new owner, applied for designation of a new field.

Robertson saw that perforations in the vertical wellbore had been made in both the Austin chalk and the Eagle Ford shale. ConocoPhillips had assumed the production was coming from the lower portion of the Austin chalk rather than the upper portion of the underlying Eagle Ford.

He knew the chalk wasn't a meaningful producer in Live Oak County. "I knew it wasn't the Austin chalk that was productive in that well; it was the Eagle Ford."

In January 2008, he rang Stoneburner. "There are some curious things going on in South Texas," Robertson told him. "I don't know if people are trying Eagle Ford, but I think it's probably worth looking at." He laid out his idea and said, "I think this could be a very large, regional, resource play."

In La Salle and McMullen counties, the Eagle Ford was at least twice as thick as anywhere else along the Gulf Coast and it had tremendous porosity and pressure, which was what kept causing near blow-outs as Lewis and others would drill through it.

Stoneburner and Charles Cusack, vice president, exploration, had Robertson work with Jana Beeson, a Petrohawk explorationist who had extensive South Texas experience. They found a well that had been drilled in 1992 by Swift Energy Co. near the gassy AWP Olmos Field in McMullen County. Swift had been producing wet gas from the tight-sand Olmos several formations above Eagle Ford and had taken the wellbore about 4,000 feet deeper into Eagle Ford.

From the log, Stoneburner says, "it was just amazing in its petrophysical appearance. It had great porosity, great resistivity. The gamma ray suggested it had a lot of relatively coarse-grained material within the rock.

"When we saw that gamma ray, the resistivity log and the density-neutron log—it took us about a month to get the density-neutron log—it was the revelation that this could be a really, really good reservoir because it just--.

"I mean, I have never seen—before or since—a thick, continuous, high-quality, shale reservoir than what we saw on that log. That got us extremely excited."

The log demonstrated the rock's petrophysical characteristics. The group set out to now learn more about the geochemical characteristics of the reservoir.[214]

They would need a physical sample of the rock.

There was a well that Phillips Petroleum had drilled through Eagle Ford in 1952 in neighboring La Salle County. Robertson went to the library of core and other rock samples held by the Bureau of Economic Geology's headquarters at the University of Texas in Austin.[215]

Mark Collette, reporter for the *Corpus Christi Caller-Times*, described Robertson's journey in the newspaper's 2012 tribute to him: "The brown boxes sat like building blocks stacked 15 feet high in endless rows of towering metal shelves at...(the) campus in Austin. Hidden here was the final piece of the puzzle that would change South Texas forever. It lay in shards in one of more than a half-million...cardboard boxes. It was an infinitesimal clue, a mere smattering of dust in a sprawling warehouse the size of three football fields...," Collette wrote.

"Gregg Robertson knew where to look. Row 57, Bay H, Shelf 4. There the manila pouches of...pebbles sat in their box. They probably went unnoticed since 1952...when a Phillips Petroleum drillbit brought the cuttings up from a layer of sediment deposited on the sea floor more than 66 million years ago."

Robertson took some of the sample and sent it off for analysis.[216] He quickly received the results. Total organic content was 1.1%, thus it held hydrocarbons. The shale was dark gray to grayish black. It was not naturally fractured, but it was fissile, meaning it could be broken; it could be fraced.

---

[214] The latter would show total organic content—that is, how much carbon is in the rock—and the thermal maturity—how thoroughly the rock had been "cooked," which indicates what type of hydrocarbon is present.

[215] The Austin library is part of a nearly 2-million-box collection of donated subsurface material housed there and in Houston and Midland. The rock samples are from wells drilled worldwide. The Houston facility was BP Plc's research center; it donated it to the bureau in 2002, along with 400,000 boxes of rock samples.

[216] As long as enough sample remains, the library allows taking a portion. The sample is not returned, as it is destroyed during the process of analysis.

Robertson and Beeson had also pulled data from vertical wells others had drilled through Eagle Ford and logs of horizontal attempts by Lewis, EOG and Apache Corp., which went 0-for-27 in horizontal attempts on old UPR acreage northeast of Live Oak County.[217] Along the way, he and Beeson would report their findings to Cusack, who would ask for more investigation.

Once Cusack was convinced, he brought in Stoneburner, who asked for more investigation. Robertson says, "We kept jumping these hurdles and, as we jumped those hurdles, it became more and more documented."

Stoneburner was updating Wilson, so Wilson was familiar with the project when they asked him to join them in a meeting. "By the time it got to Floyd's perusal," Stoneburner says, "everybody had a high level of confidence. Floyd looked at what we had done and in, like, 15 minutes said, 'Let's go do it.'

"We knew it was going to work with just the two data points—the well log from 1992 and the samples from 1952. Some plays can be over-researched. Where do you stop? We knew the reef—the Edwards shelf margin—was going to be our updip limit. We just didn't really know how to approach it laterally on strike."

Petrohawk ordered 2-D seismic data. "With that, we were able to map this very thick, Eagle Ford facies. We knew, from looking along the entire trend from Louisiana to Mexico, that there was no place that had this thick—300 feet—of section and apparent quality."

By now, it was the spring of 2008. Steve Herod and the land team were running the $2-billion, Haynesville, lease-traffic-control room. It was time for Petrohawk to start leasing for Eagle Ford pay. Robertson would take care of that.

He signed in for 10% working interest rather than an upfront fee or a cost-free ride. He knew the mineral-rights owners already. He drove from one ranch to another. Joining him in the effort was Rob-

---

[217] Robertson says, "They went 0-for-27 because the chalk is the play there, not the Eagle Ford. It was just the wrong area to try it in." The high clay content within the Eagle Ford there has made it difficult to keep fractures open.

ert Graham, a landman with whom Robertson had worked with for a couple of decades. Burke Edwards, a financial partner of Robertson's, helped as well. They quickly put together the initial, 150,000-net-acre position for about $150 an acre.

Robertson says, "Somehow $150 was a magical figure. It wasn't too much for our risk concept, but it wasn't too little to not interest people in taking a $2-million or $3-million check. We actually bought a lot more acreage than we intended to just because it came together so easily.

"It just didn't take any time at all because you have all these large ranches." And there was no lease competition. "Almost overnight, we had a position that we were ready to start drilling."

Petrohawk spud the first well, STS 241-1H, in July—just six months after Robertson brought the idea to Stoneburner. The state permit for it and all the leasehold had been procured under the First Rock name to not draw Petrohawk-size attention to it.[218] It took more than 50 days to drill the roughly 14,500 feet of hole—about 11,300 of vertical and 3,200 of lateral.

In October, just 10 months at it, the company had a second, new shale play. And its name was on the discovery well.

Robertson says, "We drilled three exploratory wells across 30 miles. Sounds crazy to do on a frontier play, but we had a high level of confidence because of the diligence we'd done."

On the far western side of the leasehold, Henderson-Cenizo 1H came on with 9.1 million near Dora Martin 1H, which came on with 8.3 million. Near the discovery well, STS 241-1H, in the middle of the leasehold, Brown Trust 1H came on with 8.1 million plus 200 barrels of condensate.[219]

On the far eastern side, Donnell Minerals 1H came on with yet more condensate—395 barrels—and 3.6 million cubic feet of gas.

All of the leasehold was prospective. The state named the field

[218] While Petrohawk had been in and out of oil and gas properties in South Texas over the years as a result of acquisitions and divestments, it wasn't operating there at the time.
[219] Natural condensate is a gas while underground that becomes a liquid as it comes to the surface.

Hawkville. In less than a year, it had already produced 3.5 billion cubic feet of gas and 50,000 barrels of condensate.

Stoneburner says, "If ever there is a classic, from-A-to-Z, shale-exploration story, there's not a better one out there. Everybody has their own stories of how they discovered this or were involved in that. Everybody can claim certain successes.

"But, from the first thought in January 2008 to having a producing, commercial discovery in October and more than 150,000 acres put together in that short period of time, that's just how far the understanding about shale had evolved.

"Everything just fell into place."

In 2010, Petrohawk won a second position over Eagle Ford, calling it Black Hawk. Like his relationship with Robertson, it also came about as a result of Stoneburner's days in the Austin chalk. "It is the best success I've personally had total control of," Stoneburner says of the deal.

Ben Weber, with whom he had worked in the legendary Giddings Field a couple of decades before, was trying to make a play in Dewitt County about 125 miles northeast of Petrohawk's Hawkville Field. Weber and a partner, GeoSouthern Energy Corp., held 120,000 acres.

"They had drilled a couple of total dusters," Stoneburner says. "I mean, you couldn't get even get a sniff out of 'em. Drilled 'em. Fraced 'em. Just totally non-productive."

Weber asked Stoneburner in late 2009 if he had an idea of how to do the completions better. "They had already done one well and it was an abysmal failure. When you looked at the completion, you could see why. I had worked with Ben over the years and we at Petrohawk were always open with technology-sharing."

Stoneburner told Weber and Meg Molleston with GeoSouthern how to complete the well. "Before they left the office, I said, 'By the way, if you ever want to sell this, just let me know.'"

Weber went on to make a 1,500-barrel-a-day well with a bonus of some 2.5 million cubic feet of gas. He called Stoneburner again. "You want to take a look at this? You're welcomed to."

Sitting in a Weber Energy office in Dallas with Cusack, Beeson and Scotty Tuttle, another Petrohawk geologist, "we looked at the data for about 10 minutes, saw the production, saw the logs, saw the core, saw everything. I said, 'We gotta buy this.'

"I walked into Ben's office and offered him $3,000 an acre—with no authority whatsoever. Floyd certainly didn't know this.

"You know, that's just how flat we were as an organization and how quickly we made decisions. If I had walked out of that office and we had pondered it for another month, there's no telling what it might have cost or he might have sold it to someone else. I got his attention at $3,000 an acre, which was a fair price."

The leasehold was in the super-NGL-rich window of the Eagle Ford. "We ended up buying an area that people have paid $40,000 an acre or more for since then. It is the best part of the play, bar none."

Steve Herod says, "People probably thought that $3,000 an acre was over the top, but we thought it was a terrific deal. As it turned out, it was. It was hugely economic."

In its Black Hawk in Dewitt County, Petrohawk's first five completions in Eagle Ford came on with between 13.2- and 16.9 million cubic feet equivalent, approximately 72% to 84% condensate. Among them, Krause 1H came on with 1,150 barrels and 3.1 million cubic feet of gas. Three subsequent wells' IPs averaged 3.6 million and 1,485 barrels.

And the deal proved to be most critical to the company's worth, entering 2011, when BHP Billiton Ltd. was shopping for shale.

BAKKEN: 2010

← ← ← ← ← → → → → → →

"We kind of looked at it as 'we built the factory.'
From there, we needed to invest
$13 billion just to drill the inventory...."
—Bud Brigham

I n April 2010, Brigham Exploration sold more stock—this time at $18 per share, which had recovered to roughly the stock's value at the June 2008 high. The company's public debt was $159 million and cash on hand was some $378 million. Its bank facility, with a $110-million borrowing base, remained untapped.

Bud Brigham was asked if he had received calls to sell. "There is, as you can expect, a lot of interest," he said at the time.

By 2011, in just six years, 21-year-old Brigham Exploration had been transformed from a Gulf Coast, short-reserve-life, hit-or-miss, gas-focused producer to a long-reserve-life, high-margin, oil-resource leader. Some 83% of its proved reserves were in the Williston Basin; in the heart of the Bakken play, it held 364,000 net acres. The wells were expected to pay out in fewer than 18 months at roughly $75 oil and make some 600,000 barrels equivalent each, more than 90% of that oil.

And oil had reached $100 again; it was now $110.

Dave Pursell and fellow analysts with Tudor, Pickering, Holt & Co. noted, in early 2010, the operator's uninterrupted run of enormous Bakken wells. After its first 11 attempts that came on with fewer than 1,000 barrels, its next 100 had come on with more than 1,000.

They called the stock their top E&P pick: "This is the name to own."

There was also yet more pay. There was the uppermost layer of the four Three Forks benches underlying Bakken. Also, Continental Resources, which determined that in 2008, proceeded to demonstrate in mid-2011 that production from the second Three Forks bench was yet another payzone without interfering with production from the middle Bakken or Three Forks 1.

In late 2010, Bud Brigham had let investment-banking firm Jefferies & Co. know that he would be open to talking to a potential acquirer. The company's stock price was now about $25, up 25-fold from March 2009. Its Bakken position was teed up for sale.

"We kind of looked at it as 'we built the factory,'" he says. "From there, we needed to invest $13 billion just to drill the inventory that we had delineated and we were a $3.5-billion company. So it made sense for us to bring in a much larger company that had a lower cost of capital and a much larger balance sheet—a company that could run the factory we had built and appreciate and take care of our people."

Production was 21,000 barrels equivalent a day net to its interest and indications were that this could grow to as much as 100,000 during the next five years.

Norway-based Statoil ASA had already zeroed in on Brigham Exploration, among others, when looking at companies it might take in to further increase its upside exposure to U.S.-shale plays. On Dec. 13, 2010, it let Jefferies know it was interested in entering the Bakken. Statoil and Brigham signed an agreement to discuss it further.

The international super-major's journey into the new, world-class, U.S., unconventional-resource plays had begun in 2008 in western Pennsylvania in Chesapeake Energy's acreage over the wet-gas Marcellus play. In 2010, it ventured to South Texas in a 50/50 deal with Talisman Energy Inc. in the wet-gas-plus-oil window of the Eagle Ford.

The third leg of its strategy took it to Austin, Texas, a city more known for state politics, music and film, college football, computer-maker Dell Inc. and natives who urge "Keep Austin Weird." Tucked along the Colorado River was Brigham Exploration and an unconventional-resource exploration team with play-leading experience in the oily Bakken.

In the Marcellus, Statoil was a nonoperator; Chesapeake was operator. In its newly gained position in the Eagle Ford, it was a nonoperator; but, in the terms of its venture with Talisman, it would become operator of 50% of the joint assets by the end of 2013.

It needed a U.S.-based, shale team.

The entry to the Marcellus play had represented real assets to Statoil but also an education. The arrangement included embedding Statoil personnel within Chesapeake's team for hands-on experience with drilling these shale-gas wells. In the South Texas deal, it gained more production and reserves—and experience.

If buying Brigham, it would gain its Bakken assets as operator as well as its personnel who knew how to make oil from this tight rock—not just smaller-molecule gas and NGL.

Statoil's debt-to-equity ratio was only 14% and it had about $15 billion of cash on hand. It had sold its retail-fuel business for $900 million, its assets offshore Brazil for $3.1 billion, 40% of its interest in a Canadian oil-sand project for $2.3 billion and some Norwegian midstream properties for $3 billion.

By September 2011, Brigham Exploration and Statoil managers had met in Houston, New York City, Austin and Norway during the previous nine months. The Statoil board offered $34.50 in cash per Brigham share. Brigham countered with $40 to which Statoil chief executive Helge Lund replied, "…Perhaps negotiations of a potential acquisition should cease."

He and Bud Brigham then met in London on Oct. 14, 2011, where Lund offered $36.50. The deal was signed on Oct. 16. Statoil and Brigham issued the press release the next morning. Statoil would pay $4.4 billion in cash for Brigham shares and assume Brigham's $300 million of debt, for a total deal value of $4.7 billion.

The merger was completed on Dec. 1.

Brigham had turned $25,000 of start-up capital in 1990 into a $4.7-billion enterprise. On a per-net-acre basis, Statoil was paying $8,000. Brigham had picked up its leasehold for $100 an acre or less.

Torstein Hole, Statoil senior vice president, U.S. onshore, was in Williston, North Dakota, meeting Brigham employees based there and area community members the day the deal was announced. Until the Bakken deal, Statoil had had an operated position in the U.S. only in the Gulf of Mexico where the sole mineral-rights owner is the federal government. Onshore the U.S., it would work with surface- and sub-surface-rights owners ranging from resident or absent landowners to trusts to native-American nations as well as with local, state and federal officials.

Hole said at the time, "It is part of our policy to have a good relationship with all stakeholders. Brigham is very well aligned with the way we want to work. We will also learn from them as we extend our operatorship in other areas as well.

"...So far...shale production in other places in the world has not taken off to the same degree as it has in the U.S. but...we know there are resources elsewhere in the world."

HAYNESVILLE
&
EAGLE FORD: 2011

← ← ← ← ← → → → → →

> *"...Only the largest companies*
> *could get their hands around the size*
> *Petrohawk had become."*
> *—Floyd Wilson*

For Petrohawk, the road to the BHP Billiton Ltd. buy-out was a short one as well, beginning in February 2011 and ending in July. It had exited the Fayetteville play in December, selling its 299 billion cubic feet equivalent of proved reserves there to ExxonMobil Corp. for $725 million. The proceeds would continue to fund its monster drilling obligations on more than 1 million net acres over the Haynesville and Eagle Ford.

A couple of months after Petrohawk's Fayetteville exit, Chesapeake sold its position there to BHP for $4.75 billion. In the deal, Chesapeake agreed to continue to operate the property for up to one year for the Australia-based, natural-resource conglomerate. At the time, BHP didn't have a U.S.-shale team yet.

Floyd Wilson had an idea; he contacted BHP through an investment banker, offering BHP a tutorial on U.S. shales. "They took us up on it," Wilson says. "I felt like they were a potential partner. I knew they were looking for an entry spot and Petrohawk would be a good one for them.

"I reached out to them and they were looking. It was 'right place, right time' for both companies."

BHP had been sitting on $16 billion of cash that it was thrice unable to convert into ownership of minerals company Rio Tinto Plc or into buying Potash Corp. in 2010. Meanwhile, its stock, which had just exceeded $100 in the spring of 2011, had gained 743% in a 10-year run and dividends paid in that timeframe totaled more than the cost of the share 10 years earlier.

Meanwhile, in June 2011, Petrohawk was looking at $4.50 gas, federal and state commentary about possibly outlawing fracing, and the possibility of outspending cash flow for several more years to make the rest of the wells—thousands of them—possible in its Haynesville and Eagle Ford leasehold. The outspend at the current gas price was looking like $1.7 billion in 2011, $1 billion in 2012 and $125 million in 2013 before turning a cash-flow-positive $1.7 billion in 2015. Its five-year capex would require some $15 billion.

On the other hand, liquids production from the Eagle Ford was strong and gas futures could go up: Other political commentary was favoring greater use of natural gas over coal in power generation and over oil in transportation, as natural gas is a lower-carbon fuel.

In the Chesapeake deal in the Fayetteville, BHP had clearly shown an interest in building a U.S.-shale business. Would it be interested in taking ownership of Petrohawk's world-class Haynesville and Eagle Ford? A deal would include Petrohawk personnel who knew how to operate a shale program, including in the Fayetteville.

When Herod saw BHP's valuation of Chesapeake's Fayetteville package, which included some 420 miles of gas-gathering pipe, it was fantastic. Without at least deducting for the lower-value pipe asset for which an assigned value was not revealed, the deal was about $11,445 per flowing thousand cubic feet a day and $9,800 per net acre.

And Fayetteville makes dry gas. What would BHP pay for shale like Eagle Ford that makes liquids too? Herod says, "I sent an e-mail to Floyd with that announcement and I said, 'They're the one.' If they would pay that much to Chesapeake for the Fayetteville, they would be a really good candidate to buy all of Petrohawk."

Oil and gas producers had begun citing the Eagle Ford as among the Top 3 plays they were in—or would have liked to be in. It gives up gas, NGL and oil—and prices for oil and NGL had grown since March 2009.[220]

Demand for Eagle Ford assets was strong. On June 1, 2011, Marathon Oil Corp. announced a plan to buy 141,000 net acres for $3.5 billion in cash from Hilcorp Resources Holdings LP, a venture started only a year earlier with $600 million in cash from private-equity firm KKR & Co. LP and $400 million of Hilcorp's existing Eagle Ford position.

Major E&Ps based abroad had already bought into the play for billions as well: China's CNOOC Ltd. for $2.2 billion, Korea's KNOC for $1.55 billion, India's Reliance Industries Ltd. for $1.15 billion, and Talisman and Statoil for a combined $1.55 billion.

On July 6, securities analyst Rehan Rashid reported that the play's production potential could be worth at least $85 billion and likely more than $200 billion. Wilson says, "It turned into something even larger than we envisioned. We knew it was going to be good, but we didn't realize how good it was going to be and how much areal extent it would have."

From the day his start-ups were formed, Wilson would tell anyone it was for sale—at the right price. Soon, Wilson got a call from investment banker Greg Pipkin at Barclays Capital about whether he might talk about a deal with BHP. "I felt like they were a potential partner," Wilson says. "I knew they were looking for an entry spot and I knew Petrohawk would be a good one for them."

His past start-ups—Hugoton Energy and 3Tec Energy—were sold to what would become large-cap E&Ps; in the case of Petrohawk, this start-up *became* a large-cap E&P. Petrohawk had 3.4 trillion cubic feet equivalent of proved reserves; adding in probable and possible reserves, then 35 trillion.

The Fayetteville property BHP bought from Chesapeake held 10

---

[220] The other two in the Top 3 were the Marcellus and Bakken; all remained the Top 3 in early 2013. Horizontals in the Permian Basin, however, are expected to trump them all.

trillion of proved, probable and possible. If BHP paid $4.75 billion for that, Wilson could reasonably expect an offer of some $16.6 billion for Petrohawk. Gas was about $5 when BHP made the offer to Chesapeake; three months later, it was about $4. Deducting for that, a bid would be at least $13.3 billion.

But Petrohawk's shale portfolio included higher-value liquids, so a good bid could be somewhere between $13.3- and $16.6 billion.

Wilson hadn't sold a company before for more than nine figures; the company's worth was now 11 figures. "I kept my conversations current with the larger companies around the world," he says. "We had become large enough that only the largest companies could get their hands around the size Petrohawk had become."

BHP made an offer. At first, it was $37.50 a share; it valued Petrohawk at about $14.7 billion, including assumption of $3 billion of debt. Wilson asked for $40. Mike Yeager, chief executive of BHP's oil- and gas-production unit, readily remarked that $40 sounded like too much; the BHP board came back with $38.75.

Sold.

From a 2003 start-up, Petrohawk went for $15.1 billion, consisting of $12.1 billion in cash and $3 billion of debt assumption. The $38.75-a-share valuation was three times the company's pre-2008 stock price.[221]

Herod says he had been won over by just the initial offer of $37.50 a share. The company's stock was trading at about $23 at the time. "It took me about three seconds to be convinced, based on the price they were talking about, that we needed to take it."

He also believed that a three-week, deal-or-no-deal deadline was necessary. "BHP wanted, like, six weeks (to conduct due diligence). We told them three weeks, max. 'If you can't get there in three weeks, you're never gonna get there.' We held real firm on that and that was important. It kept their feet to the fire."

The deal was signed at BHP's U.S. office in Houston the after-

---

[221] The extra $1.25 per share amounted to about $407 million—more than what Wilson sold his Hugoton Energy for in 1998 and nearly what he sold 3Tec for 2003.

noon of July 14, 2011. Wilson says, "We had been focused in the entire tenure of Petrohawk on finding the appropriate exit point.

"When we started, we were dealing in the consolidation business—multiple, conventional fields, generally mature with proved reserves—and tried to build a drilling business around the assets. We assumed a normal growth trajectory for that type of business—selling in three, four, five years.

"We made our total, structural, strategic, corporate change in 2007, moving away from conventional assets, selling all that stuff. It was now a horizontal, frac-stimulated, shale-resource world. And it soon became obvious that we would outpace any company our size."

The 10-minute deal Dick Stoneburner did with Ben Weber in 2010 for what Petrohawk named its Black Hawk area in the Eagle Ford was critical to BHP's valuation of Petrohawk, Herod says. The company's assets had come to consist of the huge, dry-gas Haynesville position and two sizable positions in the Eagle Ford: the liquids-heavy Black Hawk and the wet-gas Hawkville Field in McMullen and La Salle counties.[222]

Herod says, "We would not have gotten the valuation without Black Hawk. I mean, Hawkville was good but, you know, gas prices were down and half of it was dry gas. Haynesville, again, dry gas.

"We wouldn't have sold if we hadn't gotten that type of valuation. We'd probably still be sitting here. We had the foresight and the Petrohawk style of 'when you know it's right, you go do it.'

"Our $3,000 an acre (we paid for it) turned out to be, of course, terrific."[223]

---

[222] A third Eagle Ford position, Red Hawk Field in Zavala County in the southernmost window of the play, turned out to be non-commercial. Herod says, "It didn't work there."
[223] Weber's partner in the acreage, GeoSouthern, kept its interest. In late 2013, Devon Energy bid $6 billion for the 82,000 net acres that were producing some 53,000 barrels of oil equivalent—56% oil—per day, net to GeoSouthern's interest. The acreage was expected to be able to host an additional 1,200 wells.

HAYNESVILLE
&
EAGLE FORD: 2014-

← ← ← ← ← → → → → →

"...If you don't have the technology, it's worthless.
You can throw $50 million at a well
and not get what you need to get out of it."
—Rod Lewis

od Lewis, who had tried horizontal Eagle Ford wells before
Petrohawk came in with a Barnett-style job in 2008, did enjoy
upside from Petrohawk's discovery. He had some 300,000 net
acres in South Texas with about 250,000 of that prospective for Eagle
Ford. Half of it was held by production from old Olmos, Escondido
and Edwards wells.

Stoneburner says, "I know Rod very well. He readily admits that
he didn't know how to complete these wells. We ended up helping
him; we partnered with him in an area in Hawkville Field."

Lewis gives the credit to Petrohawk for proving the Eagle Ford
play. "Our team drilled many wells to the Eagle Ford, trying to make
this formation produce. I think the world of Dick (Stoneburner) and
everything he's done.

"They brought the technology, engineering and geological study
that they had learned in the Fayetteville and Haynesville shales to La
Salle County in 2008. There was a hell of an increase in technology in
just a few years.

"This wasn't the same, old, Barnett-shale-frac grandfather had pumped. There wasn't this plug-and-perf technology. There wasn't the technology to do these multi-stage fracs as efficiently. On the drilling side, there wasn't the knowledge to drill such an accurate lateral; on the frac side—the fluids, the pump brakes, the methods.

"Our deal was we'd pump as much sand concentration as we could. That was just the opposite of what you really need. You need less sand per gallon of fluid. And fluids technologies changed.

"You can have all the money in the world; if you don't have the technology, it's worthless. You can throw $50 million at a well and not get what you need to get out of it."

Petrohawk brought the technology—and enough money.

"They brought the capital budget—the wherewithal financially. They had the fortitude to come out here and try something that was going to cost a hell of a lot of money. We didn't have the knowledge or the capital to do what they did. I give them all the credit."

Meanwhile, for proving the Haynesville play, Stoneburner says, "Encana and Chesapeake were both involved in the discovery in different areas. Encana was drilling deep, exploratory wells in Red River Parish in 2006, probably 50 miles or so from where Chesapeake was targeting the Haynesville. Encana's core analysis and vertical completion of the Bossier and Haynesville in the J.W. Adcock were clearly groundbreaking events in the discovery process.

"Chesapeake was targeting the Haynesville with their early drilling in Bossier Parish. While the first wells were sub-commercial, that was very typical of most all of the shale plays; early completions were sub-optimal. Chesapeake certainly deserves a lot of the credit for the discovery. They had a technical staff that, I think, was unparalleled in evaluating these shale plays.

"It's just unfortunate that Aubrey (McClendon) decided he had to have so much of it—so much of the shale plays. It's just a kind of double-edged sword: They were so good and in the forefront of so many plays. How can you not want to go out there and get a big bite of all of them? That was probably their downfall.

"But Chesapeake was at the forefront of understanding the

Haynesville and learning how to drill it and complete it. Commercial? Not at all—but encouraging. It was a very, very challenging reservoir because of the pressure, temperature, depth.

"It was a very difficult play to break the code in. Some of their first wells weren't that great, but they were getting there."

Floyd Wilson exited Petrohawk shortly after closing the sale to BHP on Aug. 22, 2011. He had already begun work on his newest start-up, Halcon Resources Corp. "Who knows how I'll do, but I'm not ready to play golf every day yet," he said at the time.

Herod stayed on with BHP for six months and then joined Wilson at Halcon, arranging more than $3 billion in asset acquisitions—all for tight, oily rock—in Halcon's first eight months.

Stoneburner remained with BHP through year-end 2012, went on distinguished-guest-lecturer tour for the American Association of Petroleum Geologists, joined the board of Woodford-shale-play founder Newfield Exploration and took up an advisory role at energy-focused, private-equity-firm Pine Brook Partners LLC.

About that Petrohawk mindset of doing the work today and not tomorrow, the best example of it is its sale to BHP, Herod says. "We signed that deal in mid-July 2011. If you look back—and I've got charts—a week later, gas prices started falling. Two weeks later, you had the Greek financial crisis. The markets were messy.

"I honestly think that, if we had been a month later, BHP probably wouldn't have done the deal. All of the things we did to push the company along those years got us ready for a big exit. We were ready when the time came, instead of needing another three or four months.

"And we got $38.75 a share—in cash!"

Unlike his past start-ups, Wilson's newest, Halcon, was launched with a focus on unconventional-resource assets, initially that of small Ram Energy Resources Inc., which he bought in early 2012 as the publicly traded platform for Halcon. Upon news of Wilson's interest in Ram in late 2011, the stock bolted from about $3 to $12, dubbed by industry as "the Floyd Wilson premium."

Petrohawk's shift from conventional to unconventional required another mindset, Wilson says, financially and technologically. The company and its predecessors had worked proven oil and gas fields; shale plays required a different drilling and completion approach and involved buying leasehold without production. The capital for this type of acquisition wouldn't come from the neighborhood bank.

"We had a lot of really bright people at Petrohawk," he says. "One of my most important emphases in building Petrohawk was convincing people to come to work at the company. Awesome talent. Bright people. Without those people, Petrohawk wouldn't have become what it was.

"In the Haynesville, there were 10 or 15 people involved in that process; in the Eagle Ford, just a few. You don't own the idea anymore; it's a group effort. Luckily, we had the right group."

In 2004, Petrohawk had 3 billion cubic feet equivalent of proved reserves. Before buying into northwestern Louisiana in 2006—before there was a Haynesville play—it held 437 billion. Upon its sale, it had amassed 3.4 trillion—all of it in two plays that didn't exist when Wilson switched to the resource-play tack in mid-2007.

Its capital raises prior to and following the September 2008 market crisis were helpful, Wilson says. "I think we raised more money than any E&P company in 2008 and 2009. We did do equity deals at ever-lower stock prices and debt deals at ever-higher interest rates.

"We were comfortable that the use of these funds would be far more durable than the recession.

"And, as it turned out, we were, fortunately, right."

He estimates the outer limits of new, U.S., onshore, oil production remain unmapped. "It is having a real impact on our economy and on the world price of oil. And new production is possible from some of these conventional reservoirs with horizontal wells. There is still a large opportunity here.

"And the U.S. is the best place in the world to work; it has the least political risk. I won't say we have none; I wouldn't put a million acres together in the state of New York, for example. But we are far above the rest of the world in terms of political risk."

Herod, now president of Halcon, says, "I wouldn't have expected this even in the early 2000s. I don't know that anybody did. But that's what's exciting and interesting about our business: It seems like, every 10 or 15 years, everybody has said, 'There's no more oil and gas to be discovered.' And, then, there were international discoveries and the deepwater Gulf of Mexico.

"Here, the industry found a way to make these tight formations produce. The independent oil and gas companies, working with the oilfield-service companies, figured out how to make it economic.

"There's plenty of resource here in the U.S. and what all of this has done for the country is incredible, particularly on the oil side."

Stoneburner notes that fracing horizontal wells in shales required several years of application to figure out. "It's really the advent of multiple, small, isolated, induced fracturing that has changed the game. Until 2006, the industry didn't know how to complete the horizontal Barnett wells (very) commercially.

"It required the ability to induce fractures in multiple stages along the lateral, using smaller jobs in each.

"All of a sudden, you got much better productivity."

The cemented liner was the advent of the ability to isolate the fracs. "You were able to go in and do the perf-and-plug style of completion. That breakthrough allowed us to take small bites out of the well. And, with each bite, you were able to, then, pump enough sand and fluid to contact this tight rock.

"Until you were able to take small bites, you weren't effective; once we were able to take small bites, that made it work."

Also, industry had to solve for completion fluid. "The gel system didn't work in the Fayetteville. Each reservoir reacts a little differently to the type of fluid that you pump. The early Fayetteville had pretty poor results until Southwestern got to the slick-water system. That's what the Fayetteville, Barnett, Haynesville liked.

"It's not what the Eagle Ford liked. Eagle Ford likes a gel system. So each of these plays has varying, preferred fluids to optimize productivity. You had to be able to isolate each of your fracs and, then, work on your fluids and sand concentrations."

MARCELLUS: 2014-

← ← ← ← ← → → → → →

"We were—all this time—searching for
nickels and dimes and
we're sitting here with $100 bills."
—Bill Zagorski

With just a few wells in the Marcellus yet in 2007, Range Resources could see where it was going. It had already begun work on arranging markets to buy the gas and on stripping it of its high-value NGL to sell that separately.

The U.S. midstream industry of getting gas, NGL and oil to market had already been awakened by the Barnett to new, unrelenting demand for gas-transportation infrastructure. The U.S. petrochemical industry would now get a wake-up call: Unprecedented amounts of gas liquids—ethane, propane, butane and more—were heading its way.

Ray Walker says, "We were producing (from the Marcellus) a lot of highly volatile condensate—C5-plus type—at the wellhead. I had worked in the Cotton Valley around the Carthage gas-processing plant (in East Texas) in the 1990s (at UPR), so I had learned a lot about liquids, how to handle them and what was going to be required in terms of processing, transportation and markets.

"We hired a marketing guy, Greg Davis, who has been one of the absolute, key players in Pittsburgh. One of the very first conversations I had with Greg—probably in February of '07—was 'We've got to start developing markets for these liquids. We've got to figure out what we're going to do with the ethane and all of the other liquids.'"

And for the gas itself.

The northeastern U.S. was gas-short while user-heavy, including by petrochemical plants. Gas and NGL were imported into the area from the Gulf Coast and elsewhere. Many consumers in the region were anxious for supplemental dry-gas supply from the Rockies via Rockies Express, a newbuild, 1,700-mile pipe of up to 42 inches in diameter to Ohio that was completed in November 2009.

After Range made its Gulla 9, it could see the Marcellus alone would not only supply the area, but there would be surplus. For the NGL, it worked with processors, existing pipeline operators and potential buyers, eventually doing deals with a chemical manufacturer in Sarnia, Ontario, and one with a buyer in Europe; it was negotiating for a third leg that would send the liquids to the Gulf Coast.

The Pittsburgh office of one—Ray Walker—in January 2007 had grown to some 350 employees by 2014. The company's market capitalization was now $12 billion. The roughly 1 million cubic feet a day the Marcellus was making in early 2007—all by Range at the time—was now some 9 billion a day.

It took the title of largest gas field in North America.

Walker says, "And I think it has, by all rights, the real capability in the next 10 or 20 years to be the largest, gas-producing basin in the world, when you consider the potential of the (underlying) Utica, the upper Devonian, all the stacked pay. You know, it's 'Wow!'"

***

Jeff Ventura notes that, in the early days of his career, in the day of conventional wisdom "back in 1979 and through the 1980s and '90s, the common thought was that shales are a source of hydrocarbons or a seal for a conventional trap. When you explored, you looked for source, seal, reservoir, timing and all those things.

"Some people make the comment that 'Well, we always knew the gas was in the shales; we didn't know how to get it out.' I would challenge that. Granted there were exceptions, like Big Sandy Field in Kentucky that was so naturally fractured that, with just 1920s technology, it worked. But the conventional mindset was that shales were sources and seals, not reservoirs."

Mitchell Energy demonstrated that the Barnett shale is a reservoir. "It's a source, but it's also a reservoir." For others to replicate it required a new mindset and new technology—horizontal drilling, coupled with staged fracing.

And courage.

"George Mitchell was persistent enough to keep challenging, not taking 'no' for an answer. 'Could we unlock it?' Finally, they did, through (the LSF) and then, ultimately (by others), through horizontal drilling with staged fracture-stimulation."

The vertical wells Range first made in testing the Marcellus were successful, but they didn't pass Ventura's higher hurdle. "As chief operating officer, I was to build and grow Range and we couldn't do it with vertical wells. What really made the Barnett take off were the horizontal wells and staged fracs."

Bill Zagorski, who brought the Marcellus idea to Ventura, says, "If you look at all previous attempts to commercialize the Marcellus, they failed because no one applied a Barnett-style frac to it. What makes the Barnett a successful reservoir was not recognized in the Marcellus until we did that.

"I have records of early Marcellus wells back in the 1940s where they tried to shoot it with nitroglycerine. Within a mile of the Renz 1 well were some of the first three, relatively modern attempts to commercialize the Marcellus. They tried a CO_2-foam frac on one and a nitrogen-foam frac on another.

"Both of these were the standard, state-of-the-art completion techniques for shales in the Appalachian Basin down in West Virginia and Kentucky at the time. Those failed."

In the third attempt, a small frac of mostly water was applied—about 15% the volume of water and pressure pumping that Range put on Renz 1. "That well, the one fraced with water, was the only one of these wells that made any measurable amount of gas."

In 2004, he had been hoping Range would try something new—a Barnett-size LSF frac. "To me, that's one of the hardest things, being an optimistic when not everyone is. You know, not everyone can be an optimist. The people who would be designing the frac had nothing to go back to, nothing to correlate, at least not in the Marcellus."

The tendency would be to just put a small frac on it and spend only a little bit of money. "Or not doing it at all. Most anyone can get past not doing anything at all."

Also, there was no frac crew in Appalachia with Barnett experience. "We had to import it. But Range did it the Barnett way. It would have taken forever to get it to work if we hadn't been optimistic.

"Picture yourself in Jeff's and the others' shoes, after they spent $6.5 million (on the Renz 1, prior to fracing it in the Marcellus), someone telling them to do this size frac. It was really new ground. Even if you thought the formation had gas, if you knew some respected companies had failed in the next county, who wants to take that to their boss?"

In a way, developing the Marcellus has been similar to developing the old, vertical, coalbed-methane plays, he adds. "We would start out drilling 100 (wells) a year and getting a lot of gas; then, we would increase it to 300 or 400 wells. The idea was to drill as many wells as you could and keep the cost as low as you can. You would build production volume through lots of small wells. Repeatable, small wells.

"That's really what we do now. We build companies through lots of frac stages. And we're drilling hundreds fewer wells and making 10,000 times the gas. That's what's happened here.

"You can have a career of 10,000 wells. I used to think all that stuff was important. I still keep all my books and records of all the things we've found.

"But, at the end of the day, five or six horizontal wells in the Marcellus really makes all of that obsolete. It's incredible. Not just here; that's in the whole U.S. oil and gas industry. It's just amazing.

"We were—all this time—searching for nickels and dimes and we're sitting here with $100 bills."

***

After selling most of his Barnett position to Devon in mid-2006, Trevor Rees-Jones went to Pennsylvania. "Now, this was in the fall of 2006. There was some activity going on," he says. "The problem was that we couldn't tell what any wells were producing because the requirements for reporting production up there wasn't as developed as in Texas.

"Nobody could figure out what was going on. It was all rumor and you know how that goes. Nine out of 10 of those in the Barnett were false. When one of these plays is developing, there is hype that, 90% of the time, turns out to be untrue.

"So you've got to be real careful."

Michael Radler, co-founder of Jetta Operating Co., joined Rees-Jones in the Marcellus; the pair quickly leased in Lycoming County, Pennsylvania, for $150 an acre.

"For a hundred years, you could lease in Pennsylvania for $5 an acre. By the time we got up there, landman groups were putting acreage together for $100, $200, $300 an acre. That's a lot more than $5 but a whole lot less than what you can sell it for—$8,000 or $9,000— if it works. We were able to do this because we had the money now that we didn't have in the early days of the Barnett.

"And we guessed right: For natural gas—both dry gas and liquids-rich gas—I don't know that there's going to end up being a better play than the Marcellus. It's huge.

"We were so attuned to the conventional—the high-risk nature of a conventional mindset—that it was hard for us to grasp what was happening in the early years of development of the Barnett. It's beyond belief what has happened.

"Drilling conventional reservoirs had gone on for 150 years. That the unconventional-resource plays of this century have been a game changer really wasn't recognized until the Barnett was repeated in two and then three and then more places.

"There were people who thought it couldn't be repeated. Well, there are definitely more Barnetts now.

"I think it's just the beginning. I don't know what the next 10 years will hold. I would be surprised if everything has already been found."

***

There was an evening in early 2008 when Jeff Ventura was standing in the parking lot of a Hilton hotel southwest of Pittsburgh on the edge of Washington County where Range had set up its Marcellus office. He would often stay at his mother's home when visiting the area, but Range was about to test its eleventh horizontal in the Marcellus. Based on the flow rate, the well looked strong. For the brief test, the gas was going to be flared.

He wanted to be nearby. "I could see it from the Hilton," he says. "I knew we finally had the big-time breakthrough we were looking for when we got that well."

He and Zagorski both grew up in western Pennsylvania; they joke today that the two biggest wells in the play might end up being under their childhood homes.

"There's an irony for myself, personally," Ventura says. "My grandfather on my mother's side was born in the 1890s and he worked in the oil fields in and around Pittsburgh in the early part of the 1900s. I remember him telling me the story that he got out of the oil fields because they had played out. He got into coal mining for Consol (Energy Inc.) and ended up being a mine foreman."

Ventura's father had worked for Gulf Oil, whose headquarters were in Pittsburgh when Chevron bought it in the 1980s. "And, then, I got into the business and had to move away to Texas, Oklahoma, Louisiana, the Rockies. Yet, the biggest U.S. gas discovery is back in this area where it all began in the 1850s with the Drake well.

"After having explored all over the world and all over the U.S., the biggest discovery is just right back there at home."

The Marcellus proved to not only have a larger geographic footprint than the Barnett, but that it is better rock. Walker says, "When we started modeling it—creating economic scenarios of what we thought southwestern Pennsylvania would be like—we thought it was going to produce like the Barnett extension into southern Johnson County. It was about the same depth. It seemed to be about the same pressure, the Btu, the thermal maturity. All of this seemed to be about the same."

The estimated ultimate recovery of the early Johnson County wells was around 2.5 billion cubic feet equivalent each. "We thought that might be a reasonable expectation for the Marcellus."

That would be good enough; in fact, it would be excellent.

"But what we've learned since is that the Marcellus is just a whole lot higher-quality-matrix rock. It's got order-of-magnitude more permeability—still in the nanodarcy range but a lot more—and it has a lot different shape of porosity.

"We now have the technology across the industry to do things like the 'focused-ion-beam-scanning electron microscope.' That's a bunch of words that essentially mean we can now analyze the rock on an almost molecular level. We can determine what sort of porosity, what's the shape of the porosity and how well it's connected.

"What we see is that the Marcellus is just head and shoulders above everything else—whether it's Haynesville, Woodford or whatever; it's just the best there is.

"The average Marcellus well today—and they're still getting better—is more than 10 Bcf equivalent (in estimated ultimate recovery) in an area that we thought was going to be 2.5 starting out."

And the physical size—in areal extent plus thickness—makes it the largest gas field in geographic and geologic footprint as well.

"It's the largest hydrocarbon basin in North America. And some of the areas that we thought early on might be substandard are now, from some of our and others' testing, showing that some of the lowest-producing areas of the Marcellus, for instance, are better than the core, sweet spot of the Barnett.

"It's just great rock. It's got good pressure. It's got the right mineralogy, the right thermal maturity. And it's a massive basin."

He adds that other aspects of simply taking Barnett technology into the Marcellus didn't seamlessly translate. "From a high-level view, it did. But there were small, yet important, points that didn't, like targeting early on in the hottest-gamma-ray part. That didn't necessarily work early on because we didn't really understand the best way to get the right kind of fracture initiation. But, in the overall sense, absolutely, it did translate.

"From a purist standpoint, that's how we got it to work. We basically brought technology, rigs, frac crews and everything else straight from Fort Worth to Pittsburgh.

"That's what made it happen."

FAYETTEVILLE: 2014-

← ← ← ← ← → → → → → →

"Think about doing anything 10,000 times...
That's where the 'manufacturing' think comes in."
—*Richard Lane*

H arold Korell's visit with George Mitchell in early 2007 quickly paid off in the Fayetteville. At year-end 2007, Southwestern Energy was making some 325 million cubic feet a day,
gross, or an average of about 680,000 a day from 478 wells of which
415 were horizontal. Proved reserves in its acreage were 716 billion.

By year-end 2008, gross production was 720 million a day.[224]
New horizontals were coming on with an average of 2.8 million from
lateral lengths averaging about 3,600 feet. They were costing about $3
million now. It had more than 1,200 wells; of the 604 wells spud that
year, all but 18 were horizontal.

By year-end 2012, it held 3 trillion cubic feet of proved reserves
in the Fayetteville, making for it 1.33 billion a day from 2,186 net
wells. Horizontal-well cost had declined to $2.5 million each with lat-
eral lengths now averaging 4,833 feet. They were being drilled in five
days—improved from the initial 18 days and for a lateral half as long.

Gross production by all Fayetteville producers had pushed to
some 2.6 billion a day.[225] Southwestern's market cap had grown from

---

[224] Net acreage had exceeded 900,000 but Korell sold 55,631 to XTO Energy, bringing
Southwestern's net to about 875,000.
[225] By then, the Fayetteville hosted more than 4,000 producing wells drilled by Southwestern and others.

about $200 million in 2000 to some $13 billion in 2013. The stock price had grown 4,347%.

Richard Lane says of the journey, "There were the technical things. The other thing to remember is that Arkansas wasn't ready for this." The state's rules on oil and gas drilling were based on old, conventional, vertical programs. Except for Southwestern's ongoing work in its legacy acreage, there was little drilling.

John Thaeler says, "They had to create all new rules to deal with shale exploration. How do you form units and space them? How many wells per unit do you get? It was a learning process for all of us, but it turned out pretty well. The development of the shale has been very orderly and the state has benefited from it."

Also, it fell to Southwestern to educate communities about what drilling for natural gas involved. Lane says, "We set some high bars on how you go about making sure that you do things right and, more importantly, that everybody can benefit from what you're doing.

"You're really changing the landscape. You're not only providing more natural gas for the country and great jobs for folks, you're setting up a model of how you can go about doing this in a good fashion for everybody. There's a lot of thought and effort that went into building that program.

"Like any company, we made some mistakes. But we 'fessed up to our mistakes when we made them and then we tried to make 'em right. We always kept a dialogue."

Internally, the Fayetteville required every part of the company to step up. These are thousands of wells and unlike what the company had made in the past. "It's a totally different beast—a whole new demand and pressure on the organization to do that. You learn new things and you learn to think about things in ways that you never thought about them before."

Arkansas lacked much of the oilfield equipment and services Southwestern needed to drill the enormous play in the north-central area of the state. "We would have a discovery in South Louisiana and, if you prayed, there would be follow-ups to it. It would be fantastic. You didn't worry about where the frac water would come from or the rig, sand, whatever. In Louisiana, Texas or Oklahoma, you could call somebody up and get a frac job. Well (in central Arkansas), we couldn't."

Southwestern had to scrutinize the entire supply chain; where the most money would be made was in growing the production and reducing the cost. Southwestern bought a sand quarry. It bought and operated its own drilling rigs.

"Think about doing anything 10,000 times," Lane says. "If you save a buck here and a buck there 10,000 times, it adds up quickly. That's where the 'manufacturing' think comes in. You control your destiny by driving down cost."

And it was particularly helpful when gas prices weakened, beginning in mid-2008. "That's why a company like Southwestern can say today, 'Gas prices are weak, but we can still survive.'"

The Fayetteville also proved that the Barnett wasn't an exception. When Amoco, Burlington and Devon figured out the enormous Fruitland-coal play in the San Juan Basin in the 1980s, others rushed to coalbeds across the U.S. to duplicate it. While several met with commercial success, such as in the Raton Basin in southwestern Colorado, none has been of the productive magnitude of the Fruitland.

Some early Barnett enthusiasts doubted the Barnett success could be duplicated. "The Fayetteville shale is the one that said, 'The Barnett is not alone.' There must be more of them."

***

Lane retired from Southwestern Energy in 2008 and, after a year off, jumped back into oil and gas exploration, forming his own company, Vitruvian Exploration LLC, to apply horizontal, fraced wells to the Mississippian-age limestone in northern Oklahoma. Thaeler joined Lane in a second venture, Vitruvian Exploration II LLC, in 2012, working on the liquids-rich, southern end of the Woodford shale in southern Oklahoma.

Thaeler says of the early shale era, "It was a debate for quite a while: Was natural fracturing necessary for an economic shale-gas development? The advantage of natural fracturing is it would have the capacity to store more gas and, if you induced additional fractures, you would create more pathways into your wellbore.

"Theoretically, you should have better wells. Industry found out that pressure regimes change; it was hard to get your fracture-stimulation propagated. You ended up with poorer wells. We learned that we had to stay away from faults; you don't go near them."

"Now, with oil or these unconventional plays with gas liquids, those molecules are bigger. We're going through that same debate again—whether or not natural-fracture systems are important."

In southern Oklahoma, the oil window of the Woodford shale is 450 feet thick.[226] It's hard to miss. But where to best land the wells isn't simple. "It's not homogenous. Conditions changed during the deposition of that shale. So you hear people talking about 'Where's the best zone to drill that horizontal?' It's a whole lot easier in a 400-foot-thick shale than a 20-foot shale, but certain depths and areas may be better.

"This industry constantly evolves. You do what you can with what you have and then somebody figures out there's something else. I can't wait to see what the next big thing is. I know we have a lot of work still to do with these resource plays. At the same time, I'm sure there's somebody out there working on something new and different.

"In the right environment, which is capitalistic, smart and hard-working people can do incredible things. This industry is blessed with a lot of smart, creative people. And, given the proper incentives and motivation, they can do incredible things. We have positively changed the future of this country. We can become energy self-reliant. We can bring back manufacturing jobs. It's what industry strives to do and it is incredibly rewarding.

"I want to see us do it again and again.

"Look at what Silicon Valley has done to change the world. This shale revolution is no different: Creative people taking something to

---

[226] The oil-window play is known as "the Scoop," an acronym for "South-Central Oklahoma oil province."

another level and, suddenly, you have a whole new industry. Without that type of creativity and drive, countries don't go anywhere."

Lane notes, "We have this enormous federal debt and the U.S. dollar is in a tenuous place. The fact that we are controlling our own destiny on oil and gas and reversing the import/export profile, if we didn't have that, with all these other things that are going on, it's a scary picture.

"Crude oil is priced in U.S. dollars by the global market. What if our imports were rising?"

Harold Korell is now Southwestern's chairman, having retired as chief executive officer in 2009 and as executive chairman in 2010. He notes he grew up in a small town in Wyoming; other Southwestern Energy team members, like many of the industry's leaders, are from small towns across the U.S.

"And, at the end of the day, we discovered and, then, captured the opportunity (of the Fayetteville) and ran with it.

"Everyone has benefited from this effort—the employees; the mineral owners who, just through this year, have received over $1 billion in royalty payments; people who are now in high-paying jobs in Arkansas and other places; the shareholders; the state, whose economy held up through the financial crisis; and America. We are now benefiting from affordable natural-gas prices.

"For me, this has been an incredible journey: I have lived the 'American Dream' with the American shales. We're just country boys and, somehow, what we pursued in our careers worked out. I hope we continue to have a country where a person can have these kinds of opportunities, so generations in the future can have this experience.

"At the end of the day, we did something good for the world."

BAKKEN: 2014-

← ← ← ← ← → → → → →

"There is no problem that's too big to be solved...
If you believe this, it empowers you
to take on just about anything."
—Bobby Lyle

Bud Brigham says, "One of our advantages in the Bakken play was that we were looking at the economics. A lot of companies in our business tend to focus on costs and work really hard just to push down costs, instead of focusing on the return on capital. We looked at the cost of going to more frac stages and what kind of incremental production and reserves we might get."

It also didn't shy away from spending on premium proppant, choosing for its Bakken wells to use high-strength ceramic, which was increasingly in short supply during the 2000s as producers who were spending $5- to $15 million on shale-play wells didn't want the fractures, at the end of the day, to close in on less expensive sand.

"Even though it cost more, we could see significantly better performance from our wells relative to other operators' wells that were, often, just down the road, where they chose to use sand.

"The sand would crush over time."

Brigham Exploration's aggressiveness in trying more and more frac stages came to be known in the Bakken and other shale plays as fracing "Brigham-style." East of the Nesson anticline, it put its Jack Cvancara 19-18 1H on 36 stages for 4,357 barrels and 4 million cubic

257

feet of gas on May 8, 2010. The company ultimately went to as many as 38 stages in wells.[227]

Brigham keeps the chart in his new office in Austin just down the street from his old office that is now Statoil's. One old-technology, uncontrolled frac job cost about $1.5 million. Multi-stage fracs would start at about $6 million, including the swell packers and ceramic proppant. "So, of a total well cost of about $10 million, about 60% of that was the completion cost."

Were the higher-rate wells that Brigham's growing number of frac stages were producing just moving the production up in time for the Wall Street mindset of "pay me now" or would these wells actually make more oil over time as well?

The latter, Brigham says. "I remember some competitors state that they were reluctant to go to more stages, saying, 'Well, they're not increasing the EUR (estimate of ultimate recovery); they're just increasing the early production.' They were saying that, ultimately, their wells were going to produce the same reserves by doing a single frac as our wells would produce with multiple fracs.

"In time, obviously, we proved them way, way wrong. Time has proven that, with more stages, it's not just pulling the production forward; it's actually increasing the reserves ultimately produced.

"I think we led the way in the play. If you look at our results, our wells were significantly outperforming those of our competitors."

Only its first 11 Bakken attempts came on with fewer than 1,000 barrels; its next 150 that were spud in the field by the day Statoil assumed ownership in December 2011, all came on with more than 1,000. Its success rate: 100%.[228]

He credits Lyco Energy for inspiring the modern Bakken play in North Dakota by what it achieved in Montana. "Lyco—what they made is just an amazing field, Elm Coulee, the 'sleeping giant.' It was a little different reservoir than what we were targeting.

---

[227] It, as part of Statoil, and other operators have since gone to 40 and more stages.

[228] The rate excludes a lone, outlier, step-out look at Bakken in Mercer County. Of 32 attempts in Mercer County in state history in any formation by any operator, only one well made a meaningful amount of oil—just 11,394 barrels.

"We were stepping out into the basin center, which turned out to be the play that was most expansive for the Bakken. You could consider us and Continental as first movers into the middle of the basin.

"Continental was out there. We spent some time with those guys and they were really ahead of us in the play. Others were already there, but Continental deserves a lot of credit for being the first innovative mover in the North Dakota Bakken."

Ironically, as the largest oil and gas producers were leaving the onshore U.S. and the shallow Gulf of Mexico for new prizes abroad and in the deepwater Gulf, relatively small E&P companies remaining in the Lower 48 found new, huge, oil and gas fields.

"It's really remarkable. When I think about when I began my career in 1983, up until that time everybody wanted to get on with a major oil company because that was the place to learn, get exposure to new technology and innovate. It's really flip-flopped.

"The independents are doing this. The majors—they're just not the companies making that happen domestically. It's not the Chevrons; it's not the Shells; it's not the ExxonMobils. It's the smaller companies that are more entrepreneurial and able to innovate.

"Hats off to companies like EOG. Continental is another that manages to be entrepreneurial. And that hallmark separates the winners from losers."

By mid-2013, North Dakota hosted more than 5,500 wells actively producing from the Bakken. Among these, fewer than 300 were completed before 2004. Overall, the state's dry-hole rate had declined from 97% through 1985 to 1.9% since 2006.

Oasis Petroleum made 195 of the new wells—most of them coming on with more than 1,000 barrels and one for a whopping 4,095 plus 5 million cubic feet of gas. Whiting Petroleum made 807— most of them also with an IP of more than 1,000 barrels.

East of the Nesson anticline, Brigham's Alger Field discovery held 180 wells by mid-2013. Just south, Whiting's Sanish Field held 425. East of that, EOG's Parshall Field held 242. Just south, Van Hook Field hosted 128.

Along the Nesson, Bailey Field at the southern end held 131 wells. West of the Nesson, Brigham's Camp Field held 54.[229]

The USGS released a new Bakken assessment in 2013 to include the reserve potential of the underlying Three Forks formation, which Continental had proven in the first two benches by then. By 2013, the USGS noted, more than 450 million barrels of oil had been produced from the Bakken and Three Forks since just 2008. It now estimated the two formations held 7.4 billion barrels of undiscovered, technically recoverable oil—twice the 2008 estimate of the Bakken alone.

The 1995 assessment of the Williston Basin's future potential, based on technology at the time, had been just 151 million barrels.

***

Back in 1990, Bud Brigham thought 3-D was the future. And it was. But he, like any other member of the domestic and international oil and gas industry, could not have imagined a whole new business of 10,000-foot horizontals with 30-plus frac stages in super-tight rock.

"At the time, I thought it would have been 3-D alone taking it to the next level. I could not see what would be the next technology."

Where is technology going now? What could industry be doing in the next 20 years? Brigham says, "We're very early in figuring out how to optimally break up and produce the tremendous amount of oil that's in place in these reservoirs. Even with this multi-stage fracing—and everybody's doing an excellent job—we're recovering maybe eight to 12% of the oil in place.

"In the conventional oil and gas fields, historically, you saw initial recoveries of maybe 15%. It went to 25% and to 40% with subsequent recovery methods. I think we're really just getting started in the unconventional plays."

Taylor Reid, the ex-Burlington manager who went on to cofound Bakken-focused Oasis Petroleum, notes that the modern Bakken play evolved from horizontals with open-hole or "blind" fracs

---

[229] Figures are for wells for which data had been released by North Dakota by mid-2013.

to multi-stage fracs with swell packers, isolating sections of the lateral and fracing in a manner that focuses the water and proppant in discrete areas of the wellbore.

"The success of fraced horizontals in Elm Coulee Field, combined with the success of fraced horizontals in the Barnett, kicked off a new wave of drilling across the U.S.," Reid says. "It started in North Dakota (in the 1980s) with horizontals in the upper Bakken and then (in the 1990s) in Red River B—both without stimulation. Then Lyco applied fraced horizontals to the middle Bakken and EOG put in multi-stage, controlled fracs."

Garry Tanner, the ex-Enerplus chief operating officer, works again for a private-equity-investment firm, Quantum Energy Partners LP. In poring over business-plan pitches for investment consideration, Tanner is keen to the U.S.-shale plays.

The idea of more and more frac stages was the breakthrough in North Dakota, he says. "Just rubble-izing the rock, getting more of that horsepower in there in something that—to us in 2006—looked tighter than a drum and would never produce. It ultimately made Brigham, Oasis and many others a fortune. The technology opened up the rock with oil you didn't think you could ever get to.

"If you had told me in 2005, when we bought Lyco, that people would think about 30- or 40-stage fracs, that's just something that was beyond our thinking—and I think industry's too. Remember, we, at Enerplus, were fretting about going from two frac stages to four."

***

Upon buying Lyco, Tanner had enlisted Ward Polzin to run Enerplus' new U.S. business. Lyco had three rigs working for it in Elm Coulee Field. Enerplus retained three employees. "So we had as many employees as rigs," Tanner says. "We basically had to build a business unit from scratch."

Tom Lantz, the Halliburton engineer working with Lyco on Elm Coulee Field, stayed with the play to run the Bakken operation for Enerplus, which brought in Polzin as country manager. Tanner had met Polzin while Polzin worked for Calgary-based, asset-transaction firm Scotia Waterous in its Houston office. "(Scotia was) parading him around as this bright guy who knew the U.S. market. Ward and I had a great conversation; I thought he could be an excellent fit for us.

"After that meeting, we started pursuing him to run that business. One of the Scotia managing directors who had been in the meeting told me later, 'I felt like somebody was hitting on my wife and I couldn't do anything about it.'"

With a bachelor's in petroleum engineering from the Colorado School of Mines and an MBA from Rice University, Polzin went on from Enerplus in early 2008 to head asset-transaction advisory for Tudor, Pickering, Holt & Co. He was on the TPH team that represented CNOOC in its entry to the U.S. onshore via a joint venture with Chesapeake in the Eagle Ford in late 2010, followed by a JV with Chesapeake in the then-nascent Niobrara-shale play in 2011.

When joining Enerplus in the Bakken in Montana in early 2006, Polzin didn't see yet what the Bakken would become. "That was really the first unconventional-oil play," Polzin says. "It was pre-Barnett really. Lyco (in 2000) was the first to put in a fraced horizontal of scale in oil-bearing, tight rock. I think we saw that horizontal fracs of scale could change things.

"But we hadn't seen the evolution yet. Elm Coulee Field, obviously, was a sleeping giant. The porosity was much better in that area, so it had a kind of conventional aspect to it. It was tighter than anything we had ever done, but it wasn't as tight as in North Dakota.

"We could apply this horizontal frac into tighter rock and make it work. 'But, man, I don't know if it'll work in North Dakota because it's really tight over there.' That was the thinking at the time. We (at Enerplus) drilled some North Dakota wells in the early days right there with Harold Hamm.

"But, boy, he had the vision and much better than we did. And we were different too; Enerplus was still a royalty trust. We couldn't take that kind of risk."

He credits EOG with finding the enormous Parshall Field, "but that was geologically unique. I give them credit for what they do so well—finding the sweet spot of the sweet spot. No doubt they did. But in terms of making this ubiquitous—making it work almost everywhere—Continental deserves that credit."

In early 2008, EOG and Whiting were making the Bakken work east of the Nesson; the play was still foundering west of the Nesson. "We thought that Parshall was going to work because it has this unique pressure regime. And, up and down the anticline, it was going to work because it has a unique fracturing regime. But can we go to the basin center? The key thing here for the evolution of these shale plays is what people call the 'basin center.'

"'Can we go to the basin center?' The basin center is the deepest part, so it has the greatest pressure, but it usually doesn't have any natural fracturing and it's usually tighter. That would be Williams and McKenzie counties. Where I left it in early 2008, the question was 'Can we make it work with the lack of natural fractures in the really tight spot in the center of the basin? Probably not.'

"And then I've been proven wrong. It's working quite well."

Despite all that Lyco had demonstrated in Richland County, Montana, which had already made 43 million barrels of oil and 28 billion cubic feet of associated gas upon Lyco's exit in 2005, there were doubts. "A lot of people were skeptical, even after the Barnett, even after the Fayetteville—the early, gas-resource plays. They were skeptical of that tight *oil* would ever make a resource play. The Bakken dispelled that."

Commercial oil production from a shale is an exponentially greater challenge: Simply, a molecule of oil is larger than a molecule of natural gas; it is harder to extract it from a tight rock.

"Think about an interstate," says Dave Pursell, the petroleum engineer and head of securities research for Tudor, Pickering, Holt. "What may limit your drive is that one, small section where it draws into just one lane. That one lane may be just a quarter-mile, but you're going to be stuck for a while.

"Now, if every other vehicle is a tractor-trailer, you'll be stuck a long while. If they're all motorcycles, then not so long. The gas molecule gets through that same, small pore easier than oil does."

***

In 1954, one well was producing from the Bakken in North Dakota, making about 150 barrels a day. In 1994, at the end of the unfraced, horizontal attempts, there were more than 250 Bakken wells, producing 20 barrels a day each.

Upon Continental Resources' re-entry of the old Robert Heuer 1-17 to make a fraced horizontal in the middle Bakken in March 2004, the rock was giving up eight barrels a day from each of some 200 old holes. Daily Bakken production in the state was 1,640 barrels.[230]

When Brigham went to 20 frac stages in January 2009, nearly 900 wells were producing from the middle Bakken in the state, averaging 113 barrels a day each for gross output of 100,000 a day. By February 2014, some 6,000 wells were online, making 872,000 barrels a day.[231]

Cumulative oil production from North Dakota's Bakken through year-end 2012 was 546 million barrels. The old, shallower, Madison play had made 931 million. In third place with 142 million was Red River B that Burlington and Continental proved in the mid-1990s.

Continental Resources' Harold Hamm says, "This whole thing that's going on—the entire energy revolution, if you will—in America has to do with one thing and that's our ability to drill down two miles and turn right and drill two or three miles farther with horizontal wellbores, making contact in a thin, eight to 10 feet of tight rock, staying in a narrow zone for 10,000 or more feet.

"Once we were able to do that, though we might have a very low-perm rock, we were able to drain that sufficiently to be commercial. And not just in the Bakken but particularly in the Bakken.

"The Bakken is so important because it is across the entire Willis-

---

[230] Others had been plugged; they were finished.

[231] Bakken and Three Forks production from North Dakota had grown to more than 900,000 barrels a day in November 2013; however, severe, winter weather interrupted many oil-field operations. North Dakota Department of Mineral Resources director Lynn Helms reported in mid-February that the state's lows were as much as 31 degrees below zero and it had already experienced four major snow events and five major wind events. He added, "...From Williston to Bismarck, it was the ninth-snowiest December since 1890."

ton Basin and it's oil. And the oil is very high-quality. It's light, sweet, premium. You know, these gas plays are very significant—the Marcellus, the Barnett.

"But we're not fighting wars in the Middle East over natural gas. It's all about oil. And that's what this contains: 90% oil."

Hamm believes the U.S. unconventional-resource story is in only the second or, perhaps, third inning. "We're sure not in the sixth inning. You know, think about Pioneer (Natural Resources Co.)'s Wolfcamp (oil play in the Permian Basin) they announced a while back. I wanted to say, 'Well, welcome to the game.' There's been very little horizontal drilling in the Permian. Very little. Everybody's basically done fracs on verticals in stacked pay. They're hadn't been very much horizontal there. So now they've finally gotten in the game.

"We're still early on there and certainly still early in the Bakken. I mean, we talk about recoveries. Our estimate in 2010 in the Bakken was about 3.5% (of the oil in place) and that would give us about 24 billion barrels. We've seen some folks giving estimates of 10% recoveries now with the density they're doing, particularly where they're putting wells in the middle Bakken and in the first and second Three Forks formation.

"So if they've got eight, 10, maybe 12 wells in those units, they're thinking, maybe, they can get up to 10%, which, if you can, you're talking about a whole lot of reserves. And we're just now setting up pilots for secondary recovery. We haven't even talked about tertiary work yet.

"So it's very early in the game yet."

***

In 2013, Bud Brigham started his newest E&P—privately held Brigham Resources LLC. Producers were figuring out more and more layers of the nomenclature-befuddling, enormous Permian Basin in West Texas. "We think West Texas is going to continue to blossom," Brigham says. "It has just a tremendous number of tight reservoirs with world-class source rocks.

"I mean, it's almost like a mini-Saudi Arabia and, in our view, they've just scratched the surface."

In the Bakken, operators had to go horizontal and to multi-stage fracs to make it work "and, boy, did we. I mean, they are some of the highest-rate-of-return wells in the country."

But transfer to the Permian Basin has been slowed by the fact that many of its formations make commercial wells with just a vertical wellbore. "So operators have not been as motivated to go horizontal, move along the learning curve, refine that technology and determine the optimal horizontal recipe there.

"That's one of the reasons we're so excited about getting to work there. We think we can take our expertise that we've gained in the Bakken, having completed hundreds of horizontal wells in a play that was a harder nut to crack, and apply that to West Texas.

"We're going to find more oil-resource plays around the country, but we don't expect there to be as many as the gas plays just because not as many rocks will be able to produce that larger molecule."

Brigham and some former team members put together—with private-equity investors Warburg Pincus LLC, Pine Brook Partners LLC and Yorktown Partners LLC—some $650 million in 2013 to work in the Permian and other U.S. resource plays. "This renaissance is too exciting to walk away from," Brigham says.

"We want to get in front of at least four to six resource plays around the country. Some will be early, emerging; they will be riskier. But, if we can have some success, they could, potentially, be triples or even homeruns.

"We're also going to have several plays that are more proven, like singles and doubles."

The amount of start-up capital Brigham's new venture has raised is an indicator of the new onshore-U.S. oil and gas regime. He started with $25,000 in 1990 to build a $4.7-billion company, beginning with one small working interest in a well. At the time, $650 million of start-up capital would have bought 100% working interest in roughly 1,300 conventional wells. In the 2013 oil-resource world of $5-million-plus wells, $650 million might buy about 130 wells.

"That's how the business has changed," Brigham says. "The price of poker has gone up substantially. Now wells are from $2- to $10 million as opposed to $200,000 to maybe $1 million—so an order-of-10 magnitude.

"And the same thing with acreage. We were putting together options for $10 or $50 an acre in 1990. Now, in these resource plays, we're paying several hundred dollars to, sometimes, more than $5,000 per acre. It takes more capital to be successful today, domestically."

Jack Stark, Continental's senior vice president, exploration, says, "If you look at the Bakken play (Burlington attempted in North Dakota) in the late 1980s and early 1990s, they were drilling horizontal wells in the upper-Bakken shale and completing them without (fracture) stimulation.

"You look back on that now and have to ask, 'Why were they doing that?' Well, it's because the technology wasn't there to do these stimulations yet.

"In this industry, the technologies that are developed are quickly shared. Service companies facilitate this transfer. If they believe they've got a technology that could be utilized in a given situation, they bring it to the table. For instance, the technology Devon was using for stimulating Barnett wells in Texas quickly translated to other resource plays, like the Bakken. It is a highly efficient industry. We build off each other. If we try something and it works, it doesn't stay proprietary very long."

Tom Lantz, the ex-Halliburton and ex-Enerplus engineer, joined the Montana porosity trend's discoverer Dick Findley after leaving Enerplus. Together, with additional partners, their American Eagle Energy Corp. is making Bakken and Three Forks wells in far northwestern North Dakota in Divide County.

Lantz notes that fracture stimulation in the early Sleeping Giant wells were limited-entry. "The price of oil was not where it is today. It was about $20, so your well cost was especially important. With a limited-entry frac, you're just spacing perforations along the lateral. You then try to pump the job and break down the entire lateral at one time, just all at one time.

"It was a technique that had been used in vertical wells that had a lot of pay-section. But, often, all of your frac power would tend to only go in that one area that had the least resistance.

"The Bakken in the (Sleeping Giant area) is of a bit better quality than the Bakken in other areas. It was a more forgiving formation, if you will. We actually produced from some of these wells for a short time before they were fraced.

"So, when we made these limited-entry completions, we were still getting pretty decent wells. It was enough to encourage us to keep going. And they produced very little water; they were completely filled with oil (and solution gas). It was a better reservoir quality."

When considering the Sleeping Giant play, all of the science suggested it should work. But would it work?

"The conventional wisdom at that time was that you could never effectively produce oil from anything that was this low in permeability. You just couldn't do it. You couldn't do it *economically*. We did a lot of modeling. At the time, the only thing that was being produced from anything with this little permeability was natural gas, which is easier because it can flow more easily than oil.

"In the Barnett shale at the time, they were doing okay, but the results weren't great and that was gas. This Bakken play was oil.

"At the end of the day, one of the things I did was draw on—and we had drawn on all of our collective experiences—that I had worked in the North Sea with Phillips (Petroleum) and one of the ways we completed some of those wells was with fracturing, using this limited-entry technique.

"So we tried it. We didn't have a convincing Plan B or C. The technique of isolating zones along the lateral hadn't really been developed at the time. Somebody in the Bakken play in Saskatchewan had this idea of modifying sliding sleeves that were being used in vertical wells in stacked-pay formations to produce from multiple zones and apply it in a lateral wellbore.

"It allowed us to isolate areas along the lateral and pump the frac at smaller rates. We could pump them at four or five barrels (of frac fluid) a minute rather than 40 or 50 barrels a minute.

"So you're pumping more individual jobs (along the lateral) and inducing more fractures at much smaller rates. Once industry did that, it started having much more success—and not just in the Bakken but in the Barnett and in other plays. That technology rolled out pretty fast. It is the technique of the day now.

"It's a classic illustration of how innovation develops. It takes something that you've done before and some smart guys getting in there, tweaking and redesigning some existing equipment or knowledge and applying it in a different place."

Lantz recalls that, before Brigham Exploration entered the Bakken play in North Dakota, he and a Halliburton colleague went to its Austin office to talk about their experience and the services the firm could offer. "I thought we would be meeting with one or two guys. We walked into the conference room and it was filled with people, wanting to learn about the Bakken.

"The interesting aspect of this is that their early results were pretty miserable. But they stuck with it, tweaking, and the main breakthrough, in their case, was in continuing to increase the number of stages and the size of the fracs.

"It was a tremendous amount of money to do it, but they started to see some returns, some success. They deserve a lot of credit. They fought that battle for a quite a while. They, basically, started from scratch as far as the knowledge of how to go about doing this—oil from a low-permeability, low-porosity rock.

"They built a knowledge base very quickly and stuck with it."

Across the Bakken, there is still more work to do, he adds. "It's becoming evident that—even with the improved completion techniques—at best, you might be recovering 15% or 20% of the oil in place. There's a huge target left there.

"Is there some way to produce more of it? That's where the industry is right now."

Mitchell Energy's work in the Barnett was a breakthrough in countering conventional wisdom about getting natural gas out of a tight rock that lacked, open, natural fractures, Lantz says; the Bakken was the breakthrough in getting oil out of tight rock.

"It got people thinking differently. It got them thinking, 'Oh, we could actually get oil out of this kind of rock.'"

***

Oasis' Taylor Reid says the business plan for the company when it was formed in 2006 was to deploy the engineering, operations and acquisition expertise he, Tommy Nusz and fellow team members had developed at Burlington—and to focus on oil instead of gas.

"The basins we spent most of our time looking at were the Williston and the Permian. These basins have stacked pay; there is a lot of oil in place that could really set up well for resource, manufacturing plays.

"It just so happened that the Williston is where we got traction. We had experience in both, but we had a lot of experience in the Williston, so it worked out well.[232]

"You have this massive resource and, through primary depletion, you're probably only going to get maybe 15% of the oil in place. So there's a big prize to figure out how to get more out of the ground. Operational enhancements and the application of evolving technology will, ultimately, help us get more out of the ground."

Might industry circle back to putting horizontals in the Bakken shale itself but now frac it?

"We've talked about it in some areas. We haven't done that yet. There are some wells being drilled that way around the old Lyco position around the edges of the Sleeping Giant trend, primarily by Slawson (Exploration). Slawson was drilling in that original, upper-Bakken-shale play back in the late '80s and '90s. So they're familiar with it.

"It is of interest."

The new, unconventional-resource tack is contrarian to that of the old, conventional plays. "You had to find it with seismic or other methods and, then, it tended it to be more limited in scope. As you go

---

[232] Oasis' IPO was priced at $14 a share in June 2010; in March 2014, a share was $42.

to resource plays, you have oil and gas in place over vast areas. If you can figure out a way to economically recover the resource, you're going to be able to repeat it hundreds and thousands of times.

"And, then, the focus is on recovery and economics. How tightly do you space wells? How do you improve stimulation? How do you get costs down? How do you transport your product out because there's never been that volume of production from that area before?

"Instead of a small play where you drill it up with eight to 10 wells in a year or two, you're drilling this for 10 or more years."

He adds that the culture within an E&P company is a crucial differentiator. "Mitchell Energy was willing to try new things. That's very important. Companies that discover new plays—Burlington, Mitchell, the others—they apply new technology and learn from what they're doing. Something that is under-appreciated is the time it takes for technology to evolve. It may take 10 years to figure it out.

"It was like this in the Bakken. You had the upper-shale play and it stopped working. Then, the middle Bakken evolved with the application of fracture stimulation—first with fracs with liners in Elm Coulee and, later, with swell packers and staged fracs across other parts of the basin.

"The resource is still there; there's technology that, over time, will make them work. It doesn't happen overnight."

Continental's Jack Stark adds, "This is probably the most remarkable turning point—at least in my career—in this industry. It's reflected in the growth that we've seen in oil production domestically in just the last year. If you look at the (U.S. Energy Information Administration) website and just look at crude oil production in the United States, it shows that, in (2012), we increased daily production about 1 million barrels. It's the highest one-year increase in production that's ever been experienced in the U.S.

"We grew to about 10 million barrels a day in the '70s and then, after the '80s, it was really tailing down. It was on a precipitous decline. It didn't look like it would ever turn.

"Then you get this uptake here in the last couple of years. It's just remarkable. In fact, it's gotten to where we've reduced our imports such that China is now the No. 1 importer and the U.S. is No. 2.

"Who would have thought that we could turn around our production decline—and that quickly. It's caught the world by surprise. I mean the Saudis chose to cut back (daily) production about 1 million barrels last year.

"Who would have thought it, huh?"

***

Dick Findley, who developed the Sleeping Giant idea, says of the challenge of making oil and gas plays, "It's one thing to make the discovery; it's something else to make it economic. For Elm Coulee Field, the credit has to go to Bobby Lyle and his team at Lyco and to Tom Lantz and the team at Halliburton for the idea of putting horizontal drilling and fracture stimulation together.

"It's critical to have the geology—defining the field and coming up with the idea of concentrating on the middle member of the Bakken as opposed to the shale. That was a different kind of thinking.

"But that geology is worthless unless it's economic.

"It's profound—the technology that came out of Elm Coulee. Nobody believed you could produce oil out of a low-permeability rock. Nobody believed that. They had been doing it out of (tight-gas formations), but gas is a much smaller molecule than oil. Elm Coulee opened industry's eyes—and worldwide—to that you can produce oil out of an unconventional reservoir.

"Now we have other, oil-rich, unconventional-resource plays."

Findley grew up on the Gulf Coast in Corpus Christi, southwest of Houston. "My whole world, growing up, was about 'How am I going to get on the beach today?' When I was a senior in high school, my dad asked me what my plans were. I hadn't thought about it."

His father had attended Texas A&M and had wanted to be a geologist. "He was drafted in World War II and became an accountant. So I got to thinking about geology."

His sister's brother-in-law, Pete Boone, was working on a doctorate in geology at A&M; Boone was preparing to do his field work and needed an assistant. "I went out in the field with him. I crawled all over the mountains and hills of (far) West Texas for the entire summer after I finished high school. I decided that was what I wanted to do. He took me to A&M and got me enrolled. I wanted to be an oil geologist and an independent (operator).

"I was lucky; I got to do that."

Lyco's Bobby Lyle says that, if he had a favorite well in the Sleeping Giant play, it would probably be that first horizontal, Burning Tree State 36-2H. "Each one of them, they're like your kids," he says. "You love them all, but each has unique characteristics. We would reflect on and learn from each one and apply what we learned to the next well.

"But that first well—notwithstanding the fact that we were not able to take it out to the full (lateral) length that we had hoped for—gave us the encouragement to move forward.

"It has to rank as my favorite.

"If that well had been a marginal producer, our story would have been entirely different. The ultimate result from the field would not have changed, but it certainly would have been delayed. And, from our standpoint, it would have been materially different because we would have had to, basically, start over. That would have been hard.

"The Burning Tree State gave us the encouragement we needed to take the next step and truly step out to try to prove our concept."

After figuring out that the hole could be kept within the upper half of just a 30-foot zone for at least 9,500 feet, more efficiencies were sought.[233] "You start scratching your head and doodling on a piece of paper and say, 'Well, I wonder if we can drill in two directions out of the same vertical well? Interesting idea. Well, I wonder if we can drill in three directions? Interesting idea.' We weren't the only ones asking those questions; others were asking them as well."

And, while, it proved to be possible, Lyco and others determined

---

[233] Yet-longer laterals are not physically impossible. Instead, horizontal wells are traditionally no more than 10,000 feet—two miles—in lateral length due to states' rules and operators' concerns about diminishing returns.

that a short lateral of about 4,500 feet in length—rather than a long lateral—was more economic in Elm Coulee.

Lyle emphasizes the importance of good relationships. "If I hadn't had a prior relationship with Cameron Smith, he would have never thought to bring Dick Findley and Bob Robinson to my office. Had he not done that, it would have been a different story for us and for Bob and Dick. Good relationships are critical in business. It is especially important in the oil and gas industry where so much of what we do is based on trust, integrity and standing behind your word.

"No written contract will ever replace that."

Lyle is proud of the boldness Lyco demonstrated when it took on the Sleeping Giant idea. "We were just a small company, but we had technical people who were fearless, very smart and willing to undertake something that had never been done before.

"I think technology will open up additional opportunities, even in the Bakken. It's hard to believe we drilled that first (Elm Coulee Field) well just in 2000. People over the decades had said the Bakken wasn't commercial. They told me, 'You can't make any money in the Bakken. Don't even try.'

"We found ourselves at the intersection of a technological breakthrough and a reservoir just waiting for the application of that technology. Even in the Bakken, there will be other breakthroughs that will allow companies to extract even more oil from that reservoir.

"And technology will bring to bear opportunities in other basins where we know there is oil and gas, but where we haven't quite figured out how to get it out economically."

Among his current projects, Lyle, with San Antonio-based Central Montana Resources LLC, is working on the Heath shale just west of Elm Coulee Field. There, Halliburton is assisting in figuring out what may finally make this long-known, long-tried, source-rock work.

"We're still trying to figure out the reservoir," Lyle says. "It's a complicated son of a gun. Some days, I wonder when the breakthrough will occur. I scratch my head about it, but someone will figure it out. And, when that happens, the impact on domestic, recoverable reserves could be significant. The Heath has a lot of oil in it.

"Whether I'm still alive when it's figured out is a big question mark. But it will be figured out. And, when that happens, it will be a great, great resource play.

Lyle and the SMU engineering school, which bears his name, have a motto: No problem too big. "If you turn a group of brilliant minds loose on a problem like the Bakken or the Heath—whether it is young people working on it in a university context or professionals working on it in a business setting—the problem will be solved.

"You put the right, creative people together as a team with the right resources, provide a deadline and the problem will get solved.

"That's why I want young men and women to get excited about engineering, math and science and for kids to get energized by having fun while seeking and finding answers to questions like those we dealt with in Sleeping Giant and beyond. In 1997, people were saying we couldn't make money in the Bakken. We said, 'We can.' And we did.

"There is no problem that's too big to be solved. We're limited only by our creativity and our imagination. I believe that, if you can dream it, you can do it. If you believe this, it empowers you to take on just about anything.

"The other thing is to trust your intuition. It took a while for me to really believe that. I will never forget going to the Wattenberg Field (in the D-J Basin of northeastern Colorado) and people said, 'You can't make any money in the Wattenberg Field.' But we did.

"And when we went to the Texas Panhandle, people said, 'You can't produce black oil in the Panhandle.' But we did. They said it was a gas field. I said, 'I understand that but, in order to produce casing-head gas, you have to have oil.'

"I believed we could do it. And we did."

He had recently spoken to a group of MBA students whose undergraduate degrees were in engineering. They wanted to know how they could best use their engineering knowledge in running a business. He told them, "It's been a long time since I sat down and solved an engineering problem, working with formulae, but the discipline of engineering has absolutely served me well throughout my career.

"The discipline is in focusing, discovery, problem identification and the belief that there is a solution—not giving up while there is at least one more alternative to consider.

"It is the boldness of thinking beyond the conventional ways of doing things and to create solutions that others may have never considered or not been willing to pursue. These aren't things you find in many textbooks. But they are there in the engineering discipline.

"Where it leads, there is no limit."

THE MONEY

← ← ← ← ← → → → → →

*"I concluded that the industry needed something
like $50 billion a year of external capital."*
—Ralph Eads

arnett- and Marcellus-play leader Trevor Rees-Jones credits
Chesapeake's Aubrey McClendon for accelerating development of new unconventional resources by leasing aggressively.
He also notes that McClendon led industry in advocating greater U.S.
use of new gas supply. "I'm thankful for what he's done to move a lot
of these plays forward, even though he's beaten me to leases in certain
places.

"And he showed the oil and gas business how to get a deal done.
It only begins with Statoil. He was the first to invite them to the party;
everybody else followed in his footsteps.

"I think the industry owes him a debt of gratitude."

Steve Herod concurs with crediting McClendon. "Chesapeake
brought bigger, more-well-financed companies into the onshore business so, when the time came for a company like Petrohawk to sell,
there were plenty of potential buyers around to be interested."

In the fall of 2008, capital markets had closed. Stock portfolios
were showing red across the board. Long before then, however,
McClendon had known it would take more capital to fully develop the
new, U.S.-shale potential than stock and debt markets could capitalize
or that producers could fund from cash flow.

He called an old friend from his Duke University days. Ralph Eads, who received a bachelor's in economics, was now chairman of securities firm Jefferies & Co.'s energy investment-banking group. McClendon told Eads in 2007 that he had another shale play under way. Already, Chesapeake, which McClendon had co-founded in 1989, had made a meaningful position for itself in the Barnett, Woodford and Fayetteville and it had found itself on top of the Marcellus as a result of its acquisition of Triana Energy in 2005.[234]

He had gone to Eads in 2007 with a proposition.

Eads says, "After the Barnett, a number of companies, particularly Chesapeake and EOG, were saying, 'Well, if it works here, where else might this work?' Aubrey told me, 'I can't tell you the details, but we found another big shale play,' which was the Haynesville. 'And we're working on another one,' which was the Marcellus.

"I sat down with a piece of paper and added up how much capital just Chesapeake was going to need. I said, 'There's no way.'

"I mean, I'm a financier, right? This is what I worry about: How to finance things. I said, 'There's no way you can get that kind of money from the capital markets, Aubrey. We have to come up with a different way to finance this. We have to go where the money is; we have to go to the industry.'"

That would be fellow oil and gas producers. Eads got to work. He determined that a "carry" would be essential in the scale of joint venture that he knew the shale players would need. "It's favorable from a tax point of view.

"The other thing is that it's risk-sharing. You have to get the wells drilled. The buyer's point of view is 'If I'm paying in carry, I'm not paying you until you deliver me a well.' So, instead of just buying a bunch of acreage, the buyer is saying, 'No, I'm buying wells.'

"It's a different kind of risk-sharing and that's important: The carry had the function of tax-efficiency and spreading the payments

---

[234] Enerplus, which had looked at Triana when choosing to buy Lyco's oily, Bakken portfolio in 2005, added Marcellus properties to its U.S. business unit in 2009 by buying a $406-million, joint-venture package from Rees-Jones' Chief Oil & Gas.

out over time and it was risk-sharing. It meant that the seller had to actually drill the well for the buyer."

Eads looked across all the plays—the Barnett, Bakken, Woodford, Fayetteville, Marcellus and Haynesville; this was pre-Eagle Ford. After considering the capital Chesapeake would need to fully develop its position, he did the math for what all of the industry needed.

Then, he deducted cash flow. "It was $10 trillion. The U.S. GDP is $15 trillion. And the reserve potential was 2,000 trillion cubic feet of gas. I concluded that the industry needed something like $50 billion a year of external capital.

"Chesapeake needed about 20% of that. I knew the equity and debt markets couldn't give Chesapeake that; they couldn't give the rest of them that either."

The stock market is near-sighted and debt markets can't invest in just acreage; it has to invest in proven oil and gas reserves.

Eads would have to build a market.

The Jefferies staff, which includes geologists and engineers, began gathering and entering data on each play into a database. With that database, Eads and other Jefferies team members went on a world tour, explaining the shale plays to E&P-company officers in Europe, China, Japan, India and elsewhere, with a presentation that, over the years, has grown into a 189-page report.

"It's a very fat book that takes you through the technical and economic attributes, the above-ground issues—water, permitting, tax regimes. It became a study piece that we gave to all the companies we visited. We literally went around the world, telling people that this was a major development in the industry, it was going to transform the business in North America and they needed to be in this business."

From the feedback, Eads determined who was interested and in what. "Then, we connected the dots."

By 2013, of the 20 largest shale-play joint ventures, Jefferies arranged 17. Eads says, "The industry's been doing JVs for time immemorial; the industry has been built on partnerships. What was different here is combining the U.S. independent with non-U.S., major, oil and gas companies."

Altogether, including outright sales, it went on to advise sellers in 40 deals, totaling more than $125 billion, including advising XTO Energy in its $41-billion sale to ExxonMobil.[235]

"These transactions were all based on companies positioning themselves to participate in the most important development in the oil and gas industry of the past 30 years. Since deepwater (exploration and development) technology (in the 1980s), this would be the only other really big thing that's happened.

"A lot of people were naysayers early on about the shales. 'Oh, no. They're not going to work. The wells aren't going to perform' and so forth. We developed a strong, technical point of view that said, 'No, these plays are not only good today, they're going to get better because the industry's in its infancy in terms of understanding it.'

"I think our advantage was that we had the technical insight. I think we realized before anybody that the liquids part of the Eagle Ford was going to work. The early conventional wisdom was that, if you had liquids in the reservoir, the wells were going to load up and they wouldn't produce because the molecule is bigger (than gas). The pressure would decline; the well would die.

"We have an engineer here, Milton Gillespie, who found an old, vertical, fraced Eagle Ford well that produced past the 'bubble point.' He said, 'If it'll do it on a vertical basis, it'll do it on a horizontal basis.'

"That insight was critical. We did a lot of deals because we understood that there would be gas liquids and oil too. We realized that this was going to be a lot bigger; the wells were going to get better over time, not worse. And there were going to be more plays—more places where it would work.

"It was a real paradigm shift in this industry and any time you see change in an industry—any industry—it requires that companies adapt. Some companies adapted better than others."

Potential new U.S.-shale players' options by 2008 were to partner in existing plays, buy it or try to build one. "The point I always started

---

[235] The deal consisted of $31 billion of ExxonMobil shares and assumption of $10 billion of XTO debt.

with was that these assets provide a return superior to any large-scale, oil- and gas-investment opportunity on the planet. Today, it's still true. You look at the Eagle Ford: Pound for pound, it makes a higher return than anything else you can do in the oil and gas business.

"My second point was that this is going to go global because North America isn't the only place that has shales. That was particularly important to the Chinese; there's a ton of shale in China. I said, 'This is a great investment opportunity, but there's also an opportunity here to understand this important, emerging technology. And the most expeditious way to do it is to find a partner; if you don't find a partner who understands these plays, you have to build it or buy it.'"

ExxonMobil opted to buy—taking in XTO. Statoil rose up the shale-play curve through its Marcellus and Eagle Ford joint ventures and then bought Brigham Exploration.

"I think Statoil was very early to recognize the technical merit of the whole thing. Statoil ended up buying some of the very best assets because they were one of the first to understand it technically and embrace it. They were the first to see (our) presentation, start doing the work and say, 'Hey, this makes sense. Let's do this.'

"The investment climate outside of North America was becoming less attractive. They looked around the world and said, 'North America's becoming more attractive and the rest of the world's becoming less attractive. Let's go to North America.'"

Bill Marko, a managing director at Jefferies, notes that the news of the Statoil joint venture with Chesapeake in the Marcellus was stunning. It was November 2008. "Gas prices were falling and the financial markets were dead. Nobody had any confidence. And Statoil was saying, 'Hey, I want to do this deal.'

"It was big money in a really bad time. That put the shale plays on the international radar. And, then, they were followed by ExxonMobil, announcing it would buy XTO. These were world-class-type companies saying, 'Hey, this is big. This is important. I'm going to make a big commitment. I believe in it.'

"Statoil put it on the map and, once Exxon weighed in (in 2009), it was really on the map."

Eads says, "In 1981, when I started in this business, if you would have said that, 30 years into my career, the industry would have figured out how to power the planet for another 50 years, I would have said that was impossible. We had had natural-gas rationing in this country. Everyone was scrambling to build nuclear-power plants.

"Now, we can sustain humanity as we know it for a good long while, while we figure out other technological solutions to how we deal with our energy needs after that. It's a pretty amazing thing. It has lots of implications economically, socially and politically. And it hasn't even gone global yet; this is just based on what we've found here in the U.S.

"Whether other countries use their shale or not, it's there.

"This industry—what it does is hard, hard work with great ingenuity. Any time you get depressed about the world, what you need to know is that somebody will think of something to fix the problem."

***

CNOOC brought in Tudor, Pickering, Holt to represent it in its joint venture with Chesapeake in the Eagle Ford and Niobrara plays. Ward Polzin, who was head of asset-transaction advisory for TPH at the time, says CNOOC's entry into the U.S.-shale plays best demonstrated to him that the world had changed.[236]

"Statoil had done the Marcellus deal, but CNOOC's entry onshore the U.S. was a cultural moment where a river was crossed," he says. CNOOC had attempted in 2005 to buy U.S.-based Unocal Corp., drawing protest from some members of Congress; CNOOC would have become the operator of Unocal's U.S. oil and gas assets.[237]

"Today, we just don't think anything of it," Polzin notes. "Now Sinochem (Group) is doing deals in the Permian Basin, Sinopec

---

[236] Polzin returned to oil and gas exploration in 2013 as chief executive officer of start-up Centennial Resource Development LLC.

[237] Chevron stepped up with a competing, winning bid for Unocal. Its offer was of stock, while CNOOC's was of cash. Unocal shareholders preferred the stock offer, which averted the capital-gains-tax hit that would have resulted from a cash sale.

(Ltd.)'s in the Tuscaloosa Marine shale and PetroChina (Co. Ltd.)'s in Canada. The world changed rapidly. It was a bit of a seminal moment.

"I remember our discussion about it internally. There were others who wanted to work with us on these JVs and, frankly, we just thought it was so intriguing: 'How cool to work with the Chinese and see if we could get that done?'

"I would pause on it.

"In today's world, it's not a big deal but, relative to where we sat then, it was a big deal."[238]

Like Jefferies, as the 2000s marched on, TPH realized the most aggressive buyers of the shale plays—as they became more and more enormous and hungrier and hungrier for money—weren't going to be other, large, U.S. independents that were already in the shale plays.

Instead, U.S. assets had come into greater favor among non-U.S. operators in comparison with exploration abroad. "In 2000, I wouldn't have seen that, but you started to see more and more difficulty in trying to do things overseas. The terms (for operating) were being changed. Host countries were making it harder for it to be economic. Roadblocks were being put up.

"And here come the U.S.-shale plays." And it could be repeated; it wasn't just the Barnett and Bakken that would work. Fayetteville and Woodford were working and, within 10 months in 2007 and 2008, three more were proven: Marcellus, Haynesville and Eagle Ford.

Maynard Holt, a co-founder of TPH and head of E&P investment banking, says, "So much of the world believed that the Barnett was unique. When you replay the tape, we sat around in the industry for quite a long time thinking, 'Look at that.' Not many people were jumping ahead to 'Gosh, I probably ought to get a lease in Appalachia or maybe the Bakken.'"

Pre-shale, the traditional school of thought about future, meaningful, new U.S. gas supply was that it would have to come from the

---

[238] Chinese-owned oil companies' entry to owning U.S. oil and gas assets via JV was cleared by Washington in 2010 in part because the companies would not be majority owners or operators of the assets in this structure.

Rockies or the deepwater Gulf. Another myth that has been turned on its head is that future U.S. gas supply will have to be supplemented with imports. "And, then, 'Whoa! No!'[239]

"And, then, for a long time, everybody thought, 'Well, NGL prices. They're always half of oil prices and they'll hold up. We can just produce that to make up for what we're not making off (new, lower) gas prices.' Well, that myth was blown up too.

"And, then, we had this myth that U.S. oil production couldn't grow. We're on a roll here of—every three years or so—breaking down another one of these golden rules."

Polzin adds that making Barnetts and Bakkens abroad may take a while. "You have to have the right geology, of course, but you have to have the right above-ground facilities too: What's the government's take and are the oilfield services there? Three years ago, someone would have said the next shale plays would be in Argentina, Poland and China. Geology hasn't panned out well in Poland and getting the services in there is challenging.

"I heard a quote a couple years ago that it cost $50 million to procure a first frac crew in a new country. The international part of this story is going to develop glacially slow."

Holt notes, "All of this has happened in the U.S. because of the incredible economic incentive that resides here to figure this stuff out. These plays were not found on government land. They were found on private property and that incentive does not exist outside of the U.S. Take the (U.S. Bureau of Land Management) and put it in another country and, then, think about trying to develop a shale play there."

What's next in the U.S.?

Polzin says, "There have been comments that all the shales have been found. Conceptually, I can kind of agree with that. But my twist is that it doesn't mean we haven't found the next *economic* shale. Maybe we have found the big ones that go on forever, but we have tons of

---

[239] By March 24, 2014, the federal government had approved seven permits to export U.S. natural gas to countries in addition to those participating in the Free Trade Agreement. Meanwhile, U.S. oil producers were asking it to permit excess, new, light, sweet, oil as U.S. refineries have limited capacity for light, sweet oil.

little ones to find, applying this horizontal technology to more types of rock. It may not be shale. It may be tight-sand and shale technology applied to a different rock."

Holt adds, "The Barnett-to-Bakken lesson is that every time someone has said, 'We can't get any more out of the Permian. We can't get any more out of Appalachia. We can't get any more out of the Midcontinent,' well, that's never been the winning side of the bet."

BARNETT: 2014-

← ← ← ← ← → → → → →

"...What I heard...is 'You should short gas
because we're going to have a lot of it.'"
—Dave Pursell

D ave Pursell says the Barnett breakthrough came with treating this shale like one would a tight sand, such as the Cotton Valley. "People said, 'Well there's not going to be any natural fracturing in the Barnett. So what's George Mitchell doing?'

"It didn't fit the model because the model was that you had to have a lot of natural fracturing. The tight-sandstone fracing coupled with horizontal-well (technology demonstrated in) the (naturally fractured) Austin chalk all melded to create what is now the Barnett. And it's expanded exponentially.

"Were it not for George Mitchell, we would not be here. We would probably be heading this way. Somebody would have figured it out, but he figured it out when it didn't matter. He figured it out before gas prices started taking off. Really, gas prices just spurred acceleration (of the shale plays), but he was working on this and people thought he was nuts."

Pursell and other members of the research team at energy investment-banking firm Simmons & Co. International Inc.—prior to Pursell joining colleague Dan Pickering at what became TPH—had initiated coverage of Mitchell Energy in February 2001. By then, George Mitchell was 81.

"We always had funny titles for our initiations up until the day they were released, when the real title would go on it. The internal title was 'Mitchell Energy: The Old Man and the Shale.' They just kept at it when people were saying, 'You're crazy.'

"We wouldn't be where we are today without George Mitchell. Would we be getting close? Probably. But we wouldn't be producing as much gas yet. And look at the oil side of this.

"The renaissance in U.S. oil production is not just from oil shale because much of what's happening in West Texas (in the Permian Basin) is just tight rock. It may or may not be a shale; it's really just tight rock. And the best place to find oil in low-quality rock is where you found it in high-quality rock.

"The Eagle Ford had been drilled through hundreds, if not thousands, of times. Every one of these places they are drilling in West Texas has been penetrated over and over again in the past several decades. You know the areal extent; you have some data.

"This isn't rank exploration; there's very little hydrocarbon risk. You know there's oil or gas there; the question is 'Can you get it out of this more difficult rock?'

"The risk of drilling and it not containing hydrocarbons goes away, but the producibility risk is much higher. And areas where you find oil that is producible are fewer than for gas. You have this much larger molecule trying to flow through very tiny pores.

"The Barnett was the laboratory. Your typical Barnett well, the optimal lateral length was 2,500 or 3,000 feet with five or six frac stages in it. There is nobody completing a well like that in the Eagle Ford or the Bakken today; they're doing 8,000-foot laterals and 35 frac stages. You're putting in as many frac stages as you can pump.

"To take this to where we are now, you had to be smart and be able to react. That's why Shell and ExxonMobil and BP were not leaders in this. That's why it's George Mitchell, EOG and private guys who developed this. They're entrepreneurial. They don't need five committee meetings and five levels of permission to change the completion procedure. They can say, 'Let's try this on this well and see if it works. Okay, let's try this again.'

"There's this 'operational research' that is on the fly that is allowing these plays to develop. It's a critical piece in this development. If you and I have 1,000 potential well locations, we're going to say, 'Okay, let's take our first 50 wells and let's spend a little science money on the wells. Let's try some variants; let's vary some things on the individual completions to see what works.'

"That's important because, by the time we get to well No. 50, if we have a reasonably optimized understanding of what works and what doesn't work, then we can apply that to the next 950 wells.

"There is a net-present-value advantage to being quick and flexible. If you and I work for Exxon or Shell or BP or—well, let's not point at any one of them because they're all like this—we would get that acreage and have 1,000 locations. We would drill four or five wells and cut some core, ship it to a core lab, wait six or nine months for the results, kind of scratch our navel, try to do some stimulation optimization and find out that we don't have enough information.

"These horizontal wells can have eight unknowns. Until you actually go out and drill some and produce them, you don't know what those variables are.

"So, as a major, we've sat there and spent a bunch of money. We've wasted a year and a half staring at our navel and now acreage is going to start expiring before we can get to it and it is not in our corporate DNA to be nimble and flexible around completion procedures.

"You saw that over and over again where the majors just couldn't react quickly enough. And that's why it's going to be difficult to take this international. The Chesapeakes, the EOGs, the Mitchells and the private guys were able to make these work because they were nimble and able to focus on what mattered."

Pursell published in March 2007 that he had been incontrovertibly won over by the Barnett shale—and concerned about the future of U.S. gas prices. "We wrote that you could grow supply in the Barnett with a flat rig count and that this was a problem for gas prices. It was the most controversial report I have written.

"An oilfield-service executive called me and said, 'I read your stuff. I've always respected it. You must be the dumbest human being on the planet to think this and I don't even know what to think about you now, since you actually wrote it down and published it.'

"I had blasphemed in The Church of Almighty Depletion. The conventional thinking was that the gas production could never grow without more rigs, that you're going to have to continue to take the rig count higher, blah, blah, blah. What I had done is made a scaled-down model of 10 new Barnett wells per year to make the math easy. I laid everything out.

"I said, 'Well, where am I wrong?' He said, 'I don't know, but you must be wrong.'

"It was this circular argument; he couldn't find where I was wrong. Finally he said, 'Damn it. I'm a member of Mensa.' When a guy pulls the Mensa card on you, you say, 'I don't know what to say to that other than that we appear to disagree.'"

Pursell and his colleagues went on to determine and publish that the U.S. rig count would have to decline by 350 rigs to prevent more gas production. "We wrote that, if there are other Barnetts out there, this boded poorly for gas prices. When Aubrey (McClendon) was talking about the (new) Haynesville (play in the spring of 2008), what I heard him saying, basically, is "You should short gas because we're going to have a lot of it.'

"It was absolutely over from the gas-price perspective. And then came the Eagle Ford and the Marcellus, which was kind of piling insult onto injury from a supply standpoint.

"These guys should get a presidential award: They have single-handedly done more for the U.S. economy than anyone else I can think of because of cheap gas and new oil."

***

Dan Pickering was becoming a Barnett believer in 2003 during an EOG Resources earnings call. With a bachelor's in petroleum engineering from the University of Missouri and an MBA from the University of Chicago, Pickering had worked for Arco Alaska Inc. before becoming an energy-securities analyst and co-founding TPH.

"All of the questions were about the Barnett," he says. "They had hosted a lunch with analysts the following day. I remember asking Mark Papa if the hype around the Barnett was appropriate. He said, in a nutshell, 'Yes, it is.'

"That was the light bulb. The folks closest to it—who weren't trying to play it up much—were basically saying, 'Yeah, it's worth a lot of attention.' For me that was a 'wait a second' moment: We really needed to pay attention here because something is different."

As for the Bakken, Pickering's "wow" moment was in 2007. "We did a phone call with a private company. They were making pretty decent wells far south of where production had been. It was one of those moments when your ears perk up like 'I know what this smells like. It smells like what we've been seeing on the (shale-gas) side.'

"As an engineer, you know you can create fractures that will flow in the short term. The question is 'Are they going to flow in the long term?' They were making impressive wells and from source rock. 'Wow! This is coming out of source rock.' But you didn't know enough about the flow to have a lot of confidence. When you saw it, you had to be a little skeptical."

Expectations were that Bakken production would peak at 400,000 barrels a day and decline. "Instead, it became 800,000 barrels a day and it hasn't stopped. People began to realize, 'Hey, guys: We could meaningfully lower our oil imports. And we're adding jobs because natural-gas prices are cheap.'

"It finally dawned on the general populous in 2012. Industry observers could see this in 2011."

How long will the Bakken last?

"When will it peak? How fast are you going to drill it? In 2015, it will probably be producing a million barrels a day (at current oil prices). How long are we going to drill the Bakken? Twenty years for sure, but it's not crazy to think that we're going to be active there for 50 years. I think about the shale story as being measured in decades, not years or quarters."

In a yet-higher oil-price regime and with lower drilling and completion costs, there is yet more Bakken oil to be made. "The fringe areas of the Bakken still have oil but, instead of being 500,000-barrel wells, they're 100,000-barrel wells. It doesn't make sense to drill $7- or $8- or $9-million wells to get 100,000 barrels.

"The oil's there and the science still works, but you would need a lot higher oil price to drill that well."

***

Larry Nichols notes that Devon Energy's early horizontals in the Barnett had roughly 2,000-foot laterals. "The capacity of rigs has improved dramatically over time. These early wells were relatively short in lateral reach and took us forever. We were averaging 31 days for those early wells. It's down to about 12 days now and for a lateral that is twice or three times as long as what we were drilling.

"Rigs with enough horsepower weren't there at the time. Helmerich & Payne (Inc.) started making these new-technology FlexRigs. It's a dramatic change of economics.

"Another change is that there is real-time geoseismic now as you're drilling. The formation you're drilling isn't perfectly flat. They wiggle. You can chase that formation now as it moves up and as it moves down. That's a dramatic change. And how to drill these horizontals continues to evolve.

"It has been gradual. It isn't a sudden evolution. You're able to drill a little farther; the next well, a little farther. Then you're able to drill far enough and say, 'Hey, let's do multi-stage fracs. We have enough lateral there that we need to frac this thing more than once.' Every well is a bit of an experiment with a lesson from the last well."

Devon has some 4,500 now producing from Barnett and roughly 4,000 more locations to drill when gas prices improve.

"It's technology. There is a point you can make about this industry that has happened repeatedly over time and will in the future: Technology has proven us wrong.

"Right after World War I, the U.S. Geological Survey or someone came out with a study that said, 'All the oil's been discovered.' This went on for decades; you could regularly find some professor or some government agency with a new study that said, 'Everything's been discovered. We have reached peak oil and supply is going down.'

"It's been proven wrong for a hundred years now and it's because of technology. The Gulf of Mexico used to be called the Dead Sea; that was based on what technology would allow you to discover at that time. Lo and behold, the industry is producing oil and gas from the deepwater Gulf now.

"The world has huge amounts of oil and gas. Government is the major barrier to producing it. Mexico is a perfect example—political restraint.[240] In Nigeria, there is total chaos; there's just rampant fraud and lack of security. In Venezuela, the problem is expropriation."

Devon divested all of its holdings outside North America, beginning in 2009. "It's entirely driven by the opportunity we have here. We looked at the Cana (Woodford) Field, for example. It's out here in western Oklahoma, off Interstate 40. It's oil and it's in Oklahoma—an area where you can start and stop drilling as economic conditions dictate. It's in a politically safe area."

Devon also exited the Gulf of Mexico. "You're drilling these $200-million holes (net to your share of the cost); some were going to be dry. These are huge, multi-billion-dollar projects. We had a discovery in 2002. It took 10 years to get it online—10 years before you could get any return. And it's a huge, geologic risk because you're right at the edge of technology.

"You compare that with drilling a relatively little well in Oklahoma where you can get it on in 30 or 45 days. When we looked at the risk-reward ratio of the prospects we saw onshore the U.S. versus offshore, the deepwater Gulf made no sense at all."

He notes that investors should consider, when investing in an oil and gas play, that not all acreage is the same. A "manufacturing play" is a popular term. Nichols says it's not that simple.

"Relative to the history of the industry, it's getting close to that, but it's not like these machines that are mindlessly grinding things out.

---

[240] Since the April 2013 interview, Mexico repealed its 80-year-old law that had prohibited foreign ownership of its oil and gas resources.

You've got a machine and it's just pumping out one Coke can and another and there's nobody there.

"These wells are different. Some areas are karsted. The rock-stress changes across that field. Pressure changes a bit. Not all the acreage in the field is the same.[241] Whether it's the Barnett or any other play, you might say, 'Well, Barnett acreage is going for X and so-and-so owns Y amount of acreage; therefore, they're worth X times Y.' Well, the Barnett fades; it pinches out as you go west. In some of those western counties, you can say, 'I have acreage in the Barnett.' But it's never going to be economic.

"The same for the Eagle Ford or the Bakken: There are good areas and marginal areas. It is a trap to think that each is homogeneous.

"A second trap is to not recognize that technology is evolutionary. What we did in 2002 to combine horizontals with hydraulic fracturing in the Barnett was a huge step but, if we look at the horizontal wells and the fracturing we're doing today, it has become radically more sophisticated. Technology evolves; periodically, it takes giant steps forward.

"And, after that, there are thousands of little steps. It's not a light switch that is off and then on. It's a light that gets a little bit brighter and brighter."

***

The UPR team that developed the LSF technique while working the tight, Cotton Valley sandstone in East Texas in the mid-1990s tried some horizontals in the rock too, Ray Walker notes. They encountered the early issue of horizontal in tight rock like what Mitchell Energy experienced in its few horizontal-Barnett attempts.

"We did only about three of them and they were so expensive that they didn't really work," Walker says. "It wasn't a completion problem; it was a drilling problem. It took a long time to drill these horizontals. Today, they're doing them routinely out there.

---

[241] Karsted is where the rock has collapsed.

"It was just a technology issue. I look at all we learned in the 1990s about measuring a frac job in real time—being able to figure out where your fracs were being induced as you were pumping. And then I look at what that taught us about the (LSF) fracs. Both of these were applied in the Barnett in the vertical wells and then in the horizontals. It's amazing how all of these pieces came together.

"If you think about how far we've come in just the past 10 years and how far we came 10 years before that, you see us moving this industry forward every 10 years. If we continue on this same pace, 10 years from now there's no telling what it will look like.

"New technologies are coming about every day—new ways to do what we do. We're going to find better ways to drill, faster ways to drill. The rigs that are drilling in the Marcellus are now three times faster than three years ago. Frac jobs are three times faster.

"Three years ago, we were doing three frac stages in a 24-hour period, which seemed unbelievably quick at the time; today, we are routinely get nine frac jobs done in a 24-hour period."

***

John Thaeler adds that another lesson of the Mitchell Energy journey as told by Dan Steward in the documentary of Mitchell's work in the Barnett, was "don't out-smart yourself."

"It's a constant learning curve. We might get good at something, but it doesn't mean we completely understand. We always have to challenge ourselves. Dan Steward talked about how George Mitchell was always challenging everyone as to why something's happening, how it's actually happening and what you can do to make your wells better.

"And don't out-smart yourself, which we all do because we all think we're so damn smart."

In the book, Steward tells a story about H.A. Smith 1, a Barnett well the production team declined to complete in 1985, deeming it a dry hole. It was Mitchell Energy's first test of the Barnett in Denton County in trying to extend the play east of Wise County.

Steward writes, "The consensus at the time was to plug the well, get the core analysis and review." By the following Monday, plugs were set and the rig was being taken down.

"It was normal procedure on Monday mornings to review logs of new wells with Mr. Mitchell...After listening to our discussion...Mr. Mitchell explained that, regardless of what our subsequent analysis showed, we were going to attempt a Barnett completion in this well."

The company was putting together some 100,000 acres of lease-hold in Denton County. The rig was to be put back together, plugs drilled out and casing run. When it was fraced, it wasn't a great well, but it was an acceptable one. And it held the lease.[242]

Steward concludes, "I believe Mr. Mitchell's point was that, in the early stages of a play, you shouldn't out-smart yourself by thinking you know more than you do. He was exactly right. Important lessons were learned that kept repeating themselves in the Barnett play: Don't apply conventional exploration/exploitation logic, don't be afraid to try different approaches to problems and don't out-smart yourself."

---

[242] The well, which was put into sales 16 years later, came online with 700,000 cubic feet of gas; as of April 2013, it had made 364 million cubic feet. Steward says it still isn't "a great well" but Devon made five horizontals on the lease "and I believe they are quite satisfied."

GEORGE MITCHELL

← ← ← ← ← → → → → → →

"One still has to wonder how many companies...
would have devoted that level of time
and resources...with such an uncertain outcome."
—*Dan Steward*

George Mitchell could see in 1982 that the company's North Texas unit was going to run out of gas prospects. Steward says Mitchell told the North Texas group, "basically, 'It's up to y'all to find a replacement for the (Bend-conglomerate gas production) and you have 10 years to do it. And, if y'all don't think you're capable of doing that, let me know and we'll replace you with people who can.'

"We said, 'No, sir. We think we can do this.'

"People will fight something," Steward says, "and say, 'Well, that won't work and that won't work. We can't do that.' He wanted to know that the people who were going to be looking at this didn't have that attitude. I don't think that was harsh at all; he was looking to the survival of the company that was paying a lot of employees.

"We had some people who, into 1997, thought we were within 50 to 100 wells of having drilled the Barnett up. They didn't think we could go to closer spacing or go outside of our core area or that we could do anything to get costs down and reserves up. That was just where they were, which was not a good attitude for the team. They changed.

296

"But, as late as '97, there were people in the company who weren't convinced the Barnett was a replacement. Looking back and knowing what you know about shales today, it can be very easy to second-guess what was done then. But, at the time we were doing this, our knowledge was very small compared with what it is now."

In his book about the 17-year science project, he concludes, "One still has to wonder how many companies in our industry would have devoted that level of time and resources to a play, under those circumstances, with such an uncertain outcome."

Kent Bowker, the Mitchell Energy geologist who prompted reconsideration of the Barnet gas-in-place math, says, "The breakthrough in the Barnett was a complete change in industry's thinking of how petroleum systems work. We're producing gas out of a source rock and doing it in volumes that no one would have ever thought possible.

"I knew the Barnett was going to be big, but I never imagined that it would completely change the way we look at everything— geologically and geo-politically.

"And it was started by a small company no one paid much attention to. It didn't happen in Shell's lab or ExxonMobil's lab; this happened because of a bunch of guys in The Woodlands and Fort Worth who worked for a mid-size independent."

***

In Mitchell Energy's 50th-anniversary annual report in April 1996, employees slipped in an extra page after Mitchell had signed off on it, saluting him for the company's first 50 years. They wrote, "He will learn of it only after the report has been distributed and it is too late for him to say, 'Thank you, but no.'"

The salute is as follows:

George Mitchell was asked a few years ago to name his proudest accomplishment. His answer was that his role in creating the Houston Advanced Research Center was most important because of HARC's potential to benefit not only the Houston area, but the rest of the state, as well.

If asked the next day, he might very well have pointed to his accomplishments in the energy field: Building a company that has produced 2 trillion cubic feet of gas, created jobs for thousands and discovered hundreds of new fields.

But he might have said that he was proudest of building The Woodlands.

Or he could have said that his greatest satisfaction has come from rearing, with wife Cynthia, a large, close family, now grown into productive, responsible adults.

If, in the end, he selected HARC or energy or The Woodlands or his family, he'd be skipping over his role in helping to revitalize his home town of Galveston. Or chairing a task force of leading Texans to help his beloved Texas A&M plan its future. Or establishing programs that he hopes will come up with solutions to the many problems associated with unlimited population growth in the face of limited resources.

He is a restless, energetic and thoughtful citizen of the world, with achievements spanning the arts and sciences, industry and commerce, education and government. He's led the Texas Independent Producers & Royalty Owners and he's an All-American Wildcatter. He and Cynthia give the Mitchell Prize to encourage research into environmental and growth issues. The University of Houston has awarded him an honorary doctorate. He has received high recognition from organizations ranging from the Horatio Alger Association to Texas A&M to the Boy Scouts, including election to the Texas Business Hall of Fame. He and Cynthia have provided a major endowment to the Houston Symphony. The list goes on and on.

Mitchell was born poor in Galveston, the son of immigrant Greek parents. Still, as with many aspiring immigrants, so it was with the Mitchell family: In America, the keys to the future lie in family, education, hard work, enterprise.

At age 16, he went off to Texas A&M. A mountainous academic load was no great problem, but he almost had to leave the university because of trouble meeting tuition and other expenses. He earned a degree in petroleum engineering (emphasis on geology), then soon went into World War II army service. He left the army in 1946 as a captain, became a geology and engineering consultant and started his whirlwind career of broad-ranging accomplishment.

If George Mitchell were given to sentiment, he might pause to reflect on the good things he's done. But that's not his style. Instead, with characteristic intensity, he continues to devote himself to building, solving, creating.

***

George Mitchell said in April 2011 that he and the Barnett team didn't realize they were changing the world by their work. "We didn't realize the magnitude. We knew that we were going to need to produce more gas (to fulfill the gas-supply contract) to Chicago and our reserves had begun to fall. We knew we were right on the big tectonic belt (in the Fort Worth Basin) that, maybe, the gas supply in the whole Bend conglomerate came from.

"Something in that area. 'Where was the source of gas for all the Bend Arch fields?' That's what we were seeking.

"After about 17 years and $250 million of effort, we finally figured out that the (light-sand frac) was the best solution. We had tried every conceivable technique of fracturing and trying to improve the production. We finally concluded, after 17 years of effort, that the (LSF) was the best thing to use.[243]

"It's amazing how it began to catch fire. (After Mitchell Energy's merger with Devon) a lot of our top people got better offers with other companies, smaller companies. They began to spread out all over the industry—and all within the independents; no major companies were involved until later.

"Then Exxon came in and made that big deal (to buy XTO) and some of the others have made big deals. Now the Chinese have made a big deal. So it's really caught fire all over the world. It's amazing what's happening—the gas supply and not only that: It has even helped oil supply. It's really caught the whole country by storm."

---

[243] By the time Mitchell Energy merged with Devon, Mitchell had made 850 Barnett producers.

Mitchell, while still invested in Devon Energy with shares he received in the merger, went on to invest in the early days of the Fayetteville play in Arkansas and in the Marcellus in Pennsylvania.

"We picked up 50,000 acres in Pennsylvania. We were studying the geology and looking at the 3-D (seismic findings) as well as everything else. The Marcellus covers a large area. It covers half of Pennsylvania, part of the adjoining states, all the way up into New York.

"It's going to be, probably, the largest field of all. It's very similar to the Barnett. When it was laid down, it was pretty much about the same time as the Barnett—about 400 million years ago in a petroliferous type of formation.

"When we were going to drill our first four wells just to see what the Marcellus (had in Pennsylvania), we made a location where we thought was the best part of the state. And then we drilled the next well eight miles away, the third well eight miles in the other direction and the fourth well eight miles in the other direction.

"I began to think that half the state was going to make gas. After it's all developed, we'll find out."

Mitchell was impressed with the Bakken oil play as well. "I drilled a well in the Bakken back in '83, a wildcat, but we never could make oil out of it. The Bakken (today) looks very promising. And it's oil, so that's a big help too."

He hoped the U.S. will use its new gas supply. "If you get three miles per gallon on heavy trucks, get (natural-gas) fuel for them. Let's figure out how to do that. I think you can find a lot of gas use can be devised to take the excess gas that is coming out of the shales.

"We have to get everything organized. The gas production can help take care of some of (our) oil needs. Oil is still deficient. Gas— there's too much of it now. But the demand is such that I think we'll use up all the excess gas.

"I think there's a lot of work that's still to be done."

Mitchell said that asking Dan Steward in 2005 to document the Barnett work was to have "the technology written up for the records, so that everybody could see what we did and to have this type of record available for everybody to look at and to use.

"I've been busy now for 65 years, drilling wells all over the nation, and now we've had a consequence that came out if it that's been important. And it's been documented as to exactly how it worked, so other people could study the formula we used and what we accomplished and improve on it to help get our (U.S. energy) supply back in balance."

Mitchell's advice to this and future generations of oil and gas industry members: "Explore!"

Globally acclaimed geoscientist Michel Halbouty "used to tell me all the time--. Mike was a great geologist and he would say, 'Come on! Explore! Do something.' So, when I found the Barnett field, I said, 'Mike, I found this field because of you. You kept me drilling wildcats all over the place.' It made him happy.

"If you're an explorationist, be bold and really work at it.

"Twenty years ago, you'd say, 'Well, the independents will be out of business by (now).' But, right now, they're doing more work than they ever did because of this discovery that we put together. You have to keep the incentive going and the talent will come out.

"Let's see how we can all do better."

ACKNOWLEDGEMENTS

← ← ← ← ← → → → → →

My family very kindly forgave me for missing our usual celebrations during most of 2013. Between Easter and Thanksgiving, I made it to one birthday party. A nephew says he was convinced I really was working hard on the book when he learned in October that I had not played golf since July.

A friend from my newspaper days, Master Sgt. John A. Sullivan, retired, Louisiana National Guard, made many, much-appreciated, food and other runs for me, giving me dozens of extra hours toward staying on task.

Hart Energy very generously gave me leave to work on this project. My thinking had been that it would be a roughly six-month endeavor. Thankfully, I was quite wrong as a result of the abundance of information industry members and additional sources provided.

Linda Bomke, vice president, The Mitchell Family Corp., loaned me the office copy of Dan Steward's book, which was out of print in 2013 and continues to be unavailable for purchase as of this writing. Dan's book was crucial in walking through the geological and engineering challenges of the early work in the Barnett and he was tireless in helping me get the science and timetable behind the Mitchell Energy story right.

Dick Findley is who found my porosity/permeability mix-up. I was certain it was in the work, but I had not yet located it by early October. It was in Dick's portion and he came upon it during fact-check. Despite my extraordinarily daft *faux pas*, he continues to be encouraged by that I seem to be capable of learning.

Dan and Dick each also participated in the pre-reader group, reviewing the entire work for sensibility and additional corrections, along with Dr. Bobby Lyle, Steve Herod, Dick Stoneburner, Bud Brigham, Steve Antry (chairman and chief executive officer, Eagle Energy Exploration LLC) and Peggy Williams (geologist and editorial director, Hart Energy). Their expert challenge of the content has provided confidence in its worth as a lasting resource.

Liza Karakashian with Verbal Ink arranged expedited transcription of the interview files. Edgar Online Inc. provided tremendously search-friendly archives of SEC filings.

The cadence of the opening paragraphs is borrowed from historian David McCullough in his narration of *Seabiscuit*. Mid-afternoon pep rallies were provided by *Secretariat*.

Fellow editor and long-time friend Jodi Wetuski Phillips apparently whispered to me in June that I should briefly suspend my research and start writing. In December, I looked in my appointment book for when we had last visited. I checked the book's Word file; it had been created that day at 3:54 p.m.

When interviewing George Mitchell in 2011, I had been certain of a twinkle in his eyes. Of course, there were boom lights behind me at the time that had been set up by the videographer. But I was sure the twinkle remained as we were parting.

In his obituary, his family wrote of "stargazing on warm summer nights in Galveston" and that his childhood dream had been to be an astronomer. After selling Mitchell Energy, "the twinkle of starlight was rekindled in his imagination."

Still driven by a burning curiosity and a fascination of what may lie at the edge of what is knowable, he founded the George P. and Cynthia Woods Mitchell Institute for Fundamental Physics and Astronomy at Texas A&M. With the Board of the Carnegie Institute of Science, he co-funded an initiative to build the first of six, massive mirrors for the Giant Magellan Telescope, an unprecedented, high-risk engineering project that proved the technology existed to open new horizons in astronomy. Although he will never peer into the depths of the universe with these new scientific tools, those who do see farther will benefit from his vision and commitment. He dreamed big.

The shale-play founders and leaders who were interviewed for this work were earnest in their candor and their patience. If not for their frankness and generosity with their time, this documentary would not have been possible. If not for their and others' earnest pursuit of geologic truth and engineering possibility, there would not yet be a story to be told.

—Nissa Darbonne,
April 2014

SOURCES

← ← ← ← ← → → → → →

The vast amount of companies' historical fiscal data, portfolio positions and outlooks cited in this work are sourced from their digital filings with the U.S. Securities and Exchange Commission and accessed via Edgar-Online.com.

Stock-price data are from Nasdaq and the New York Stock Exchange for stocks that no longer trade, e.g. BEXP (Brigham Exploration Co.) For stocks that continue to trade, historical pricing, volume, splits, dividends and other details are sourced from Yahoo! Finance and Fidelity.com as well as for the Dow Jones Industrial Average and the Arca Oil & Gas Index. IPO pricing data are from Edgar-Online.com.

Historical oil and gas prices are sourced from the U.S. Energy Information Administration's daily record of Cushing, Oklahoma, Crude Oil Futures Contract 1, beginning April 4, 1983, and its daily record of Natural Gas Futures Contract 1, beginning Jan. 13, 1994.

Historical data for North Dakota wells are sourced from the Excel index and PDF files on record with the North Dakota Industrial Commission, Oil and Gas Division. Montana annual drilling summaries, annual production summaries and historical well files are from the Montana Board of Oil and Gas.

Haynesville-well data are supplemented with records from the Louisiana Department of Natural Resources; historical Fayetteville production data, from the Arkansas Oil and Gas Commission; historical Barnett production data, from the Texas Railroad Commission; historical U.S. production, from the EIA.

SEC filings that were reviewed total more than 1,200. Additional sources are cited below; these and data from SEC filings are referenced in the bibliography that follows.

Interviews (in order of appearance)

—George Mitchell, April 7, 2011.

—Ray Walker, executive vice president and chief operating officer, Range Resources Corp., April 29, 2013.

—Dick Findley, chairman, American Eagle Energy Corp., March 18, 2013.

—Taylor Reid, president and chief operating officer, Oasis Petroleum Inc., April 24, 2013.

—Cameron Smith, advisor, Warburg Pincus LLC, March 18, 2013.

—Bobby Lyle, chairman, Lyco Holdings Corp., Jan. 25, March 11 and March 14, 2013.

—Kent Bowker, executive vice president, geology, Titan River Energy LLC, April 25, 2013.

—Dan Steward, geologist, Republic Energy Inc., March 12, August 14 and August 18, 2013.

—Larry Nichols, executive chairman, Devon Energy Corp., April 17, 2013.

—Tony Vaughn, executive vice president, exploration and production, Devon Energy Corp., April 17, 2013.

—Tom Lantz, chief operating officer, American Eagle Energy Corp., April 3, 2013.

—Harold Hamm, chairman and chief executive officer, Continental Resources Inc., Sept. 3, 2013.

—Garry Tanner, managing director, Quantum Energy Partners LP, Aug. 23, 2013.

—Jack Stark, senior vice president, exploration, Continental Resources Inc., March 19, 2013.

—Trevor Rees-Jones, president and chief executive officer, April 15, 2013.

—Dave Pursell, managing director and head of securities research, Tudor, Pickering, Holt & Co., April 25, 2013.

—Harold Korell, chairman, Southwestern Energy Co., March 27, 2013.

—John Thaeler, chief operating officer, Vitruvian Exploration LLC, April 10, 2013.

—Richard Lane, president and chief executive officer, Vitruvian Exploration LLC, April 10, 2013.

—Bud Brigham, chairman, Brigham Resources LLC, June 14, 2010, and April 23, 2013.

—Bill Zagorski, vice president, geology, Marcellus-shale division, Range Resources Corp., April 26, 2013.

—Jeff Ventura, president and chief executive officer, Range Resources Corp., May 17, 2013.

—Dick Stoneburner, senior advisor, Pine Brook Partners LP, March 11, 2013.

—Floyd Wilson, chairman and chief executive officer, Halcon Resources Corp., Sept. 17, 2011.

—Steve Herod, president, Halcon Resources Corp., March 27, 2013.

—Rod Lewis, chief executive officer, Lewis Energy Corp., April 19, 2013.

—Gregg Robertson, president, First Rock Inc., March 25, 2013.

—Ward Polzin, chief executive officer, Centennial Resource Development LLC, April 15, 2013.

—Ralph Eads, vice chairman, energy investment banking, Jefferies & Co., May 15, 2013.

—Bill Marko, managing director, Jefferies & Co., March 15, 2013.

—Maynard Holt, co-president and head of E&P investment banking, Tudor, Pickering, Holt & Co., April 15, 2013.

—Dan Pickering, co-president and head of TPH Asset Management, Tudor, Pickering, Holt & Co., March 28, 2013.

Books, Papers, Presentations & Articles

Barnett

—*The Barnett Shale Play: Phoenix of the Fort Worth Basin, A History*, Dan Steward, Fort Worth Geological Society and North Texas Geological Society, 2007.

—"Proppants? We Don't Need No Proppants," M.J. Mayerhofer, M.F. Richardson, R.N. Walker Jr., D.N. Meehan, M.W. Oehler and R.R. Browning Jr., Society of Petroleum Engineers annual technical conference and exhibition, Oct. 5-8, 1997.

—"Proppants, We Still Don't Need No Proppants—A Perspective of Several Operators," Ray N. Walker Jr., Jeffery L. Hunter, Al C. Brake, Paul A. Fagin and Nick Steinsberger, Society of Petroleum Engineers annual technical conference and exhibition, Sept. 27-30, 1998.

—"Waterfracs: Results from 50 Cotton Valley Wells," Michael J. Mayerhofer and D. Nathan Meehan, Society of Petroleum Engineers technical conference and exhibition, Sept. 27-30, 1998.

—"Barnett shale rising star in Fort Worth Basin," Vello A. Kuuskraa, George Koperna, James W. Schmoker and John C. Quinn, *Oil & Gas Journal*, May 25, 1998.

—"A Case History for Massive Hydraulic Fracturing the Cotton Valley Lime Matrix, Fallon and Personville Fields," H.G. Kozik/Mitchell Energy Corp. and S.A. Holditch/Texas A&M University, Journal of Petroleum Technology, Volume 33, Number 2, February 1981.

—"Breaking Into The Barnett," Nissa Darbonne, *Oil and Gas Investor*, April 2006.

— "The Barnett Barrels Along," Robert Ransone, *Oil and Gas Investor*, December 2003.

—"Recent developments of the Barnett Shale play, Fort Worth Basin," Kent A. Bowker, *West Texas Geological Society Bulletin*, Volume 42, No. 6 (2003).

—"Mississippian Barnett Shale, Fort Worth basin, north-central Texas: Gas-shale play with multi-trillion cubic foot potential," Scott L. Montgomery, Daniel M. Jarvie, Kent A. Bowker and Richard M. Pollastro, *AAPG Bulletin*, February 2005.

—"The Barnett Shale: Visitors Guide to the Hottest Gas Play in the US," Jeff Hayden and Dave Pursell, Pickering Energy Partners Inc., October 2005.

—"The Barnett Shale: Still the Hottest Gas Play in the U.S.," Dave Pursell, David Heikkinen and Marshall Carver, Pickering Energy Partners Inc., Dec. 20, 2006.

—"The Yin and Yang of Production Growth, Rig Count, and Gas Storage," Dave Pursell, Pickering Energy Partners Inc., March 8, 2007.

—"Newark, East (Barnett Shale) Field, Discovery Date: 10-15-1981," field data, Texas Railroad Commission, Jan. 23, 2012.

—"Newark, East (Barnett Shale) Total Natural Gas, 1993 through April 2013," Texas Railroad Commission, April 25, 2013.

Bakken

—"A Brief History of Oil Production from the Bakken Formation in the Williston Basin," Stephan Nordeng, *Geo News*, January 2010.

—"The Bakken: A Question of Maturity," Stephan Nordeng and Julie LeFever, Williston Basin Petroleum Conference, April 2008.

—*Obscurity to Fame in the Oil Business*, Michael S. Johnson, undated.

—"In Pursuit of Bakken," Nissa Darbonne, *Oil and Gas Investor*, August 2010.

—"The New Bakken Play in Eastern Montana," Stephen A. Sonnenberg, *AAPG Search and Discovery*, July 16, 2012.

—"Characterization of the Bakken System of the Williston Basin from Pores to Production; The Power of a Source Rock/Unconventional Reservoir Couplet," Anne Grau and Robert H. Sterling, *AAPG Search and Discovery*, Article #40847, December 12, 2011.

—"Bakken Horizontal Best Practices Review," Charles Wiley, Mike Eberhard, Bob Barree and Tom Lantz, Halliburton corporate presentation, October 2005.

—"Improved Horizontal Well Stimulations in the Bakken Formation, Williston Basin, Montana," Charles Wiley, Bob Barree, Mike Eberhard and Tom Lantz, Society of Petroleum Engineers annual technical conference and exhibition, Sept. 26-29, 2004.

—"The Department Of Mineral Resources Assessment Of The Bakken Formation," Ed Murphy, *DMR Newsletter*, Volume 36, No. 1.

—"North Dakota Geological Survey Circular No. 16, Summary of the Henry O. Bakken No. 1, Williams County, North Dakota," Sidney B. Anderson, July 1953.

—"What Are Prospects In Williston Basin's East Side?" Clarence B. Folsom Jr. and Sidney B. Anderson, *Oil & Gas Journal*, Dec. 12, 1955.

—"Oil Exploration and Development in the North Dakota Williston Basin: 1994-1995," Thomas J. Heck, *Miscellaneous Series No. 84*, North Dakota Geological Survey, 1996.

—"Mississippian stratigraphy of northern Montana," J.W. Nordquist, *4th Annual Field Conference Guidebook*, Billings Geological Society, 1953.

—"3 to 4.3 Billion Barrels of Technically Recoverable Oil Assessed in North Dakota and Montana's Bakken Formation—25 Times More Than 1995 Estimate," U.S. Geological Survey, April 10, 2008.

—"Assessment of Undiscovered Oil Resources in the Bakken and Three Forks Formations, Williston Basin Province, Montana, North Dakota, and South Dakota," U.S. Geological Survey, April 2013.

—"North Dakota Annual Oil Production, 1951-2012," North Dakota Department of Mineral Resources, June 2013.

—"Containment of Hydraulic Fracture Treatments in the Viewfield Bakken Oilfield of SE Saskatchewan," Barry Hassen, Youssouf Zotskine and Dale Gulewicz, Canadian Society for Unconventional Resources, February 2013.

—"Director's Cut," monthly briefing, Lynn Helms, North Dakota Industrial Commission, Department of Mineral Resources," Feb. 14, 2014.

—"Robert-Heuer 1-17R Well Dedication," proclamation by North Dakota Gov. Jack Dalrymple, Oct. 27, 2011.

—"Statoil's Bakken," Nissa Darbonne, *Oil and Gas Investor*, December 2011.

—"Emerging Plays," Nissa Darbonne, *Oil and Gas Investor*, January 2012.

—"The Bakken Is Back," Peggy Williams, *Oil and Gas Investor*, April 2004.

—"Jefferies Analyst: Bakken 'Will Be One Of The Largest Oil Discoveries In North America," Nissa Darbonne, *Oil and Gas Investor*, Sept. 24, 2009.

—"ND Monthly Bakken Oil Production Statistics, including Bakken, Sanish, Three Forks, and Bakken/Three Forks Pools," North Dakota Department of Natural Resources, Oil & Gas Division.

—"North Dakota Cumulative Oil Production by Formation Through December 2012," North Dakota Department of Natural Resources, Oil & Gas Division.

—"Elm Coulee Idea Opened New Play; Learning curve continues," Louise S. Durham, AAPG *Explorer*, August 2009.

—"Experience Paid Off at Parshall; Explorer of the Year saw Elm Coulee similarities," Louise S. Durham, AAPG *Explorer*, June 2009.

Fayetteville
—"Assessment of Undiscovered Natural Gas Resources of the Arkoma Basin Province and Geologically Related Areas," U.S. Geological Survey, Fact Sheet 2010-3043, June 2010.
—"Landowners, Others Seeing the Impact of Energy Investment," Garry Hoffmann, *Arkansas Business*, Aug. 27, 2007.
—*Arkansas: Reasonably Forseeable Development Scenario for Fluid Minerals*, U.S. Department of the Interior, Bureau of Land Management, March 2008.
—"Our History," Southwestern Energy Co., Swn.com, 2013.
—*Revisiting the Economic Impact of the Natural Gas Activity in the Fayetteville Shale: 2008-2012*, Center for Business and Economic Research, Sam M. Walton College of Business, University of Arkansas, May 2012.

Marcellus
—"Range's Path to Discovery and Commercialization of the Marcellus Shale—the Largest Producing Gas Field in the U.S.," Jeff Ventura, American Association of Petroleum Geologists annual convention and exhibition, May 20, 2013.
—"Practical Problems in Well Testing Devonian Shale Gas Wells," J.A. Murtha and D.E. Lancaster, Society of Petroleum Engineers eastern regional meeting, October 1989.
—"A Case Study of the Evaluation, Completion, and Testing of a Devonian Shale Gas Well," D.E. Lancaster, F.K. Guidry, R.L. Graham, J.B. Curtis, J.S. Shaw and T.H. Blake, *Journal of Petroleum Technology*, May 1989.
—*Elmworth: Case Study of a Deep Basin Gas Field*, introduction by John Masters, American Association of Petroleum Geologists, Memoir 38, 1984.
—"Company Timeline," Range Resources Corp., Rangeresources.com.
—"Corporate History of the East Ohio Gas Co.: The Spirit of Progress," East Ohio Gas Co., Dom.com (Dominion Resources Inc.)
—"Optimal Development of Utica Shale Gas Wells," George J. Koperna Jr., Jonathan Kelafant and Vello A. Kuuskraa, AAPG *Search and Discovery*, 2008.
—"Pennsylvania Natural Gas Production Up 62% y/y to 3.3 Tcf, NGI Reports," press release issued by *Natural Gas Intelligence*, Feb. 21, 2014.
—"Rockies pipeline reverses flow for Marcellus shale gas and wins FERC ruling," George Lobsenz, IHS Unconventional Energy Blog, Dec. 17, 2013.

Haynesville & Eagle Ford
—"Geologic analysis of the Upper Jurassic Haynesville Shale in east Texas and west Louisiana: Discussion," Marvin D. Brittenham, *AAPG Bulletin*, March 2013.
—"Floyd-Opoly," Nissa Darbonne, *Oil and Gas Investor*, November 2011.

—"Petrohawk Energy Corporation Announces Plans to Divest Gulf Coast Division and Grows Mid-Continent Resource Presence," Petrohawk Energy Corp., Business Wire, June 25, 2007.
—"The Wildcatter: Corpus Christi's Gregg Robertson, key member of Eagle Ford discovery, named 2012 Newsmaker of the Year," Mark Collette, *Corpus Christi Caller Times*, Dec. 29, 2012.
—"Petrohawk/Eagle Ford," Dick Stoneburner, Independent Petroleum Association of America and Texas Independent Producers & Royalty Owners Association membership meeting, July 8, 2009.
—"Petrohawk and KCS Are Fracing The Hosston Code," Nissa Darbonne, *Oil and Gas Investor*, August 2006.
—"Dirty Chalk," Nissa Darbonne, *Oil and Gas Investor*, August 2011.
—"Recipe for Growth," Leslie Haines, *Oil and Gas Investor*, May 2000.
—"South Texas Freebird," Steve Toon, *Oil and Gas Investor*, June 2011.
—"The Application of Petrohawk Operating Company to Adopt Temporary Field Rules for the Hawkville (Eagleford Shale) Field, La Salle County, Texas," Texas Railroad Commission, Nov. 4, 2009.
—"The Application of Apache Corporation to Consider Adoption of Temporary Field Rules for the Giddings (Eagleford) Field, Lee, Brazos and Burleson Counties, Texas," Texas Railroad Commission, Aug. 13, 2008.

Additional
—*The Prize: The Epic Quest for Oil, Money, and Power*, Daniel Yergin, Simon & Schuster, 1991.
—"National Oil and Gas Assessment 2013, Assessment Updates," U.S. Geological Survey, Energy.usgs.gov.
—Written testimony to the U.S. Senate, Committee on Energy and Natural Resources, Stephen A. Holditch, Oct. 4, 2011.
—Written testimony to the U.K. House of Lords, Economic Affairs Committee, Chris Wright, Oct. 20, 2013.
—"Hydraulic Fracturing of Oil and Gas Wells in Kansas," Daniel R. Suchy and K. David Newell, Kansas Geological Survey, PIC-32, May 15, 2012.
—"DOE's Unconventional Gas Research Programs 1976-1995: An Archive of Important Results," Strategic Center for Natural Gas and Oil, National Energy Technology Laboratory, U.S. Department of Energy, Jan. 31, 2007.
—"Translating Lessons Learned From Unconventional Natural Gas R&D To Geologic Sequestration Technology," Vello A. Kuuskraa and Hugh D. Guthrie, *Journal of Energy & Environmental Research*, 2.1, 2002.
—"The Reservoir Engineering Aspects of Horizontal Drilling," F.M. Giger, L.H. Reiss, A.P. Jourdan, Society of Petroleum Engineers technical conference

and exhibition, Sept. 16-19, 1984.

—"Natural Gas Regulation: The History of Regulation," NaturalGas.org, 2013.

—"Shale Gas Holds Global Opportunities," Stephen A. Holditch, *American Oil & Gas Reporter*, August 2010.

—"George Phydias Mitchell—The Father We Knew, May 21, 1919-July 26, 2013," the Mitchell family, *Houston Chronicle*, July 30, 2013.

—"Small-Scale Geologic Structures within Cedar Hills Red River B Field, Bowman and Slope Counties, North Dakota," Paul E. Diehl, *NDGS Newsletter*, Volume 28, Number 2.

—"History of the Cedar Creek Anticline, Southeast Montana," John Davis, Denbury Resources Inc., *AAPG Search and Discovery*, Article #90169, October 2013.

—"The Cedar Creek Anticline, 43 Years of History and Development, 1921-1964," Thomas A. Gwynn, North Dakota Geological Society and Saskatchewan Geological Society, Williston Basin Symposium, September 1964.

—"Big Stick/Four Eyes Fields: Structural, Stratigraphic and Hydrodynamic Trapping Within Mission Canyon Formation, Williston Basin," John J. Breig, *AAPG Search and Discovery*, Article #91033, August 1988.

—"Table 11.1b World Crude Oil Production: Persian Gulf Nations, Non-OPEC, and World," U.S. Energy Information Administration, *Monthly Energy Review*, March 2014.

—"LNG Revisited," Nissa Darbonne, Oil and Gas Investor, July 2001.

—"Applications Received by DOE/FE to Export Domestically Produced LNG from the Lower-48 States, as of March 24, 2014," U.S. Department of Energy, Office of Fossil Energy, Energy.gov, March 24, 2014.

—"Statement by Harold Hamm, Chairman and Chief Executive Officer, Continental Resources, Inc., Senate Energy and Natural Resources Committee Hearing, January 30, 2014," Energy.senate.gov.

—"Fifty Year History of the Texas Austin Chalk Trend," Holifield Energy Company LLC, Holifieldenergy.homestead.com.

—*2009 Annual Report of the State Oil & Gas Supervisor*, California Department of Conservation, Division of Oil, Gas, & Geothermal Resources, 2010.

—*Something from Nothing: Joe B. Foster and the People Who Built Newfield Exploration Company*, Arthur L. Smith, Bright Sky Press, 2011.

—"2009 is the 150th Anniversary of Oil," Oil 150, Oil Region Alliance of Business, Industry & Tourism, Pennsylvania, 2009.

—"U.S. M&A," Nissa Darbonne, *Oil and Gas Investor*, October 2005.

—"Gobble or Go," Nissa Darbonne, *Oil and Gas Investor*, March 2005.

—"Exit Here," Nissa Darbonne, *Oil and Gas Investor*, October 2004.

—"In Harper We Trusted," *Canada's Oil & Gas Sector*, a special report by *Oil and*

Gas Investor and Global Business Reports, *Oil and Gas Investor*, October 2007.
—"Obituary: Frank Pitts, Dallas energy pioneer," Alan Peppard, *The Dallas Morning News*, Aug. 15, 2009.
—"About," Alta Resources LLC, Alta-resources.com, 2013.
—"Money by the Numbers," Nissa Darbonne, *Oil and Gas Investor*, September 2010.
—"East Texas Gas Manufacturing," Nissa Darbonne, *Oil and Gas Investor*, August 2003.
—"Three Legends Talking," Nissa Darbonne, *Oil and Gas Investor*, November 2011.
—"North American Shale Transactions Since 2008," Bill Marko, Jefferies & Co., April 2013.
—"J.B. Hunt (1927-2006)," Huntventures.net, 2013.
—*Damage Survey and Assessment of Fort Worth Tornado, 28 March 2000*, C.W. Letchford, H.S. Norville, and J. Bilello, Wind Science & Engineering Program, Texas Tech University, for the National Institute for Standards and Technology, August 2000.
—"William F. Buckley, Sr.: An Inventory of His Papers at the Benson Latin American Collection," University of Texas.
—"La Salle County," John Leffler, Texas State Historical Association, 2013.
—"The Beginning of a 'New Town,'" New Town (North Dakota) Chamber of Commerce, 2013.
—"Treasury Announces Guaranty Program for Money Market Funds," press release, U.S. Department of Treasury, Sept. 19, 2008.
—"Lehman throws in the keys," William Cohan, Money.CNN.com, Dec. 14, 2008.
—"WWII by the Numbers, Charting and Graphing D-Day and WWII Data," The National WWII Museum, 2013.
—"Burlington Resources Company History," ConocoPhillips.com, 2013.
—"BEG Facilities," Bureau of Economic Geology, University of Texas at Austin, Beg.utexas.edu, 2013.
—"Northwest Arkansas Developer Gary Combs Dies," Rob Keys, *Arkansas Business*, Aug. 13, 2012.
—"Tim G. Graham," Huntventures.net, 2013.
—"Witt Stephens (1907-1991), Ernest Dumas, *The Encyclopedia of Arkansas History & Culture*, The Central Arkansas Library System, 2013.
—"W.R. 'Witt' Stephens, CEO, 1933-1956," Stephens Inc., Stephens.com.
—"Outcrops versus Exposures, an Essay," Andrew Alden, Geology.About.com, 2013.
—Lewisairlegends.com.

—"Annual Report 2013," Smithsonian National Air and Space Museum.

—"Land Run of 1889," *Encyclopedia of Oklahoma History and Culture*, Oklahoma Historical Society, 2010.

—"Oklahoma City," *Encyclopedia of Oklahoma History and Culture*, Oklahoma Historical Society, 2010.

—"Galveston, TX," David G. McComb, Texas State Historical Association, 2013.

—*Isaac's Storm: A Man, a Time, and the Deadliest Hurricane in History*, Erik Larson, Vintage Books, 2000.

Additional Sources

—Linda Bomke, vice president, The Mitchell Family Corp.

—David Miller, managing partner, EnCap Investments LP.

—Bruce Hicks, assistant director, oil and gas division, Department of Mineral Resources, North Dakota Industrial Commission.

—Jonathan Cogan, office of communications, Energy Information Administration, U.S. Department of Energy.

—Madeline Robinson and Kelly Robinson, Kelly Oil & Gas Inc..

—Chris Wright, chairman and chief executive officer, Liberty Resources LLC.

—Erik Hoover, executive vice president, operations, Brigham Resources LLC.

—Scott Rees, chairman and chief executive officer, Netherland, Sewell & Associates Inc.

—Jeff Dietert, managing director and head of research, Simmons & Co. International Inc.

—ConocoPhillips Co., via Burlington Resources Inc., conference-call transcript, Dec. 13, 2005.

—Southwestern Energy Co. for Southwestern Energy earnings-call transcripts, April 30, 2004, and July 30, 2004.

—SeekingAlpha.com for earnings-call transcripts for EOG Resources Inc. (Aug. 3 and Oct. 30, 2007), Brigham Exploration Co. (Nov. 7, 2007, and Nov. 6, 2009), Exco Resources Inc. (Jan. 30, 2008), Cabot Oil & Gas Corp. (Oct. 26, 2007, and Feb. 14, 2008) and Comstock Resources Inc. (Feb. 12, 2008).

—Chip Minty, manager, media relations, and Cindy Allen, senior communications specialist, Devon Energy Corp.

—Brad Sylvester, vice president, investor relations, Southwestern Energy Co.

—Matt Pitzarella, director of corporate communications and public affairs, Mike Mackin, communications manager, and Mark Windle, communications specialist, Range Resources Corp.

—Mary Ann Osko, director, public relations, Continental Resources Inc.

—Debbie Mangum, executive assistant, Oasis Petroleum Inc.

—Doug Hock, manager, media relations, Encana Oil & Gas (USA) Inc.

—Jill McMillan, director, communications and investor relations, EnLink Midstream Partners LP.

—Tom Tarrant, managing director, marketing, Jefferies LLC.

—(J.B.) Hunt Ventures.

***

Chapter 1, Barnett: 1996

—p. 2: "A nation...just 44 months." "WWII by the Numbers, Charting and Graphing D-Day and WWII Data," The National WWII Museum, 2013.

—p. 2: "Oil had established...would not be overcome." *The Prize: The Epic Quest for Oil, Money, and Power*, Daniel Yergin, Simon & Schuster, 1991.

—p. 2: "George...in 1946." Mitchell Energy & Development Corp., Form 10-K, April 30, 1996.

—p. 2: "The 27-year-old...of better means." An amalgamation primarily based upon "George Phydias Mitchell—The Father We Knew," May 21, 1919-July 26, 2013," the Mitchell family, *Houston Chronicle*, July 30, 2013.

—p. 2: "With his degree...North Texas acreage." Mitchell Energy & Development Corp., Form 10-K, April 30, 1996.

—p. 2: "Mitchell was well...tourism industry." "Galveston, TX," David G. McComb, Texas State Historical Association, 2013.

—p. 2, footnote No. 2: Author's e-mail conversation with Linda Bomke, vice president, The Mitchell Family Corp.

—p. 3: "...unnamed hurricane of 1900." *Isaac's Storm: A Man, a Time, and the Deadliest Hurricane in History*, Erik Larson, Vintage Books, 2000.

—p. 3: "A geologist, John A. Jackson...on 400,000 acres." Mitchell Energy & Development Corp., Form 10-K, April 30, 1996.

—p. 3: "Fifty years later...the Wise County area." Ibid.

—p. 3: "And another tip...of completion operations." Author's interview of Ray Walker, executive vice president and chief operating officer, Range Resources Corp., April 29, 2013.

—p. 3: "In September 1981...was this shale." *The Barnett Shale Play: Phoenix of the Fort Worth Basin, A History*, Dan Steward, Fort Worth Geological Society and North Texas Geological Society, 2007.

—p. 3, footnote No. 5: *Isaac's Storm: A Man, a Time, and the Deadliest Hurricane in History*, Erik Larson, Vintage Books, 2000.

—p. 3, footnote No. 7: *The Barnett Shale Play: Phoenix of the Fort Worth Basin, A History*, Dan Steward, Fort Worth Geological Society and North Texas Geological Society, 2007.

—p. 4: "This rock is so tight...acreage that was part of the contract." Ibid.

—p. 4: "We needed to produce...anxious to get something done." Author's interview of George Mitchell, April 7, 2011.

—p. 5: "In 1980, Mitchell wasn't...too low for it to be profitable." "Natural Gas Regulation: The History of Regulation," NaturalGas.org, 2013.

—pp. 5-6: "Soon, natural gas...by a dramatic decline." "Translating Lessons Learned From Unconventional Natural Gas R&D To Geologic Sequestration Technology," Vello A. Kuuskraa and Hugh D. Guthrie, *Journal of Energy & Environmental Research*, 2.1, 2002.

—p. 6: "In 1978, Congress developed...year-end 1992." Ibid.

—pp. 6-7: "In 1981, to replace...would unlock it all?" *The Barnett Shale Play: Phoenix of the Fort Worth Basin, A History*, Dan Steward, Fort Worth Geological Society and North Texas Geological Society, 2007.

—p. 6, footnote No. 11, references to dates of oil- and gas-price deregulation: Jonathan Cogan, office of communications, Energy Information Administration, U.S. Department of Energy.

—p. 7: "Generally, industry thought...to get onboard." From myriad interviews.

—pp. 7-8: "After that Slay well...In the stubborn Barnett, not so much." An amalgamation based upon Steward's *The Barnett Shale Play* and the author's interviews of Steward and of Ray Walker.

—p. 7, footnote No. 13, reference to the Slay well: Steward's *The Barnett Shale Play*.

—p. 8: "Walker had been involved...southeast of Fort Worth." The interview, Ray Walker.

—p. 9: "UPR had been formed...active explorers in the 1990s." Union Pacific Resources Group Inc., Form 10-KA, March 8, 1995, and Form 10-K, March 21, 1997.

—p. 9: "The Cotton Valley was the first...on a large scale in the U.S." "A Case History for Massive Hydraulic Fracturing the Cotton Valley Lime Matrix, Fallon and Personville Fields," H.G. Kozik/Mitchell Energy Corp. and S.A. Holditch/Texas A&M University, Journal of Petroleum Technology, Volume 33, Number 2, February 1981.

—p. 11: "In their trials...undergone the MHF treatment." "Proppants? We Don't Need No Proppants," M.J. Mayerhofer, M.F. Richardson, R.N. Walker Jr., D.N. Meehan, M.W. Oehler and R.R. Browning Jr., Society of Petroleum Engineers annual technical conference and exhibition, Oct. 5-8, 1997.

—p. 12: "Among producers trying it...Valence Operating Co." "Proppants, We Still Don't Need No Proppants—A Perspective of Several Operators," Ray N. Walker Jr., Jeffery L. Hunter, Al C. Brake, Paul A. Fagin and Nick Steinsberger,

Society of Petroleum Engineers annual technical conference and exhibition, Sept. 27-30, 1998.

—pp. 12-13: "Mitchell Energy had made a...practically nothing within 24 months." Kozik and Holditch, "A Case History for Massive Hydraulic Fracturing the Cotton Valley Lime Matrix, Fallon and Personville Fields."

—p. 13, footnote No. 22: "Hydraulic Fracturing of Oil and Gas Wells in Kansas," Daniel R. Suchy and K. David Newell, Kansas Geological Survey, PIC-32, May 15, 2012.

—p. 14, footnote No. 23: Written testimony to the U.S. Senate, Committee on Energy and Natural Resources, Stephen A. Holditch, Oct. 4, 2011.

Chapter 2, Bakken: 1996
—pp. 15-16: "Dick Findley had an idea...interval for a decade by now." Author's interview of Dick Findley, chairman, American Eagle Energy Corp., March 18, 2013.

—pp. 16-17: "In the mid-1990s, railroad operator...to more than 15,000 feet." "Burlington Resources Company History," ConocoPhillips.com, 2013.

—pp. 17-18: "Burlington had a strong management team...They didn't frac them." Author's interview of Taylor Reid, president and chief operating officer, Oasis Petroleum Inc., April 24, 2013.

—pp. 18-19: "On Sept. 25...were deemed dry holes." Well files, North Dakota Department of Mineral Resources, Oil & Gas Division, and author's calculations.

—p. 18, footnote No. 27: "The Reservoir Engineering Aspects of Horizontal Drilling," F.M. Giger, L.H. Reiss, A.P. Jourdan, Society of Petroleum Engineers technical conference and exhibition, Sept. 16-19, 1984.

—p. 18, footnote Nos. 29 and 30: Historical well data from North Dakota's Department of Mineral Resources, Oil & Gas Division.

—pp. 19-20: "But the horizontal, unfraced...no longer economically viable." "Oil Exploration and Development in the North Dakota Williston Basin: 1994-1995," Thomas J. Heck, *Miscellaneous Series No. 84*, North Dakota Geological Survey, 1996.

—p. 19, footnote No. 31: Historical well data from North Dakota's Department of Mineral Resources, Oil & Gas Division.

—p. 20: "At year-end 1993...$16.69 a barrel for its oil." Burlington Resources Inc., Form 10-K, Feb. 14, 1994.

—p. 21: "In the spring of 1995...mention Bakken." Burlington Resources Inc., Form 10-K, Feb. 9, 1995.

—p. 22: "But pick carefully...structural closures." Historical well data from North Dakota's Department of Mineral Resources, Oil & Gas Division.

—p. 22, footnote No. 32: Author's calculation from historical well data from North Dakota's Department of Mineral Resources, Oil & Gas Division.

—p. 23, footnote No. 35: An amalgamation of data from Findley and Jack Stark, senior vice president, exploration, Continental Resources Inc.

—p. 25: "The well flowed back...April 20, 1996." *Montana Oil and Gas Annual Review* 1996, Volume 40.

—p. 25, footnote No. 37: An amalgamation of data from North Dakota's Department of Mineral Resources.

—p. 25, footnote No. 39: As per Findley.

—p. 26, footnote No. 40: "Outcrops versus Exposures, an Essay," Andrew Alden, Geology.About.com, 2013.

—pp. 26-27: "The county is flanked by...in the 1920s." "History of the Cedar Creek Anticline, Southeast Montana," John Davis, Denbury Resources Inc., *AAPG Search and Discovery*, Article #90169, October 2013, and "The Cedar Creek Anticline, 43 Years of History and Development, 1921-1964," Thomas A. Gwynn, North Dakota Geological Society and Saskatchewan Geological Society, Williston Basin Symposium, September 1964.

—p. 29: "Others drilling in Richland...Luff Exploration Co." *Montana Oil and Gas Annual Review* 1996, Volume 40.

Chapter 3, Barnett: 1996, Part Two

—p. 31: "When Steinsberger...The Woodlands, north of Houston." Steward's *The Barnett Shale Play*.

—p. 31, footnote No. 47: An amalgamation primarily based upon "George Phydias Mitchell—The Father We Knew," May 21, 1919-July 26, 20013," the Mitchell family, *Houston Chronicle*, July 30, 2013.

—p. 32: "Understanding this, George Mitchell...the company's overall worth." Mitchell Energy & Development Corp., Form 10-K, April 26, 1994.

—pp. 32-33: "Into 1994, the situation...'what we have been experiencing.'" Mitchell Energy & Development Corp., Form 10-K, April 21, 1995.

—p. 33: "Buckle up: Rather than...but still promising, Barnett-shale play." Mitchell Energy & Development Corp., Form 10-Q, Sept. 14, 1995.

—pp. 33-34: "He wrote, 'Fifty years'...from North Texas alone." Mitchell Energy & Development Corp., Form 10-K, April 30, 1996.

—p. 34: "Another surprise came...The Woodlands Corp." Mitchell Energy & Development Corp., Form 10-K, April 2, 1998.

—p. 34: "In early 1998, gas prices...more than 250 were in the Barnett." Ibid.

—p. 34: "In a study with...horizontal well in 1991." Steward's *The Barnett Shale Play*.

—p. 34, footnote No. 50: An amalgamation from Mitchell Energy & Develop-

ment Corp., Form 10-K, April 1, 1997, and Form 10-K, April 2, 1998.
—p. 35: "In April 1998, the company disclosed...'by as much as 20%.'" Mitchell Energy & Development Corp., Form 10-K, April 1, 1997, and Form 10-K, April 2, 1998.
—p. 35, footnote No. 53: Miller Exploration Co., Form S-1, Nov. 17, 1997.

Chapter 4, Bakken: 1996, Part Two
—p. 36: "Dick Findley...Taconic Petroleum Corp." Author's interview of Dick Findley, chairman, American Eagle Energy Corp., March 18, 2013.
—p. 36: "A New York-based...and MBAs with capital." An amalgamation primarily from the author's interview of Cameron Smith, advisor, Warburg Pincus LLC, March 18, 2013, and "William F. Buckley, Sr.: An Inventory of His Papers at the Benson Latin American Collection," University of Texas Libraries.
—p. 37: "Using 3-D seismic...were dry holes." An amalgamation primarily from the author's interviews of Bobby Lyle, chairman, Lyco Holdings Corp., Jan. 25, March 11 and March 14, 2013, and *Montana Oil and Gas Annual Review* 1995, Volume 39.
—pp. 37-39: "Lyle says, 'Cameron'...was already looking in Montana." Interviews of Bobby Lyle.
—p. 43, footnote No. 61: "Table 11.1b World Crude Oil Production: Persian Gulf Nations, Non-OPEC, and World," U.S. Energy Information Administration, *Monthly Energy Review*, March 2014.

Chapter 5, Barnett: 1999
—pp. 44-45: "1998 was the newest...'than once thought,' the company reported." Mitchell Energy & Development Corp., Form 10-K, April 16, 1999.
—p. 44, footnote No. 62: Author's conversation with Scott Rees, chairman and chief executive officer, Netherland, Sewell & Associates Inc.
—p. 44, footnote No. 63: Mitchell Energy & Development Corp., Form 10-Q, Dec. 6, 1999.
—p. 45: "Chevron Corp. had tried...'he was so far-sighted.'" Author's interview of Kent Bowker, executive vice president, geology, Titan River Energy LLC, April 25, 2013.
—p. 45: "Mitchell Energy's Barnett team...sections into consideration." An amalgamation from Steward's *The Barnett Shale Play* and "Recent developments of the Barnett Shale play, Fort Worth Basin," Kent A. Bowker, *West Texas Geological Society Bulletin*, Volume 42, No. 6 (2003).
—p. 48: "Based on new economics...cost to improve the productivity." Mitchell Energy & Development Corp., Form 10-K, April 16, 1999.
—p. 48: "In the fall of 1999...half of this over Barnett." Mitchell Energy & Development Corp., Form 10-Q, Dec. 6, 1999.

—p. 48: "But no one showed up...particularly in the Barnett." Mitchell Energy & Development Corp., Form 10-K, April 28, 2000.

—pp. 48-50: "The company's two classes...had only followed Mitchell Energy's stock." An amalgamation from Mitchell Energy & Development Corp., Form 10-K, April 28, 2000; Form 10-Q, June 5, 2000; Form 10-Q, Sept. 11, 2000; and Form 10-KT (recasting for new fiscal year), Oct. 13, 2000.

—p. 49, footnote No. 65: Mitchell Energy & Development Corp., Form 10-K, April 28, 2000.

—p. 50, footnote No. 67: An amalgamation from Bronco Drilling Co., Form S-1, June 1, 2005; Union Drilling Inc., Form S-1, Aug. 15, 2005; and historical U.S. gas-production data, U.S. Energy Information Administration.

—p. 51: "In November 2000...'north-central Texas.'" Patterson-UTI Energy Inc., Form 8-K, Dec. 1, 2000.

—p. 51: "Four months later...active in the Barnett." PXP Producing Co. LLC (Pogo Producing Co.), Form 10-K, March 2, 2001.

—pp. 51-52: "A week later...550,000 net acres in North Texas." Mitchell Energy & Development Corp., Form 10-K, March 9, 2001.

—pp. 52-53: "Larry Nichols wanted...and enterprise value." Author's interview of Larry Nichols, executive chairman, Devon Energy Corp., April 17, 2013; Devon Energy Corp., Form S-4, Aug. 30, 2001; and supplemental Devon corporate data.

—p. 53: "By early 2001, oil and gas...'$2.50 per Mcf.'" Mitchell Energy & Development Corp., Form 10-A, May 14, 2001.

—p. 53: "The figure was remarkable...LNG-import plant instead." An amalgamation primarily from "LNG Revisited," Nissa Darbonne, Oil and Gas Investor, July 2001, and Cheniere Energy Inc., Form S-3, Oct. 12, 2001.

—p. 54: "When George Mitchell...before the deal was announced." An amalgamation from the interview of Larry Nichols and Devon Energy Corp., Form S-4, Aug. 30, 2001.

—p. 54: "Three week later...Western Canadian Sedimentary Basin." Devon Energy Corp., Form 425, Sept. 4, 2001.

—pp. 54-55: "To make it clear...'preeminent North American independent.'" Ibid.

—p. 55: "Completing both deals...again, No. 1." Devon Energy Corp., Form 425, Sept. 4, 2001.

—p. 55, footnote No. 72: Devon Energy Corp., Form DEF 14A, April 9, 2002, and Form DEF 14A, April 24, 2013.

—p. 56: "Tony Vaughn, Devon executive...south of there." Author's interview of Tony Vaughn, executive vice president, exploration and production, Devon Energy Corp., April 17, 2013.

Chapter 6, Bakken: 2000

—p. 58: "Tom Lantz had joined...relocated to Houston." Author's interview of Tom Lantz, chief operating officer, American Eagle Energy Corp., April 3, 2013.
—p. 60: "Lyle says...'the test well.'" Author's interviews of Bobby Lyle, chairman, Lyco Holdings Corp., Jan. 25, March 11 and March 14, 2013.
—p. 60: "Findley recalls...'drill it horizontal.'" Author's interview of Dick Findley, chairman, American Eagle Energy Corp., March 18, 2013.
—p. 62, footnote No. 79: Mobil Corp., Form 10-K, March 13, 1995, and Belden & Blake Corp., Form 10-K, March 31, 1995.
—pp. 63-64: "In 2000, only six wells...almost entirely for Lyco." *Montana Oil and Gas Annual Review* 2000, Volume 44; *Montana Oil and Gas Annual Review* 2001, Volume 45; and *Montana Oil and Gas Annual Review* 2002, Volume 46.

Chapter 7, Barnett: 2002

—p. 65: "Of Mitchell Energy's...for the company." Steward's *The Barnett Shale Play*.
—pp. 65-66: "Tony Vaughn...'had done for 20 years.'"Author's interview of Tony Vaughn, executive vice president, exploration and production, Devon Energy Corp., April 17, 2013.
—p. 65, footnote No. 82: Steward's *The Barnett Shale Play*.
—p. 66: "Like Vaughn...'amalgamation of knowledge.'" Author's interview of Larry Nichols, executive chairman, Devon Energy Corp., April 17, 2013.
—p. 68: "In early 2003...1 million a day." Devon OEI Operating Inc., Form 425, Feb. 25, 2003.
—p. 68: "Later that year...1.5 million a day." "The Barnett Barrels Along," Robert Ransone, *Oil and Gas Investor*, December 2003.
—pp. 68-69: "In February 2004...'future of Barnett expansion.'" Devon Energy Corp., Form 8-K, Feb. 5, 2004.
—p. 69: "By January 2005...making 80%." Devon Energy Corp., Form 8-K, Feb. 2, 2005.
—p. 69: "By now, Devon was nearly...largest gas field in Texas." "Devon Energy Reports Results of Midstream Divestitures," Devon Energy Corp. press release, Jan. 20, 2005.
—p. 69: "...making some 1.1 billion...Ninety rigs were at work in the play." An amalgamation from Texas Railroad Commission Newark East Field data, Jan. 25, 2013; XTO Energy Inc., Form 10-K, March 7, 2005; and DTE Energy Co., Form 8-K, March 10, 2005.
—p. 69: "About a fifth...down to 20 acres." Devon Energy Corp., Form 8-K, Aug. 5, 2004; Form 10-K, March 9, 2005; and Form 8-K, Aug. 4, 2005.

Chapter 8, Bakken: 2003

—p. 70: "Otherwise, mention was only...southwestern North Dakota." Burlington Resources Inc., Form 10-K, March 17, 2000.

—p. 70: "In July 2003, Whiting...barrels of oil apiece." Whiting Petroleum Corp., Form S-1, July, 25, 2003.

—pp. 70-71: "A month later, American...'porosity and permeability.'" American Oil & Gas Inc., Form 10-QSB, Aug. 14, 2003, and *Montana Oil and Gas Annual Review* 2002, Volume 46.

—pp. 71-72: "Now, Lyco had lots...came on with more than 1,000 barrels." *Montana Oil and Gas Annual Review* 2003, Volume 47; *Montana Oil and Gas Annual Review* 2004, Volume 48; and *Montana Oil and Gas Annual Review* 2005, Volume 49.

—p. 71, footnote No. 88: SM Energy Co., Form 10-K, Feb. 27, 2004.

—p. 72: "Lyle says...'largest-producing county.'" Author's interviews of Bobby Lyle, chairman, Lyco Holdings Corp., Jan. 25, March 11 and March 14, 2013.

—pp. 72-73: "Continental Resources joined...'expected to take three years.'" Continental Resources Inc., Form 10-K, March 30, 2004.

—p. 73: "In 2004, Elm Coulee...to fifth (3.1 million)." *Montana Oil and Gas Annual Review* 2005, Volume 49, and *Montana Oil and Gas Annual Review* 2006, Volume 50.

—p. 73: "Besides the 27 million...30 million cubic feet a day." *Montana Oil and Gas Annual Review* 2006, Volume 50.

—p. 73, footnote No. 90: Well files, North Dakota Department of Natural Resources, Oil & Gas Division.

—p. 73, footnote No. 91: *Montana Oil and Gas Annual Review* 2005, Volume 49.

—p. 74: "'We were...not very attractive.'" Author's interview of Harold Hamm, chairman and chief executive officer, Continental Resources Inc., Sept. 3, 2013.

—p. 74: "Lyle and Hamm agreed...added as well." Hiland Partners LP, Form S-1, Oct. 22, 2004.

—p. 75: "By July 2005...or about to be spud." Well and field data from *Montana Oil and Gas Annual Review* 2006, Volume 50; best-practices data from "Bakken Horizontal Best Practices Review," Charles Wiley, Mike Eberhard, Bob Barree and Tom Lantz, Halliburton corporate presentation, October 2005, and "Improved Horizontal Well Stimulations in the Bakken Formation, Williston Basin, Montana," Charles Wiley, Bob Barree, Mike Eberhard and Tom Lantz, Society of Petroleum Engineers annual technical conference and exhibition, Sept. 26-29, 2004.

—p. 76: "Meanwhile, Canada-based...'in the U.S. market.'" Author's interview of Garry Tanner, managing director, Quantum Energy Partners LP, Aug. 23, 2013.

—pp. 76-77: "They were insatiable...later turned out by the explorer." An amalgamation primarily from "U.S. M&A," Nissa Darbonne, *Oil and Gas Investor*, October 2005; "Gobble or Go," March 2005; and "Exit Here," October 2004.

—p. 77, footnote No. 98: "In Harper We Trusted," *Canada's Oil & Gas Sector*, a special report by *Oil and Gas Investor* and Global Business Reports, *Oil and Gas Investor*, October 2007.

—p. 78-79: "On July 18...750,000 barrels equivalent." Enerplus Corp., Form 6-K, July 19, 2005, and Form 6-K, Nov. 10, 2005.

—p. 78, footnote No. 100: Chesapeake Energy Corp., Form 8-K, Oct. 4, 2005.

—p. 78, footnote No. 102: As per Dick Findley and Bobby Lyle.

—p. 79: "More than 225 of these...Findley had mapped." Calculated from the *Montana Oil and Gas Annual Review* for years 2000-2005.

—pp. 79-80: "While he was re-entering...would sputter out." Well files, North Dakota Department of Natural Resources, Oil & Gas Division.

—p. 79, footnote No. 103: As per Lyle.

—p. 80: "With a permit...with 80 barrels." Well file, North Dakota Department of Natural Resources, Oil & Gas Division.

—p. 80, footnote No. 105: Ibid.

—p. 80, footnote No. 106: Ibid.

—p. 80, footnote No. 107: Ibid.

—p. 82: "West Texas-focused...as a dry hole." Clayton Williams Energy Inc., Form 10-K, March 16, 2006, and Form 10-K, March 16, 2007.

—p. 82: "And even with...at 19 million barrels." *Montana Oil and Gas Annual Review* 2007, Volume 51, through 2013, Volume 57.

—p. 82: "SM Energy...'end of primary development.'" SM Energy Co., Form 10-KA, March 21, 2007.

—p. 82, footnote No. 109: Clayton Williams Energy Inc., Form 10-K, March 16, 2007.

—p. 82, footnote No. 110: *Montana Oil and Gas Annual Review* 2007, Volume 51, through 2012, Volume 56, and "The New Bakken Play in Eastern Montana," Stephen A. Sonnenberg, *AAPG Search and Discovery*, July 16, 2012.

—p. 83: "Before joining Lyco...Margaret 44-15H." *Montana Oil and Gas Annual Review* 1987, Volume 31, through 2003, Volume 47.

—p. 83: "In early 2004...'unproven at this time.'" Continental Resources Inc., Form 10-Q, Aug. 16, 2004.

—p. 83: "It bought some...'to positive results.'" Continental Resources Inc., Form 10-Q, Nov. 15, 2004.

—pp. 83-84: "While it was making...customary and allowed by the state." Continental Resources Inc. and well file, North Dakota Department of Natural Resources, Oil & Gas Division.

—p. 84: "Jolette's plan was to...its first 25 days online." Well file, North Dakota

Department of Natural Resources, Oil & Gas Division.

—p. 84: "It was the first...in North Dakota." "Robert-Heuer 1-17R Well Dedication," proclamation by North Dakota Gov. Jack Dalrymple, Oct. 27, 2011.

—p. 84, footnote No. 113: Well file, North Dakota Department of Natural Resources, Oil & Gas Division.

—p. 84, footnote No. 114: Ibid.

—pp. 85-86: "Jack Stark...'easier to find than oil.'" Author's interview of Jack Stark, senior vice president, exploration, Continental Resources Inc., March 19, 2013.

—p. 85, footnote No. 115: Continental Resources Inc.

—pp. 86-87: "In 1994, North Dakota...for more mounds." "Oil Exploration and Development in the North Dakota Williston Basin: 1994-1995," Thomas J. Heck, *Miscellaneous Series No. 84*, North Dakota Geological Survey, 1996, and well files, North Dakota Department of Natural Resources, Oil & Gas Division.

—p. 87: "In Bowman County...successful as past wells." Well files, North Dakota Department of Natural Resources, Oil & Gas Division.

—pp. 87-88: "In 1194, as...in North Dakota that year." Ibid.

—p. 87, footnote No. 117: Ibid.

—p. 87, footnote No. 118: Ibid.

—p. 87, footnote No. 119: Ibid.

—p. 88: "But Thomas Heck...'important new discoveries.'" Thomas J. Heck, *Miscellaneous Series No. 84*, North Dakota Geological Survey, 1996.

—p. 88: "Eight years earlier...Cedar Hills Field." Ibid and well files, North Dakota Department of Natural Resources, Oil & Gas Division.

—pp. 88-89: "Taylor Reid...flowed naturally." Author's interview of Taylor Reid, president and chief operating officer, Oasis Petroleum Inc., April 24, 2013.

—p. 88, footnote No. 120: Well file, North Dakota Department of Natural Resources, Oil & Gas Division.

—p. 89: "North Dakota geologist...500,000 barrels each." Thomas J. Heck, *Miscellaneous Series No. 84*, North Dakota Geological Survey, 1996.

—p. 89: "Burlington followed...in May 1995." Well files, North Dakota Department of Natural Resources, Oil & Gas Division.

—pp. 89-90: "Burlington ended up...25 million barrels." Ibid, author's calculations and "Small-Scale Geologic Structures within Cedar Hills Red River B Field, Bowman and Slope Counties, North Dakota," Paul E. Diehl, *NDGS Newsletter*, Volume 28, Number 2.

—p. 90: "The state's oil production...the most since 1981." Thomas J. Heck, *Miscellaneous Series No. 84*, North Dakota Geological Survey, 1996.

—p. 90: "And the wells were incredibly...'water-flood operations in 1999.'" Burlington Resources Inc., Form 10-K, Feb. 13, 1998.

—p. 90, footnote No. 121: Well files, North Dakota Department of Natural Resources, Oil & Gas Division.

—p. 90, footnote No. 122: North Dakota Department of Natural Resources, Oil & Gas Division.

—p. 93: "...Amerada Petroleum...well in 1951." Well files, North Dakota Department of Natural Resources, Oil & Gas Division.

—p. 94: "It had followed...for 125 barrels." Ibid.

—p. 94: "It resumed a year...164 and 280 barrels." Ibid.

Chapter 9, Barnett: 2006

—p. 96: "Micro-cap Empire...the Barnett zone." Empire Energy Corp., Form 10-QSB, Aug. 14, 2001.

—p. 96: "Dan Steward...'received some attention.'" *The Barnett Shale Play: Phoenix of the Fort Worth Basin, A History*, Dan Steward, Fort Worth Geological Society and North Texas Geological Society, 2007.

—p. 97: "In the article...as 4,200 square miles." "Barnett shale rising star in Fort Worth Basin," Vello A. Kuuskraa, George Koperna, James W. Schmoker and John C. Quinn, *Oil & Gas Journal*, May 25, 1998.

—p. 97: "By mid-1999, as gas...'as a significant resource play.'" Steward's *The Barnett Shale Play.*

—pp. 97-100: "Among those chasing...tremendous amount of reserves in place." Author's interview of Trevor Rees-Jones, president and chief executive officer, April 15, 2013.

—p. 100, footnote No. 125: "Obituary: Frank Pitts, Dallas energy pioneer," Alan Peppard, *The Dallas Morning News*, Aug. 15, 2009.

—pp. 101-103: "Dan Steward knew that...Management said, 'Yeah. Let's do it.'" Author's interviews of Dan Steward, geologist, Republic Energy Inc., March 12, August 14 and August 18, 2013.

—pp. 105-106: "A micro-cap paid...Barnett might be better." TBX Resources Inc., Form 10-KSB40, Feb. 28, 2002, and Form 10-KSB, March 5, 2002.

—p. 105, footnote No. 130: Author's interview of Kent Bowker, executive vice president, geology, Titan River Energy LLC, April 25, 2013.

—p. 106: "Another paid $100,000...drilled Marble Falls wells." Micron Enviro Systems Inc., Form 10-KSB, April 7, 2004.

—pp. 106-107: "Tiny, Dallas-based...study of Barnett and other shales," Crosstex Energy Inc., Form 10-K, March 25, 2003; Progress Energy Inc., Form U-1, May 5, 2003; Republic Energy Inc.; Devon Energy Corp.; Enbridge Energy Partners LP, Form 8-K, Nov. 24, 2003; TXU Corp.; Heritage Propane Partners LP, Form S-3A, Dec. 8, 2003; Key Energy Services Inc., Form 8-K, Nov. 18, 2004; and Core Laboratories NV, Form 8-K, Feb. 24, 2005.

—p. 107: "By year-end 2004...more than 1,100." Texas Railroad Commission data.

—p. 107: "Among them, Fort Worth-based...and Hill counties." Quicksilver Resources Inc., Form 8-K, March 4, 2004; Form 8-K, Nov. 8, 2004; and Form 8-K, Feb. 25, 2005.

—pp. 107-108: "Larger-cap Denbury...fifth rig on the way." Denbury Resources Inc., Form 10-K, March 25, 2002; Form 10-K, March 24, 2003; Form 10-K, March 12, 2004; Form 8-K, Oct. 28, 2004; Form 10-Q, Nov. 9, 2004; Form 8-K, Feb. 1, 2005; Form 8-K, Feb. 24, 2005; Form 10-K, March 15, 2005; and Form 8-K, May 3, 2005.

—p. 108: "Permian Basin-focused...5.2 million a day." Parallel Petroleum Corp., Form 10-K, March 22, 2004; Form 8-K, Jan. 11, 2005; and Form 8-K, Aug. 2, 2005.

—pp. 109-110: "Large-cap Chesapeake...looking to reach 80 million by year-end." Chesapeake Energy Corp., Form 8-K, July 26, 2004; Form 8-K, Nov. 2, 2004; Form 8-K, Dec. 1, 2004; Form 8-K, Dec. 27, 2004; Form 8-K, Aug. 5, 2005; Hallwood Group Inc., Form 10-K, April 15, 2003; Form 10-Q, Nov. 14, 2003; Form 10-K, March 30, 2004; Form 10-Q, May 17, 2004; Form 10-Q, Aug. 16, 2004; Form 8-K, Sept. 1, 2004; Form 10-Q, Nov. 12, 2004; Form 10-K, March 31, 2005; and Form 10-Q, May 16, 2005.

—p. 109, footnote No. 133: Chesapeake Energy Corp., Form 8-K, March 12, 2002.

—pp. 110-112: "In 2004, large-cap XTO Energy...Production was 65 million a day." XTO Energy Inc., Form 8-K, Feb. 24, 2004; Form 8-K, April 21, 2004; Form 10-Q, Aug. 9, 2004; Form 8-K, Sept. 7, 2004; Form 8-K, Jan. 13, 2005; Form 10-K, March 7, 2005; Form 8-K, July 11, 2005; Form 8-K, July 19, 2005; Energy Transfer Partners LP, Form 424-B3, June 23, 2004; and "Money by the Numbers," Nissa Darbonne, *Oil and Gas Investor*, September 2010.

—p. 111, footnote No. 135: Encore Acquisition Co., Form S-1, Oct. 6, 2000, and Encore Acquisition Co., Form 425, Nov. 2, 2009.

—p. 111, footnote No. 136: XTO Energy Inc., Form 10-Q, Aug. 9, 2005.

—p. 112: "Burlington Resources...'because gas prices are at $14." Burlington Resources Inc., Form 10-K, March 12, 2003; Form 10-K, Feb. 26, 2004; Form 10-K, Feb. 28, 2005; Form 8-K, Oct. 27, 2005; Form DEFA-14A, Dec. 14, 2005; ConocoPhillips, Form 8-K, Dec. 13, 2005.

—pp. 113-114: "The horizontal code...'not just in Johnson County.'" EOG Resources Inc., Form 10-K, March 13, 2003; Form 10-K, March 11, 2004; Form 8-K, May 3, 2004; Form 8-K, Aug. 2, 2004; Form 10-Q, Aug. 3, 2004; Form 8-K, Oct. 26, 2004; Form 8-K, Feb. 2, 2005; Form 10-K, Feb. 25, 2005; Form 8-K, April 26, 2005; Form 8-K, Nov. 1, 2005; Form 8-K, Feb. 1, 2006; and "Breaking

Into The Barnett," Nissa Darbonne, *Oil and Gas Investor*, April 2006.

—p. 113, footnote No. 138: "Three Legends Talking," Nissa Darbonne, *Oil and Gas Investor*, November 2011.

—p. 113, footnote No. 139: United States Lime & Minerals Inc., Form 8-K, June 2, 2004.

—pp. 114-115: "Securities analyst Dave Pursell...'were among the first.'" Author's interview of Dave Pursell, managing director and head of securities research, Tudor, Pickering, Holt & Co., April 25, 2013.

—p. 114, footnote No. 142: EOG Resources Inc., Form 8-K, Feb. 2, 2006.

—pp. 115-116: "Among these was the worth...about $9 to $29." Carrizo Oil & Gas Inc., Form S-2A, Jan. 15, 2004; Form 424-B3, March 4, 2004; Form 10-Q, May 17, 2004; Form 8-K, Aug. 3, 2004; Form 8-K, Aug. 16, 2004; Form 10-Q, Aug. 16, 2004; Form 8-K, Nov. 3, 2004; Form 8-K, Nov. 12, 2004; Form 10-Q, Nov. 15, 2004; Form 8-K, March 1, 2005; and Form 10-K, March 31, 2005.

—p. 116: "John Hancock...'stocks in the portfolio.'" John Hancock Investment Trust, Form NCSR, Aug. 30, 2004, and Scudder Portfolio Trust, Form NCSRS, Sept. 1, 2004.

—p. 116: "By then, some 17 billion...only 4 billion a day." "DOE's Unconventional Gas Research Programs 1976-1995: An Archive of Important Results," U.S. Department of Energy, Jan. 31, 2007, and "Translating Lessons Learned From Unconventional Natural Gas R&D To Geologic Sequestration Technology," Vello A. Kuuskraa and Hugh D. Guthrie, *Journal of Energy & Environmental Research*, 2.1, 2002.

—p. 117: "By the spring...for the company." Devon Energy Corp., Form 8-K, May 2, 2006.

—pp. 118-119: "On May 2, 2006...an additional 1 trillion-plus." Ibid.

—p. 119: "As for Rees-Jones'...and being expanded to 375 million." Crosstex Energy Inc., Form 8-K, May 4, 2006.

Chapter 10, Fayetteville: 2000

—p. 120: "Harold Korell wasn't...eastern Oklahoma and western Arkansas." Author's interview of Harold Korell, chairman, Southwestern Energy Co., March 27, 2013.

—p. 120: "Southwestern was formed...in the 1950s as Arkansas Production Co." "Our History," Southwestern Energy Co., Swn.com.

—p. 120, footnote No. 145: *2009 Annual Report of the State Oil & Gas Supervisor*, California Department of Conservation, Division of Oil, Gas, & Geothermal Resources, 2010.

—pp. 122-123: "While based in Denver...of the Madison formation." Well files, North Dakota Department of Natural Resources, Oil & Gas Division.

—p. 123: "Tenneco had discovered...was just beneath." "Big Stick/Four Eyes Fields: Structural, Stratigraphic and Hydrodynamic Trapping Within Mission Canyon Formation, Williston Basin," John J. Breig, *AAPG Search and Discovery*, Article #91033, August 1988.

—p. 124: "Tenneco Oil was sold...auto-parts businesses." *Something from Nothing: Joe B. Foster and the People Who Built Newfield Exploration Company*, Arthur L. Smith, Bright Sky Press, 2011.

—pp. 124-125: "About 56% of...about 2.2 billion cubic feet of gas." Southwestern Energy Co., Form 10-K405, March 29, 2000, and "East Texas Gas Manufacturing," Nissa Darbonne, *Oil and Gas Investor*, August 2003.

—p. 125: "The company had lost...mineral-rights owners." Southwestern Energy Co., Form 10-K405, March 29, 2000, and Form 10-K405, March 30, 2001.

—p. 125, footnote No. 146: Total S.A., Form 20-F, March 28, 2013.

—p. 126: "Hunt had founded...north of Fayetteville." "J.B. Hunt (1927-2006)," Huntventures.net, 2013.

—p. 128: "Combs was a...and Hunts." "Northwest Arkansas Developer Gary Combs Dies," Rob Keys, *Arkansas Business*, Aug. 13, 2012.

—p. 128: "Graham and Hunt...of Combs' projects." "Tim G. Graham," Huntventures.net, 2013.

—p. 128, footnote No. 148: Southwestern Energy Co., Form 10-K, Feb. 26, 2009.

—p. 129, footnote No. 150: "Tim G. Graham," Huntventures.net, 2013.

—p. 130: "Korell's predecessor, Charles Scharlau...since 1951." Southwestern Energy Co., Form DEF-14A, April 5, 2012.

—p. 130: "Another early explorer...Stephens Inc." "Witt Stephens (1907-1991), Ernest Dumas, *The Encyclopedia of Arkansas History & Culture*, The Central Arkansas Library System, 2013, and "W.R. 'Witt' Stephens, CEO, 1933-1956," Stephens Inc., Stephens.com.

—p. 131: "Thaeler says, 'We were talking...this thing here.'" Author's interview of John Thaeler, chief operating officer, Vitruvian Exploration LLC, April 10, 2013.

—p. 132: "Lane says, 'There were very...500 feet thick out there.'" Author's interview of Richard Lane, president and chief executive officer, Vitruvian Exploration LLC, April 10, 2013.

—p. 133: "In early 2003, with its...gas prices were growing." Southwestern Energy Co., Form 8-K, March 7, 2003.

—pp. 135-136: "Aubrey McClendon...and increasing production." Chesapeake Energy Corp., Form S-1, July 7, 2000.

—p. 138: "Finally, legal advised...'increase over the next several years.'" Southwestern Energy Co., Form 10-K, Feb. 25, 2004; "Southwestern Energy Company 1Q 2004, Friday, April 30, 2004," Swn.com.; Form 8-K, July 30, 2004; and Form 8-K, Aug. 17, 2004.

—pp. 141-142: "By early 2007...half-million a day from each." Southwestern Energy Co., Form 8-K, Sept. 21, 2004; Form 8-K, Nov. 1, 2004; Form 8-K, March 2, 2005; Form 10-K, March 8, 2005; Form 10-K, March 6, 2006; Form 8-K, March 1, 2007; Form 10-K, March 1, 2007; and Form 8-K, March 2, 2007.

—p. 141, footnote No. 153: Southwestern Energy Co., Form 8-K, Feb. 28, 2006, and *Arkansas: Reasonably Forseeable Development Scenario for Fluid Minerals*, U.S. Department of the Interior, Bureau of Land Management, March 2008.

—p. 142, footnote No. 154: Southwestern Energy Co., Form 8-K, June 10, 2005.

—p. 143, footnote No. 155: "About," Alta Resources LLC, Alta-resources.com, 2013, and Petrohawk Energy Corp., Form 8-K, Nov. 30, 2007.

—p. 144: "The Mitchell Energy...than the verticals." Steward's *The Barnett Shale Play*.

Chapter 11, Bakken: 2006

—p. 145: "Continental Resources...in the Montana play." Well files, North Dakota Department of Natural Resources, Oil & Gas Division.

—p. 145: "Micro-cap, Denver-based...'formation, difficulties.'" Earthstone Energy Inc., Form 10-QSB, Aug. 15, 2005.

—pp. 145-146: "Dick Findley...'work that well.'" Author's interview of Dick Findley, chairman, American Eagle Energy Corp., March 18, 2013.

—pp. 146-147: "Growing up in the...'not have made it.'" Author's interviews of Bud Brigham, chairman, Brigham Resources LLC, June 14, 2010, and April 23, 2013.

—p. 146, footnote No. 157: "Elm Coulee Idea Opened New Play; Learning curve continues," Louise S. Durham, AAPG *Explorer*, August 2009, and *Montana Oil and Gas Annual Review* 2012, Volume 56.

—pp. 147-148: "By early 1997, Brigham...$24.7 million net of fees." Brigham Exploration Co., Form S-1, Feb. 27, 1997, and Form 424-B4, May 9, 1997.

—p. 148: "Brigham Exploration went on to...'Frio development program could disappoint us.'" Brigham Exploration Co., Form 10-K, March 30, 2000; Form 10-K, March 31, 2005; and Form 8-K, July 1, 2005.

—pp. 149-150: "In November 2005...'focus trend for us.'" Brigham Exploration Co., Form 8-K, Nov. 3, 2005.

—p. 150: "Brigham sold 7.5 million shares." Brigham Exploration Co., Form 424-B5, Nov. 18, 2005.

—p. 150: "PDC Energy brought on...PDC reported." PDC Energy Inc., Form 8-K, Nov. 22, 2005.

—p. 150: "Continental reported...'limited but encouraging.'" Continental Resources Inc., Form S-1, March 7, 2006.

—p. 150: "Micro-cap Earthstone...'in this immediate area.'" Earthstone Energy Inc., Form 10-KSB, July 14, 2006.

—pp. 150-151: "Having greater access...offering senior notes." Brigham Exploration Co., Form 8-K, Aug. 7, 2006, and Form S-3, July 31, 2006.

—p. 150, footnote No. 158: Brigham Exploration Co., Form 8-K, Nov. 3, 2005, and Form 8-K, June 1, 2006.

—p. 150, footnote No. 159: Well file, North Dakota Department of Natural Resources, Oil & Gas Division.

—p. 151: "Meanwhile, Continental brought in...$500 an acre." Continental Resources Inc., Form S-1A, Aug. 17, 2006.

—p. 151: "On Jan. 31, 2007, Brigham...was getting the well reports." Brigham Exploration Co., Form 8-K, Jan. 31, 2007, and Form 8-K, April 25, 2007; EOG Resources Inc., Form 8-K, Feb. 1, 2007; and well files, North Dakota Department of Natural Resources, Oil & Gas Division.

—p. 151: "EOG had operated in North Dakota...now had 144,212 net." Well files, North Dakota Department of Natural Resources, Oil & Gas Division; *Montana Oil and Gas Annual Review* 2003-2006, volumes 47-50; EOG Resources Inc., Form 10-K, Feb. 25, 2005; Form 10-K, Feb. 23, 2006; Form 10-K, Feb. 28, 2007.

—p. 152: "'Michael Johnson noticed...in Mountrail County.'" "A Brief History of Oil Production from the Bakken Formation in the Williston Basin," Stephan Nordeng, *Geo News*, January 2010.

—pp. 152-153: "Johnson had been an...It's new office in Williston, North Dakota." *Obscurity to Fame in the Oil Business*, Michael S. Johnson, undated.

—p. 152, footnote No. 160: Ibid.

—p. 153: "While he had been gone...landowner, Henry O. Bakken." Well files, North Dakota Department of Natural Resources, Oil & Gas Division; "Mississippian stratigraphy of northern Montana," J.W. Nordquist, *4th Annual Field Conference Guidebook*, Billings Geological Society, 1953; and "What Are Prospects In Williston Basin's East Side?" Clarence B. Folsom Jr. and Sidney B. Anderson, *Oil & Gas Journal*, Dec. 12, 1955.

—pp. 153-154: "Johnson worked for Amerada...leased already or HBPed." *Obscurity to Fame in the Oil Business*, Michael S. Johnson, undated.

—p. 153, footnote No. 161: "History of the Cedar Creek Anticline, Southeast Montana," John Davis, Denbury Resources Inc., *AAPG Search and Discovery*, Article #90169, October 2013, and "The Cedar Creek Anticline, 43 Years of History and Development, 1921-1964," Thomas A. Gwynn, North Dakota Geological Society and Saskatchewan Geological Society, Williston Basin Symposium, September 1964.

—p. 153, footnote No. 162: "North Dakota Geological Survey Circular No. 16, Summary of the Henry O. Bakken No. 1, Williams County, North Dakota," Sidney B. Anderson, July 1953, archived by the North Dakota Department of Mineral Resources.

—pp. 154-157: "Virtually nothing had been produced...it came back on with 813." Well data from author's research of files, North Dakota Department of Natural Resources, Oil & Gas Division; Johnson's narrative from *Obscurity to Fame in the Oil Business*, Michael S. Johnson, undated.

—p. 157: Also, in reference to "the mature/immature boundary," see "The Bakken: A Question of Maturity," Stephan Nordeng and Julie LeFever, Williston Basin Petroleum Conference, April 2008.

—p. 154, footnote No. 163: Well files, North Dakota Department of Natural Resources, Oil & Gas Division.

—p. 155, footnote No. 164: Ibid and "The Beginning of a 'New Town,'" New Town (North Dakota) Chamber of Commerce, undated.

—p. 156, footnote No. 165: Well files, North Dakota Department of Natural Resources, Oil & Gas Division.

—p. 157, footnote No. 166: Ibid and "Experience Paid Off at Parshall; Explorer of the Year saw Elm Coulee similarities," Louise S. Durham, AAPG *Explorer*, June 2009.

—p. 158: "Bruce Hicks...'with the AFD.'" Author's e-mail conversation with Bruce Hicks, assistant director, North Dakota Department of Mineral Resources, Oil & Gas Division.

—p. 158: "Bud Brigham had information...a 'controlled' frac." Amalgamation from well files, North Dakota Department of Natural Resources, Oil & Gas Division; Brigham Exploration Co., Form 8-K, April 25, 2007; and the author's interviews of Bobby Lyle.

—p. 159: "Until EOG's use of...for other operators." Brigham Exploration Co., Form 10-K, March 9, 2007, and well files, North Dakota Department of Natural Resources, Oil & Gas Division.

—pp. 159-160: "He worked out a deal...already made 133,430 barrels." Brigham Exploration Co., Form 8-K, April 25, 2007; Northern Oil & Gas Inc., Form 10-QSB, May 14, 2007; and well files, North Dakota Department of Natural Resources, Oil & Gas Division.

—p. 159, footnote No. 168: Well files, North Dakota Department of Natural Resources, Oil & Gas Division.

—p. 160: "On Aug. 2, 2007...and 1,675." EOG Resources Inc., Form 8-K, Aug. 2, 2007, and well files, North Dakota Department of Natural Resources, Oil & Gas Division.

—pp. 160-162: "In an earnings call...'That's all I can say.'" Earnings-call transcript, SeekingAlpha.com, EOG Resources Inc., Aug. 3, 2007.

—p. 162: "A month later, Brigham Exploration...base was $101 million." Brigham Exploration Co., Form 8-K, Sept. 28, 2007, and Form 8-K, Oct. 10, 2007; and earnings-call transcript, SeekingAlpha.com, Brigham Exploration, Nov. 7, 2007.

—pp. 162-163: "In late October 2007...'got more than that,' he added." Earnings-call transcript, SeekingAlpha.com, EOG Resources Inc., Oct. 30, 2007.

—p. 162, footnote No. 169: Well files, North Dakota Department of Natural Resources, Oil & Gas Division.

—pp. 163-164: "A week later, Brigham...'not going to drill a dry hole.'" Earnings-call transcript, SeekingAlpha.com, Brigham Exploration Co., Nov. 7, 2007.

—p. 163, footnote No. 170: Earnings-call transcript, SeekingAlpha.com, EOG Resources Inc., Oct. 30, 2007.

—p. 164: "And Parshall Field...along the anticline." Well files, North Dakota Department of Natural Resources, Oil & Gas Division.

—p. 164, footnote No. 171: Ibid.

Chapter 12, Marcellus: 2003
—p. 165: "Tevor Rees-Jones...'comparison to the Marcellus.'" Author's interview of Trevor Rees-Jones, president and chief executive officer, April 15, 2013.

—pp. 165-166: "The UPR engineer...closed its acquisition of Stroud." An amalgamation from the author's interview of Ray Walker; written testimony to the U.K. House of Lords, Economic Affairs Committee, Chris Wright, Oct. 20, 2013; e-mail conversations with Chris Wright; Range Operating Texas LLC (Stroud Energy Inc.), Form S-1, Nov. 7, 2005, Form S-1, April 6, 2006, and Form RW, July 6, 2006; Steward's *The Barnett Shale Play*; the author's site observations, 2001-2012; *Damage Survey and Assessment of Fort Worth Tornado, 28 March 2000*, C.W. Letchford, H.S. Norville, and J. Bilello, Wind Science & Engineering Program, Texas Tech University, for the National Institute for Standards and Technology, August 2000; Range Resources Corp., Form 8-K, May 16, 2006; and Union Pacific Corp., Form 10-KA, March 8, 1995.

—p. 166, footnote No. 172: Author's on-site observation.

—pp. 167-168: "Range had been formed...shallow shale since the 1820s." "Company Timeline," Range Resources Corp., Rangeresources.com; "Optimal Development of Utica Shale Gas Wells," George J. Koperna Jr., Jonathan Kelafant and Vello A. Kuuskraa, AAPG *Search and Discovery*, 2008; "Practical Problems in Well Testing Devonian Shale Gas Wells," J.A. Murtha and D.E. Lancaster, Society of Petroleum Engineers eastern regional meeting, October 1989; and "A Case Study of the Evaluation, Completion, and Testing of a De-

SOURCES

vonian Shale Gas Well," D.E. Lancaster, F.K. Guidry, R.L. Graham, J.B. Curtis, J.S. Shaw and T.H. Blake, *Journal of Petroleum Technology*, May 1989.

—p. 167, footnote No. 173: Range Resources Corp., Form 10-K, Feb. 27, 2007.

—p. 167, footnote No. 174: Range Resources Corp., Form 8-K, March 2, 2011.

—p. 167, footnote No. 175: "Corporate History of the East Ohio Gas Co.: The Spirit of Progress," East Ohio Gas Co., Dom.com (Dominion Resources Inc.)

—pp. 168-171: "In the Ohio office...'How much work do I do on it?'" Author's interview of Bill Zagorski, vice president, geology, Marcellus-shale division, Range Resources Corp., April 26, 2013; and *Elmworth: Case Study of a Deep Basin Gas Field*, introduction by John Masters, American Association of Petroleum Geologists, Memoir 38, 1984.

—p. 168, footnote No. 176: Range Resources Corp. (Domain Energy Corp.), Form S-1, April 4, 1997.

—p. 168, footnote No. 177: "2009 is the 150th Anniversary of Oil," Oil 150, Oil Region Alliance of Business, Industry & Tourism, Pennsylvania, 2013.

—p. 171: "Range's capital budget...reinstated dividends." Range Resources Corp., Form 10-K, March 3, 2004.

—p. 171: "Jeff Ventura had just joined...'the next Barnett.'" Author's interview of Jeff Ventura, president and chief executive officer, Range Resources Corp., May 17, 2013, and Range Resources Corp., Form DEF-14A, April 21, 2004.

—p. 172: "The company was wildcatting...in Appalachia." Range Resources Corp., Form 8-K, April 19, 2006.

—p. 173, footnote No. 178: "Newark, East (Barnett Shale) Field, Discovery Date: 10-15-1981," field data, Texas Railroad Commission, Jan. 23, 2012.

—p. 174: "The frac crew gathered for a photo." "Range's Path to Discovery and Commercialization of the Marcellus Shale–the Largest Producing Gas Field in the U.S.," Jeff Ventura, American Association of Petroleum Geologists annual convention and exhibition, May 20, 2013.

—p. 174: "Until Oct. 18, 2004...85 wells in the region." Range Resources Corp., Form 8-K, Oct. 19, 2004.

—p. 175: "And its position...1.7 million net, acres." Range Resources Corp., Form 10-K, March 2, 2005.

—p. 175, footnote No. 179: Range Resources Corp., Form 8-K, June 4, 2004.

—p. 176: "And the company's...was $254 million." Range Resources Corp., Form 10-K, March 2, 2005.

—p. 176: "In 2006, its capex...now $429 million." Range Resources Corp., Form 10-K, Feb. 23, 2006.

—p. 177: "By then, Range's capex...Permian Basin and Barnett." Range Resources Corp., Form 10-K, Feb. 27, 2007.

—p. 179: "In December 2007...4.7 million." Range Resources Corp., Form 8-K,

Dec. 10, 2007.

—p. 179: "It now had proved...wells in the new year." Range Resources Corp., Form 8-K, Feb. 11, 2008, and Form 8-K, Feb. 27, 2008.

—p. 180, footnote No. 180: "National Oil and Gas Assessment 2013, Assessment Updates," U.S. Geological Survey, Energy.usgs.gov, and "Pennsylvania Natural Gas Production Up 62% y/y to 3.3 Tcf, NGI Reports," press release, *Natural Gas Intelligence*, Feb. 21, 2014.

Chapter 13, Haynesville: 2007

—p. 181: "As Range Resources...was heading to 3 billion a day." *Revisiting the Economic Impact of the Natural Gas Activity in the Fayetteville Shale: 2008-2012*, Center for Business and Economic Research, Sam M. Walton College of Business, University of Arkansas, May 2012, and "Newark, East (Barnett Shale) Total Natural Gas, 1993 through April 2013," Texas Railroad Commission, April 25, 2013.

—p. 181: "Petrohawk...'technology wasn't there yet.'" Author's interview of Dick Stoneburner, senior advisor, Pine Brook Partners LP, March 11, 2013.

—p. 181: "Otherwise, Petrohawk...1,895 acres." Petrohawk Energy Corp. (Beta Oil & Gas Inc.), Form PRER-14A, March 17, 2004.

—pp. 182-183: "Wilson began his career...'this old rule of thumb.'" "Floyd-Opoly," Nissa Darbonne, *Oil and Gas Investor*, November 2011.

—pp. 183-184: "Three years later...of proved reserves." Petrohawk Energy Corp., Form 8-K, Feb. 28, 2007.

—p. 184: "But, by way of one...Wilson chose shale." Petrohawk Energy Corp., Form 8-K, Aug. 9, 2006, and "Petrohawk Energy Corporation Announces Plans to Divest Gulf Coast Division and Grows Mid-Continent Resource Presence," Petrohawk Energy Corp., Business Wire, June 25, 2007.

—p. 187: "By 2006, among Petrohawk's...463 billion of proved reserves." Petrohawk Energy Corp., Form 8-K, Dec. 20, 2005, and Form 8-K, Aug. 9, 2006.

—p. 187: "The company went to work...up from those as well." "Petrohawk and KCS Are Fracing The Hosston Code," Nissa Darbonne, *Oil and Gas Investor*, August 2006.

—p. 187, footnote No. 183: Additional information on dentritic fracturing, "Fifty Year History of the Texas Austin Chalk Trend," Holifield Energy Company LLC, Holifieldenergy.homestead.com

—p. 188: "Wilson says, "The Haynesville...'play yet.'" Author's interview of Floyd Wilson, chairman and chief executive officer, Halcon Resources Corp., Sept. 17, 2011.

—p. 188: "Instead, Petrohawk aimed...then 2,500." "Floyd-Opoly," Nissa Darbonne, *Oil and Gas Investor*, November 2011.

—p. 188: "KCS also happened...took the offer." Petrohawk Energy Corp., Form 8-K, Aug. 9, 2006, and "Landowners, Others Seeing the Impact of Energy Investment," Garry Hoffmann, *Arkansas Business*, Aug. 27, 2007.

—p. 188: "Steve Herod...by June 2007." "Petrohawk Energy Corporation Announces Plans to Divest Gulf Coast Division and Grows Mid-Continent Resource Presence," Petrohawk Energy Corp., Business Wire, June 25, 2007.

—p. 189: "Floyd Wilson had seen...June 25, 2007." Ibid.

—p. 189: "Herod says, 'In a shale...treadmill for opportunities.'" Author's interview of Steve Herod, president, Halcon Resources Corp., March 27, 2013.

—pp. 190-191: "There, Randy Miller...analyzed the data." Stoneburner and "Geologic analysis of the Upper Jurassic Haynesville Shale in east Texas and west Louisiana: Discussion," Marvin D. Brittenham, *AAPG Bulletin*, March 2013.

—p. 190, footnote No. 185: "Geologic analysis of the Upper Jurassic Haynesville Shale in east Texas and west Louisiana: Discussion," Marvin D. Brittenham, *AAPG Bulletin*, March 2013.

—p. 191: "In 2004, it had entered...at about 9,600 feet." Chesapeake Energy Corp., Form 8-K, May 12, 2004.

—p. 192: "On Sept. 27, 2007, Chesapeake spud...cubic feet a day." Well files from the Louisiana Department of Natural Resources.

—p. 192, footnote No. 186: Ibid.

—p. 192, footnote No. 187: Ibid.

—p. 193: "A land rush began...new 3Tec public." 3Tec Energy Corp. (Middle Bay Oil Co. Inc.), Form DEF-14A, May 15, 1998, and Form 10-KSB40A, Oct. 16, 1998; 3Tec Energy Corp., Form 10-KSB40, March 30, 2000.

—p. 193: "That fall, 3Tec...of $250 million." 3Tec Energy Corp., Form 10-KSB40, March 30, 2000.

—pp. 194-195: "In January 2008, Herod...was now 150,000 net acres." Petrohawk Energy Corp., Form 10-K, Feb. 27, 2008; Form 8-K, Jan. 25, 2008 and Form 8-K, Nov. 30, 2007.

—p. 195-196: "On Nov. 7, 2007, small-cap...'always a bad sign.'" Earnings-call transcripts, SeekingAlpha.com, for Exco Resources Inc., Jan. 30, 2008; Cabot Oil & Gas Corp., Oct. 26, 2007, and Feb. 14, 2008; and Comstock Resources Inc., Feb. 12, 2008; GMX Resources Inc., Form 8-K, Nov. 8, 2001; and Cubic Energy Inc., Form 10-QSB, Feb. 12, 2008.

—p. 195, footnote No. 192: Earnings-call transcript, SeekingAlpha.com, for Cabot Oil & Gas Corp., Feb. 14, 2008.

—pp. 196-197: "The slide stated...'petrophysical characteristics.'" Petrohawk Energy Corp., Form 8-K, March 12, 2008.

—p. 197: "In that announcement, on March 24...$675 million." Chesapeake Energy Corp., Form 8-K, March 24, 2008.

—p. 197, footnote No. 194: Newfield Exploration Co., Form 8-K, July 28, 2005.

—p. 199: "The city, with a...Entertainment Corp." "History of Shreveport," Eric Brock for the Greater Shreveport Chamber of Commerce, undated, and "Major Employers," Greater Bossier Economic Development Foundation, Gbedf.org.

—p. 200: "In early August 2008, Petrohawk reported...averaging 19.3 million cubic feet a day." Petrohawk Energy Corp., Form 8-K, Aug. 6, 2008; and Form 10-K, Feb. 25, 2009.

—p. 201: "It had grown its land...some six times its pre-existing leasehold." Petrohawk Energy Corp., Form 10-K, Feb. 25, 2009.

—p. 202, footnote No. 195: "Land Run of 1889," *Encyclopedia of Oklahoma History and Culture*, Oklahoma Historical Society, 2010.

Chapter 14, Bakken: 2008

—p. 203: "But Brigham Exploration...1.15 million cubic feet of gas." Well files, North Dakota Department of Natural Resources, Oil & Gas Division.

—p. 203: "Bud Brigham reported...'horizontal Bakken wells.'" Brigham Exploration Co., Form 8-K, Sept. 11, 2008.

—p. 203: "Halliburton...'to complete a well.'" Halliburton Co., Form 8-K, Oct. 21, 2008.

—p. 204: "'We were optimistic...a game changer.'" Author's interviews of Bud Brigham, chairman, Brigham Resources LLC, June 14, 2010, and April 23, 2013.

—p. 204: "In early 2008, west of Nesson...with 565 barrels." Well files, North Dakota Department of Natural Resources, Oil & Gas Division.

—p. 204: "The completion report...two months later." Ibid.

—p. 204: "Now, Brigham had...by year-end 2009." Brigham Exploration Co., Form 8-K, July 16, 2008, and Sept. 11, 2008.

—p. 204: "Meanwhile, Continental...lower-Bakken shale." Continental Resources Inc., Form 8-K, Feb. 26, 2008.

—p. 204, footnote No. 196: Continental Resources Inc., Form 10-K, March 17, 2008, Form 8-K, May 5, 2008 and Form 8-K, July 29, 2008, and "Emerging Plays," Nissa Darbonne, *Oil and Gas Investor*, January 2012.

—p. 205: "All the while, Whiting...upper-shale play." "3 to 4.3 Billion Barrels of Technically Recoverable Oil Assessed in North Dakota and Montana's Bakken Formation—25 Times More Than 1995 Estimate," U.S. Geological Survey, April 10, 2008.

—p. 205: "Since then, by 2008, the fraced...east of Nesson." *Montana Oil and Gas Annual Review* 2007, Volume 51, and well files, North Dakota Department of Natural Resources, Oil & Gas Division.

—p. 205: "The 1995 estimate...'(structural) occurrences.'" "3 to 4.3 Billion Barrels of Technically Recoverable Oil Assessed in North Dakota and Montana's

Bakken Formation—25 Times More Than 1995 Estimate," U.S. Geological Survey, April 10, 2008.

—pp. 205-206: "Two weeks later, the 16th...these people to act." "The Department Of Mineral Resources Assessment Of The Bakken Formation," Ed Murphy, *DMR Newsletter*, Volume 36, No. 1.

—pp. 206-207: "Stephan Nordeng...'resource must as well.'" "A Brief History of Oil Production from the Bakken Formation in the Williston Basin," Stephan Nordeng, *Geo News*, January 2010.

—p. 207: "Citing the USGS report...30,000 barrels a day." Enbridge Energy Partners LP, Form 8-K, April 29, 2008.

—p. 207: "All oil production...already 172,000." "North Dakota Annual Oil Production, 1951-2012," North Dakota Department of Mineral Resources, June 2013.

—p. 207: "Soon, micro-cap Earthstone...all of this new oil." Earthstone Energy Inc., Form 10-KSB, July 11, 2008.

—p. 207: "EOG...to the Gulf Coast." EOG Resources Inc., Form 8-K, May 4, 2009.

—p. 207: "XTO...some $1,150 an acre." XTO Energy Inc., Form 8-K, May 30, 2008; Form 8-K, June 12, 2008; and Form 8-K, July 18, 2008.

—p. 207: "Hess...drilling for it." Hess Corp., Form 10-Q, Aug. 8, 2008, and Marathon Oil Corp., Form 8-K, July 31, 2008.

—p. 207, footnote No. 197: XTO Energy Inc., Form 8-K, June 12, 2008, and Form 8-K, July 22, 2008..

—p. 208: "In 2008, by the morning...modern Bakken play." Author's calculation from well files, North Dakota Department of Natural Resources, Oil & Gas Division.

—p. 208: "Hurricane Ike...awoke to more news." Author's and family's on-site observations.

—p. 208: "At 12:45 a.m. CDT...protection." "Lehman throws in the keys," William Cohan, Money.CNN.com, Dec. 14, 2008.

—p. 208: "A U.S. dollar...worth 99 cents." "Treasury Announces Guaranty Program for Money Market Funds," press release, U.S. Department of Treasury, Sept. 19, 2008.

—p. 209: "Brigham Exploration was hit...'financing sources.'" "In Pursuit of Bakken," Nissa Darbonne, *Oil and Gas Investor*, August 2010, and Brigham Exploration Co., Form 10-Q, Nov. 6, 2008.

—pp. 209-210: "His first, big, east-of-Nesson...throughout North America." Brigham Exploration Co., Form 8-K, Oct. 31, 2008.

—p. 210: "In December 2008...4.5 years of the new play." Brigham Exploration Co., Form 8-K, Dec. 5, 2008, and author's calculation from well files, North

Dakota Department of Natural Resources, Oil & Gas Division.

—p. 210: "There still hadn't...east of Nesson by now." Author's calculation from well files, North Dakota Department of Natural Resources, Oil & Gas Division.

—p. 210: "In January 2009, he went ahead...with 1,160 barrels." Well file, North Dakota Department of Natural Resources, Oil & Gas Division.

—p. 210, footnote No. 200: Ibid.

—p. 211: "In 2008, the company...to at least $100." "In Pursuit of Bakken," Nissa Darbonne, *Oil and Gas Investor*, August 2010.

—p. 211: "...the price at which Brigham...on Bakken wells." Brigham Exploration Co., Form 8-K, Oct. 31, 2008.

—pp. 211-212: "In May, the company sold...as much as 40% in the region." "In Pursuit of Bakken," Nissa Darbonne, *Oil and Gas Investor*, August 2010, and Brigham Exploration Co., Form 8-K, May 28, 2009.

—p. 211, footnote No. 201: Author's ongoing observation of industry commentary.

—pp. 212-213: "The company completed two more...big wells west of Nesson." Well files, North Dakota Department of Natural Resources, Oil & Gas Division; and Brigham Exploration Co., Form 8-K, May 28, 2009, and Form 8-K, July 20, 2009.

—p. 213: "It also brought in...more than 1,000 barrels." Brigham Exploration Co., Form 8-K, Aug. 27, 2009, and well files, North Dakota Department of Natural Resources, Oil & Gas Division.

—p. 213: "Securities analyst Subash...'in North America.'" "Jefferies Analyst: Bakken 'Will Be One Of The Largest Oil Discoveries In North America," Nissa Darbonne, *Oil and Gas Investor*, Sept. 24, 2009.

—p. 213: "Brigham went back...$110 million of bank debt." "In Pursuit of Bakken," Nissa Darbonne, *Oil and Gas Investor*, August 2010.

—pp. 213-214: "The company was going to 28...for a record 5,133 barrels equivalent." Brigham Exploration Co., Form 8-K, Aug. 27, 2009; well file, North Dakota Department of Natural Resources, Oil & Gas Division; earnings-call transcript, SeekingAlpha.com, Brigham Exploration Co., Nov. 6, 2009; supplemented from the author's interview of Bud Brigham, April 23, 2013.

—p. 214: "Through year-end...in the Williston Basin." Brigham Exploration Co., Form 10-K, March 1, 2010.

—p. 214, footnote No. 204: Well file, North Dakota Department of Natural Resources, Oil & Gas Division.

Chapter 15, Eagle Ford: 2008

—p. 215: "When Floyd...found another one." Author's interview of Dick Stoneburner, senior advisor, Pine Brook Partners LP, March 11, 2013.

—p. 215: "On Oct. 21, 2008...'at 9.1 MMcfe/d.'" Press release, Petrohawk Energy Corp., PRNewswire, Oct. 21, 2008.

—p. 215: "'Floyd is...done quicker.'" Author's interview of Steve Herod, president, Halcon Resources Corp., March 27, 2013.

—p. 216: "Leading up to the...line of credit." "Floyd-Opoly," Nissa Darbonne, *Oil and Gas Investor*, November 2011.

—p. 216: "...the company had quietly...yet more superior there." Press release, Petrohawk Energy Corp., PRNewswire, Oct. 21, 2008.

—p. 216, footnote No. 206: "Floyd-Opoly," Nissa Darbonne, *Oil and Gas Investor*, November 2011.

—p. 216, footnote No. 207: Ibid.

—p. 216, footnote No. 208: Petrohawk Energy Corp., Form 8-K, Aug. 4, 2009.

—p. 217: "For months...spread was enormous." Author's interview of Rod Lewis, chief executive officer, Lewis Energy Corp., April 19, 2013, and "La Salle County," Texas State Historical Association, 2013.

—p. 217: "Drilling in La Salle...in 1940." "La Salle County," John Leffler, Texas State Historical Association, 2013.

—p. 217: "His fascination...for $13,000." "South Texas Freebird," Steve Toon, *Oil and Gas Investor*, June 2011.

—p. 217, footnote No. 209: Lewisairlegends.com and "Annual Report 2013," Smithsonian National Air and Space Museum.

—p. 223: "Robertson had explored...in the 1970s." "The Wildcatter: Corpus Christi's Gregg Robertson, key member of Eagle Ford discovery, named 2012 Newsmaker of the Year," Mark Collette, *Corpus Christi Caller Times*, Dec. 29, 2012.

—pp. 223-224: "For Petrohawk...4,000 feet deeper into Eagle Ford." Author's interview of Gregg Robertson, president, First Rock Inc., March 25, 2013, supplemented by the author's interview of Dick Stoneburner.

—p. 225: "There was a well...'66 million years ago.'" "The Wildcatter: Corpus Christi's Gregg Robertson, key member of Eagle Ford discovery, named 2012 Newsmaker of the Year," Mark Collette, *Corpus Christi Caller Times*, Dec. 29, 2012.

—p. 225, footnote No. 215: "BEG Facilities," Bureau of Economic Geology, University of Texas at Austin, Beg.utexas.edu, 2013.

—p. 227: "The state permit...attention to it." "The Wildcatter: Corpus Christi's Gregg Robertson, key member of Eagle Ford discovery, named 2012 Newsmaker of the Year," Mark Collette, *Corpus Christi Caller Times*, Dec. 29, 2012.

—p. 227: "It took more than...3,200 of lateral." Petrohawk Energy Corp., Form 8-K, April 21, 2009, and "Petrohawk/Eagle Ford," Dick Stoneburner presentation to the Independent Petroleum Association of America and Texas Independent Producers & Royalty Owners Association membership meeting, July 8, 2009.

—pp. 227-228: "On the far western side...50,000 barrels of condensate." Petrohawk Energy Corp., Form 8-K, April 21, 2009, and Form 8-K, Aug. 4, 2009; and "The Application of Petrohawk Operating Company to Adopt Temporary Field Rules for the Hawkville (Eagleford Shale) Field, La Salle County, Texas," Texas Railroad Commission, Nov. 4, 2009.

—p. 229: "In its Black Hawk...and 1,485 barrels." Petrohawk Energy Corp., Form 8-K, Aug. 3, 2010.

Chapter 16, Bakken: 2010

—p. 230: "In April 2010...said at the time." "In Pursuit of Bakken," Nissa Darbonne, *Oil and Gas Investor*, August 2010.

—p. 230: "In 2011, in just...90% of that oil." Brigham Exploration Co., Form 10-K, March 1, 2011, and Form 8-K, May 4, 2011; and "In Pursuit of Bakken," Nissa Darbonne, *Oil and Gas Investor*, August 2010.

—pp. 230-231: "Dave Pursell...'name to own.'" Author's calculation from well files, North Dakota Department of Natural Resources, Oil & Gas Division, and "In Pursuit of Bakken," Nissa Darbonne, *Oil and Gas Investor*, August 2010.

—p. 231: "Also, Continental...Three Forks 1." "Emerging Plays," Nissa Darbonne, *Oil and Gas Investor*, January 2012.

—p. 231: "Bud Brigham let...potential acquirer." Brigham Exploration Co., Form SC-TOT, Oct. 28, 2011.

—p. 231: "'We kind of looked...care of our people.'" Author's interviews of Bud Brigham, chairman, Brigham Resources LLC, June 14, 2010, and April 23, 2013.

—p. 231: "Production was...next five years." Statoil ASA, Form 6-K, Oct. 17, 2011.

—p. 231: "Norway-based Statoil...discuss it further." Brigham Exploration Co., Form SC-TOT, Oct. 28, 2011.

—pp. 231-232: "The international super-major's...midstream properties for $3 billion." "Statoil's Bakken," Nissa Darbonne, *Oil and Gas Investor*, December 2011.

—p. 232: "By September 2011...completed on Dec. 1." Brigham Exploration Co., Form SC-TOT, Oct. 28, 2011; and Statoil ASA, Form 6-K, Oct. 17, 2011, and Statoil ASA, Form 6-K, Dec. 1, 2011.

—p. 233: "Torstein Hole...'elsewhere in the world.'" "Statoil's Bakken," Nissa Darbonne, *Oil and Gas Investor*, December 2011.

Chapter 17, Haynesville & Eagle Ford: 2011

—p. 234: "It had exited the Fayetteville...Eagle Ford." Petrohawk Energy Corp.,

Form 10-K, Feb. 22, 2011.

—p. 234: "A couple of months...U.S.-shale team yet." Chesapeake Energy Corp., Form 8-K, Feb. 22, 2011.

—pp. 234-235: "Floyd...'for both companies.'" Author's interview of Floyd Wilson, chairman and chief executive officer, Halcon Resources Corp., Sept. 17, 2011.

—p. 235: "BHP had been sitting...Potash Corp. in 2010." BHP Billiton Ltd., Form 20-F, Sept. 21, 2011.

—p. 235: "Meanwhile, in June 2011...lower-carbon fuel." Petrohawk Energy Corp., Form SC-14D9, July 25, 2011, and SC-14D9A, Aug. 10, 2011.

—p. 235: "Without at least deducting...$9,800 per net acre." Author's calculation based on asset data from Chesapeake Energy Corp., Form 8-K, Feb. 22, 2011, and BHP Billiton Ltd., Form 6-K, Feb. 22, 2011.

—p. 235: "Herod says...'buy all of Petrohawk.'" Author's interview of Steve Herod, president, Halcon Resources Corp., March 27, 2013.

—p. 236: "Demand for Eagle Ford...$1.55 billion." "North American Shale Transactions Since 2008," Bill Marko, Jefferies & Co., April 2013.

—p. 236: "On July 6, securities...more than $200 billion." "Dirty Chalk," Nissa Darbonne, *Oil and Gas Investor*, August 2011.

—p. 236: "Soon, Wilson got a call...a deal with BHP." Petrohawk Energy Corp., Form SC-14D9, July 25, 2011, and SC-14D9A, Aug. 10, 2011.

—pp. 236-237: "Petrohawk had 3.4 trillion...and $16.6 billion." Ibid and "Floyd-Opoly," Nissa Darbonne, *Oil and Gas Investor*, November 2011; and author's calculation.

—p. 237: "BHP made an offer...pre-2008 stock price." Petrohawk Energy Corp., Form SC-14D9, July 25, 2011, and SC-14D9A, Aug. 10, 2011.

—p. 238, footnote No. 222: Devon Energy Corp., Form 8-K, Nov. 22, 2013.

Chapter 18, Haynesville & Eagle Ford: 2014-
—p. 239: "Rod Lewis...Edwards wells." Author's interview of Rod Lewis, chief executive officer, Lewis Energy Corp., April 19, 2013.

—p. 239: "Stoneburner says...'Hawkville Field.'" Author's interview of Dick Stoneburner, senior advisor, Pine Brook Partners LP, March 11, 2013.

—p. 240: Encana Corp. and Chesapeake Energy Corp. references are supplemented by "Geologic analysis of the Upper Jurassic Haynesville Shale in east Texas and west Louisiana: Discussion," Marvin D. Brittenham, *AAPG Bulletin*, March 2013.

—p. 241: "Floyd Wilson exited...at the time." Petrohawk Energy Corp., Form SC-14D9, July 25, 2011; "Floyd-Opoly," Nissa Darbonne, *Oil and Gas Investor*, November 2011; and Halcon Resources Corp. (Ram Energy Resources Inc.),

Form 8-K, Dec. 22, 2011.

—p. 241: "Herod stayed on...Halcon's first eight months." Petrohawk Energy Corp., Form SC-14D9, July 25, 2011, and Halcon Resources Corp. (Ram Energy Resources Inc.), Form 8-K, Dec. 22, 2011.

—p. 241: "Stoneburner remained...Brook Partners LLC." Petrohawk Energy Corp., Form SC-14D9, July 25, 2011, and Newfield Exploration Co., Form DEF-14A, March 20, 2014.

—p. 241: "About that Petrohawk mindset...'in cash!'" Author's interview of Steve Herod, president, Halcon Resources Corp., March 27, 2013.

—p. 241: "Unlike his past start-ups...for Halcon." Halcon Resources Corp. (Ram Energy Resources Inc.), Form 8-K, Dec. 22, 2011.

—p. 242: "Its capital raises...'in terms of political risk.'" Author's interview of Floyd Wilson, chairman and chief executive officer, Halcon Resources Corp., Sept. 17, 2011.

—p. 242: "In 2004, Petrohawk...mid-2007." Petrohawk Energy Corp., Form 10-K, March 26, 2004; Form 10-K, March 14, 2006; and Form SC-14D9, July 25, 2011.

Chapter 19, Marcellus: 2014-

—pp. 244-245: "Ray Walker says...'all of the other liquids.'" Author's interview of Ray Walker, executive vice president and chief operating officer, Range Resources Corp., April 29, 2013.

—p. 245: "Many consumers were...in November 2009." "Rockies pipeline reverses flow for Marcellus shale gas and wins FERC ruling," George Lobsenz, IHS Unconventional Energy Blog, Dec. 17, 2013.

—p. 245: "For the NGL...to the Gulf Coast." Range Resources Corp., Form 8-K, Feb. 26, 2014.

—p. 245: "The Pittsburgh office...gas field in North America." "Range's Path to Discovery and Commercialization of the Marcellus Shale–the Largest Producing Gas Field in the U.S.," Jeff Ventura, American Association of Petroleum Geologists annual convention and exhibition, May 20, 2013.

—pp. 245-246: "Jeff Ventura notes...'and staged fracs.'" Author's interview of Jeff Ventura, president and chief executive officer, Range Resources Corp., May 17, 2013.

—pp. 246-247: "Bill Zagorski...'with $100 bills.'" Author's interview of Bill Zagorski, vice president, geology, Marcellus-shale division, Range Resources Corp., April 26, 2013.

—pp. 248-249: "After selling most of his...'has already been found.'" Author's interview of Trevor Rees-Jones, president and chief executive officer, April 15, 2013.

Chapter 20, Fayetteville: 2014-
—p. 252: "At year-end 2007...lateral half as long." Southwestern Energy Co., Form 8-K, Feb. 28, 2008; Form 8-K, Feb. 27, 2009; and Form 8-K, Feb. 21, 2013.
—p. 252: "Gross production by all...2.6 billion a day." *Revisiting the Economic Impact of the Natural Gas Activity in the Fayetteville Shale: 2008-2012*, Center for Business and Economic Research, Sam M. Walton College of Business, University of Arkansas, May 2012.
—p. 253: "Richard Lane says of...there was little drilling." Author's interview of Richard Lane, president and chief executive officer, Vitruvian Exploration LLC, April 10, 2013.
—p. 253: "John Thaeler says...'benefited from it.'" Author's interview of John Thaeler, chief operating officer, Vitruvian Exploration LLC, April 10, 2013.
—p. 256: "Harold Korell...'good for the world.'" Author's interview of Harold Korell, chairman, Southwestern Energy Co., March 27, 2013.

Chapter 21, Bakken: 2014-
—p. 257: "Bud Brigham says...'crush over time.'" Author's interviews of Bud Brigham, chairman, Brigham Resources LLC, June 14, 2010, and April 23, 2013.
—p. 257: "Brigham Exploration's aggressiveness...'Brigham-style.'" "Characterization of the Bakken System of the Williston Basin from Pores to Production; The Power of a Source Rock/Unconventional Reservoir Couplet," Anne Grau and Robert H. Sterling, *AAPG Search and Discovery*, Article #40847, December 12, 2011.
—pp. 257-258: "East of the Nesson...May 8, 2010." Well file, North Dakota Department of Natural Resources, Oil & Gas Division.
—p. 258: "Only its first 11...Its success rate: 100%." Author's calculation from well files, North Dakota Department of Natural Resources, Oil & Gas Division.
—p. 258, footnote No. 228: Ibid.
—pp. 259-260: "By mid-2013...Camp Field held 54." Ibid.
—p. 260: "The USGS released...just 151 million barrels." "Assessment of Undiscovered Oil Resources in the Bakken and Three Forks Formations, Williston Basin Province, Montana, North Dakota, and South Dakota," U.S. Geological Survey, April 2013, and "3 to 4.3 Billion Barrels of Technically Recoverable Oil Assessed in North Dakota and Montana's Bakken Formation—25 Times More Than 1995 Estimate," U.S. Geological Survey, April 10, 2008.
—pp. 260-261: "Taylor Reid...'controlled fracs.'" Author's interview of Taylor Reid, president and chief operating officer, Oasis Petroleum Inc., April 24, 2013.
—pp. 261-262: "Garry Tanner...'do anything about it.'" Author's interview of Garry Tanner, managing director, Quantum Energy Partners LP, Aug. 23, 2013.

—pp. 262-263: "With a bachelor's...'It's working quite well.'" Author's interview of Ward Polzin, chief executive officer, Centennial Resource Development LLC, April 15, 2013.

—p. 263: "...had already made 43 million...upon Lyco's exit in 2005." *Montana Oil and Gas Annual Review* 2006, Volume 50.

—p. 263: "Commercial oil production...'easier than oil does.'" Author's interview of Dave Pursell, managing director and head of securities research, Tudor, Pickering, Holt & Co., April 25, 2013.

—p. 264: "In 1954, one well...proved in the mid-1990s." ND Monthly Bakken Oil Production Statistics, including Bakken, Sanish, Three Forks, and Bakken/Three Forks Pools," well files, and "North Dakota Cumulative Oil Production by Formation Through December 2012," all from the North Dakota Department of Natural Resources, Oil & Gas Division; and author's supplemental calculations.

—pp. 264-265: "Continental Resources' Harold Hamm...'early in the game yet.'" Author's interview of Harold Hamm, chairman and chief executive officer, Continental Resources Inc., Sept. 3, 2013.

—p. 264, footnote No. 231: "Director's Cut," monthly briefing, Lynn Helms, North Dakota Industrial Commission, Department of Mineral Resources," Feb. 14, 2014.

—p. 267: "Jack Stark, Continental's...'it doesn't stay proprietary very long.'" Author's interview of Jack Stark, senior vice president, exploration, Continental Resources Inc., March 19, 2013.

—pp. 267-270: "Tom Lantz...'out of this kind of rock.'" Author's interview of Tom Lantz, chief operating officer, American Eagle Energy Corp., April 3, 2013.

—pp. 272-273: "Dick Findley...'I got to do that.'" Author's interview of Dick Findley, chairman, American Eagle Energy Corp., March 18, 2013.

—pp. 273-276: "Lyco's Bobby Lyle...'there is no limit.'" Author's interviews of Bobby Lyle, chairman, Lyco Holdings Corp., Jan. 25, March 11 and March 14, 2013.

Chapter 22, The Money

—p. 277: "Barnett- and Marcellus-play...'debt of gratitude.'" Author's interview of Trevor Rees-Jones, president and chief executive officer, April 15, 2013.

—p. 277: "Steve Herod concurs...'around to be interested.'" Author's interview of Steve Herod, president, Halcon Resources Corp., March 27, 2013.

—pp. 277-281: "Long before then, however...'go to North America.'" Author's interview of Ralph Eads, vice chairman, energy investment banking, Jefferies & Co., May 15, 2013.

—p. 278, footnote No. 234: Enerplus Corp., Form 6-K, Aug. 20, 2009.

—p. 281: "Bill Marko...'on the map.'" Author's interview of Bill Marko, managing director, Jefferies & Co., March 15, 2013.

—pp. 282-283: "CNOOC brought in...'was a big deal.'" Author's interview of Ward Polzin, chief executive officer, Centennial Resource Development LLC, April 15, 2013.

—p. 282, footnote No. 237: ChevronTexaco Corp. (Unocal Corp.), Form 425, April 7, 2005.

—pp. 283-284: "Maynard Holt...'these golden rules.'" Author's interview of Maynard Holt, co-president and head of E&P investment banking, Tudor, Pickering, Holt & Co., April 15, 2013.

—p. 284, footnote No. 239: "Applications Received by DOE/FE to Export Domestically Produced LNG from the Lower-48 States, as of March 24, 2014," U.S. Department of Energy, Office of Fossil Energy, Energy.gov, March 24, 2014, and "Statement by Harold Hamm, Chairman and Chief Executive Officer, Continental Resources, Inc., Senate Energy and Natural Resources Committee Hearing, January 30, 2014," Energy.senate.gov.

Chapter 23, Barnett: 2014-

—p. 286: "Dave Pursell says...'he was nuts.'" Author's interview of Dave Pursell, managing director and head of securities research, Tudor, Pickering, Holt & Co., April 25, 2013.

—p. 286: "...initiated coverage of Mitchell Energy in February 2001." Author's e-mail conversation with Jeff Dietert, managing director and head of research, Simmons & Co. International Inc.

—p. 288: "Pursell published in March 2007...future of U.S. gas supply." "The Yin and Yang of Production Growth, Rig Count, and Gas Storage," Dave Pursell, Pickering Energy Partners Inc., March 8, 2007.

—pp. 289-290: "Dan Pickering...'to drill that well.'" Author's interview of Dan Pickering, co-president and head of TPH Asset Management, Tudor, Pickering, Holt & Co., March 28, 2013.

—pp. 291-293: "Larry Nichols notes...'brighter and brighter.'" Author's interview of Larry Nichols, executive chairman, Devon Energy Corp., April 17, 2013.

—pp. 293-294: "The UPR team...'in a 24-hour period.'" Author's interview of Ray Walker, executive vice president and chief operating officer, Range Resources Corp., April 29, 2013.

—p. 294: "John Thaeler adds...'we're so damn smart.'" Author's interview of John Thaeler, chief operating officer, Vitruvian Exploration LLC, April 10, 2013.

—p. 295: "In the book...'don't out-smart yourself.'" *The Barnett Shale Play: Phoenix of the Fort Worth Basin, A History*, Dan Steward, Fort Worth Geological Society and North Texas Geological Society, 2007.

—p. 295, footnote No. 242: Steward's *The Barnett Shale Play* and supplemental data from Steward.

Chapter 24, George Mitchell

—pp. 296-297: "George Mitchell...'compared with what it is now.'" Author's interviews of Dan Steward, geologist, Republic Energy Inc., March 12, August 14 and August 18, 2013.

—p. 297: "In his book...'such an uncertain outcome.'" *The Barnett Shale Play: Phoenix of the Fort Worth Basin, A History*, Dan Steward, Fort Worth Geological Society and North Texas Geological Society, 2007.

—p. 297: "Kent Bowker...'for a mid-size independent.'" Author's interview of Kent Bowker, executive vice president, geology, Titan River Energy LLC, April 25, 2013.

—pp. 297-299: "In Mitchell Energy's 50th...'to building, solving, creating.'" Mitchell Energy & Development Corp., Form 10-K, April 30, 1996.

—pp. 299-301: "George Mitchell said...'we can all do better.'" Author's interview of George Mitchell, April 7, 2011.

Acknowledgements

—p. 303: "Still driven...He dreamed big." "George Phydias Mitchell—The Father We Knew, May 21, 1919-July 26, 2013," the Mitchell family, *Houston Chronicle*, July 30, 2013.

INDEX

← ← ← ← ← → → → → →

Formations, basins, structures, fields and wells are also cited with the play to which they are related. Materials, techniques and other related to completions are additionally cited under "Completion."

3Tec Energy Corp., 182-184, 187-188, 193-194, 236-237
A.J. Hodges Industries Inc., 87
Adexco Production Co., 181
Adix 25-1H, 209-210
Adrian College, 45
Advanced Resources International Inc., 5, 97
AIG, 208
Albin 31X-28, 63
Albin FLB 2-33, 23-28, 40, 60, 63
Alger Field, 212, 259
Alliant Energy Corp., 70
Allison, Jay, 196
Alta Resources LLC, 143, 195
Amerada Hess Corp., 145
Amerada Petroleum Corp., 93, 145, 152-153, 207
American Association of Petroleum Geologists, 146, 157, 241
American Eagle Energy Corp., 267
American Exploration Co., 29
American Hunter Exploration Ltd., 19, 155
American Oil & Gas Inc., 70-71
Ames Field, 85
Amoco Corp., 12, 66, 111, 125, 254
Anadarko Basin, 17
Anadarko Petroleum Corp., 165, 194
Anderson 28 1H, 212
Anderson Exploration Ltd., 54-55
Anderson, J.C., 55
Anderson, Sidney B., 153
Antelope Field, 25
Antero Resources Corp., 111
Antrim (Michigan) shale, 35, 103, 107

Apache Corp., 52, 153, 226
Arco/Atlantic Richfield Co., 114-115, 121, 289
Arkansas Oil & Gas Commission, 129
Arkansas Western Gas Co., 128
Arkansas Western Production Co., 120
Arkoma Basin, 120, 124, 126, 129-133, 138-139
Armstrong Operating Inc., 29, 63-64
Aspect Energy LLC, 195
Atlas Resources Inc., 168
Atlas Shrugged II: The Strike, i
Atlas Shrugged, i
Atoka sandstone, 125, 129-130
Austin chalk, 18, 135-137, 166-167, 177, 185-186, 190, 217-219, 223-224, 228, 286
Austin Field, 88
AWP Olmos Field, 224
Aydin, Jack, 163
Baden, Bruce, 166
Bailey Field, 260
Baker Hughes Inc., 8, 11
Bakken, Henry O., 153

———

Bakken and additional Williston Basin formations
Bakken, i-ii, 16-29, 37, 40-42, 59-64, 70-71, 73-75, 78-84, 86-88, 91-94, 112, 123, 142, 145-146, 149-164, 203-211, 213-214, 230-233, 236, 257-258, 259-272, 274-275, 278-279, 283-285, 287, 290, 293, 300
Banff sand, 84

347

THE AMERICAN SHALES

Reid, Taylor, 17-18, 20-21, 88, 90,
    260-261, 270
Reliance Industries Ltd., 236
Renz 1, 169-170, 172-176, 178, 246-
    247
Renz 2, 175
Republic Energy Inc., 99, 106
Rettig 34, 221
Rhome Newark fault system, 68,
    104-105
Rice University, 262
Ridgeley sandstone, 169
Rimco, 147
Rio Tinto Plc, 235
Risan 1-34H, 162
Rising Star Energy LLC, 192
Rivera, Diego, 1
Robert Heuer 1-17, 83, 92-94, 264
Robertson, Gregg, 223-227
Robertson, Rock, 223
Robinson, Bob, 21, 23-30, 39-41,
    58, 61, 63, 72, 78, 123, 274
Robinson, Charles "Red," 23
Rockies Express, 245
Rodessa formation, 191
Rosewood Resources Inc., 146
Ross Field, 156, 160
Roxoil Drilling Inc., 2
Ruegsegger 24H 1, 82
S.A. Holditch & Associates Inc.,
    114
Salina formation, 170
Samson Resources Co., 19
San Joaquin Valley, 120
San Juan Basin, 17, 52-53, 66-67,
    109, 126, 254
Sanish Field, 155, 159, 164, 210,
    212, 259
Sanish formation, 23, 25
Scharlau, Charles, 130
Schlumberger Ltd., 8, 115, 221
Scoop play, 255
Scotia Waterous, 262
Scudder Portfolio Trust, 116
Section 29 tax credits, 6, 50, 52, 116
Setback D Unit 1H, 114

Shelby, Philip, 130-131
Shell Oil Co., 19, 27, 58, 153, 198,
    259, 287-288, 297
ShoBiz Pizza, 109
Shore Oil Co., 193
Silverston Field, 80
Simmons & Co. International Inc.,
    286
Simpson, Bob, 110, 117
Sinclair Oil Corp., 111
Sinochem Group, 282
Sinopec Ltd., 282
Skinner formation, 86
Slawson Exploration Co. Inc., 19,
    71, 73, 209, 270
Sleeping Giant, 15, 29, 37, 41, 43,
    63, 73-75, 78, 82, 123, 258,
    267-268, 270, 272-275
Sligo Field, 191
SM Energy Co., 71, 82
Smackover formation, 37, 195-197
Smith, Cameron, 30, 36-37, 39-40,
    274
Snyder Oil Co., 168
Society of Petroleum Engineers,
    11-12
Sorenson 29-32 1-H, 214
SourceGas LLC, 128
Southern Methodist University, 38,
    42, 146, 275
Southern Union Co., 120
Southland Royalty Co., 16-17, 83-
    84, 92, 110
Southwestern Energy Co., 120,
    124-126, 130-132, 134-135,
    138-139, 142, 144, 183, 188-
    189, 217, 243, 252-254, 256
Stages, frac (also see *Pumping,
    pressure*) , ii, 59, 75, 79, 81, 92-
    93, 108, 114-115, 157, 160,
    164, 178, 200, 203-204, 209-
    210, 212-214, 216, 221, 240,
    243, 246-247, 257-258, 260-
    261, 264, 266, 269, 271, 287,
    291, 294-295
Stanford University, 17

ABOUT THE AUTHOR

← ← ← ← ← → → → → →

Nissa Darbonne is editor-at-large for *Oil and Gas Investor* magazine. Prior to joining Hart Energy in 1998, she was the business editor for *The Daily Advertiser* (Lafayette, Louisiana), focusing on regional industry, including oil and gas extraction and transportation, and a government correspondent to *The Morning Advocate* (Baton Rouge, Louisiana). She received her B.A. in English and Journalism from the University of Southwestern Louisiana, now known as the University of Louisiana at Lafayette. She lives in Houston.

For the readers' forum, see
TheAmericanShales.com.

Praise for *The American Shales*

"This is an excellent written account of how things went down. I thoroughly enjoyed walking through the history of the shales by the way of the pages of your manuscript."

—Dan Steward, geologist and author,
The Barnett Shale Play: Phoenix of the Fort Worth Basin, A History

"The amount of research seems staggering to me but, more importantly, complete. The way you have documented the Bakken play is accurate. This also gives me confidence the other plays, which I did not know intimately, are accurate as well."

—Dick Findley, geologist and chairman,
American Eagle Energy Corp.

"I think you have captured a very, very important part of the history of our industry and I commend you on a job well done. It is organized in a way that is logical and easy to read and understand."

—Dr. Bobby B. Lyle, founder and chairman,
Lyco Holdings Inc.

"This should be required reading in every energy program in any educational institution that has one...It is a marvelous tool to get someone up to speed on the state of this industry, i.e. 'How did we get here?'"

—Steve Antry, chairman and chief executive officer,
Eagle Energy Exploration LLC

"Very thorough and well researched...You got some great interviews and access to the key players...and made the technical material accessible."

—Peggy Williams, geologist and editorial director,
Hart Energy

Made in the USA
Monee, IL
25 May 2023

34560962R00218